Embodied Conversational Agents

Embodied Conversational Agents

edited by

Justine Cassell,

Joseph Sullivan,

Scott Prevost, and

Elizabeth Churchill

The MIT Press Cambridge, Massachusetts London, England

This book was set in Caecilia and Matrix by The MIT Press.
Printed and bound in the United States of America.

Library of Congress Cataloging-in-Publication Data

Embodied conversational agents / edited by Justine Cassell ... [et al.].
   p. cm.
Includes bibliographical references and index.
ISBN 0-262-03278-3
   1. Intelligent agents (Computer software) 2. Human-computer interaction. I. Cassell, Justine, 1960–
QA76.76.I58 E43 2000
006.3—dc21   99-089951

Contents

III Evaluation

I
Introduction

I

Nudge Nudge Wink Wink:

Elements of Face-to-Face Conversation for Embodied

Conversational Agents

Justine Cassell

It will not be possible to apply exactly the same teaching process to the machine as to a normal child. It will not, for instance, be provided with legs, so that it could not be asked to go out and fill the coal scuttle. Possibly it might not have eyes. But however well these deficiencies might be overcome by clever engineering, one could not send the creature to school without the other children making excessive fun of it.
—Alan Turing, "Computing Machinery and Intelligence," 1950

The story of the automaton had struck deep root into their souls and, in fact, a pernicious mistrust of human figures in general had begun to creep in. Many lovers, to be quite convinced that they were not enamoured of wooden dolls, would request their mistresses to sing and dance a little out of time, to embroider and knit, and play with their lapdogs, while listening to reading, etc., and, above all, not merely to listen, but also sometimes to talk, in such a manner as presupposed actual thought and feeling.
—E. T. A. Hoffmann, "The Sandman," 1817

1.1 Introduction

Only humans communicate using language and carry on conversations with one another. And the skills of conversation have developed in humans in such a way as to exploit all of the unique affordances of the human body. We make complex representational gestures with our prehensile hands, gaze away and towards one another out of the corners of our centrally set eyes, and use the pitch and melody of our voices to emphasize and clarify what we are saying.

Perhaps because conversation is so defining of humanness and human interaction, the metaphor of face-to-face conversation has been applied to human-computer interface design for quite some time. One of the early arguments for the utility of this metaphor gave a list of features of face-to-face conversation that could be applied fruitfully to human-computer interaction, including mixed initiative, nonverbal communication, sense of presence, rules for transfer of control (Nickerson 1976). However, although these features have gained widespread recognition, human-computer conversation has only recently become more than a metaphor. That is, just lately have designers taken the metaphor seriously enough to attempt to design computer interfaces that can hold up their end of the conversation, interfaces that have bodies and know how to use them for conversation, interfaces that realize conversational behaviors as a function of the demands of dialogue and also as a function of emotion, personality, and social convention. This book addresses the features of human-human conversation that are being implemented in this new genre of *embodied conversational agents*, and the models and functions of conversation that underlie the features.

One way to think about the problem that we face is to imagine that we succeed beyond our wildest dreams in building a computer that can carry on a face-to-face conversation with a human. Imagine, in fact, a *face-to-face Turing test*. That is, imagine a panel of judges challenged to determine which socialite was a real live young woman and which was an automaton (as in Hoffmann's "The Sandman"). Or, rather, perhaps to judge which screen was a part of a video conferencing setup, displaying the human being filmed in another room, and which screen was displaying an autonomous embodied conversational agent running on a computer. In order to win at this Turing test, what underlying models of human conversation would we need to implement, and what surface behaviors would our embodied conversational agent need to display?

The chapters assembled here demonstrate the breadth of models and behaviors necessary to natural conversation. Four models, in particular, that inform the production of conversational behaviors are employed by the authors in this volume, and those are *emotion*, *personality*, *performatives*, and *conversational function*. All of these models are proposed as explanatory devices for the range of verbal and nonverbal behaviors seen in face-to-face conversation, and therefore implemented in embodied conversational agents (ECAs). In what follows, I examine these nonverbal behaviors in depth, as background to the underlying models presented in each chapter. But first, I describe briefly the nature of the models themselves.

Several authors address the need for models of personality in designing ECAs. In the work of André et al. (chap. 8), where two autonomous characters carry on a conversation that users watch, characters with personality make information easier to remember because the narration is more compelling. Their characters, therefore, need to be realized as distinguishable individuals with their own areas of expertise, interest profiles, personalities, and audiovisual appearance, taking into account their specific task in a given context. Each character displays a set of attitudes and actions, consistent over the course of the interaction, and revealed through the character's motions and conversations and interactions with the user and with other characters.

Ball and Breese (chap. 7) propose that the user's personality should also be *recognized*, so that the agent's personality can match that of the user. Churchill et al. (chap. 3) focus more generally on how to create *personable* characters. They suggest that success will be achieved when users can create thumbnail personality sketches of a character on the basis of an interaction. They also point out that personality should influence not just words and gestures, but also reactions to events, although those reactions should be tempered by the slight unpredictability that is characteristic of human personality.

What behaviors realize personality in embodied conversational agents? The authors in this book have relied on research on the cues that humans use to read personality in other humans: verbal style, physical appearance and nonverbal behaviors. These will be addressed further below. The importance of manipulating these behaviors correctly is demonstrated by Nass, Isbister, and Lee (chap. 13), who show that embodied conversational agents that present consistent personality cues are perceived as more useful.

Several authors also address the need for models of emotion that can inform conversational behavior. In the chapter by Badler et al. (chap. 9), the emotional profile of the ECA determines the style of carrying out actions that is adopted by that character. In the chapter by Lester et al. (chap. 5), where the ECA serves as tutor, the character exhibits emotional facial expressions and expressive gestures to advise, encourage, and empathize with students. These behaviors are generated from pedagogical speech acts, such as cause and effect, background information, assistance, rhetorical links, and congratulation, and their associated emotional intent, such as uncertainty, sadness, admiration, and so on.

Ball and Breese (chap. 7) describe not only generation of emotional responses in their ECA but also recognition of emotions on the part of the human user, using a Bayesian network approach. The underlying model of emotion that they implement is a simple one, but the emotion recognition that this model is capable of may be carried out strictly on the basis of observable features such as speech, gesture, and facial expression.

Like Lester et al., Poggi and Pelachaud (chap. 6) generate communicative behaviors on the basis of speech acts. However, Poggi and Pelachaud concentrate on one particular communicative behavior—facial expression—and one particular kind of speech act—performatives. Performatives are a key part of the communicative intent of a speaker, along with propositional and interactional acts. They can be defined as "the reason the speaker is communicating a particular thing—what goal the speaker has in mind," and they include acts such as "wishing, informing, threatening." Because Poggi and Pelachaud generate facial expression directly from this aspect of communicative intention, they can be said to be engaging not in speech to text but, on the contrary, in *meaning to face*.

Many of the authors in this volume discuss conversational function as separate from speech acts, emotion, and personality. Cassell et al. (chap. 2) propose a model of conversational function. In general terms, all conversational behaviors in the FMTB conversational model must support conversational functions, and any conversational action in any modality may convey several communicative goals. In this framework, four features of conversation are proposed as key to the design of embodied conversational agents:

- the distinction between propositional and interactional functions of conversation
- the use of several conversational modalities, such as speech, hand gestures, facial expression
- the importance of timing among conversational behaviors (and the increasing co-temporality or synchrony among conversational participants)
- the distinction between conversational behaviors (such as eyebrow raises) and conversational functions (such as turn taking)

All of the models described so far are proposed as ways of predicting *conversational behaviors and actions*. That is, each model is a way of *realizing* a set of conversational surface behaviors in a principled way. In what follows, we turn to those conversational behaviors and actions. We concentrate on the nonverbal behaviors, which are what distinguish embodied conversational agents from more traditional dialogue systems (for a good overview of the issues concerning speech and intonation in conversational interfaces and dialogue systems, see Luperfoy n.d.). In particular, we focus here on hand gesture and facial displays[1] and ignore other aspects of nonverbal behavior (such as posture, for example).

1.2 Overview of Nonverbal Behaviors

What nonverbal behaviors, then, do we find in human-human conversation? Spontaneous (that is, unplanned, unselfconscious) *gesture* accompanies speech in most communicative situations and in most cultures (despite the common belief to the contrary, in Great Britain, for example). People even gesture while they are speaking on the telephone (Rimé 1982). We know that listeners attend to such gestures in face-to-face conversation, and that they use gesture in these situations to form a mental representation of the communicative intent of the speaker (Cassell, McNeill, and McCullough 1999), as well as to follow the conversational process (Bavelas et al. 1995). In ECAs, then, gestures can be realized as a function of models of propositional and interactional content. Likewise, faces change expressions continuously, and many of these changes are synchronized to what is going on in concurrent conversation (see Pelachaud, Badler, and Steedman 1996; Poggi and Pelachaud, chap. 6). Facial displays are linked to all of the underlying models mentioned above and described in this book. That is, *facial displays* can be realized from the interactional function of speech (raising eyebrows to indicate attention to the other's speech), emotion (wrinkling one's eyebrows with worry), personality (pouting all the time), performatives (eyes wide while imploring), and other behavioral variables (Picard 1998). Facial displays can replace sequences of words ("she was dressed [wrinkle nose, stick out tongue]?") as well as accompany them (Ekman 1979), and they can help disambiguate what is being said when the acoustic signal is degraded. They do not occur randomly but rather are synchronized to one's own speech or to the speech of others (Condon and Osgton 1971; Kendon 1972). *Eye gaze* is also an important feature of nonverbal conversational behavior. Its main functions are (1) to help regulate the flow of conversation; that is, to signal the search for feedback during an interaction (gazing at the other person to see whether he or she follows), (2) to signal the search for information (looking upward as one searches for a particular word), to express emotion (looking downward in case of sadness), or (3) to indicate personality characteristics (staring at a person to show that one won't back down) (Beattie 1981; Duncan 1974).

Although many kinds of gestures and a wide variety of facial displays exist, the computer science community until very recently has for the most part only attempted to integrate one kind of gesture and one kind of facial display into human-computer interface systems—that is, *emblematic* gestures (e.g., the "thumbs up" gesture, or putting one's palm out to mean "stop"), which are employed in the absence of speech, and *emotional* facial displays (e.g., smiles, frowns, looks of puzzlement). But in building embodied conversational agents, we wish to exploit the power of gestures and facial displays that function in conjunction with speech.

For the construction of embodied conversational agents, then, there are types of gestures and facial displays that can serve key roles. In natural human conversation, both facial displays and gesture add redundancy when the speech situation is noisy, give the listener cues about where in the conversation one is, and add information that is not conveyed by accompanying speech. For these reasons, facial display, gesture, and speech can profitably work together in embodied conversational agents. Thus, in the remainder of this chapter, I will introduce those nonverbal behaviors that are integrated with one another, with the underlying structure of discourse and with models of emotion and personality.

Let's look at how humans use their hands and faces. In figure 1.1, Mike Hawley, one of my colleagues at the Media Lab, is shown giving a speech about the possibilities for communication among objects in the world. He is known to be a dynamic speaker, and we can trace that judgment to his animated facial displays and quick staccato gestures.

As is his wont, in the picture, Mike's hands are in motion, and his face is lively. As is also his wont, Mike has no memory of having used his hands when giving this talk. For our purposes, it is important to note that Mike's hands are forming a square as he speaks of the mosaic tiles he is proposing to build. His mouth is open and smiling, and his eyebrows raise as he utters the stressed word in the current utterance. Mike's interlocutors are no more likely to remember his nonverbal behavior than he is. But they do register those behaviors at some level and use them to form an opinion about what he said, as we will see below.

Gestures and facial displays such as those demonstrated by Mike Hawley can be implemented in ECAs as well. Let's deconstruct exactly what people do with their hands and faces during dialogue, and how the respective functions of the three modalities are related.

1.3 Kinds of Gesture

1.3.1 Emblems

When we reflect on what kinds of gestures we have seen in our environment, we often come up with a type of gesture known as *emblematic*. These gestures are culturally specified in the sense that one single gesture may differ in inter-

Figure 1.1
Hawley talking about mosaic tiles.

pretation from culture to culture (Efron 1941; Ekman and Friesen 1969). For example, the American "V for victory" gesture can be made either with the palm or the back of the hand toward the listener. In Britain, however, a "V" gesture made with the back of the hand toward the listener is inappropriate in polite society. Examples of emblems in American culture are the thumb-and-index-finger ring gesture that signals "okay" or the "thumbs up" gesture. Many more of these "emblems" appear to exist in French and Italian culture than in America (Kendon 1993), but in few cultures do these gestures appear to consti-tute more than 10 percent of the gestures produced by speakers. Despite the paucity of emblematic gestures in everyday communication, it was solely ges-tures such as these that interested interface designers at one point. That is, computer vision systems known as "gestural interfaces" attempted to invent or co-opt emblematic gesture to replace language in human-computer interaction. However, in terms of *types*, few enough different emblematic gestures exist to make untenable the idea of co-opting emblems as a gestural language. And in terms of *tokens*, we simply don't seem to make that many emblematic gestures on a daily basis. In ECAs, then, where speech is already a part of the interaction, it makes more sense to concentrate on integrating those gestures that accompany speech in human-human conversation.

1.3.2 Propositional Gestures

Another conscious gesture that has been the object of some study in the interface community is the so-called propositional gesture (Hinrichs and Polanyi 1986). An example is the use of the hands to measure the size of a symbolic space while the speaker says "it was this big." Another example is pointing at a chair and then pointing at another spot and saying "move that over there." These gestures are not unwitting and in that sense not spontaneous, and their interaction with speech is more like the interaction of one grammatical constituent with another than the interaction of one communicative channel with another. In fact, the demonstrative "this" may be seen as a placeholder for the syntactic role of the accompanying gesture. These gestures can be particularly important in certain types of task-oriented talk, as discussed in the well-known paper "Put-That-There: Voice and Gesture at the Graphics Interface" (Bolt 1980). Gestures such as these are found notably in communicative situations where the physical world in which the conversation is taking place is also the topic of conversation. These gestures do not, however, make up the majority of gestures found in spontaneous conversation, and I believe that in part they have received the attention that they have because they are, once again, *conscious, witting* gestures available to our self-scrutiny.

1.3.3 Spontaneous Gestures

Let us turn now to the vast majority of gestures—those that, although unconscious and unwitting, are the gestural vehicles for our communicative intent with other humans, and potentially with our computer partners as well. These gestures, for the most part, are not available to conscious access, either to the person who produced them or to the person who watched them being produced. The fact that we lose access to the form of a whole class of gestures may seem odd, but consider the analogous situation with speech. For the most part, in most situations, we lose access to the *surface structure* of utterances immediately after hearing or producing them (Johnson, Bransford, and Solomon 1973).

That is, if listeners are asked whether they heard the word "couch" or the word "sofa" to refer to the same piece of furniture, unless one of these words sounds odd to them, they probably will not be able to remember which they heard. Likewise, slight variations in pronunciation of the speech we are listening to are difficult to remember, even right after hearing them (Levelt 1989). That is because (so it is hypothesized) we listen to speech in order to extract meaning, and we throw away the words once the meaning has been extracted. In the same way, we appear to lose access to the form of gestures (Krauss, Morrel-Samuels, and Colasante 1991), even though we attend to the information that they convey (Cassell, McNeill, and McCullough 1999).

The spontaneous unplanned, more common *co-verbal* gestures are of four types:

- *Iconic* gestures depict by the form of the gesture some feature of the action or event being described. An example is a gesture outlining the two sides of a triangle while the speaker said, "the biphasic-triphasic distinction between gestures is the first cut in a hierarchy."

  Iconic gestures may specify the viewpoint from which an action is narrated. That is, gesture can demonstrate who narrators imagine themselves to be and where they imagine themselves to stand at various points in the narration, when this is rarely conveyed in speech, and listeners can infer this viewpoint from the gestures they see. For example, a participant at a computer vision conference was describing to his neighbor a technique that his lab was employing. He said, "and we use a wide field cam to [do the body],'" while holding both hands open and bent at the wrists with his fingers pointed toward his own body and the hands sweeping up and down. His gesture shows us the wide field cam "doing the body" and takes the perspective of somebody whose body is "being done." Alternatively, he might have put both hands up to his eyes, pantomiming holding a camera and playing the part of the viewer rather than the viewed.

- *Metaphoric* gestures are also representational, but the concept they represent has no physical form; instead, the form of the gesture comes from a common metaphor. An example is the gesture that a conference speaker made when he said, "we're continuing to expound on this" and made a rolling gesture with his hand, indicating ongoing process.

  Some common metaphoric gestures are the "process metaphoric" just illustrated and the "conduit metaphoric," which objectifies the information being conveyed, representing it as a concrete object that can be held between the hands and given to the listener. Conduit metaphorics commonly accompany new segments in communicative acts; an example is the box gesture that accompanies "In this [next part] of the talk I'm going to discuss new work on this topic."

Metaphoric gestures of this sort contextualize communication, for example, by placing it in the larger context of social interaction. In this example, the speaker has prepared to give the next segment of discourse to the conference attendees. Another typical metaphoric gesture in academic contexts is the metaphoric pointing gesture that commonly associates features with people. For example, during a talk on spontaneous gesture in dialogue systems, I might point to Phil Cohen in the audience while saying, "I won't be talking today about the pen gesture." In this instance, I am associating Phil Cohen with his work on pen gestures.

- *Deictic* gestures spatialize, or locate in the physical space in front of the narrator, aspects of the discourse; these can be discourse entities that have a physical existence, such as the overhead projector that I point to when I say "this doesn't work," or nonphysical discourse entities. An example of the latter comes from an explanation of the accumulation of information during the course of a conversation. The speaker said, "we have an [attentional space suspended] between us and we refer [back to it]." During "attentional space," he defined a big globe with his hands, and during "back to it" he pointed to where he had performed the previous gesture.

  Deictic gestures populate the space in between the speaker and listener with the discourse entities as they are introduced and continue to be referred to. Deictics do not have to be pointing index fingers. One can also use the whole hand to represent entities or ideas or events in space. In casual conversation, a speaker said, "when I was in a [university] it was different, but now I'm in [industry]," while opening his palm left and then flipping it over toward the right. Deictics may function as an interactional cue, indexing which person in a room the speaker is addressing, or indexing some kind of agreement between the speaker and a listener. An example is the gesture commonly seen in classrooms accompanying "yes, [student X], you are exactly right" as the teacher points to a particular student.

- *Beat* gestures are small batonlike movements that do not change in form with the content of the accompanying speech. They serve a pragmatic function, occurring with comments on one's own linguistic contribution, speech repairs, and reported speech.

Beat gestures may signal that information conveyed in accompanying speech does not advance the "plot" of the discourse but rather is an evaluative or orienting comment. For example, the narrator of a home repair show described the content of the next part of the TV episode by saying "I'm going to tell you how to use a caulking gun to [prevent leakage] through [storm windows] and [wooden window ledges] . . ." and accompanied this speech with several beat gestures to indicate that the role of this part of the discourse was to indicate the relevance of what came next, as opposed to imparting new information in and of itself.

Beat gestures may also serve to maintain conversation as dyadic: to check on the attention of the listener and to ensure that the listener is following (Bavelas et al. 1992).

These gesture types may be produced in a different manner according to the emotional state of the speaker (Badler et al., chap. 9; Elliott 1997). Or they may differ as a function of personality (André et al., chap. 8; Churchill et al., chap. 3; Nass, Isbister, and Lee, chap. 13). Their content, however, is predicted by the communicative goals of the speaker, both propositional and interactional (Cassell et al., chap. 2). The fact that they convey information that is not conveyed by speech, and that they convey it in a certain manner, gives the impression of cognitive activity over and above that required for the production of speech. That is, they give the impression of a *mind*, and therefore, when produced by embodied conversational agents, they may enhance the believability of the interactive system. But exploiting this property in the construction of ECAs requires an understanding of the *integration* of gesture with speech. This is what we turn to next.

1.4 Integration of Gesture with Spoken Language

Gestures are integrated into spoken language at the level of the phonology, the semantics, and the discourse structure of the conversation.

1.4.1 Temporal Integration of Gesture and Speech

First, a short introduction to the physics of gesture: iconic and metaphoric gestures are composed of three phases. And these *preparation*, *stroke*, and *retraction* phases may be differentiated by short holding phases surrounding the stroke. Deictic gestures and beat gestures, on the other hand, are characterized by two phases of movement: a movement into the gesture space and a movement out of it. In fact, this distinction between biphasic and triphasic gestures appears to correspond to the addition of semantic features—or iconic meaning—to the representational gestures. That is, the number of phases corresponds to type of meaning: representational versus nonrepresentational. And it is in the second phase—the stroke—that we look for the meaning features that allow us to interpret the gesture (Wilson, Bobick, and Cassell 1996). At the level of the word, in both types of gestures, individual gestures and words are synchronized in time so that the "stroke" (most energetic part of the gesture) occurs either with or just before the intonationally most prominent syllable of the accompanying speech segment (Kendon 1980; McNeill 1992).

This phonological co-occurrence leads to co-articulation of gestural units. Gestures are performed rapidly, or their production is stretched out over time, so as to synchronize with preceding and following gestures and the speech these gestures accompany. An example of gestural co-articulation is the relationship between the two gestures in the phrase "do you have an [account] at this [bank]?": during the word "account," the two hands sketch a kind of box in front of the speaker; however, rather than carrying this gesture all the way to completion (either both hands coming to rest at the end of this gesture, or maintaining the location of the hands in space), one hand remains in the "account" location while the other cuts short the "account" gesture to point at the ground while saying "bank." Thus, the occurrence of the word "bank," with its accompanying gesture, affected the occurrence of the gesture that accompanied "account." This issue of timing is a difficult one to resolve in ECAs, as discussed by Lester et al. (chap. 5), Rickel and Johnson (chap. 4), and Cassell et al. (chap. 2).

At the level of the turn, the hands being in motion is one of the most robust cues to turn taking (Cassell et al., chap. 2; Duncan 1974). Speakers bring their hands into gesture space as they think about taking the turn, and at the end of a turn the hands of the speaker come to rest, before the next speaker begins to talk. Temporal integration, then, is key to the interpretation of gesture in the context of speech. Gestures that are mistimed will lead listeners in human conversation to misinterpret who has the turn and/or what is intended to be said. Timing is just as important to ECAs, and the issue of how to time graphical to speech output is a difficult one.

1.4.2 Semantic Integration

Speech and the nonverbal behaviors that accompany it are sometimes redundant, and sometimes they present complementary but nonoverlapping information. This complementarity can be seen at several levels.

In the previous section, I wrote that gesture is co-temporaneous with the linguistic segment it most closely resembles in meaning. But what meanings does gesture convey, and what is the relationship between the respective meanings of gesture and of speech? Gesture can convey redundant or complementary meanings to those in speech; in normal adults, gesture is almost never contradictory to what is conveyed in speech (politicians may be a notable exception, if one considers them normal adults). At the semantic level, this means that the semantic features that make up a concept may be distributed across speech and gesture. As an example, take the semantic features of manner of motion verbs: these verbs, such as "walk," "run," and "drive," can be seen as being made up of the meaning "go" *plus* the meanings of how one got there (walking, running, driving). The verbs "walking" and "running" can be distinguished by way of the speed with which one got there. And the verb "arrive" can be distinguished from "go" by whether one achieved the goal of getting there, and so on. These meanings are semantic features that are added together in the representation of a word. Thus, I may say "he drove to the conference" or "he went to the conference" + drive gesture.

McNeill has shown that speakers of different languages make different choices about which features to put in speech and which in gesture (McNeill n.d.). Speakers of English often convey path in gesture and manner in speech, while speakers of Spanish put manner in gesture and path in speech. McNeill claims that this derives from the typology of Spanish versus English.

In my lab, we have shown that even in English a whole range of features can be conveyed in gesture, such as path, speed, telicity ("goal-achievedness"), manner, aspect. One person, for example, said "Road Runner [comes down]" while she made a gesture with her hands of turning a steering wheel. Only in the gesture is the manner of coming down portrayed. She might just as well have said "Road Runner comes down" and made a walking gesture with her hands. Another subject said "Road Runner just [goes]" and with one index finger extended made a fast gesture forward and up, indicating that the Road Runner zipped by. Here both the path of the movement (forward and up) and the speed (very fast) are portrayed by the gesture, but the manner is left unspecified (we don't know whether the Road Runner walked, ran, or drove). This aspect of the relationship between speech and gesture is an ongoing research issue in psycholinguistics but has begun to be implemented in ECAs (Cassell and Stone 1999).

Even among the blind, semantic features are distributed across speech and gesture—strong evidence that gesture is a product of the same generative process that produces speech (Iverson and Goldin-Meadow 1996).

In general, however, we can say that speech and gesture join together to convey the communicative intent of a speaker. Gesture conveys those concepts for which it is best suited (concepts that can be mapped onto space, or that are more easily expressed through a medium that allows simultaneity than a medium that depends on linearity). And a particular language conveys those concepts for which it is best suited. Gesture and speech may redundantly express concepts that are difficult to convey, or that the speaker believes the hearer will have difficulty understanding. This allocation of content across media is also an issue in automatic document generation, and several of the chapters in this volume take advantage of the insights discovered in that prior work.

1.4.3 Discourse Integration

For many gestures, occurrence is determined by the discourse structure of the talk. In particular, *information structure* appears to play a key role in where one finds gesture in discourse. The information structure of an utterance defines its relation to other utterances in a discourse and to propositions in the relevant knowledge pool. Although a sentence like "George withdrew fifty dollars" has a clear semantic interpretation that we might symbolically represent as *withdrew(george, fifty-dollars)*, such a simplistic representation does not indicate how the proposition relates to other propositions in the discourse. For example, the sentence might be an equally appropriate response to the questions "Who withdrew fifty dollars?," "What did George withdraw?," "What did George do?," or even "What happened?" Determining which items in the response are most important or salient clearly depends on which question is asked. These types of salience distinctions are encoded in the information structure representation of an utterance.

Following Halliday and others (Hajicova and Sgall 1987; Halliday 1967), one can use the terms *theme* and *rheme* to denote two distinct information structural attributes of an utterance. The theme/rheme distinction is similar to the distinctions *topic/comment* and *given/new*. The theme roughly corresponds to what the utterance is about, as derived from the discourse model. The rheme corresponds to what is new or interesting about the theme of the utterance. Depending on the discourse context, a given utterance may be divided on semantic and pragmatic grounds into thematic and rhematic constituents in a variety of ways. That is, depending on what question was asked, the contribution of the current answer will be different.[3]

In English, intonation serves an important role in marking information as rhematic and as contrastive. That is, pitch accents mark which information is new to the discourse. Thus, the following two examples (from Cassell et al. 1994) demonstrate the association of pitch accents with information structure (primary pitch accents are shown in boldface type):

```
1. [Q:] Who withdrew fifty dollars?
2. [A:] (George)_RHEME (withdrew fifty dollars)_THEME
3. [Q:] What did George withdraw?
4. [A:] (George withdrew)_THEME (fifty dollars)_RHEME
```

In speaking these sentences aloud, one notices that even though the answers to the two questions are identical in terms of the words they contain, they are uttered quite differently. In the first, the word "George" is stressed, and in the second it is the phrase "fifty dollars" that is stressed. This is because in the two sentences different elements are marked as rhematic, or difficult for the listener to predict.

Gesture also serves an important role in marking information structure. When gestures are found in an utterance, the vast majority of them co-occur with the rhematic elements of that utterance (Cassell and Prevost n.d.). In this sense, intonation and gesture serve similar roles in the discourse. Intonational contours also time the occurrence of gesture (Cassell and Prevost n.d.). Thus, the distribution of gestural units in the stream of speech is similar to the distribution of intonational units, in the following ways.

- First, gestural domains are isomorphic with intonational domains. The speaker's hands rise into space with the beginning of the intonational rise at the beginning of an utterance, and the hands fall at the end of the utterance along with the final intonational marking.

- Second, the most effortful part of the gesture (the "stroke") co-occurs with the pitch accent, or most effortful part of enunciation.

- Third, gestures co-occur with the rhematic part of speech, just as we find particular intonational tunes co-occurring with the rhematic part of speech. We hypothesize that this is so because the rheme is that part of speech that contributes most to the ongoing discourse and that is least known to the listener beforehand. It makes sense that gestures, which may convey additional content to speech and may flag that part of the discourse as meriting further attention, would be found where the most explanation is needed in the discourse. This does not mean that one never finds gestures with the theme, however. Some themes are *contrastive*, marking the contrast between one theme and another. An example is "In the cartoon you see a manhole cover. And then the rock falls *down on that manhole cover*." When thematic material is contrastive, then gesture may occur in that context. Although we know that intonation and gesture function in similar ways, and are synchronized to one another, how to implement this property in ECAs is still an unsolved issue, due in part to the difficulty of reconciling the demands of graphics and speech synthesis software.

In sum, then, gestures of four types co-occur with speech in particular rule-governed ways. These associations mark the status of turn taking, identify particular items as rhematic (particularly important to the interpretation of the discourse), and convey meanings complementary to those conveyed by speech. Are these results true only for North America?

1.4.4 Cultural Differences

It is natural to wonder about the cultural specificity of gesture use. We often have the impression that Italians gesture more and differently than do British speakers. It is true that, as far as the question of quantity is concerned, speakers from some language communities demonstrate a greater number of gestures per utterance than others. This phenomenon appears to be linked to the fact that some cultures may embrace the use of gesture more than others; many segments of British society believe that gesturing is inappropriate, and therefore children are encouraged to not use their hands when they speak. But the effect of these beliefs and constraints about gesture is not as strong as one might think. In my experience videotaping people carrying on conversations and telling stories, many speakers claim that they never use their hands. These speakers are then surprised to watch themselves on video, where they can be seen gesturing. In fact, every speaker of every language that I have seen videotaped (French, Spanish, Italian, Tagalog, Soviet Georgian, Chinese, Japanese, to name a few) has gestured. That is, all except for one American man who made one single gesture during his entire twenty-minute narration, a gesture that he himself aborted by grabbing the gesturing hand with the other hand and forcefully bringing it down to his lap.

As far as the nature of gesture is concerned, as mentioned above, emblems do vary widely from language community to language community. Americans make a "V for victory" with their palm oriented either out toward the listener or toward themselves. For British speakers, the "V for victory" with the palm oriented toward the self is exceedingly rude. Italian speakers demonstrate a wide variety of emblematic gestures that can carry meaning in the absence of speech, while both American and English speakers have access to a limited number of such gestures. But remember that emblematic gestures still make up less than 20 percent of the gestures found in everyday conversation. The four types of spontaneous gestures described, however, appear universal.

Interestingly, and perhaps not surprisingly, the *form* of metaphoric gestures appears to differ from language community to language community. Conduit metaphoric gestures are not found in narrations in all languages: neither Chinese nor Swahili narrators use them, for example (McNeill 1992). These narratives do contain abundant metaphoric gestures of other kinds but do not depict abstract ideas as bounded containers. The metaphoric use of space, however, appears in all narratives collected, regardless of the language spoken. Thus, apart from emblematic gestures, the use of gesture appears to be more universal than particular. Nevertheless, the ways in which hand gestures and other nonverbal behaviors are produced do certainly differ from culture to culture. And, as Nass, Isbister, and Lee (chap. 13) show, cultural identification in ECAs is important to users' estimation of their abilities. This topic remains, then, an important one for future research.

1.5 Kinds of Facial Displays

Let us turn now to the use of the face during conversation. Like hand gestures, facial displays can be classified according to their placement with respect to the linguistic utterance and their significance in transmitting information (Scherer 1980). When we talk about facial displays, we are really most interested in precisely timed changes in eyebrow position, expressions of the mouth, movement of the head and eyes, and gestures of the hands. For example, raised eyebrows + a smiling mouth is taken to be a happy expression (Ekman and Friesen 1984), while moving one's head up and down is taken to be a nod. Some facial displays are linked to personality and remain constant across a lifetime (a "wide-eyed look"). Some are linked to emotional state, and may last as long as the emotion is felt (downcast eyes during depression). And some are synchronized with the units of conversation and last only a very short time (eyebrow raises along with certain performatives, such as "implore").

In addition to characterizing facial displays by the muscles or part of the body in play, or the amount of time that they last, we can also characterize them by their function in a conversation. Some facial displays have a phonological function—for instance, lip shapes that change with the phonemes uttered. It has been shown that such lip shapes can significantly improve the facility with which people understand "talking heads" (Bregler et al. 1993; Massaro et al., chap. 10). Some facial displays fulfill a semantic function, for example, nodding rather than saying "yes." Some facial displays, on the other hand, have an envelope,[4] or conversational-process-oriented function. Examples are quick nods of the head while one is listening to somebody speak, or a glance at the other person when one is finished speaking. Still other functions for facial displays are to cement social relationships (polite smiles) and to correspond to grammatical functions (eyebrow raises on pitch-accented words).

Note that the same movements by the body can have two (or more) different functions. Smiles can serve the function of emotional feedback, indicating that one is happy, or they can serve a purely social function even if one is not at all happy. Nods of the head can replace saying "yes" (a content function) or simply indicate that one is following, even if one does not agree with what is being said (an envelope function).[5]

1.5.1 Cultural Differences

Like emblem gestures, facial displays with a semantic function can vary from culture to culture. To indicate agreement, for example, one nods in the United States but shakes one's head in Greece or Albania. However, like beat gestures, facial displays with a dialogic function are similar across cultures. Thus, although generally one looks less often at one's interlocutor in Japanese conversation, conversational turns are still terminated by a brief glance at the listener. And, even though semantic agreement is indicated by a shake of the head in Greece, feedback is still accomplished by a nod. As with gesture, then, there are more similarities in the use of the face than there are differences, at least with respect to the regulatory conversational function of these behaviors.
In the remainder of this chapter, we concentrate on the facial behaviors whose description has more universal validity.

1.6 Integration of Verbal Displays with Spoken Language

As with hand gesture, facial displays are tightly coupled to the speech with which they occur.

1.6.1 Temporal Synchronization

Synchrony occurs at all levels of speech: phonemic segment, word, phrase or long utterance. Different facial motions are isomorphic to these groups (Condon and Osgton 1971; Kendon 1974). Some of them are more adapted to the phoneme level, like an eye blink, while others occur at the word level, like a frown. In the example "Do you have a checkbook with you?," a raising eyebrow starts and ends on the accented syllable "check," while a blink starts and ends on the pause marking the end of the utterance. Facial display of emphasis can match the emphasized segment, showing synchronization at this level (a sequence of head nods can punctuate the emphasis, as when one nods while saying the word "really" in the phrase "I REALLY want this system to work"). Moreover, some movements reflect encoding-decoding difficulties and therefore coincide with hesitations and pauses inside clauses (Dittman 1974). Many hesitation pauses are produced at the beginning of speech and correlate with avoidance of gaze, presumably to help the speaker concentrate on what he or she is going to say.

1.6.2 Facial Display Occurrence

As described above, facial displays can be classified according to their placement with respect to the linguistic utterance and their significance in transmitting information. Some facial displays have nothing to do with the linguistic utterance but serve a biological need (wetting the lips or blinking), while some are synchronized with phonemes, such as changing the shape of one's lips to utter a particular sound. The remaining facial displays that have a dialogic function are primarily movements of the eyes (gaze), eyebrow raises, and nods. In the following section, we discuss the co-occurrence of these behaviors with the verbal utterance.

Facial behavior can be classified into four primary categories depending on its role in the conversation (Argyle and Cook 1976; Chovil 1992; Collier 1985). The following describes where behaviors in each of these four categories occur, and how they function.

- *Planning:* Planning eye movements correspond to the first phase of a turn when speakers organize their thoughts. The speaker has a tendency to look away in order to prevent an overload of visual and linguistic information. On the other hand, during the execution phase, when speakers know what they are going to say, they look more often at listeners. For a short turn (of a duration of less than 1.5 seconds), this planning look-away does not occur, and the speaker and listener maintain mutual gaze.

- *Comment:* Accented or emphasized linguistic items are punctuated by head nods; the speaker may also look toward the listener at these moments. Eyebrow raises are also synchronized with pitch accents.

- *Control:* Some eye movements regulate the use of the communication channel and function as synchronization signals. That is, one may request a response from a listener by looking at the listener and suppress the listener's response by looking away; these behaviors occur primarily at the ends of utterances and at grammatical boundaries. When the speaker wants to give up the floor, she gazes at the listener at the end of the utterance. When the listener wants the floor, she looks at and slightly up at the speaker.

- *Feedback:* Facial behaviors may be used to elicit feedback and to give it. Speakers look toward listeners during grammatical pauses and when asking questions, and these glances signal requests for verbal or nonverbal feedback, without turning the floor over to the listener. Listeners respond by establishing gaze with the speaker and/or nodding. The feedback-elicitation head movements are referred to as *within turn* signals. If the speaker does not emit such a signal by gazing at the listener, the listener can still emit a *back-channel* or feedback signal, which in turn may be followed by a *continuation* signal by the speaker. But the listener's behavior is dependent on the behavior of the speaker; one is much less likely to find feedback in the absence of a feedback elicitation signal (Duncan 1974).

In the description just given, facial behavior is described as a function of the turn-taking structure of a conversation rather than as a function of information structure. This is the way that facial behavior has been described in most literature; in fact, gaze behavior has come to represent *the* cue to turn organization and has been described as if it were entirely predicted by turn organization.

However, turn taking only partially accounts for the gaze behavior in discourse. Our research shows that a better explanation for gaze behavior integrates turn taking with the information structure of the propositional content of an utterance (Cassell, Torres, and Prevost n.d.). Specifically, the beginning of themes are frequently accompanied by a look-away from the hearer, and the beginning of rhemes are frequently accompanied by a look-toward the hearer. When these categories are co-temporaneous with turn construction, then they are strongly—in fact, absolutely—predictive of gaze behavior. That is, when the end of the rheme corresponds to the end of the turn, then speakers always look toward their listeners in our data.

Why might there be such a link between gaze and information structure? The literature on gaze behavior and turn taking suggests that speakers look toward hearers at the ends of turns to signal that the floor is "available"—that hearers may take the turn. Our findings suggest that speakers look toward hearers at the beginning of the rheme—that is, when new information or the key point of the contribution is being conveyed. Gaze here may focus the attention of speaker and hearer on this key part of the utterance. And, of course, signaling the new contribution of the utterance and signaling that one is finished speaking are not entirely independent. Speakers may be more likely to give up the turn once they have conveyed the rhematic material of their contribution to the dialogue. In this case, gaze behavior is signaling a particular kind of relationship between information structure and turn taking.

It is striking, both in the role of facial displays in turn taking and in their association with information structure, the extent to which these behaviors coordinate and regulate conversation. It is clear that through gaze, eyebrow raises, and head nods both speakers and listeners collaborate in the construction of synchronized turns and efficient conversation. In this way, these nonverbal behaviors fill the function that Brennan and Hulteen (1995) suggest is needed for more robust speech interfaces.

1.7 Another Example

Let us now end with another example from life. This excerpt from a human speaking will show the rules we have just discussed, in action.

Figure 1.2 shows Seymour Papert talking about embedding computing in everyday objects and toys. He breathes in, looks up to the right, then turns toward the audience and says, "A kid can make a device that will have real behavior (. . .) that two of them [will interact] in a– to– to do a [dance together]." When he says "make a device" he looks upward; at "real behavior" he smiles; on "will interact" he looks toward the audience, raises his hands to chest level, and points with each hand toward the other as if the hands are devices that are about to interact. He holds that pointing position through the speech disfluency

Figure 1.2
". . . will interact."

and then, while saying "dance together," his hands move toward one another and then away, as if his fingers are doing the tango (not shown). He then looks down at his hands, looks to the side, and pauses, before going on.

Now, because this is a speech and not a conversation, some of the integration of verbal and nonverbal behavior is different, but some is also strikingly similar. For example, although nobody else is taking a turn, Papert still gazes away before taking the turn and gazes toward his audience as he begins to speak. Likewise, he gazes away at the end of this particular unit of the discourse and then turns back as he continues. Papert also still uses all four kinds of gestures (beat gestures, in fact, although not illustrated here, are particularly frequent in speeches). His gestures are still aligned with the most prominent phonological units of his speech, and there is co-articulation such that the first gesture, a deictic, perseverates through his speech disfluency, allowing the second gesture, an iconic, to co-occur with the semantic unit it most resembles.

1.8 Conclusion

One of the motivations for embodied conversational agents—as for dialogue systems before them—comes from increasing computational capacity in many objects and environments outside the desktop computer—smart rooms and intelligent toys—in environments as diverse as a military battlefield or a children's museum, and for users as different from one another as we can imagine. It is in part for this reason that we continue to pursue the dream of computers without keyboards, which can accept natural untrained input and respond in kind. In situations such as these, we will need natural conversation, multiple modalities, and well-developed characters to interact with.

We still cannot build an embodied conversational agent with anything like the conversational skills of Mike Hawley or Seymour Papert. Our models of emotion, of personality, of conversation are still rudimentary. And the number of conversational behaviors that we can realize in real time using animated bodies is still extremely limited. But, as we begin to understand the abilities that underlie human conversation, and to appreciate the behaviors that make up human conversation, we approach the day when a face-to-face Turing test will become imaginable.[6]

Notes

Research leading to the preparation of this chapter was supported by the National Science Foundation (award IIS-9618939), AT&T, Deutsche Telekom, and the other generous sponsors of the MIT Media Lab. Thanks to Andrew Donnelly for so ably handling the administrative aspects of this project, to all of the students of the Gesture and Narrative Language research group for dedication above and beyond the call of duty to this book as to every other project we undertake, and to David Mindell and Cathy O'Connor for providing intellectual and physical contexts for writing. Finally, profound and heartfelt thanks to David McNeill for introducing me to this field, sharing his passion about the topic, and teaching me so much about scholarship and academic community.

1. Following Takeuchi and Nagao (1993), we use the term "facial display" rather than "facial expression" to avoid the automatic connotation of emotion that is linked to the latter term.

2. Square brackets indicate the extent of speech that is accompanied by a nonverbal behavior.

3. This description is, of course, an oversimplification of a topic that is still the subject of vigorous debate. I do not pretend to a complete theory that would, in any case, be beyond the scope of this chapter.

4. We call these behaviors "envelope" to convey the fact that they concern the outer envelope of communication, rather than its contents (Cassell and Thórisson 1999). A similar distinction between content and envelope is made by Takeuchi and Nagao (1993) when they refer to the difference between "object-level communication" (relevant to the communication goal) and "meta-level processing" (relevant to communication regulation).

5. Content nods tend to be fewer and produced more emphatically and more slowly than envelope nods (Duncan 1974).

6. Parts of this chapter appeared in somewhat different form in Cassell (2000).

References

Argyle, M., and M. Cook. 1976. *Gaze and mutual gaze*. Cambridge: Cambridge University Press.

Bavelas, J., N. Chovil, L. Coates, and L. Roe. 1995. Gestures specialized for dialogue. *Personality and Social Psychology Bulletin* 21(4):394–405.

Bavelas, J., N. Chovil, D. Lawrie, and A. Wade. 1992. Interactive gestures. *Discourse Processes* 15:469–489.

Beattie, G. W. 1981. Sequential temporal patterns of speech and gaze in dialogue. In T. A. Sebeok and J. Umiker-Sebeok, eds., *Nonverbal communication, interaction, and gesture: Selections from Semiotica*, 298–320. The Hague: Mouton.

Bolt, R. A. 1980. Put-That-There: Voice and gesture at the graphics interface. *Computer Graphics* 14(3):262–270.

Bregler, C., H. Hild, S. Manke, and A. Waibel. 1993. Improving connected letter recognition by lipreading. In *Proceedings of the International Conference on Acoustics, Speech, and Signal Processing* (IEEE-ICASSP) (Minneapolis, Minn.).

Brennan, S., and E. Hulteen. 1995. Interaction and feedback in a spoken language system: A theoretical framework. *Knowledge-Based Systems* 8(2–3):143–151.

Cassell, J. 2000. More than just another pretty face: Embodied conversational interface agents. *Communications of the ACM*. Forthcoming.

Cassell, J., and S. Prevost. N.d. Embodied natural language generation: A framework for generating speech and gesture. Forthcoming.

Cassell, J., and M. Stone. 1999. Living hand to mouth: Theories of speech and gesture in interactive systems. In *Proceedings of the AAAI Fall Symposium on Psychological Models of Communication in Collaborative Systems* (Cape Cod, Mass.), 34–42.

Cassell, J., and K. Thórisson. 1999. The power of a nod and glance: Envelope vs. emotional feedback in animated conversational agents. *Journal of Applied Artificial Intelligence* 13(3):519–538.

Cassell, J., D. McNeill, and K. E. McCullough. 1999. Speech-gesture mismatches: Evidence for one underlying representation of linguistic and nonlinguistic information. *Pragmatics and Cognition* 7(1):1–34.

Cassell, J., C. Pelachaud, N. Badler, M. Steedman, B. Achorn, T. Becket, B. Douville, S. Prevost, and M. Stone. 1994. Animated conversation: Rule-based generation of facial expression, gesture and spoken intonation for multiple conversational agents. *Computer Graphics SIGGRAPH Proceedings 1994*, 413–420. New York: ACM SIGGRAPH.

Cassell, J., O. Torres, and S. Prevost. N.d. Turn taking vs. discourse structure: How best to model multimodal conversation. In Y. Wilks, ed., *Machine conversations*. The Hague: Kluwer. Forthcoming.

Chovil, N. 1992. Discourse-oriented facial displays in conversation. *Research on Language and Social Interaction* 25:163–194.

Collier, G. 1985. *Emotional expression*. Hillsdale, N.J.: Lawrence Erlbaum Associates.

Condon, W. S., and W. D. Osgton. 1971. Speech and body motion synchrony of the speaker-hearer. In D. H. Horton and J. J. Jenkins, eds., *The perception of language*, 150–184. New York: Academic Press.

Dittman, A. T. 1974. The body movement-speech rhythm relationship as a cue to speech encoding. In S. Weitz, ed., *Nonverbal communication*. New York: Oxford University Press.

Duncan, S. 1974. Some signals and rules for taking speaking turns in conversations. In S. Weitz, ed., *Nonverbal communication*. New York: Oxford University Press.

Efron, D. 1941. *Gesture and environment*. New York: King's Crown Press.

Ekman, P. 1979. About brows: Emotional and conversational signals. In M. von Cranach, K. Foppa, W. Lepenies, and D. Ploog, eds., *Human ethology: Claims and limits of a new discipline*, 169–249. New York: Cambridge University Press.

Ekman, P., and W. Friesen. 1969. The repertoire of nonverbal behavioral categories—Origins, usage, and coding. *Semiotica* 1:49–98.

———. 1984. *Unmasking the face*. Palo Alto, Calif.: Consulting Psychologists Press.

Elliott, C. 1997. I picked up Catapia and other stories: A multimodal approach to expressivity for "emotionally intelligent" agents. In *Proceedings of the First International Conference on Autonomous Agents* (Marina del Rey, Calif.), 451–457.

Hajicova, E., and P. Sgall. 1987. The ordering principle. *Journal of Pragmatics* 11:435–454.

Halliday, M. 1967. *Intonation and grammar in British English*. The Hague: Mouton.

Hinrichs, E., and L. Polanyi. 1986. Pointing the way: A unified treatment of referential gesture in interactive contexts. In A. Farley, P. Farley, and K. E. McCullough, eds., *Proceedings of the Parasession of the Chicago Linguistics Society Annual Meetings (Pragmatics and Grammatical Theory)*. Chicago: Chicago Linguistics Society.

Iverson, J., and S. Goldin-Meadow. 1996. Gestures in blind children. Unpublished manuscript, Department of Psychology, University of Chicago.

Johnson, M., J. Bransford, and S. Solomon. 1973. Memory for tacit implications of sentences. *Journal of Experimental Psychology* 98(1):203–205.

Kendon, A. 1972. Some relationships between body motion and speech. In A. W. Siegman and B. Pope, eds., *Studies in dyadic communication*. New York: Pergamon Press.

———. 1974. Movement coordination in social interaction: some examples described. In S. Weitz, ed., *Nonverbal communication*. New York: Oxford University Press.

———. 1980. Gesticulation and speech: Two aspects of the process. In M. R. Key, ed., *The relation between verbal and nonverbal communication*. The Hague: Mouton.

———. 1993. Gestures as illocutionary and discourse structure markers in southern Italian conversation. In *Proceedings of the Linguistic Society of America Symposium on Gesture in the Context of Talk*.

Krauss, R., P. Morrel-Samuels, and C. Colasante. 1991. Do conversational hand gestures communicate? *Journal of Personality and Social Psychology* 61(5):743–754.

Levelt, W. 1989. *Speaking: From intention to articulation*. Cambridge, Mass.: The MIT Press.

Luperfoy, S. N.d. *Spoken dialogue systems*. Cambridge, Mass.: The MIT Press. Forthcoming.

McNeill, D. 1992. *Hand and mind: What gestures reveal about thought*. Chicago: University of Chicago Press.

———. N.d. Models of speaking (to their amazement) meet speech-synchronized gestures. In D. McNeill, ed., *Language and gesture: Window into thought and action*. Hillsdale, N.J.: Lawrence Erlbaum Associates. Forthcoming.

Nickerson, R. S. 1976. On conversational interaction with computers. In R. M. Baecker and W. A. S. Buxton eds., *Readings in human computer interaction*, 681–693. Los Altos, Calif.: Morgan Kaufman.

Pelachaud, C., N. Badler, and M. Steedman. 1996. Generating facial expressions for speech. *Cognitive Science* 20(1):1–46.

Picard, R. 1998. *Affective computing*. Cambridge, Mass.: The MIT Press.

Rimé, B. 1982. The elimination of visible behavior from social interactions: Effects of verbal, nonverbal and interpersonal variables. *European Journal of Social Psychology* 12:113–129.

Scherer, K. R. 1980. The functions of nonverbal signs in conversation. In R. N. St. Clair and H. Giles, eds., *The social and psychological contexts of language*, 225–243. Hillsdale, N.J.: Lawrence Erlbaum Associates.

Takeuchi, A., and K. Nagao. 1993. Communicative facial displays as a new conversational modality. In *Proceedings of InterCHI* (Amsterdam), 187–193.

Wilson, A., A. Bobick, and J. Cassell. 1996. Recovering the temporal structure of natural gesture. In *Proceedings of the Second International Conference on Automatic Face and Gesture Recognition* (IEEE) (Killington, Vt.).

II
Systems

2

Human Conversation as a System Framework:

Designing Embodied Conversational Agents

Justine Cassell, Tim Bickmore, Lee Campbell, Hannes Vilhjálmsson, and Hao Yan

2.1 Introduction

Embodied conversational agents (ECAs) are not just computer interfaces represented by way of human or animal bodies. And they are not just interfaces where those human or animal bodies are *lifelike* or *believable* in their actions and their reactions to human users.

Embodied conversational agents are specifically *conversational* in their behaviors, and specifically humanlike in the way they use their bodies in conversation. That is, embodied conversational agents may be defined as those that have the same properties as humans in face-to-face conversation, including:

- the ability to recognize and respond to verbal and nonverbal input
- the ability to generate verbal and nonverbal output
- the ability to deal with conversational functions such as turn taking, feedback, and repair mechanisms
- the ability to give signals that indicate the state of the conversation, as well as to contribute new propositions to the discourse

The design of embodied conversational agents puts many demands on system architecture. In this chapter, we describe a conversational framework expressed as a list of conversational properties and abilities and then demonstrate how it can lead to a set of *architectural* design constraints. We describe an architecture that meets the constraints, and an implementation of the architecture that therefore exhibits many of the properties and abilities required for real-time natural conversation.

Research in computational linguistics, multimodal interfaces, computer graphics, and autonomous agents has led to the development of increasingly sophisticated autonomous or semi-autonomous virtual humans over the last five years. Autonomous self-animating characters of this sort are important for use in production animation, interfaces, and computer games. Increasingly, their autonomy comes from underlying models of behavior and intelligence rather than simple physical models of human motion. Intelligence also refers increasingly not just to the ability to reason, but also to "social smarts"—the ability to engage a human in an interesting, relevant conversation with appropriate speech and body behaviors. Our own research concentrates on social and linguistic intelligence—"conversational smarts"—and how to implement the type of virtual human that has the social and linguistic abilities to carry on a face-to-face conversation. This is what we call embodied conversational agents.

Our current work grows out of experience developing two prior systems: Animated Conversation (Cassell et al. 1994) and Ymir (Thórisson 1996). Animated Conversation was the first system to produce automatically context-appropriate gestures, facial movements, and intonational patterns for animated agents based on deep semantic representations of information, but it did not provide for real-time interaction with a user. The Ymir system focused on integrating multimodal input from a human user, including gesture, gaze, speech, and intonation, but was only capable of limited multimodal output in real time.

We are currently developing an embodied conversational agent architecture that integrates the real-time multimodal aspects of Ymir with the deep semantic generation and multimodal synthesis capability of Animated Conversation. We believe the resulting system provides a reactive character with enough of the nuances of human face-to-face conversation to make it both intuitive and robust. We also believe that such a system provides a strong platform on which to continue development of embodied conversational agents. And we believe that the conversational framework that we have developed as the underpinnings of this system is general enough to inform development of many different kinds of embodied conversational agents.

2.2 Motivation

A number of motivations exist for relying on research in human face-to-face conversation in developing embodied conversational agent interfaces. Our most general motivation arises from the fact that conversation is a primary skill for humans, and a very early learned skill (practiced, in fact, between infants and mothers who take turns cooing and burbling at one another (Trevarthen 1986)), and from the fact that the body is so well equipped to support conversation. These facts lead us to believe that embodied conversational agents may turn out to be powerful ways for humans to interact with their computers. However, an essential part of this belief is that in order for embodied conversational agents to live up to their promise, their implementations must be based on actual study of human-human conversation, and their architectures must reflect some of the intrinsic properties found there.

Our second motivation for basing the design of architectures for ECAs on the study of human-human conversation arises from an examination of some of the particular needs that are not met in current interfaces. For example, we consider ways to make dialogue systems robust in the face of imperfect speech recognition, to increase bandwidth at low cost, and to support efficient collaboration between human and machines and between humans mediated by machines. We believe that it is likely that embodied conversational agents will fulfill these needs because these functions are exactly what bodies bring to conversation. But these functions, then, must be carefully modeled in the interface.

Our motivations are expressed in the form of "beliefs" because, to date, no adequate embodied conversational agent platform has existed to test these claims. It is only now that implementations of "conversationally smart" ECAs exist that we can turn to the evaluation of their abilities (see, e.g., Nass, Isbister, and Lee, chap. 13; Oviatt and Adams, chap. 11; Sanders and Scholtz, chap. 12).

In the remainder of this chapter, we first present our conversational framework. We then discuss how this framework can drive the design of an architecture to control an animated character who participates effectively in conversational interaction with a human. We present an architecture that we have been developing to meet these design requirements and describe our first conversational character constructed using the architecture—Rea.[1] We end by outlining some of the future challenges that our endeavor faces, including the evaluation of this design claim.

2.3 Human Face-to-Face Conversation

To address the issues and motivations outlined above, we have developed the Functions, Modalities, Timing, Behaviors (FMTB) conversational framework for structuring conversational interaction between an embodied conversational agent and a human user. In general terms, all conversational behaviors in the FMTB conversational framework must support conversational functions, and any conversational action in any modality may convey several communicative goals. In this section, we motivate and describe this framework with a discussion of human face-to-face conversation. Face-to-face conversation is about the exchange of information, but in order for that exchange to proceed in an orderly and efficient fashion, participants engage in an elaborate social act that involves behaviors beyond mere recital of information-bearing words. This spontaneous performance, which so seamlessly integrates a number of modalities, is given unselfconsciously and without much effort. Some of the key features that allow conversation to function so well are

- the distinction between propositional and interactional functions of conversation
- the use of several conversational modalities
- the importance of timing among conversational behaviors (and the increasing co-temporality or synchrony among conversational participants)
- the distinction between conversational behaviors and conversational functions

2.3.1 Interactional and Propositional Functions of Conversation

Although a good portion of what goes on in conversation can be said to represent the actual thought being conveyed, or propositional content, many behaviors serve the sole purpose of regulating the interaction (Goodwin 1981; Kendon 1990). We can refer to these two types of contribution to the conversation as behaviors that have a *propositional* function and behaviors that have an *interactional* function, respectively. Propositional information includes meaningful speech as well as hand gestures and intonation used to complement or elaborate upon the speech content. Interactional information, likewise, can include speech or nonspeech behaviors.

Both the production and interpretation of propositional content rely on knowledge about what one wishes to say and on a dynamic model of the discourse context that includes the information previously conveyed and the kinds of reasons one has for conveying new information. Interactional content includes a number of cues that indicate the state of the conversation. They range from nonverbal behaviors such as head nods to regulatory speech such as "huh?" or "do go on."

One primary role of interactional information is to negotiate speaking turns. Listeners can indicate that they would like to receive the turn, for example, by raising their hands into space in front of their bodies or by nodding excessively before a speaker reaches the end of a phrase. Speakers can indicate they want to keep the turn, for example, by keeping their hands raised or by gazing away from the listener. These cues are particularly useful for the speaker when pauses in speech may tempt the listener to jump in.

Turn-taking behavior along with listener feedback, such as signs of agreement or simple "I am following" cues, are good examples of the kind of parallel activity that occurs during face-to-face conversation. Speakers and listeners monitor each other's behavior continuously throughout the interaction and are simultaneously producing and receiving information (Argyle and Cook 1976) and simultaneously conveying content and regulating the process of conveying content.

2.3.2 Multimodality

We can convey multiple communicative goals via the same communicative behaviors or by different communicative behaviors carried out at the same time. What makes this possible is the fact that we have at our disposal a number of modalities that can overlap without disruption. For example, a speaker can add a certain tone to the voice while raising the eyebrows to elicit feedback in the form of a head nod from the listener, all without interrupting the production of content. The use of several different modalities of communication—such as hand gestures, facial displays, eye gaze, and so forth—is what allows us to pursue multiple goals in parallel, some of a propositional nature and some of an interactional nature. It is important to realize that even though speech is prominent in conveying content in face-to-face conversation, spontaneous gesture is also integral to conveying propositional content. In fact, speech and gesture are produced simultaneously and take on a form that arises from one underlying representation (Cassell, chap. 1; McNeill 1992). What gets conveyed through speech and what gets conveyed through gesture are therefore a matter of a particular surface structure taking shape. For interactional communicative goals, the modality chosen may be more a function of what modality is free—for example, is the head currently engaged in looking at the task, or is it free to give a feedback nod?

2.3.3 Timing

The existence of such quick behaviors as head nods, which nonetheless have such an immediate effect on the other conversational participant, emphasizes the range of time scales involved in conversation. While we have to be able to interpret full utterances to produce meaningful responses, we are also sensitive to instantaneous feedback that may modify our production as we go.

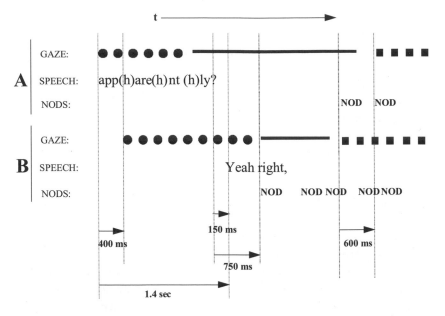

Figure 2.1
A wide variety of time scales in human face-to-face conversation. Circles indicate gaze moving toward other; lines indicate fixation on other; squares are withdrawal of gaze from other; question mark shows rising intonation (from Thórisson 1996, adapted from Goodwin 1981).

In addition, the *synchrony* among events, or lack thereof, is meaningful in conversation. Even the slightest delay in responding to conversational events may be taken to indicate unwillingness to cooperate or a strong disagreement (Rosenfeld 1987). As demonstrated in figure 2.1, speakers and listeners attend to and produce behaviors with a wide variety of time scales. It is remarkable how over the course of a conversation, participants increasingly synchronize their behaviors to one another. This phenomenon, known as entrainment, ensures that conversation will proceed efficiently.

2.3.4 Conversational *Functions* Are Carried Out by Conversational *Behaviors*
Even though conversation is an orderly event, governed by rules, no two conversations look exactly the same and the set of behaviors exhibited differs from person to person and from conversation to conversation. It is the functions referred to above that guide a conversation. Typical discourse functions include

conversation invitation, turn taking, providing feedback, contrast and emphasis, and breaking away. Therefore, to successfully build a model of how conversation works, one can not refer to surface features, or conversational behaviors alone. Instead, the emphasis has to be on identifying the fundamental phases and high-level structural elements that make up a conversation. These elements are then described in terms of their role or function in the exchange.

This is especially important because particular behaviors, such as the raising of eyebrows, can be employed in a variety of circumstances to produce different communicative effects, and the same communicative function may be realized through different sets of behaviors. The form we give to a particular discourse function depends on, among other things, current availability of modalities such as the face and the hands, type of conversation, cultural patterns, and personal style. For example, feedback can be given by a head nod, but instead of nodding, one could also say "uh huh" or "I see," and in a different context a head nod can indicate emphasis or a salutation rather than feedback. Table 2.1 shows some important conversational functions and the behaviors that realize them.

From the discussion above, it should be clear that we make extensive use of the body when engaged in face-to-face conversation. This is natural to us and has evolved along with language use and social competence. Given that this elaborate system of behaviors requires minimal conscious effort, and that no other type of real-time human-to-human interaction, such as phone conversation, can rival face-to-face interaction when it comes to "user satisfaction," one has to conclude that the affordances of the body in conversation are unique.

The ability to handle natural conversational interaction is particularly critical for real-time embodied conversational agents. Our FMTB conversational framework, then, relies on the interaction among the four properties of conversation described above (co-pursuing of interactional and propositional functions, multimodality, timing, distinction between conversational behaviors and conversational functions). Below, we review some related work before turning to a demonstration of how this model provides a natural design framework for embodied conversational architectures.

2.4 Related Work

We have argued that embodied conversational agents must be designed from research on the use and function of the verbal and nonverbal modalities in human-human conversation. Other authors in this volume adhere to this principle to a greater or lesser extent. Other work in interface design has also followed this path in the past, in particular, work in the domain of *multimodal*

Table 2.1 Some examples of conversational functions and their behavioral realization

Communicative Function	Communicative Behavior
Initiation and termination	
React to new person	Short glance at other
Break away from conversation	Glance around
Farewell	Look at other, head nod, wave
Turn taking	
Give turn	Look, raise eyebrows (followed by silence)
Want turn	Raise hands into gesture space
Take turn	Glance away, start talking
Feedback	
Request feedback	Look at other, raise eyebrows
Give feedback	Look at other, nod head

interfaces. Research on multimodal interfaces has concentrated more on the question of understanding the verbal and nonverbal modalities, whereas embodied conversational agents must both understand and generate behaviors in different conversational modalities. In what follows, we review some previous research in the fields of conversational interfaces and multimodal interfaces before turning to other embodied conversational agent work that resembles our own.

2.4.1 Synthetic Multimodal Conversation

"Animated Conversation" (Cassell et al. 1994) was a system that automatically generated context-appropriate gestures, facial movements, and intonational patterns. In this case, the domain was an interaction between a bank teller and customer. In order to avoid the issues involved with understanding human behavior, the interaction took place between two autonomous graphical agents and the emphasis was on the production of nonverbal behaviors that emphasized and reinforced the content of speech. In "Animated Conversation," although both turn-taking conversational behaviors and content-conveying conversational behaviors were implemented, no distinction was made between conversational behaviors and the functions they fulfilled. Each function was filled by only one behavior. Because there was no notion of conversational function, the interactional and propositional distinction could not be explicitly made. This was not a problem for the system, since it did not run in real time, and there was no interaction with a real user, but it made it impossible to extend the work to actual human-computer interaction.

André et al. (chap. 8) also implement a system for conversation between synthetic characters for the purpose of presenting information to a human, motivated by the engaging effect of teams of newscasters or sportscasters. Two domains are explored: car sales and "RoboCup Soccer," with an emphasis on conveying character traits as well as domain information. In the car domain, they use goal decomposition to break a presentation into speech acts; and personality and interest profiles in combination with multi-attribute utility theory to organize the presentation of automotive features and values. The result is a sequence of questions, answers, and comments between a seller and one or two buyers. The modalities explored are primarily speech and intonation; although there are some pointing hand gestures. The conversational behaviors generated by this system either fulfill a propositional goal, or convey personality or emotional traits; interactional goals are not considered.

2.4.2 Conversational Interfaces

Nickerson (1976) was one of the pioneers of modeling the computer interface on the basis of human conversation. He provided a list of features of face-to-face conversation that could be fruitfully applied to human-computer interaction, including mixed initiative, nonverbal communication, sense of presence, and rules for transfer of control. His concern was not even necessarily systems that carried on conversations with humans, but rather a model that allowed management and explicit representation of turn taking so the user's expectations could be harnessed in service of clearer interaction with the computer.

Brennan (1990) argues that human-computer interaction literature promulgates a false dichotomy between direct manipulation and conversation. From observations of human-human conversation, Brennan develops guidelines for designers of both GUI and conversational interfaces. Key guidelines include modeling shared understandings and provisions for feedback and for repair sequences. The work of both Nickerson and Brennan was essential to our FMTB model.

Badler et al. (chap. 9) present a conversational interface to an avatar control task. Avatars interact in the Jack-MOO virtual world, controlled by natural language commands such as "walk to the door and turn the handle slowly." They developed a Parameterized Action Representation to map high-level action labels into low-level sequences of avatar activity. Humans give orders to their avatars to act and speak, and the avatars may converse with some fully automated characters in the virtual world. Thus, the human interface is effectively command and control, while the multimodal conversation occurs between avatars and automatic characters. No interactional functions such as turn taking are considered in this system. In addition, there is a hard mapping between conversational behaviors and conversational functions, making the use of the different modalities somewhat inflexible.

2.4.3 Multimodal Interfaces

One of the first multimodal systems based on the study of nonverbal modalities in conversation was Put-That-There (Bolt 1980). Put-That-There used speech recognition and a six-degrees-of-freedom space-sensing device to gather user gestural input and allow the user to manipulate a wall-sized information display. Put-That-There used a simple architecture that combined speech and deictic gesture input into a single command that was then resolved by the system. For example, the system could understand the sentence "Move that over there" to mean move the sofa depicted on the wall display to a position near the table by analyzing the position of the pointing gestures of the user. In each case, however, the speech drove the analysis of the user input. Spoken commands were recognized first, and the gesture input only used if the user's command could not be resolved by speech analysis alone. Certain words in the speech grammar (such as "that") were tagged to indicate that they usually co-occurred with a deictic (pointing) gesture. When these words were encountered, the system analyzed the user's pointing gestures to resolve deictic references.

Koons extended this work by allowing users to maneuver objects around a two-dimensional map using spoken commands, deictic hand gestures, and eye gaze (Koons, Sparrel, and Thórisson 1993). In his system, nested frames were employed to gather and combine information from the different modalities. As in Put-That-There, speech drove the analysis of gesture: if information was missing from speech, the system would search for the missing information in the gestures and/or gaze. Time stamps united the actions in the different modalities into a coherent picture. Wahlster used a similar method, depending on typed text input to guide the interpretation of pointing gestures (Wahlster 1991).

These examples exhibit several features common to command-and-control-type multimodal interfaces. They are speech-driven, so the other input modalities are only used when the speech recognition produces ambiguous or incomplete results. Input interpretation is not carried out until the user has finished an utterance, meaning that the phrase level is the shortest time scale at which events can occur. The interface only responds to complete, well-formed input, and there is no attempt to use nonverbal behavior as interactional information to control the pace of the user-computer interaction.

These limitations were partially overcome by Johnston (1998), who described an approach to understanding user input based on unification with strongly typed multimodal grammars. In his pen and speech interface, either gesture or voice could be used to produce input and either one could drive the recognition process. Multimodal input was represented in typecast semantic frames with empty slots for missing information. These slots were then filled by considering input events of the correct type that occurred about the same time.

On a different tack, Massaro et al. (chap. 10) use nonverbal behavior in Baldi, an embodied character face, to increase the intelligibility of synthetic speech; they prove efficacy by testing speech readers' recognition rate with Baldi mouthing monosyllables. The output demonstrates improved intelligibility when lip shapes are correct, and the authors have also shown the utility of such a system for teaching spoken conversation to deaf children.

Missing from all these systems, however, is a distinction between conversational behavior and conversational function. This means, in addition, that there can be no notion of why a particular modality might be used rather than another, or what goals are achieved by the congruence of different modalities. The case of multiple communicative goals (propositional and interactional, for example) is not considered. Therefore, the role of gesture and voice input cannot be analyzed at more than a sentence-constituent replacement level.

2.4.4 Embodied Conversational Interfaces

Lester et al. (chap. 5) do rely on a notion of semantic function (reference) in order to generate verbal and nonverbal behavior, producing deictic gestures and choosing referring expressions as a function of the potential ambiguity of objects referred to and the proximity of those objects to the animated agent. This system is based on an understanding of how reference is achieved to objects in the physical space around an animated agent and the utility of deictic gestures in reducing potential ambiguity of reference. However, the generation of gestures and the choice of referring expressions (from a library of voice clips) are accomplished in two entirely independent (additive) processes, without a description of the interaction between or function filled by the two modalities.

Rickel and Johnson (1999; chap. 4) have designed a pedagogical agent, Steve, that can travel about a virtual ship, guiding a student to equipment, and then using gaze and deictic gesture during a verbal lesson about that equipment. The agent handles verbal interruption and provides verbal and nonverbal feedback (in the form of nods and headshakes) of the student's performance. Although Steve does use both verbal and nonverbal conversational behaviors, there is no way to time those behaviors with respect to one another at the level of the word or syllable. Nonverbal behaviors are hardwired for function: Steve cannot reason about which modalities might be better suited to serve particular functions at particular places in the conversation.

In contrast to these other systems, our current approach handles both multimodal input and output and is based on conversational functions that may be either interactional or propositional in nature. The basic modules of the architecture described in the next section were developed in conjunction with Churchill et al. (chap. 3). The architecture grows out of previous work in our research group on the Ymir architecture (Thórisson 1996). In this work, the main emphasis was on the development of a multilayer multimodal architecture that could support fluid face-to-face dialogue between a human and a graphical agent. The agent, Gandalf, recognized and displayed interactional information such as gaze and simple gesture and also produced propositional information, in the form of canned speech events. In this way, it was able to perceive and generate turn-taking and back-channel behaviors that lead to a very natural conversational interaction. This work provided a good first example of how verbal and nonverbal function might be paired in a conversational multimodal interface. However, Gandalf had limited ability to recognize and generate propositional information, such as providing correct intonation for speech emphasis on speech output, or a gesture co-occurring with speech. The approach we use with Rea combines lessons learned from both the Gandalf and Animated Conversation projects.

2.5 Embodied Conversational Agent Architecture

The FMTB model described above can be summarized as follows: multiple (interactional and propositional) communicative goals are conveyed by conversational functions that are expressed by conversational behaviors in one or several modalities. This model, which also serves as a strong framework for system design, is lacking in other embodied conversational agents. We have therefore designed a generic architecture for ECAs that derives directly from the FMTB conversational framework described above. We feel that it is crucial that ECAs be capable of employing the same repertoire of conversational skills as their human interactants, both to obviate the need for users to learn how to interact with the agent and to maximize the naturalness and fluidity of the interaction. We believe that in order to enable the use of conversational skills, even the very architecture of the system must be designed according to the affordances and necessities of conversation. Thus, in our design we draw directly from the rich literature in linguistics, sociology, and human ethnography described in the previous section to derive our requirements, based on our FMTB conversational framework.

In general terms, the conversational model that we have described leads to the following set of ECA architectural design requirements:

- Understanding and Synthesis of Propositional and Interactional Information. Dealing with both propositional and interactional functions of conversation requires models of the user's needs and knowledge and of the user's conversational process and states. Producing propositional information requires a planning module to plan how to present multisentence output and manage the order of presentation of interdependent facts. The architecture must include both a static domain knowledge base and a dynamic discourse knowledge base. Understanding interactional information, on the other hand, entails building a model of the current state of the conversation with respect to conversational process (who is the current speaker and who is the listener, has the listener understood the speaker's contribution, and so on).

- Multimodal Input and Output. Since humans in face-to-face conversation send and receive information through gesture, intonation, and gaze as well as speech, the architecture also should support receiving and transmitting this information and should be modular so that new input and output modalities can easily be added as new technologies are developed.

- Timing. Because of the importance of working with different time scales, and of synchrony among behaviors, the system must allow the embodied conversational agent to watch for feedback and turn requests, while the human can send these at any time through various modalities. The architecture should be flexible enough to track these different threads of communication in ways appropriate to each thread. Different threads have different response-time requirements; some, such as feedback and interruption, occur on a subsecond time scale. The architecture should reflect this fact by allowing different processes to concentrate on activities at different timescales.

- Conversational Function Model. Explicitly representing conversational functions rather than simply a set of conversational behaviors provides both modularity and a principled way to combine different modalities. Functional models influence the architecture because the core modules of the system operate exclusively on functions (rather than sentences, for example), while other modules at the edges of the system infer functions from input and realize functions for outputs. This also produces a symmetric architecture because the same functions and modalities are present in both input and output.

Based on our previous experience with Animated Conversation and Ymir, we have developed an architecture that handles both real-time response to interactional cues and understanding and generation of propositional content. The interactional and propositional functions are capable of being filled by conversational behaviors in several modalities.

The architecture follows sequential processing of user input (see fig. 2.2). First, the Input Manager collects input from all modalities and decides whether the data requires an instant reaction or deliberative discourse processing. Hardwired Reaction handles quick reactions to stimuli such as the appearance or side-to-side movement of the user. These stimuli then provoke a modification of the agent's behavior without much delay. For example, the agent's gaze can seamlessly track the user's movement. The Deliberative Discourse Processing module handles all input that requires a discourse model for proper interpretation. This includes many of the interactional behaviors as well as all propositional behaviors. Last, the Action Scheduler is responsible for scheduling motor events to be sent to the animated figure representing the agent. A crucial function of the scheduler is to prevent collisions between competing motor requests. Each of the modules in the architecture is described next.

2.5.1 Input Manager

In order to support integration of multimodal input from the user, the Input Manager obtains data from the various input devices, converts it into a form usable by other modules in the system, and routes the results to the Deliberative Module. Some interactional information can also be forwarded directly to the Action Scheduler module by way of the Hardwired Reaction module to minimize system response time (e.g., changing the character's gaze to

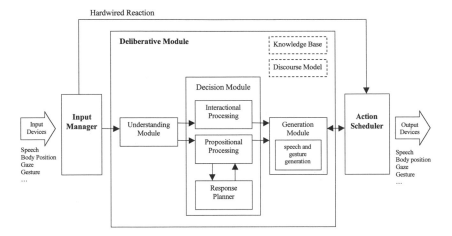

Figure 2.2
Overall architecture.

track a change in the user's location). The Input Manager will typically receive information from devices that provide speech text, user gesture, location, and gaze information, and other modalities. In all cases, the features sent to the Input Manager are time-stamped with start and end times in milliseconds.

2.5.2 Hardwired Reactions

Hardwired reactions enable the character to respond immediately to certain unimodal user inputs that require fast reaction but do not require any inferencing or reference to the discourse model. Examples include tracking the user's location with the character's eyes and responding to the user suddenly entering or leaving the interaction space.

2.5.3 Deliberative Module

In order to maintain coherence in the conversation and track the user's focus, the Deliberative Discourse Processing module maintains a discourse model of the entities introduced in the conversation, the previous statements made by the user and the agent, and other information (e.g., the user's ultimate and intermediate communicative goals in terms of housing requirements in the real estate domain). The components of this module are grouped together so that they can reference and update these data structures.

The Deliberative Module performs the action selection function of the architecture, which determines what the agent's contribution to the conversation should be at each moment in time. It receives asynchronous updates from the Input Manager and uses information about the domain (static knowledge base) and current discourse state to determine the conversational action to perform.

The processing is split into three main components: Understanding, Decision, and Generation (see fig. 2.2). The Understanding Module is responsible for fusing all input modalities into a coherent understanding of what the user is doing and for translating a set of behaviors into a discourse function, interactional or propositional. It passes these on to the Decision Module in the form of speech acts.

The processing within the Decision Module is split between the processing of interactional communicative acts (those that contribute to the management of the conversational situation) and the processing of propositional communicative acts (those that contribute to the content of the discussion).

The Interactional Processing submodule is responsible for updating the conversational state—namely, whether a conversation with a user has started, who has the turn, and whether the interaction has been put on hold while the user momentarily attends to something else (see fig. 2.3). The Propositional Processing submodule is responsible for choosing adequate responses to propositional input (for example, answering questions) and for communicating with the Response Planner if necessary.

It is important for both the interactional and propositional processes to have access to a common discourse model because interactional information plays a role in validating discourse history updates. For example, the propositional submodule will send off to the Generation Module a speech act to be realized. However, only when the interactional part detects that the agent has successfully concluded an utterance without an interruption from the user does the system consider whether to add the new proposition to the shared knowledge or discourse history.

The Response Planner is responsible for formulating sequences of actions, some or all of which will need to be executed during future execution cycles, to carry out desired communicative or task goals. The Generation Module is responsible for turning discourse functions (such as giving up the turn or con-

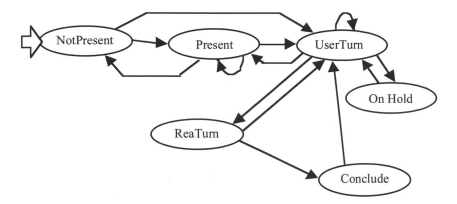

Figure 2.3
Interactional conversational states.

veying a communicative goal) that have been chosen by the Decision Module into actual surface behaviors by producing a set of coordinated primitive actions (such as speech, gesture, facial expression, or a combination of the above) and sending the actions to the Action Scheduler for performance.

2.5.4 Action Scheduling Module
The Action Scheduler is the motor controller for the embodied agent, responsible for coordinating output actions at the lowest level. It takes a set of atomic modality-specific commands and executes them in a synchronized way. This is accomplished through the use of event conditions specified on each output action which define when the action should be executed.

2.5.5 Architecture Summary
In moving from studying conversation between humans to implementing computer systems, we are moving from a rich description of a naturally occurring phenomenon to a parametric implementation. In the process, certain aspects of the phenomenon emerge as feasible to implement, and certain aspects of the phenomenon emerge as key functions without which the implementation would make no sense. The FMTB conversational model is a way of gathering those functions that are essential to the implementation and that can be used

as a design framework for the architecture. In the next section, we address the implementation that comes out of an architecture designed in this way.

2.6 Implementation

We are developing an embodied conversational agent within this architecture that is capable of having a real-time face-to-face conversation with a human. The agent, named Rea (for Real Estate Agent), plays the role of a real estate salesperson who interacts with users to determine their needs, shows them around virtual properties, and attempts to sell them a house. We chose the domain of real estate because of the amount of talk with a social function that it provokes (and because we couldn't pass up the phrase "an experiment in virtual realty"!). That is, in order to put clients enough at ease that they will be able to conceive of parting with the amount of money needed to purchase a house, realtors engage in a lot of talk with a mixed social or interactional function and a propositional function. This domain, then, allowed us to work toward an agent capable of dealing with multiple communicative goals: both interactional and propositional contributions to the discourse, made by way of conversational behaviors carried out in several modalities.

Rea has a fully articulated 3-D graphical body and communicates using both verbal and nonverbal modalities. She is able to describe features of a house using a combination of speech utterances and gestures, and can also respond to users' verbal and nonverbal input. When the user makes cues typically associated with turn-taking behavior such as gesturing, Rea allows herself to be interrupted, then takes the turn again when she is able. She is able to initiate conversational repair when she misunderstands what the user says. Rea's speech and gesture output are actually generated in real time from the same underlying knowledge base and description of communicative goals, using the SPUD ("Sentence Planning Using Description") natural language generation engine (Stone 1998; Stone and Doran 1997). The following is an excerpt from a sample interaction:

Lee approaches the projection screen. Rea is currently turned side on and is gazing idly about. As Lee moves within range of the two cameras mounted above the screen, Rea turns to face him and says:
REA> Hello. How can I help you?
LEE> I'm looking to buy a place near MIT.
Rea nods, indicating that she is following.
REA> I have a house to show you.

*A picture of a house appears on-screen behind Rea who blinks
and looks at the house and then at Lee.*
REA> It's in Somerville.
LEE> Tell me about it.
Rea looks up and away while she plans what to say.
REA> It's big.
Rea makes an expansive gesture with her hands.
*Lee brings his hands up as if he is about to speak and so Rea
does not continue; instead, she is waiting for him to speak.*
LEE> Tell me more about it.
REA> Sure thing. It has a nice garden.
*Rea sketches a curved gesture with her hands indicating that
the garden extends along two sides of the house.*
LEE> How far is it?
REA> It is five minutes to the Porter Square T station.
*Rea makes it clear that it is five minutes **on foot** from the T
station by making a walking gesture with her fingers.*
LEE> How big is the house?
REA> It has four bedrooms, three bathrooms . . .
Lee interrupts Rea who stops speaking immediately.
LEE> Wait. Tell me, where is the master bedroom?
REA> I'm sorry, I didn't catch that. What did you ask me?
LEE> Where is the master bedroom?
REA> It's upstairs.
Rea points up.
LEE> Where is the master bathroom?
REA> It's next to the bedroom.
*Rea brings her hands together to indicate the relationship
between the bedroom and the bathroom.*
And the house tour continues . . .

The system currently consists of a large projection screen on which Rea is displayed and in front of which the user stands. Two cameras mounted on top of the projection screen track the user's head and hand positions in space. Users wear a microphone for capturing speech input. A single SGI™ Octane computer runs the graphics and conversation engine of Rea, while several other computers manage the speech recognition and generation and image processing (fig. 2.4). The system is implemented in C++ and CLIPS (CLIPS 1994), a rule-based expert system programming language. The modularity of the system design is made possible by using KQML performatives, a common message protocol for interagent communication (Finin and Fritzon 1994), to send and receive messages between different modules.

In the following sections, we discuss in detail our implementation of the embodied conversational agent architecture in the Rea system. In the discussion of Rea's implementation, we will follow our discussion of the architecture, moving from the Input Manager through the discourse processing module to the Action Scheduler and graphics generation.

2.6.1 Input Sensors

The function of the Input Manager in the architecture is to handle both verbal and nonverbal inputs from different devices and prepare them for understanding.

In Rea, the Input Manager currently receives three types of input:

- Gesture Input: STIVE vision software (Azarbayejani, Wren, and Pentland 1996) uses two video cameras to track flesh color and produce 3-D position and orientation of the head and hands at ten to fifteen updates per second.
- Audio Input: A simple audio processing routine detects the onset, pauses, and cessation of speech.
- Grammar-Based Speech Recognition: Speech is also piped to a PC running IBM's ViaVoice98™, which returns text from a set of phrases defined by a grammar.

Data sent to the Input Manager is time-stamped with start and end times in milliseconds. The various computers are synchronized to within a few milliseconds of each other using NTP (Network Time Protocol) clients. This synchronization is key for associating verbal and nonverbal behaviors. Low-level gesture and audio detection events are sent to the Deliberative Module immediately. These events are also stored in a buffer so that when recognized speech arrives, a high-level multimodal KQML frame can be created containing mixed speech, audio, and gesture events. This is sent to the Understanding Module for interpretation.

2.6.2 Discourse Processing

The deliberative processing module is the core part of the architecture. It handles both interactional and propositional facets of the discourse. In Rea, all of

Figure 2.4
Rea says, "It is next to the bedroom."

the deliberative processing modules are written in CLIPS. Although propositional and interactional elements are considered in an integrated fashion at
many points in the system, we will describe them here separately for expository purposes.

2.6.2.1 *Interactional Discourse Processing* The processing of interactional information in Rea involves some speech but primarily the handling of all non-
speech-content inputs and outputs.

The Understanding Module receives a KQML frame from the Input Manager
that contains tagged user input, including information from the vision system
about the presence or absence of the user and whether he or she is gesturing or
not, and information from the audio threshold detector about whether the user
has started speaking, has paused, or has finished speaking. The Understanding
Module looks at the current conversational state (as shown in fig. 2.3) and the last

known state of all inputs in deciding how to map a particular input into a discourse function. For example, if the user has paused in his or her speaking and the conversational state is UserTurn (user has the floor) and Rea does not take the turn within 0.8 seconds, then a WantingFeedback functional descriptor is created, indicating that the user's utterance should be acknowledged if possible.

The Decision Module is the center of volition for Rea, since all of its inputs are input discourse functions describing user actions, and its outputs are output discourse functions for Rea to execute. Upon receipt of an interactional message from the Understanding Module, the Decision Module consults the current conversational state and decides on an output action and/or conversational state change. For example, if the conversational state is UserTurn and the Decision Module receives a WantingFeedback message, then a GiveFeedback interactional output message is constructed and sent to the Generation Module for execution, and the state remains UserTurn.

The Generation Module maps requests for output discourse functions into specific output behaviors, based on channel availability, and defines the synchronization requirements for the Action Scheduler to execute. For example, if the interactional output function GiveFeedback is received and Rea's head is not currently being used for a higher-priority behavior, then an Action Scheduler command is generated and sent to cause Rea to nod her head (if her head had been busy, feedback could also have been generated by means of a paraverbal, such as "uh huh").

2.6.2.2 *Propositional Discourse Processing* The processing of propositional information primarily involves the understanding and processing of speech inputs and the generation of speech and gestural outputs.

As mentioned above, the Understanding Module receives a KQML frame from the Input Manager that contains tagged user input. The Understanding Module's main propositional task is to convert speech input into a valid speech act after resolving referring expressions. The KQML tags from the speech recognizer describe the contents of the utterance and the type of speech act being performed (following Ferguson et al. 1996), in addition to the identification of all discourse entities.

When the Understanding Module has finished binding the discourse entities of the new utterance to existent knowledge base entries, it tries to fill in a speech act template. The template type is chosen according to the incoming speech act tag, but the templates may have preconditions associated with them that have to be fulfilled in order for them to be selected. This way, the choice of template can be sensitive to the discourse model states.

Once the speech act template has been selected and filled in, it is sent to the Decision Module that then needs to evaluate its effect and choose a response. The evaluation may update facts in the dynamic knowledge base and/or create an obligation that the agent needs to attend to. The agent can then perform simple plan reasoning to come up with one or more speech acts to achieve the obligation or communicative goal. The agent commits to the execution of that plan by intending to execute the first speech act of the plan. When it is time to act, the relevant speech act template is filled out and handed to the Generation Module for realization, along with any interactional functions that need to be executed in order to contribute successfully to the conversation.

In Rea, the communicative goal of a speech act can be accomplished by a speech utterance or by the combination of a speech utterance and an appropriate gesture (or gestures). The task of the Speech and Gesture Generation Module is to construct the communicative action that achieves given goals. These propositional goals need to convey domain propositions that encode specified kinds of information about a specified object. The communicative action generated must also fit the context specified by the discourse model, to the best extent possible. We use the SPUD generator to carry out this generation task.

Figure 2.5 shows the structure of the simultaneous speech and gesture generation process in the Generation Module. An utterance generation process starts when the Decision Module sends out a generation speech act. The generation speech act is usually in the "Describe(object, aspect)" form. The request formulator first converts it into a communicative goal that can be understood by the SPUD generator.

The structure of context, private and shared knowledge, syntactic frames, and the lexicon construct the basic background knowledge base upon which SPUD can draw for its communicative content. The lexical items in speech and constraints on movements in gestures are treated equally as lexicalized descriptors in the knowledge base. The organization of the background knowledge base defines the common ground, in terms of the sources of information that the user and Rea share. It also describes the relationship between Rea's privately held information and the questions of interest to the user that information can be used to settle. Necessary syntactic and semantic constraints about utterances are also specified in the background knowledge base.

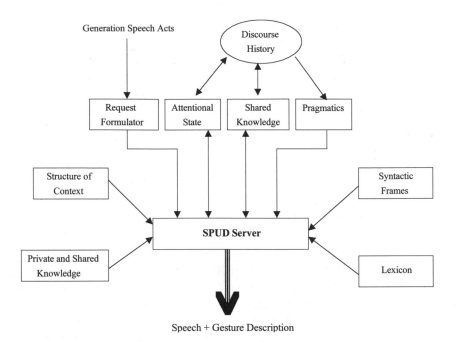

Figure 2.5
Speech and gesture generation.

During the conversation, SPUD gets dynamic updates from Rea's Discourse Model to keep on top of the changing state and context of conversation. These updates include the current attentional state of the discourse (Grosz and Sidner 1986), shared knowledge update to the common ground (Clark and Marshall 1981), and pragmatics by which SPUD looks to prove before an entry can be used.

Based on the communicative goal, background knowledge base, and the updated context of current conversation, SPUD builds the utterance element by element; at each stage of construction, SPUD's representation of the current incomplete utterance specifies its syntax, semantics, interpretation, and fit to context. If a generation process is successful, a speech utterance along with appropriate gesture descriptions are generated. The gestures generated by the generation process can convey the same piece of meaning that is conveyed by the speech utterances. The use of gestures in this condition will increase the expressiveness and robustness of the communication. The gestures can also complement the speech utterances—namely, they can convey additional information that is not conveyed by the speech itself. In this case, the communicative load is distributed to both the speech and gestures. The generation process currently uses the combination of the following two kinds of rules to determine whether to generate a complementary or a redundant gesture:

- grouping rules that determine which aspects of an object or an action can be articulated together
- appropriateness rules that determine which aspects/semantics are appropriate or easier to be expressed via the gesture channel, and if appropriate, which gesture can best represent the semantics

Finally, a KQML frame containing the description is sent to the Action Scheduler for execution.

2.6.3 Output System

The multimodal and real-time architectural requirements call for a careful design of the output system. In particular, an embodied conversational agent needs a near-perfect coordination between speech and nonverbal behavior such as gesturing. The slightest mismatch will not only look unnatural, but could in fact convey something different from what was intended. The modularity and extensibility of the architecture require well-defined interfaces between the various components of the output system and have inspired the implementation of a plug-in style motor skill mechanism.

The output system in Rea consists of three main components: a scheduling component, an animation component, and a rendering component. They map into the ECA architecture as Action Scheduler and output devices, respectively. The scheduler receives requests for the activation of various behaviors from the Generation Module. The requests include interdependencies among the behaviors, such as requirements about one behavior finishing before another one starts. The scheduler is therefore responsible for successfully sequencing pending behaviors. The animator assigns a behavior ready to be executed to a motor skill that then becomes responsible for animating the joints of the model by communicating with the renderer (fig. 2.6).

2.6.3.1 Scheduler A behavior description with its preconditions and manner of execution are sent to the scheduler in a KQML message. The Generation Module

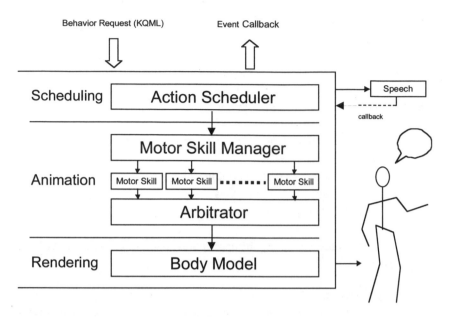

Figure 2.6
The three layers of the output system: scheduling, animation, and rendering.

typically sends the scheduler a set of behaviors that together, when properly triggered, are meant to carry out a single function, for example an invitation to start a conversation. The scheduler can be instructed to notify the Generation Module through KQML callback messages when certain events occur, such as completion of an output behavior sequence.

Execution of behaviors in the scheduler is event-driven because it is often difficult to accurately predict output behavior execution timings, making it impossible to plan out completely synchronized execution sequences in advance. In addition, some behaviors can produce meaningful events while they are being executed (e.g., the speech synthesis behavior can produce an event after each word is produced) and thus allow other behaviors to be started or stopped when these events occur. Figure 2.7 shows an example of an event-driven plan executed by the Action Scheduler with dependencies among the individual behaviors.

The specification sent to the Action Scheduler contains a description of each individual behavior to be executed (a ":content" clause), along with a pre-

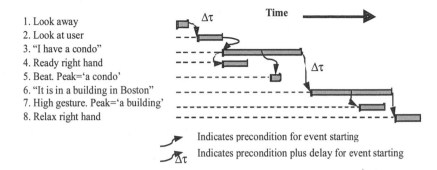

1. Look away
2. Look at user
3. "I have a condo"
4. Ready right hand
5. Beat. Peak='a condo'
6. "It is in a building in Boston"
7. High gesture. Peak='a building'
8. Relax right hand

Indicates precondition for event starting

Indicates precondition plus delay for event starting

Figure 2.7

Example of synchronized speech and gesture output by the Action Scheduler.

condition for the start of the behavior (a ":when" clause) and an optional symbolic label (":id"), which can be used in the preconditions of other behaviors. Figure 2.8 shows the KQML input specification for the plan shown in figure 2.7.

The Action Scheduler works by managing a set of primitive behavior objects, each of which represents a set of animations (e.g., "right arm gestures"). When a behavior is commanded to start, it first acquires the body degrees of freedom (DOF) that it requires, such as the set of the right arm and hand joints. It then goes into a starting phase in which it can perform initialization, such as moving the arm into a ready position. Most of the behavior's actions are carried out in the update phase, which ends when the behavior reaches a natural stopping point, when it is explicitly commanded to stop, or when some other behavior preempts it by grabbing one or more of its DOFs. Before returning to idle, a behavior can go through an ending phase in which it can perform any wrap-up operations needed, such as returning the arm to its rest position.

When the scheduler has a nonverbal behavior ready for execution, it passes its description over to the animator. Actions not involving the character's body are executed directly: for example, verbal behavior is sent to the speech synthesizer.

2.6.3.2 *Animator* The animator checks with the Motor Skill Manager to see if a motor skill capable of handling the request has registered with it. The task of animating joints of the model was broken up into separate motor skills in part

```
[(action :id H_AWAY :when immediate
    :content (headlook :cmd away :object user))
(action :id H_AT :when (offset_after :event H_AWAY.END :time 00:01.50)
    :content (headlook :cmd towards :object user))
(action :id S_CONDO :when (after :event H_AT.END)
    :content (speak :content "I have a condo."))
(action :when (after :event S_CONDO.START)
    :content (rightgesture :cmd ready))
(action :when (after :event S_CONDO.WORD3)
    :content (rightgesture :cmd beat))
(action :id S_BLDG :when (offset_after :event S_COND.END :time 00:01.00)
    :content (speak :content "It is in a building in Boston."))
(action :when (after :event S_BLDG.WORD4)
    :content (rightgesture :cmd compose :trajectory vertup :hand bend))
(action :when (after :event S_BLDG.END)
    :content (rightgesture :cmd relax))]
```

Figure 2.8
Action Scheduler KQML input specification for the plan shown in figure 2.7.

because the different skills called for different methods of animation. Motor skills range from straightforward ones, such as those executing a single head nod, to more elaborate ones such as those employing inverse kinematics for pointing at objects or playing key-frame animation. When a motor skill is activated, it asks the Arbitrator for the body DOFs it needs to modify. If two skills ask for the same DOF, the one with the higher priority captures it.

Depending on the implementation of particular skills, the losing skill can keep trying to capture the DOF. This feature is useful for instances where a continuous behavior is momentarily interrupted by an instantaneous one, such as when the character is tracking the user with its gaze and gets asked to glance up and away (higher priority). When the glance is completed, the tracking automatically resumes. The Arbitrator is responsible for keeping track of DOFs in use and allocating them to skills that request them.

All skills can access information about the environment, including virtual objects and the perceived user position through a shared world. Motor skills such as for controlling facing can therefore accept names of objects as parameters.

2.6.3.3 Renderer The rendering engine is abstracted away from the animator by introducing a Body Model layer that essentially maps a DOF name to the corresponding model transformation. We have implemented a Body Model that interfaces with a VRML scene graph rendered using OpenInventor from TGS.

The naming of the character's DOFs follows the H-Anim VRML Humanoid Specification for compatibility.

2.7 Evaluation

In this chapter, we have argued that architectures for embodied conversational agents can—indeed must—be built from a model of human-human conversation. And we have provided such a model in the form of a set of properties of human-human conversation that we believe are essential to allowing computers to carry on natural conversations with humans. Note that, following Nickerson (1976), it is important to point out that "an assumption that is not made, however, is that in order to be maximally effective, systems must permit interactions between people and computers that resemble interperson conversations in all respects." Instead, we have argued in this chapter that a successful model of conversation for ECAs picks out those facets of human-human conversation that are feasible to implement, and without which the implementation of an ECA would make no sense.

These claims must be evaluated. To date, empirical evaluations of any kinds of embodied interfaces have been few, and their results have been equivocal. As Shneiderman (1998) points out, ample historical evidence, in the form of a veritable junk pile of abandoned anthropomorphic systems, exists against using anthropomorphized designs in the interface. And Dehn and van Mulken (n.d.), specifically examining evaluations of recent animated interface agents, conclude that the benefits of these systems are arguable in terms of user performance, engagement with the system, or even attributions of intelligence. They point out, however, that virtually none of the systems evaluated exploited the affordances of the human bodies they inhabited: this design paradigm "can only be expected to improve human-computer interaction if it shows some behavior that is functional with regard to the system's aim." In other words, embodiment for the sake of the pretty graphics will probably not work.

But note that it is only very recently that embodied conversational agents have been implemented with anywhere near the range of conversational properties outlined above. For this reason, it is only now that we can start to carry out rigorous evaluations of the benefits of conversational embodiment. But evaluation of a system like this takes several forms. We must evaluate the adequacy of the *model* that serves as a design framework; we must evaluate the *implementation* of that design, and we must evaluate the *artifact* that results—that is, we must evaluate the ECA as human-computer interface.

2.7.1 Evaluation of Conversational Model

Our method of evaluating the FMTB conversational model is to look for lacunae in the theory that are pointed out by the implementation. For example, in the earlier Animated Conversation system, interactional and propositional functions were handled entirely separately throughout the system architecture. It was assumed that each utterance had one communicative goal. An unexpected result was that too many head nods and hand gestures were generated, since some performed an interactional and some performed a propositional function. As a result, the current conversational model allows multiple communicative goals for each utterance, of which some may be interactional and some propositional. Our evaluation of the current conversational model, FMTB, has pointed out a weak spot in the understanding of the relationship between conversational behaviors and conversational functions. In particular, it is clear that there is of yet no way of predicting what conversational behaviors will vehicle particular conversational behaviors. That is, we have no theory of the generativity of conversational behaviors from conversational functions.

One particularly difficult arena in which this is true is the generation of hand gestures. We may know that a gesture should convey propositional content, and even that the content should be "a garden that surrounds the house," and we can autonomously generate these two stages of the production process, but we have no way of predicting what shape of the hands or movement of the hands will best represent this content. For the moment, we resolve this lacuna by providing a list of conversational behaviors. We hope in the future to have a more principled method of solving the problem. We might look at this issue as being one of the *morphology* of conversational behaviors, and we see it as a topic of future research for our group.

2.7.2 Evaluation of Implementation

Our method of evaluating the implementation is simply to see what aspects of the architecture, and of the model before it, are not translated into system behaviors. And, what aspects are badly or imperfectly translated. In this evaluation, one aspect of the FMTB conversational model is strikingly difficult to implement, and that is the feature of *timing*. In fact, our evaluation of our own current implementation points out several weaknesses with respect to timing and to synchrony. First of all, with respect to speed, the natural language generation engine is not currently fast enough to provide any sense of entrainment to human users. That is, users get a sense that Rea is thinking too long before she speaks. Because we have implemented a deliberative discourse processing module and a hardwired reaction module to handle different time scales, this slowness is all the more noticeable. Sometimes Rea reacts instantly, and sometimes she takes too long. Next, with respect to synchrony, we have not yet resolved the issue of how to time gestures perfectly with respect to the speech that they accompany. Thus, for example, hand gestures may occur somewhat after the speech with which they are generated. This simply gives the impression that the system is not working correctly, or that Rea is a bit dim. The problem is due primarily to the difficulty of synchronizing events across output devices, and of predicting in advance how long it will take to execute particular behaviors. That is, it is difficult to predict—and synchronize—the timing of speech synthesis produced by a text-to-speech engine and graphical representations of hand movements produced by a rendering engine.

In order to address this problem, we are currently looking at other text-to-speech engines that may give us phoneme timings in advance, which might facilitate predicting how long it will take to utter a particular phrase. However, a more profound solution, and one that is more in line with the conversational FMTB model presented here, is to endow the Action Scheduler with more intelligence about issues of timing and synchrony. That is, we might conceive of an Action Scheduler that doesn't allow missynchronized behaviors to be generated, or that works with other kinds of timing and synchronization constraints. This is a topic for future research.

2.7.3 Evaluation of Interaction

We evaluate the quality of Rea as interface by having her interact with untrained users. Of course, an entirely free interaction with a user would allow us to know whether Rea is ready for prime time (the real estate market) but not allow us to pinpoint the source of any difficulties users might have in the interaction. Therefore, as Nass, Isbister, and Lee (chap. 13) describe, we evaluate the performance of our embodied conversational agent through a series of Wizard of Oz experiments where we manipulate one or two variables at a time. Comparing one of Rea's ancestors (see Cassell and Thórisson 1999 for further details and citations) to an identical body uttering identical words, but without nonverbal interactional behaviors, we found that users judged the version with interactional behaviors to be more collaborative and more cooperative and to exhibit better natural language (even though both versions had identical natural language abilities). On the other hand, performance on the task was not significantly different between the groups. An evaluation of one of Rea's cousins—a 3-D graphical world where anthropomorphic avatars autonomously generate the conversational behaviors described here—did show positive benefits on task performance. And users in this study preferred the autonomous version to a menu-driven version with all of the same behaviors (Cassell and Vilhjálmsson 1999).

Currently, we are conducting an evaluation that compares (a) face-to-face conversation with Rea to conversation over the telephone with a dialogue system, and (b) whether the user believes that the system (either Rea or the dialogue system) is autonomous to whether it is being manipulated by a human in real time. We will look at the effect of these conditions on users' perception of the system but also on their efficiency in carrying out a task and their performance on that task. In this way, we hope to begin to evaluate the particular conversational properties that make up our FMTB conversational model.

2.8 Conclusions

One of the motivations for embodied conversational agents—as for dialogue systems before them—comes from increasing computational capacity in many objects and environments outside of the desktop computer—smart rooms and intelligent toys, in environments as diverse as a military battlefield or a children's museum—and for users as different from one another as we can imagine. It is in part for this reason that we continue to pursue the dream of computers without keyboards that can accept natural untrained input. In situations such as these, we will need robustness in the face of noise, universality and intuitiveness, and a higher bandwidth than speech alone. We will need computers that untrained users can interact with naturally. And we believe that this naturalness of interaction can come from systems built on the basis of a strong model of human conversation.

In this chapter, we have argued that architectures for embodied conversational agents need to be based on a conversational model that describes the functionality, properties, and affordances of human face-to-face conversation. The qualitative difference in architectures designed in this way is that the human body enables the use of certain communication protocols in face-to-face conversation. The use of gaze, gesture, intonation, and body posture plays an essential role in the proper execution of many conversational behaviors—such as conversation initiation and termination, turn taking and interruption handling, and feedback and error correction—and these kinds of behaviors enable the exchange of multiple levels of information in real time. People are extremely adept at extracting meaning from subtle variations in the performance of these behaviors; for example, slight variations in pause length, feedback nod timing, or gaze behavior can significantly alter the message a speaker sends.

Of particular interest to interface designers is that these communication protocols come for "free" in that users do not need to be trained in their use; all native speakers of a given language have these skills and use them daily. Thus, an embodied interface agent that exploits them has the potential to provide a higher bandwidth of communication than would otherwise be possible. However, the flip side is that these communications protocols must be executed correctly for the embodiment to bring benefit to the interface.

We believe that Rea begins to demonstrate those correct communications protocols that will make embodied conversational agents successful as human-computer interface.

Notes

Research leading to the preparation of this article was supported by the National Science Foundation (award IIS-9618939), AT&T, Deutsche Telekom, and the other generous sponsors of the MIT Media Lab. Sincere thanks to Kenny Chang, Joey Chang, Sola Grantham, Erin Pänttäjä, Jennifer Smith, Scott Prevost, Kris Thórisson, Obed Torres, and all of the other talented and dedicated students and former students who have worked on the Embodied Conversational Agents project. Many thanks also to colleague Matthew Stone for his continued invaluable contribution to this work. Finally, thanks to Jeff Rickel and Elisabeth André for helpful comments on an earlier draft.

1. This architecture has been developed in conjunction with the Conversational Characters project at FX Palo Alto Laboratory Inc.

References

Argyle, M., and M. Cook. 1976. *Gaze and mutual gaze*. Cambridge: Cambridge University Press.

Azarbayejani, A., C. Wren, and A. Pentland. 1996. Real time 3-D tracking of the human body. In *Proceedings of IMAGE'COM 96* (Bordeaux, France), May.

Bolt, R. A. 1980. Put-That-There: Voice and gesture at the graphics interface. *Computer Graphics* 14(3):262–270.

Brennan, S. 1990. Conversation as direct manipulation: An iconoclastic view. In B. Laurel, ed., *The art of human-computer interface design*, 393–404. Reading, Mass.: Addison-Wesley.

Cassell, J., and K. Thórisson. 1999. The power of a nod and glance: Envelope vs. emotional feedback in animated conversational agents. *Journal of Applied Artificial Intelligence* 13(3):519–538.

Cassell, J., and H. Vilhjálmsson, H. 1999. Fully embodied conversational avatars: Making communicative behaviors autonomous. *Autonomous Agents and Multi-Agent Systems* 2:45–64.

Cassell, J., C. Pelachaud, N. Badler, M. Steedman, B. Achorn, T. Becket, B. Douville, S. Prevost, and M. Stone. 1994. Animated conversation: Rule-based generation of facial expression, gesture and spoken intonation for multiple conversational agents. In *Computer Graphics*, 413–420. New York: ACM SIGGRAPH.

Clark, H. H., and C. R. Marshall. 1981. Definite reference and mutual knowledge. In A. K. Joshi, B. L. Webber, and I. Sag, eds., *Elements of discourse understanding*, 10–63. Cambridge: Cambridge University Press.

CLIPS. 1994. *Reference Manual 6.0* (Technical Report Number JSC-25012). Houston, Tex.: Software Technology Branch, Lyndon B. Johnson Space Center.

Dehn, D., and S. v. Mulken. N.d. The impact of animated interface research: A review of empirical research. *Human-Computer Studies*. Forthcoming.

Ferguson, G., J. Allen, B. Miller, and E. Ringger. 1996. The design and implementation of the TRAINS-96 System: A prototype mixed-initiative planning assistant (Technical Note 96-5). University of Rochester, Department of Computer Science.

Finin, T., and R. Fritzon. 1994. KQML as an agent communication language. Paper presented at the Third International Conference on Information and Knowledge Management (CIKM '94), Gaithersburg, Maryland, November.

Goodwin, C. 1981. *Conversational organization: interaction between speakers and hearers.* New York: Academic Press.

Grosz, B., and C. Sidner. 1986. Attention, intentions, and the structure of discourse. *Computational Linguistics* 12(3):175–204.

Johnston, M. 1998. Unification-based multimodal parsing. In *Proceedings of COLING-ACL 98*, 624–630. Montreal: Morgan Kaufman Publishers.

Kendon, A. 1990. The negotiation of context in face-to-face interaction. In A. Duranti and C. Goodwin, eds., *Rethinking context: Language as interactive phenomenon*, 323–334. New York: Cambridge University Press.

Koons, D. B., C. J. Sparrel, and K. R. Thórisson. 1993. Integrating simultaneous input from speech, gaze, and hand gesture. In M. T. Maybury, ed., *Intelligent multimedia interfaces*. Cambridge, Mass.: AAAI Press/MIT Press.

McNeill, D. 1992. *Hand and mind: What gestures reveal about thought.* Chicago: The University of Chicago Press.

Nickerson, R. S. 1976. On conversational interaction with Computers. In R. M. Baecker and W. A. S. Buxton, eds., *Readings in human computer interaction*, 681–693. Los Altos, Calif.: Morgan Kaufman.

Rickel, J., and W. L. Johnson. 1999. Animated agents for procedural training in virtual reality: Perception, cognition and motor control. *Applied Artificial Intelligence* 13:343–382.

Rosenfeld, H. M. 1987. Conversational control functions of nonverbal behavior. In A. W. Siegman and S. Feldstein, eds., *Nonverbal behavior and communication*, 2d ed., 563–601. Hillsdale, N.Y.: Lawrence Erlbaum Associates.

Shneiderman, B. 1998. *Designing the user interface: strategies for effective human-computer interaction*, 3d ed. Reading, Mass.: Addison-Wesley.

Stone, M. 1998. Modality in dialogue: Planning, pragmatics, and computation. Unpublished doctoral dissertation, Department of Computer and Information Sciences, University of Pennsylvania, Philadelphia.

Stone, M., and C. Doran. 1997. Sentence planning as description using tree adjoining grammar. In *Proceedings of the 35th Annual Meeting of the Association for Computational Linguistics and 8th Conference of the European Chapter of the Association for Computational Linguistics* (Madrid, Spain), 198–205.

Thórisson, K. R. 1996. Communicative humanoids: A computational model of psychosocial dialogue skills. Ph.D. diss., Massachusetts Institute of Technology, Cambridge, Massachusetts.

Trevarthen, C. 1986. Sharing makes sense: Intersubjectivity and the making of an infant's meaning. In R. Steele and T. Threadgold, eds., *Language topics: Essays in honour of M. Halliday*, vol. 1, 177–200. Amsterdam: J. Benjamins.

Wahlster, W. 1991. User and discourse models for multimodal conversation. In J. W. Sullivan and S. W. Tyler, eds., *Intelligent user interfaces*, 45–67. Reading, Mass.: Addison-Wesley.

3

"May I Help You?":

Designing Embodied Conversational Agent Allies

Elizabeth F. Churchill, Linda Cook, Peter Hodgson, Scott Prevost,

and Joseph W. Sullivan

3.1 Introduction

In theory we create boundaries [between humans and computational artifacts], in practice we dissolve them.

—SHERRY TURKLE, *LIFE ON THE SCREEN*

In keeping with Turkle's comment, recent research suggests the intellectual distinction between *us* humans and *them* computers is dissolving. Reeves and Nass (1996), among others, have demonstrated that human interactions with computers, and indeed other forms of media, are intrinsically social in nature; we unconsciously treat computers as social actors, and the rules that govern our social interactions with other people also apply to our use of computers. Such psychosocial interactions occur whatever the visual interface of the computer. This is particularly the case when the causal mechanisms underlying reactive behaviors are opaque (Kiesler and Sproull 1997; Turkle 1995).

These observations are relevant for design of computer artifacts. It has been suggested that we should design explicitly with social interaction in mind—that is, design interfaces that make interacting with computers *even more* like interacting with other people (Dryer 1997; Reeves and Nass 1996). This suggestion translates into a broad range of possibilities, from the design of dialogue boxes that are more informative, helpful, and socially astute (Dryer 1997) to the design of embodied, conversational interface agents (e.g., André et al., chap. 8; André, Müller, and Rist 1999; Cassell et al. 1999; Churchill et al. 1999; Lester et al. 1997; Lester et al., chap. 5; McCarthy 1999; Prevost et al. 1999; Rickel and Johnson, chap. 4; Thórisson 1996). As the chapters in this book suggest, recent developments are making it increasingly likely that socially able, embodied agents will soon be commonplace.

3.2 Designing Embodied Conversational Agents

Designing with conscious consideration of *social* rules of engagement seems a promising departure from early visions of human-computer interaction that focused more heavily on models of communication as information exchange and required use of specialized languages with rigid turn taking. However, if we are to design agents with visual form and to take human-human interaction as our cue, a number of design issues become apparent that are less relevant in the design of nonembodied agents and more traditional systems. What are the appropriate methods for designing rich interactions with embodied agents? How can we draw on existing research and effectively put the pieces together to design characters that are compelling companions and helpful allies?

The aim of this chapter is to describe the process we have followed in the design of embodied conversational agents. We have found systems-centered design models inappropriate for the design of embodied interactive agents. Similarly, many user-centered interface design methods have a fairly narrow focus, concentrating on maximizing efficiency in user-interface interactions (Neilsen 1993; Preece et al. 1994). These methods are typically not broad enough to deal with many of the social and psychological factors that need to be considered when designing embodied conversational agents, although they may be appropriate for focused design of interaction details. Therefore, we have used a method that we believe is more suited to weaving together relevant research from diverse disciplines and to developing our understanding of the possibilities for embodied agent–human relationship(s). Our design focus is on supporting and staging fluid interactions, and our process involves iterative prototyping using scenarios, storyboarding, and prototype development. This scenario and storyboard process is coupled with analytic review of existing agents (embodied and nonembodied) and with consideration of relevant state-of-the-art technologies. In the next section, we will discuss this process in more detail.

3.2.1 Using Scenarios and Storyboards

Scenarios are stories about how users interact with each other and with the resources that are available (technical and otherwise) to get things done. They are action/interaction-oriented rather than abstracted, formalized representations of inputs, outputs, control flows, or information exchanges. Scenarios are fundamentally about elaborating activities in context and considering applications in use. Contexts are not represented as a set of surrounding or necessary conditions but are described as dynamic processes that exist within a broader social and cultural perspective. Scenarios can be abstract, but often are stories that encompass consideration of the motivations, actions, and expectations of individuals and groups (and, in our case, embodied agents) within a temporal, causal sequence of events (Erickson 1995).

Early on in a design phase, scenarios enable exploration of a design space. Later in the design process, application scenarios can be embedded in context scenarios for explication of specific application-related details. In tandem with this, various qualitative and quantitative evaluation techniques can be used to assess the success of the designed interactions (Sanders and Scholtz, chap. 12).

We chose to use scenarios and storyboards in our early design work on embodied agents for a number of reasons. First, observations and evaluations of use of embodied agents "in the wild" or development of multiple fully functional prototypes are not feasible in the development of novel and complex technologies of this kind. Both Karat (1995) and Neilsen (1995) make a similar point with regard to the "visionary" technologies they have developed. Therefore, analytic review of existing, broadly related systems and research, coupled with scenario-based narrative construction to build an elaborated design space, seemed appropriate for imagining where embodied conversational agents could be most effective and what the characteristics of those embodied agents could be. By keeping our focus on the level of the interaction scenario, we are able to draw on detailed research in diverse fields and choreograph methods and mechanisms to produce context-appropriate design possibilities and requirements.

Second, we are concerned with designing embodied agents who have *character* in addition to being effective. Through narrative elaboration, we engaged in a process of character development, much as the characteristics of protagonists in a novel would be developed. In this way, it is possible to make statements about our ideal embodied agent's character in terms of its knowledge, personality, and self-presentation. Scenario-based design is well suited to this process—asking questions is what scenarios are all about (Carroll 1995). By telling stories about human-agent interactions, and then posing questions, we were able to think carefully about the details of the relationship between the embodied agents and the human characters in our scenarios. Questions concerned the agents' activities, their appearance, the human collaborators, the physical space of the room in which interactions would take place, and so on.

We asked questions such as: Who is the agent? What is its role? Who will the agent be interacting with? What are its goals and desires? What is the setting for the interaction? And so on.

Finally, design is a social process, involving reflexive communication (Erickson 1995). In the case of our design meetings, given the multidisciplinary nature of our design team, design artifacts in the form of textual and graphical artifacts were a good way of focusing discussion and enabling the establishment of shared vocabularies and shared understandings. Specifically, we used images, stories, vignettes, video mock-ups, scenarios, and sketches. Thus we were able to elaborate and role play interactions, reflect on the characters involved in the interactions (both the character of the embodied agents and the humans), consider what props may be needed, and think about the digital and physical staging of interactions.

Some sample early sketches are shown in figure 3.1. These images are taken from an elaborated, narrative scenario describing two forms of computer-based, conversational ally agents: a meeting coordinator and a personal representative, interactive avatar. It has been noted elsewhere that rough sketches of this kind are often more effective early in design than are more complete prototypes (Black 1990; Erickson 1995); roughness is important for conveying ideas in formation.

These sketches show the design of a meeting-support, embodied agent. In the first frame on the top line, from left to right, a number of people sit at a table with a large display at one. On that display are meeting-relevant artifacts. In the second frame, the agent can be seen on the screen, embodied as a talking head. In the third frame, one of the meeting attendees talks directly to one of two embodied agents who are now present, one on the left of the screen and the other on the right. The lower two frames show closeups of the screen with a number of applications in use.

3.2.2 Levels of Description in Elaborated Scenarios

The questions above all address character design at the level of the narrative that unfolds in the scenario. We also evaluated scenarios in terms of how easy they would be to achieve representationally, algorithmically, and technically. In table 3.1, we outline our characterization of these different levels.

The top level is the *interaction* level. Scenarios represent an example of an interaction-level description of an embodied conversational agent system. At this level, we consider interactions between classes of embodied agent, classes

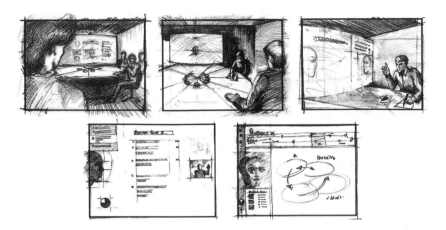

Figure 3.1
Sketching a scene with embodied agents and intelligent avatars.

Table 3.1 Levels of description for embodied agent designs

Action and interaction level	Agent, human collaborator issues plus physical and digital context characteristics
Representational and algorithmic level	Agent architecture issues; representations and algorithms (see figs. 3.7 and 3.8)
Systems level 1: software	Software systems issues Code for speech recognition, vision, speech generation, etc.
Systems level 2: hardware	Hardware systems issues Cameras, microphones, displays, computers, etc.

of users, and different interaction contexts by elaborating instances in story form. Supporting the interaction level is *the representational and algorithmic* level, where the particular agent's performance is realized and its domain and interaction competence are represented. Although embodied conversational agents can be used in a wide range of applications and user environments, a central tenet of our work is that a control architecture can be developed that factors out the common elements required for embodied agent systems. We have been successful in this; we co-developed this architecture with MIT's Gesture and Narrative Language Group, and it has been used both to create Will, our embodied agent, and also Rea (Cassell et al. 1999). An overview of the architecture is presented below.

Below this level is the *systems* level, wherein consideration is given to the software and hardware required for implementing the details specified at the algorithmic level. Certain constraints derive from systems levels as well as from the features of the social and physical environment.

To clearly establish the derivation of design decisions, our analysis of scenarios involves explicit consideration of these multiple levels. This enables discussion of whether a particular decision is driven by consideration of the psychosocial factors when trying to support a certain type of interaction or whether the decision derives from a systems or hardware level constraint. Ideally, we would like design decisions to result from the interaction level and not the systems levels. Some of these trade-offs are mentioned below in our discussion of the development of Will, an embodied conversational ally.

In addition, distinguishing between these levels also enables us to consider what occurs in the instance of a breakdown at any level and enables us to build in appropriate redundancy. For example, a breakdown in a particular communication mode (e.g., speech output) would require some other means of imparting information to achieve graceful degradation of the interaction; at the interaction level, we may wish to consider text presentation and imagine how that transition could be achieved smoothly.

In the next section, we outline some of the considerations that have emerged from our design meetings. Through consideration of these, we have designed Will, who is described in section 3.4.

3.3 The Design Space

Elaboration of scenarios as described above have enabled us to chart out a design space and begin to identify important considerations in the design of

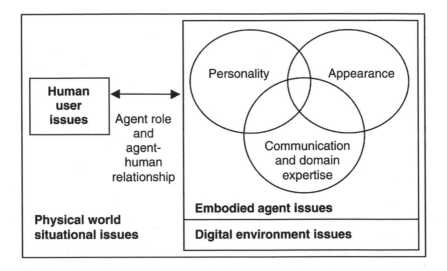

Figure 3.2
Issues in the design of an embodied agent.

any embodied agent. Figure 3.2 illustrates these issues in pictorial form. In this chapter, we focus on issues relating specifically to the design of the embodied agent. We have considered, although we have not discussed them here, design issues related to the characteristics of the embodied agent's digital domain (e.g., the display the agent appears in, what kind of control the agent has over that display and running applications, and so on), the characteristics of the physical domain in which the agent technology is located (e.g., in a room, on a wrist-watch, in a kiosk, etc.), and the characteristics of the user population with which the agent interacts (e.g., children, adults, preferred language, degree of expertise in the domain, etc.). Details of these considerations have been elaborated elsewhere (Churchill et al. 1998; Churchill et al. 1999).

In charting the design space for the embodied conversational agents, we have identified a number of interrelated issues that must be foregrounded in order to design an agent with character. These include (1) the agent's role, and its domain and interactional competencies, (2) the agent's self-presentation in terms of appearance and motion, and (3) the agent's personality.

3.3.1 Roles and Competence

In our scenarios, we have envisaged the embodied agent as ally or helper who performs tasks and provides information about complex systems. Users can avoid the complexity of the underlying system by issuing commands through speech and gesture. These ally agent interfaces can be contrasted with what Lewis (1998) has called the "environment" metaphor of interfaces. The agent metaphor presents human user-system intermediaries, while the environment metaphor presents objects the user can interact with directly. In agent interfaces, in addition to asking the character to manipulate the system ("turn the widget on"), the user can ask for help in using a particular feature ("how do I turn the widget on?") or ask what a given control does ("what does this switch do?"). As an ally, the agent will not block the user's access to the underlying system but rather will act as an independent third party; the user should always have the ability to bypass the agent if necessary.

A central concern is the believability or credibility of characters in their roles. A number of factors contribute to this, but central are domain competence (what is known) and interactional competence (how the information is communicated, and the agent's behavior toward others). We will consider each of these in turn.

Domain competence. Clearly characters should have domain competence, providing the right information for the user's current needs. By detailed scenario elaboration and task analysis, it is possible to outline at the interactional level what the embodied agent *needs* to know in order to be perceived to be competent. It is also possible to allocate tasks between the agent and the human user (a point also made in Lewis 1998). Further, we can distinguish the *necessary* and *sufficient* domain knowledge; the *desirable,* but not necessary, domain knowledge; and, finally, information that is not central to the intended interaction situation.

Considering the representational perspective, desired domain competence can be achieved through provision of a rich knowledge base. Making this tractable presents a constraint derived from the representational and systems levels (Is the system networked? If standalone, how much memory is available?), which may in turn place constraints upon which domains are currently appropriate for the introduction of embodied agents. One can see these constraints playing out in many existing agents who deal with limited domains only. A further consideration that leads back from this constraint to design at the interaction level is designing for fluidity of interaction once the boundaries of the agent's knowledge have been reached. When this occurs, the embodied agent should exhibit social competence and allow the conversation to degrade gracefully, for example, by offering alternative sources of information.

Linguistic and paralinguistic competence. The maintenance of a socially based interaction does not necessarily *require* the linguistic and paralinguistic competence of multimodal interaction. However, it may well make interactions more "natural," more intuitive, and more enjoyable. Certainly, speaking with someone directly has several advantages over written text and disembodied speech. In face-to-face situations, information can be conveyed through multiple modalities, including spoken words, intonation (roughly, the melody) of speech, facial expressions, gaze movements, gestures, and body posture. Face-to-face interaction also allows information to be transmitted continuously and bidirectionally between interlocutors so that, for example, one participant in a conversation may be signaling agreement by nodding his head, while at the same time the other participant is speaking and gesturing with her hands.

Multimodal information in face-to-face conversation can be divided into two broad categories: information-bearing propositional content, such as words and iconic gestures, and information that serves to regulate the dialogue, such as back-channel expressions and turn-taking gaze indicators. As argued elsewhere (e.g., Prevost, Bickmore, and Cassell 1998), embodied agents must convey competence at both the propositional and interactional levels of communication to adequately comprehend and simulate face-to-face human conversation, even for limited domains. For processing propositional information, rule sets that specify (1) the proper alignment of intonational contours, gestures, and facial signals and (2) the proper selection of those behaviors based on the discourse history (Cassell et al. 1994) are required. For processing interactional information, Thórisson's (1996) work has led to a model in which specific behaviors and collections of behaviors trigger conversational events.

A major challenge at the representational and algorithmic levels for embodied agents who are built around this type of design is to determine how information from multiple input modalities can be fused into a coherent understanding of the world, including, in particular, what the human collaborator is doing or communicating. Similarly, embodied agents must "understand" the potential meanings of non-verbal modalities (such as gestures), and how those meanings are affected by context and other modalities. Thus one of the key problems in understanding the various types of behaviors involved in face-to-face interactions is that some behaviors can be "understood" only in the context of other behaviors. For example, the utterance "it's over there" makes sense only when "there" is specified, either by a previous utterance or a pointing gesture. To confuse matters more, behaviors that appear similar on the surface don't always have the same function. For example, while many speakers unwittingly raise their eyebrows on emphasized (intonationally stressed) words, raising eyebrows has a very different function when a speaker shows surprise. Embodied agents must also "know" how to produce multimodal output and communicate effectively—that is, how to distribute interactional and propositional information across different output modalities (posture, gesture, backchannels, and speech).

At the systems level, we have to consider issues related to image rendering such that gestures can be produced in real time. Similarly, the perception and recognition of users and of their gestures in real time represents a strain for current technologies.

Interaction strategies and social competence. A number of issues have been raised previously when considering more social forms of human-system interface designs (Stone 1995). Interruptions by any party in the interaction should be possible without a complete disruption to the flow of the interaction. Some looking ahead or anticipation about the direction in which the conversation is going should occur. However, conversations should not be pre-scripted and required to follow predetermined paths; rather, conversations should develop in the interaction. In addition, there should be tolerance of speech errors and repairs.

To give the impression of a sentient creature, embodied agents should be able to act on their own, exhibiting autonomous and variable behavior. Embodied agents should be capable of changing the current focus of attention, of deliberating and enacting reasoned plans, and, finally, should react in *reasonable* time to input from human collaborators (where reasonable again depends on the interaction context). That agents respond in "reasonable" time to both explicit and implicit commands from a user is crucial; such responsiveness has been demonstrated in other domains to be centrally important in engendering trust and in creating a sense of co-presence or cognitive/emotional engagement in a situation (Lombard and Ditton 1997).

Much recent research has addressed how to enable embodied agents to operate autonomously (Blumberg 1996) and to be both reactive to events and able to deliberate and enact plans (Loyall and Bates 1991). Several architectures explore the balance between reactivity and deliberation in robotics—for example, 3T (Bonasso et al., 1996), RAP (Firby 1978), Cypress (Wilkins et al. 1995), and Remote Agent (Pell et al. 1997).

3.3.2 Acting and Appearing

Appearance matters, as endless racks of beauty and muscle magazines in our stores attest. In human-human interactions, beliefs about others are often based on stereotyped interpretations of surface appearance and behavior. These beliefs affect our behaviors and are used to anticipate the behavior of others. Evidence suggests this is the same for interfaces; people anticipate the behavior of embodied agents and these expectations drive their own behavior (Nass, Steuer, and Tauber 1994).

These visual indicators of the embodied agent's competencies are akin to the notion of affordances or invitation characteristics in interface and product design (Gaver 1991; Margolin 1996). They indicate the agent's availability for interaction and give external cues to human collaborators about traits, scope of effectiveness, and competencies. Therefore, a central design concern in creating embodied agents surrounds making the right impression. The conversational interface is a metaphor that can break down in frustrating ways if users overextend their expectations on the basis of that metaphor; this has been observed in other contexts of metaphoric designs in human-computer interaction (Halasz and Moran 1982). Therefore, the agent should explicitly and implicitly (through appearance and behavior) also give cues to the limits of its competence and offer the user alternatives for achieving goals and resolving difficulties.

Designing to engage through appearance. Again, a central question is how to build on these observations to set out some design heuristics for designing embodied agents' appearance. Research indicates that more *pleasant-looking* agents are deemed to have more personality (Sproull et al. 1997). Evidence also suggests that giving embodied agents *humanlike faces* may be more engaging, even though that engagement is sometimes evaluated negatively (Walker, Sproull, and Subramani 1994). Parise et al. (1996) have shown that talking to a human face, even when the face is not animated, results in more impression management than talking through text alone. Furthermore, participants in a study cooperated more with a humanlike, computer-based social agent than with a dog agent, even though they thought the dog was "cuter." These results suggest that for most interactions, we should (1) make our agents pleasing to look at, and (2) design with a face as a means of engaging the user. However, these are fairly unspecific goals. Evidence suggests that we need to carefully consider the context of placement for embodied agents and the psychosocial dynamics that are being encouraged in those contexts. For example, Parise et al. (1996) found that dog owners showed different responses to dog agents than non–dog owners! Dealing with humanlike embodied agents, Lee and Nass (1998) have demonstrated that the ethnicity of the agent affects how they are perceived; people perceived embodied agents with similar ethnicity to their own to be more like them, more attractive, more trustworthy, and more persuasive.

As an initial step to elucidating agent appearance possibilities, we elaborated some design dimensions along which embodied agents can vary and considered design options along those dimensions. The dimensions are shown in figure 3.3.

The first dimension indicates that embodiments can vary in the extent to which they are humanoid or not—that is, resembling human beings in appearance. At the far right of the dimension, we would expect to see images that look like us, with hands, feet, an expressive face with two eyes, a mouth, ears, and so on. At the far left, we may see abstract shapes (e.g., squares, circles, and triangles) and alien creatures. The images in figure 3.4 are somewhere in the middle. The shapes are configured like human bodies, and the faces resemble the emoticons that have become so familiar in e-mail exchanges and in text-based human-human communication.

The second dimension explicitly makes us consider that, across the course of an interaction or a number of interactions, the representation of the embodied agent may not be completely consistent or stable. Embodied agents may morph over time. For example, an embodied agent could at one time be a humanoid embodiment and then be a talking ball. Such a ball may not be humanoid but may serve well enough for communicating effectively in some contexts. Similarly, embodiments may not always be complete humanoid bodies but could be body parts. In figure 3.1, we showed our sketches, which included an embodiment that was simply a talking head. In other screens, no embodiment was shown. A basic requirement is that an embodiment should not occlude relevant applications and material; a disembodied voice may be sufficient for certain contexts.

In figure 3.5, the various elements that are central to creating a humanoid embodiment can be seen: the face, the hands, the feet, and the torso. By taking each of these elements, we can envisage channels of nonverbal communication: facial expressions for signaling emotion, interest, surprise, disappointment; the hands for interactional and propositional gestures; the body for posturing as a

Figure 3.3
Dimensions of agent embodiment.

Figure 3.4
Abstracted embodiments and faces.

Figure 3.5
Body elements for an embodied conversational agent.

means of indicating interest and orientation; the feet for again indicating direction of interest. Kendon (1970), among others, has shown the importance of small gestures for indicating interest, managing conversational turn taking and so on. Examining each one in turn, we can consider the contributions that are made in any interaction and the necessary degree of embodiment.

The third dimension is perhaps the most important for creating multi-modally interactive embodied agents. This concerns the extent to which an embodiment can move. At the left of our dimension are embodiments that do not move at all. At the right are embodied agents that are fully dynamic, with articulated bodies. Although many current embodiments look humanoid, animators have clearly demonstrated that objects that in the "real" world are inanimate, like cardboard boxes and desk lamps, can be made to communicate a message through movement. The human body, and by extension bodies that follow its dynamics, is well articulated for multimodal interactions, and we are particularly practiced at generating and reading movement of the body. This is the crux of the claim that interacting with an embodied agent may be more "natural," since it leverages well-practiced skills. Specific details of the role of facial expression, body posture, and body movement in human-human communication are clearly elaborated elsewhere in this volume (e.g., Cassell, chap. 1; Lester et al., chap. 5; Massaro et al., chap. 10; Poggi and Pelachaud, chap. 6).

The last two dimensions address the visual rendering of the embodied agent. Embodiments can be rendered as 2-D or 3-D. The extent to which this will affect human users' reactions is not known, but being 2-D or 3-D does not affect users' ability to comprehend gestures, as evidenced again by the genre of the animated cartoon (Klein 1993). Similarly, whether the embodied agent is a line drawing, as in many of the figures in this chapter, or photoreal is not known. In practice, the decision may lie in considering the trade-offs between task and context constraints and the constraints of rendering.

Creating characters. Developing embodied agents that look interesting or that can move and produce gestures and facial expressions is, however, only the beginning. While we have begun to lay out some relevant issues in the design of character appearance, it would be naïve to assume that we can engineer impression management from embodiment design easily. Representations of the body and of body parts are culturally coded and movement codes are read according to context and the experience of the perceiver (Klein 1993; Zarrilli 1995). As we advance in our ability to technically support fluid movement, we need to consider how the movements of our embodied agents will be read in different cultures and contexts.

3.3.3 Personality and Interindividual Differences

As described above, research strongly suggests that it doesn't take much in an interface to convey a sense of personality to a user. However, it is also fair to say that computers' "displays" of personality have to date been heavy on human interpretation and light on intended personality projection. Our research has focused largely on understanding the elements involved in the "projection" of personality such that the character personality that we intend to create can be recognized and labeled as such by users.

Personality is expressed as consistent and enduring patterns of behavior. In order to selectively and efficiently draw from modern personality theory, we relied on Revelle's (1995) classification. Revelle's system, which offers broad coverage of phenomena related to the expression of personality, enabled decomposition of our design task into readily identifiable subtasks. He classifies personality theories based on the focus they place on different aspects of personality: (1) *species-specific behavior*: how all people are the same, (2) *individual differences*: how *some* people are the *same*, and (3) *unique patterns of behavior*: no person is the same as another.

This classification describes our approach to the design issues that must be addressed. First, people have far more behavioral similarities than they have differences. Like the social competencies described above, these behaviors arise largely out of our common developmental experiences and underlie our sense of identification with and ability to relate to others. As such, these behaviors must be accounted for in any personality design methodology. In Will, our prototype embodied agent, these behaviors became localized in both the representational and systems levels. Second, some people are more alike along certain dimensions than are others and we would like to understand which features contribute to the perceived sameness of some people or their differences. Finally, we are all different because of the unique experiences in our lives. Interesting embodied agents should be a combination of all of these—mannerisms and behaviors that are familiar enough to support some degree of predictability (without repetition), and a compelling sense of uniqueness that entices a user to spend more time in the company of an embodied agent.

In addition to Revelle's classification system, we have also relied on the work of Hampson (1988, 1992) to outline a coherent model on which to base a more formal approach to personality design. In his model, personality is both *within* an individual and *between* an individual and respective interactants. It is not only projected by an individual but is also inferred by others. He considers three interdependent components: (1) actor, (2) observer, and (3) self-observer.

The *actor* denotes an individual with specific internal characteristics and dispositions. In considering the actor, personality trait theories have tended to formalize what is often described as a "commonsense" approach to personality or folk psychology (Matthews and Deary 1998). Natural language trait descriptors are employed to describe and classify personalities along dimensions that are well understood and accepted. Research indicates that traits appear to be stable, to be fairly predictive of future behavior and to span cultural boundaries, which gives credibility to this approach (Costa and McCrae 1994; Matthews and Deary 1998). This lexical-based approach has resulted in a number of formal taxonomies, parts of which have been used to create mostly single-dimension personality expression within characters (Bates, Loyall, and Reilly 1992; Elliott 1992; Rousseau and Hayes-Roth 1998).

When considering the *observer*, we note that traits are inferred on the basis of several sources of input: appearance (as described above), direct interaction (linguistic and paralinguistic competence), and observation of either goal-directed or idle behaviors. Little research evidence exists that ties traits directly to behaviors; most of the work to date has focused on a single personality variable, and with a limited range of nonverbal behaviors. Current agents with personality likewise play out the exaggeration of a single trait by the use of a small set (often one or two) of universally agreed trait-indicative behavior (i.e., a submissive trait conveyed by a slumping body posture). Certainly, nonverbal behaviors play a major role in the determination of others' personalities (Leathers 1997). Three reasons underlie this: (1) feelings and emotional states are often more accurately revealed by nonverbal behaviors; (2) congruency between the verbal and nonverbal channels can compound or increase the valence of the message being conveyed; and (3) nonverbal cues can be a more efficient means of communication.

Finally, the actor, aware of external interpretation, becomes a *self-observer* with the capacity to modify behavior to affect observer judgments (i.e., impression management). In considering the notion of the self-observer, we find that representing the capacity to self-observe and to act or react accordingly poses a significant challenge. Such a notion implies modification of personality expression according to context. This requires the ability to detect when such changes are necessary (i.e., context changes, goal needs inconsistent with existing personality), and the metaknowledge of how to effect them. It also assumes that a robust personality exists.

Design goals for personable characters. How will we know when we have an embodied agent with personality? Personality within embodied characters is as much about "being" as it is about "doing." In most embodied systems, when the character cycles into selecting the "next behavior," it is not that difficult to generate a selection process that chooses a preconfigured behavior that is appropriate to both personality profile and the current context (e.g., Bates 1994; Rousseau and Hayes-Roth 1998). The ultimate design challenge lies in creating personality expression that is much more ubiquitous in nature; numerous strands resident within multiple communication channels speak in unison about the essence of a character. With this in mind, we suggest the following set of dimensions as a means to gauge our level of success in generating truly personalized, individuated conversational agent characters.

- The embodied agent should be able to pass the "lay personality psychologist" test. A viewer *watching* an embodied agent could give a thumbnail personality sketch that corresponds closely to that intended by the character's author.
- Embodied agents may share a trait but differ on the "degree" or intensity of that trait.
- The embodied conversational agent should respond to external events in a manner that is consistent with its personality profile in general but may display unpredictable and random behaviors at a microlevel of expression. The agent may display slightly different behavioral reactions to the same event when the event is repeated.
- Embodied conversational agents with different personalities will display different reactions to the same events. As with the lay personality psychologist test, viewers would attribute behavioral differences to the different personality profiles of the characters.
- An embodied conversational agent's personality will differentially filter its perception of events. For example, a submissive agent may look for and respond to events that are threatening.
- An embodied conversational agent should be capable of modifying its personality expression or "presentation of self" to achieve some goal. An observer previously familiar with the agent would recognize the change.
- In a communicative interaction, an embodied conversational agent can make subtle changes in its personality expression that reflect a response to the personality, or a change in the needs, of the person with whom it is communicating (i.e., an interactive "dance").

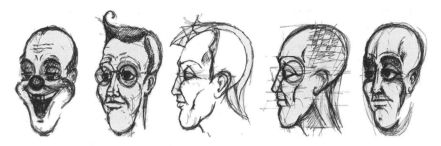

Figure 3.6
Sketching Will.

3.4 A Design Instantiation: Will, A Computer-Based Ally

Having outlined our design approach and laid out some of the design issues that were generated during our design sessions, in this section we introduce you to Will, an embodied conversational agent. We have drawn a number of characteristics from the design space elaborated above.

3.4.1 Will's Characteristics

Will is male. His job is to help presenters in a multimedia conference room set up and give their presentations. He has some knowledge of the applications that are used in presentations (e.g., video, audio, presentation applications) and of the physical room (e.g., lights, cameras). Will is a somewhat retiring character, relaxed and easygoing in his style of interaction. Will does not at this point need to build a relationship with one particular human collaborator, but he does understand the requirements of a *class* of people. Will's physical appearance developed by consulting our dimensions, developing sketches and carrying out an informal user study where users were asked to write short biographies of characters on the basis of photographs they were shown. Some example sketches are shown in figure 3.6. We imagine most people Will interacts with will speak English and will be computer literate, although not necessarily computer scientists. People will only interact with Will for short periods of time at infrequent intervals.

3.4.2 An Interaction and Cognition-Based Architecture

Will's psyche is embodied in an architecture that integrates multimodal information to enable him to see where his human collaborator is standing and to hear what he or she says. He is also able to generate appropriate speech, gestures, and facial expressions and to carry out tasks in the digital domain. This architecture was designed by taking into account interactional, social, linguistic, and multimodal competencies and issues surrounding embodied agent appearance and personality. Our understanding of the action and interaction level (see table 3.1) for Will in his role as an interface ally heavily influenced our initial architecture. Since Will's job is to assist users in using equipment in the conference room, we knew the architecture would have to address his domain of expertise and the actions he can take within that domain. Because we modeled Will as a humanlike embodied agent, both in terms of appearance and performance, we knew that we also had to address the many issues involved in human face-to-face interaction. In the sections that follow, we describe this architecture in more detail. This architecture can be used to create numerous other embodied agents, all of whom will have their own look, personality, and expertise. As noted above, this basic architecture already underlies REA's interactions (Cassell et al. 1999) as well as those of Will.

3.4.2.1 *Domain Constraints* Will's particular conference room domain imposed a number of architectural constraints. The existing interface to the room and its equipment was a menu-based touch panel display that can control lighting, a large screen display, video and audio devices, and a computer. We wanted Will to "live" in the large display and be able to tutor users in employing the existing interface. Will should be able to control the devices directly through voice commands. Because certain actions in the room are only available when the room is in specific states, Will needs to know the state of all the devices at every moment. In addition, because Will might need to explain where objects are in the room, such as the touch panel display, he needs to be able to point to various locations around the room. Given these domain constraints, it was clear that Will's architecture must account for several types of "knowledge." First, he needs to be aware of static information, such as the locations of fixed objects in the room, and dynamic information, such as the current state of the room's lighting. Because of the tutoring requirement for showing users how to use the existing touch panel interface, Will also needs some ability to plan sequences of actions. For example, to tell a user how to play a video tape, he needs to know to switch the menu panel to the source-select screen, press the VCR button, then switch to the source-control screen and press the PLAY button.

3.4.2.2 *Face-to-Face Interaction Constraints* Although architectural considerations of the domain constraints are important for ensuring that Will can interact with users while showing reasonable intelligence about his environs, we believe it is equally important for Will to understand *how* people naturally interact to form common ground, accomplish goals, and provide information. Since Will is an embodied agent, the architecture should reflect the way people interact in face-to-face situations—particularly the way we make facial expressions and gestures to help us get our points across.

As discussed earlier, we differentiate two layers of behaviors for face-to-face interactions—the propositional layer and the interactional layer. The propositional layer involves those verbal and nonverbal behaviors that contribute to the intended meaning of the corresponding speech. For example, an iconic gesture may supply information that is not present in the speech, such as a typing gesture in conjunction with the utterance "I'll send it right away," implying that the speaker intends to send "it" by e-mail. The interactional layer involves those verbal and nonverbal behaviors that regulate, coordinate, and manage the flow of information between interlocutors. For example, the direction of gaze has been shown to be correlated with turn taking in dyadic conversation (Duncan 1974), regulating control of the speaking floor. Other interactive behaviors include back channels, such as head nods, which are performed by the listener as a means of providing limited feedback without taking a full speaking turn.

The architecture for Will was designed with these face-to-face interaction issues in mind. Our main criteria for modeling face-to-face interactions in the architecture included the following (also discussed in Cassell et al., chap. 2):

- *Quick reaction time for interactional behaviors.* Interactional behaviors, such as back channels (e.g., head nods) or turn-taking gaze behaviors, need to occur immediately upon the proper stimuli in order to seem natural. We developed the architecture to support quick reactions by immediately processing certain input signals and generating appropriate reactions independent of the embodied agent's higher-level "cognitive" processing. For example, based on a simple vision system and off-the-shelf speech recognition, the embodied agent is able to turn and orient his gaze to the user as soon as she starts speaking and before the speech system has recognized the entire phrase, or even the first word.

- *Multistep deliberation.* Since the embodied agent needs to understand the content of users' requests and engage in simple dialogues to perform certain multistep tasks, the architecture had to include at least a rudimentary component for planning dialogues. For the initial architecture, we employed a number of prespecified plans for Will's tutoring tasks.

- *Parallelism.* Because face-to-face interactions are inherently continuously bidirectional (e.g., one participant in a conversation may be nodding her head while the other is actually speaking), the architecture had to reflect this processing parallelism. That is, the architecture had to support processing inputs, planning responses, and generating outputs all at the same time.

- *Rule-based control of gestures and facial expressions for interactional behaviors.* Previous research on the role of nonverbal behaviors in managing conversational interactions (Cassell et al. 1994) has led to a collection of rules for generating such behaviors in an animated, embodied agent. The architecture incorporates these rules in its reactive and deliberative processing.

- *Rule-based control of gestures and facial expressions for propositional behaviors.* We relied on prior research on the role of nonverbal behaviors in conveying propositional information (Cassell et al. 1994) to generate a set of rules for determining which types of gestures are appropriate and when they should occur. For example, an iconic gesture representing a particular concept may occur with high probability on the first occurrence of the concept in the conversation but with lower probability on subsequent mentions.

- *Input/output symmetry.* Because we wanted the system to be as intuitive as possible for users, we designed the architecture to (ultimately) support the same modalities in both the user inputs and embodied agent outputs.

- *Output synchrony.* Because the timing of nonverbal behaviors with respect to speech is crucial to understanding their meaning, we designed the architecture to support real-time on-the-fly synchronization of speech, gestures, and facial expressions. For example, the architecture must support the automatic alignment of intonational and gestural peaks.

The top-level view of a generic conversational embodied agent architecture based on these requirements is shown in figure 3.7, in which the Input Manager

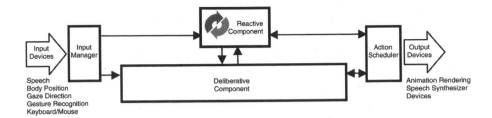

Figure 3.7
Top-level embodied conversational agent architecture.

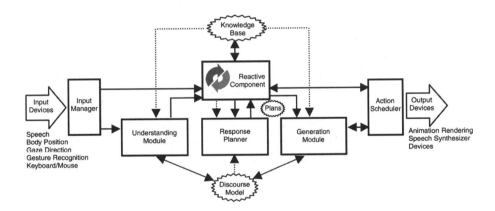

Figure 3.8
FXPAL embodied conversational agent architecture.

simply collects and distributes information from the multimodal input devices and the Action Scheduler performs the output synchronization and generates actions for the animation rendering system.

Our elaboration of this architecture for the Conversational Characters project at FX Palo Alto Laboratory is shown in figure 3.8. The Reaction Module is responsible for the "action selection" component of the architecture, which determines at each moment in time what the embodied agent should be doing and thus functions as the locus of control for the entire system. This ensures that certain interactional behaviors, such as head nods, can be performed instantaneously on the proper stimuli (e.g., user-speaking and user-looking-at-me). The Understanding Module is responsible for fusing all input modalities into a coherent understanding of the world including, in particular, what the user is doing or communicating. To perform its task, it utilizes and updates a Discourse Model (also used by the Generation Module and Response Planner) and may produce multiple outputs in the case of ambiguity.

The Response Planner formulates sequences of actions, some or all of which will need to be executed during future execution cycles, to carry out desired communicative or task goals. The Response Planner is activated when the Reaction Module sends it an action to be performed, and the plans it produces influence the Reaction Module to prefer behaviors that tend to achieve the plan steps, thereby achieving the multistep deliberation requirement. Finally, the Generation Module realizes complex action requests from the Reaction Module by producing one or more coordinated primitive actions (e.g., speech generation, gesture, facial expression, "physical" action), sending the actions to the Action Scheduler for performance. The Generation Module is responsible for enacting the rules which associate nonverbal behaviors with speech for both propositional nonverbal behaviors (e.g,. pointing) as well as some interactional nonverbal behaviors (e.g., extending the hand, palm facing up, as a means of handing over the speaking turn).

3.4.2.3 *System Considerations for the Architecture* The architecture described above was conceived by carefully considering the action and interaction level of the design process (see table 3.1). In building such a system, however, a number of technical constraints also had to be considered. The architecture shown in figure 3.8 was designed to allow input and output symmetry so that all the available output modalities (speech, gesture, facial expression) would have input counterparts. Unfortunately, with current technology, gesture and facial expression recognition cannot be performed robustly, even when the user is asked to wear motion-sensing equipment. Because we wanted the user to be relatively unencumbered (i.e., not have to wear a special body suit), we opted for two simple inputs: speech and a lightweight vision component that uses background differencing to detect the approximate location of the user in the room. Given the relatively impoverished input set, and the resulting simplicity of the interactional rules based on those inputs (i.e., gaze, gesture and face rules for signaling turn taking and back channels), we decided to implement the Action Scheduler and reactive module in a single component and to send the vision system outputs (user coordinates) and speech detection signals (speech-on/speech-off) directly to this combined component. As a result, we were able to minimize the number of processes running as well as the message passing among processes.

3.4.2.4 *Appearance and Personality Considerations* The selection of an appropriate animation rendering system was crucial for achieving the project goals for embodied agent appearance and personality. In particular, we were concerned with producing natural-looking gestures and facial expressions and being able to modulate them to effect different personality types. For example, an outgoing embodied agent might make broad pointing gestures, while an agent with a more restrained personality might point in more subtle ways.

In the interest of maximizing gesture naturalness, we chose an animation rendering system based on performance animation. The process began by capturing motion data for a set of gestures to be performed by the embodied agent. This process involved wiring up a human "performer" and using software (produced by Protozoa) to map the performer's movements onto a 3-D character model. For each gesture, we captured a range of performances that can be mapped to different personality types. This process recorded full-body performance animation data. Our goal was to be able to trigger gestures for different body parts independent of each other. Therefore, we had the additional task of "cleaning" the data for each body part so that it would represent the movement of a single body part with respect to the relative position of the body. Using this performance animation technique makes the gestures appear more natural (with proper acceleration and detail) than does using techniques where gestures are computed algorithmically.

In order to produce facial expressions, we built a polygonal model (see figure 3.9) and developed a set of morph targets for the model to represent various

Figure 3.9
Developing Will's face.

Figure 3.10
Will posing.

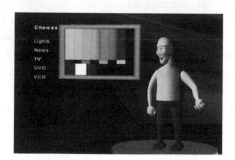

Figure 3.11
Will's world.

facial features such as lip and eyebrow positions. By combining morph targets, we can automatically generate a wide range of facial expressions and mouth shapes.

Finally, for the run-time animation system, we employed Protozoa's Alive software in an unconventional manner. The Alive system contains MIDI drivers for triggering animation events from devices such as joysticks and MIDI sliders. We integrated software drivers into the system so that our agent's Action Scheduler can trigger such events.

As a result, the Action Scheduler can trigger gestures (from the captured performance animation data), facial expressions, and head movements independently of one another, affecting the real-time animation of the 3-D model. Figure 3.10 shows some of Will's poses, and figure 3.11 shows Will in action, explaining a set of menu options.

3.4.3 Current and Future Work

Our development of Will and his environment continues. Informal evaluations of Will in action have raised a number of issues that we are currently working on. We have been experimenting with different parameter settings on nonverbal behaviors and combinations of nonverbal behaviors that are known to affect personality manifestation. We are also currently working on automating rule sets for expression of personality through nonverbal behaviors.

Our method for animating Will has proven successful, introducing more natural-looking gestures than those produced algorithmically. In particular, motion-captured gestures retain subtleties of movement such as variations in acceleration. We have been able to parameterize gestures by blending motion-capture data and to maintain some ability for co-articulation of gestures (for example, by adding a beat gesture on top of an iconic gesture). Timing of gestures can also be easily synchronized with speech by stretching or squashing the motion-captured data. Although creating new gestures is not easy, this is not a problem for the motion-capture method alone; while algorithmically generated gestures could be generated in real time given the right semantic analysis and framework, to date this has proven difficult. Finally, we are currently working on relaxing our synchronization of gestures and speech. Currently, motion-captured gestures have a single point of synchronization with speech—the start point. We are working on generating a model where gestures can be realigned at several points—for example, at the start of the gesture, on the stroke, and at the end of relaxation.

3.5 Summary

In this chapter, we have outlined our approach to the design and development of conversational, embodied agents, focusing in particular on embodied conversational allies. Our design process is scenario-based. This process enables us to pinpoint, draw together and choreograph appropriate techniques to support fluid human user-embodied agent collaborations for particular interaction contexts. Having described our iterative design approach, we presented a description of Will, an embodied agent who resides in the FXPAL Multimedia Conference Room and acts as an ally in the use of a complex audiovisual system for both FXPAL staff and visitors. Development of the architecture that underlies Will, and the development and integration of our personality models, continues. Planned evaluations include empirical tests and long-term observations of interactions with Will to understand how interactional patterns change and develop.

We are encouraged by recent research developments and believe that embodied conversational agents could be effective in many settings. By continuing to draw on research in human-human and human-agent communication and in technology design, while considering the broader context within which interactions take place, we are set to evaluate emerging possibilities for embodied agents.

References

André, E., J. Müller, and T. Rist. 1999. Employing AI methods to control the behavior of animated interface agents. *Applied Artificial Intelligence* 13:415–448.

Bates, J. 1994. The role of emotion in believable characters. *Communications of the ACM* 37(7):122–125.

Bates, J., A. Loyall, and W. S. Reilly. 1992. Integrating reactivity, goals, and emotion in a broad agent. Technical Report CMU-CS-92-142, School of Computer Science, Carnegie Mellon University, Pittsburgh, Pennsylvania.

Black, A. 1990. Visible planning on paper and screen: The impact of working medium on decision-making by novice graphic designers. *Behavior and Information Technology* 9(4):283–296.

Blumberg, B. 1996. Old tricks, new dogs: Ethology and interactive creatures. Ph.D. diss., MIT Media Lab, Cambridge, Massachusetts.

Bonasso, R. P., D. Kortenkamp, D. P. Miller, and M. Slack. 1996. Experience with an architecture for intelligent reactive agents. *Lecture Notes in Artificial Intelligence* 1037:187-202.

Carroll, J. M. 1995. *Scenario-based design: Envisioning work and technology in system development.* New York: John Wiley and Sons.

Cassell, J., and K. Thórisson. 1999. The power of a nod and a glance: Envelope vs. emotional feedback in animated conversational agents. *Journal of Applied Artificial Intelligence* 13(3):519–538.

Cassell, J., T. Bickmore, M. Billingshurst, L. Campbell, K. Chang, H. Vilhjálmsson, and H. Yan. 1999. Embodiment in conversational interfaces: Rea. I:. *Proceedings of CHI '99*, 520–527. New York: ACM Press.

Cassell, J., C. Pelachaud, M. Steedman, B. Douville, S. Prevost, and M. Stone. 1994. Animated conversation: Rule-based generation of facial expressions, gesture and spoken intonation for multiple conversational agents. In *Computer Graphics (SIGGRAPH '94)*, 413–420. (Reprinted in M. Huhns and M. Singh, eds., *Readings in agents*. San Francisco: Morgan Kaufman.)

Churchill, E. F., L. Cook, P. Hodgson, S. Prevost, and J. W. Sullivan. 1999. Designing embodied conversational agent allies. A scenario based approach. FX Palo Alto Technical Report FXPAL-TR-99-023.

Churchill, E. F., S. Prevost, T. Bickmore, L. Cook, P. Hodgson, and J. W. Sullivan. 1998. Design issues for situated conversational characters. FX Palo Alto Technical Report FXPAL-TR-98-048.

Costa, P. T., and R. R. McCrae. 1994. Set like plaster? Evidence for the stability of adult personality. In T. Heathererton and J. Weinberger, eds., *Can personality change?* Washington, D.C.: American Psychological Association.

Duncan, S. 1974. Some signals and rules for taking speech turns in conversations. In S. Weitz, ed., *Nonverbal communication*. Oxford, U.K.: Oxford University Press.

Dryer, D. C. 1997. Ghosts in the machine: Personalities for socially adroit software agents. In *Proceedings of the AAAI Fall Symposium on Socially Intelligent Agents, AAAI Press: Technical Report FS-97-02*, 31–36.

Elliott, C. 1992. The Affective Reasoner: A process model of emotions in a multi-agent system. Ph.D. diss., Institute for the Learning Sciences, Northwestern University, Evanston, Illinois.

Erickson, T. 1995. Notes on design practice: Stories and prototypes as catalysts for communication. In J. M. Carroll, ed., *Scenario-based design: Envisioning work in technology and system development*, 37–58. New York: John Wiley and Sons.

Firby, R. J. 1978. Adaptive execution in complex dynamic worlds. Ph.D. diss., Department of Computer Science, Yale University, New Haven, Connecticut.

Gaver, W. 1991. Technological affordances. In *Proceedings of the CHI '91 Conference on Computer and Human Interaction*. New York: ACM Press.

Halasz, F., and T. P. Moran. 1982. Analogy considered harmful. *Proceedings of the Human Factors in Computing Systems Conference*. Gaithersburg, Md.: National Bureau of Standards.

Hampson, S. E. 1992. The emergence of personality: A broader context for biological perspectives. In A. Gale and M. W. Eysenck, eds., *Handbook of individual differences: Biological perspectives*. Chichester, U.K.: Wiley.

———. 1988. *The construction of personality*. London: Routledge.

Karat, J. 1995. Scenario use in the design of a speech recognition system. In J. M. Carroll, ed., *Scenario-based design. Envisioning work in technology and system development*, 109–133. New York: John Wiley and Sons.

Kendon, A. 1970. Movement coordination in social interaction: Some examples described. *Acta Psychologica*, 32:100–125.

Kiesler, S., and L. Sproull. 1997. "Social" human-computer interaction. In B. Friedman, ed., *Human values and the design of computer technology*. Cambridge, U.K.: Cambridge University Press CSLI Publications.

Klein, N. 1993. *7 minutes. The life and death of the American animated cartoon*. London: Verso.

Laurel, B. 1997. Interface agents; metaphors with character. In J. M. Bradshaw, ed., *Software agents*, 67–78. Cambridge, Mass.: The MIT Press.

Leathers, D. G. 1997. *Successful nonverbal communication*. Boston: Allyn and Bacon.

Lee, E., and C. Nass. 1998. Does the ethnicity of a computer agent matter? An experimental comparison of human-computer interaction and computer-mediated communication. In *Proceedings of the Workshop on Embodied Conversational Characters*, 67–76. (Available as FXPAL Technical Report FXPAL-TR-99-027.)

Lester, J. C., S. A. Converse, S. E. Kahler, S. T. Barlow, B. A. Stone, and R. S. Bhoga. 1997. The Persona Effect: Affective impact of animated pedagogical agents. In *Proceedings of CHI '97*, 359–366. New York: ACM Press.

Lewis, M. 1998. Designing for human agent interaction. In *AI Magazine* (Summer):67–78.

Lombard, M., and T. Ditton. 1997. At the heart of it all: The concept of presence. *Journal of Computer Mediated Communication* 3(2). Available: <www.ascusc.org/jcmc/vol3/issue2/lombard.html>.

Loyall, A. B., and J. Bates. 1991. Hap: A reactive, adaptive architecture for agents. CMU Technical Report CMU-CS-91-147.

Margolin, V. 1996. Expanding the boundaries of design: the product environment and the new user. In V. Margolin and R. Buchanan, eds., *The idea of design. A design issues reader.* Cambridge, Mass.: The MIT Press.

Matthews, G., and I. Deary. 1998. *Personality traits.* Cambridge, U.K.: Cambridge University Press.

McCarthy, L. 1999. Human-systems interaction for virtual environment team training. *Virtual Reality; Research, Development and Applications* 4:38–48.

Nass, C., J. Steuer, and E. R. Tauber. 1994. Computers are social actors. In *Proceedings of CHI '94,* 72–78. New York: ACM Press.

Neilsen, J. 1993. *Usability engineering.* San Diego: Academic Press.

———. 1995. Scenarios in discount usability engineering. In J. M. Carroll, ed., *Scenario-based design: Envisioning work in technology and system development,* 59–84. New York: John Wiley and Sons.

Parise, S., L. Sproull, S. Kiesler, and K. Waters. 1996. My partner is a real dog: Cooperation with social agents. In *Proceedings of CSCW '96,* 399–408. New York: ACM Press.

Pell, B., D. E. Bernard, S. A. Chien, E. Gat, N. Muscettola, P. P. Nayak, M. D. Wagner, and B. C. Williams. 1997. An autonomous spacecraft agent prototype. *Proceedings of the First International Conference on Autonomous Agents.* New York: ACM Press.

Preece, J., Y. Rogers, H. Sharp, D. R. Benyon, S. Holland, and T. Carey. 1994. *Human-computer interaction.* Reading, Mass.: Addison-Wesley.

Prevost, S., T. Bickmore, and J. Cassell. 1998. Interactional competency for conversational characters. In *Proceedings of the AAAI Workshop on Representations for Multi-Modal Human-Computer Interaction.* Menlo Park, Calif.: AAAI Press.

Prevost, S., P. Hodgson, L. Cook and E. Churchill. 1999. Face-to-face interfaces. In *Extended abstracts of CHI '99,* 244–245. New York: ACM Press.

Reeves, B., and C. Nass. 1996. *The media equation: How people treat computers. Television and new media like real people and places.* Cambridge, U.K.: Cambridge University Press.

Revelle, W. 1995. Personality processes. *Annual Review of Psychology* 46:295–328.

Rousseau, D., and B. Hayes-Roth. 1998. A social-psychological model for synthetic actors. *Proceedings of the 2nd International Conference on Autonomous Agents,* 165–172. New York: ACM Press.

Sproull, L., M. Subramani, S. Kiesler, J. Walker, and K. Waters. 1997. When the interface is a face. In B. Friedman, ed., *Human values and the design of computer technology*. Cambridge, U.K.: Cambridge University Press CSLI Publications.

Stone, A. R. 1995. *The war of desire and technology at the close of the mechanical age*. Cambridge, Mass: The MIT Press.

Thórisson, K. 1996. Communicative humanoids: A computational model of psychosocial dialogue skills. Ph.D. diss., Massachusetts Institute of Technology, Cambridge, Massachusetts.

Turkle, S. 1995. *Life on the screen: Identity in the age of the Internet*. New York: Simon and Schuster.

Walker, J., L. Sproull, and R. Subramani. 1994. Using a human face in an interface. In *CHI '94*, 85–91. New York: ACM Press.

Wilkins, D. E., K. L. Myers, J. D. Lowrance, and L. P. Wesley. 1995. Planning and reacting in uncertain and dynamic environments. *Journal of Experimental and Theoretical AI* 7(1):197–227.

Zarilli, P.B., ed. 1995. *Acting re(considered)*. London: Routledge.

4

Task-Oriented Collaboration with Embodied Agents in Virtual Worlds

Jeff Rickel and W. Lewis Johnson

4.1 Introduction

We are working toward animated agents that can collaborate with human students in virtual worlds. The agent's objective is to help students learn to perform physical, procedural tasks, such as operating and maintaining equipment. Like most of the previous research on task-oriented dialogues, the agent (computer) serves as an expert that can provide guidance to a human novice. Research on such dialogues dates back more than twenty years (Deutsch 1974), and the subject remains an active research area (Allen et al. 1996; Lochbaum 1994; Walker 1996). However, most of that research has focused solely on verbal dialogues, even though the earliest studies clearly showed the ubiquity of nonverbal communication in human task-oriented dialogues (Deutsch 1974). To allow a wider variety of interactions among agents and human students, we use virtual reality (Durlach and Mavor 1995); agents and students cohabit a three-dimensional, interactive, simulated mock-up of the student's work environment.

Virtual reality offers a rich environment for multimodal interaction among agents and humans. Like standard desktop dialogue systems, agents can communicate with humans via speech, using speech synthesis and recognition software. As in previous simulation-based training systems, a simulator controls the behavior of the virtual world. Agents can perceive the state of the virtual world via messages from the simulator, and they can take action in the world by sending messages to the simulator. However, an animated agent that cohabits a virtual world with students has a distinct advantage over previous disembodied tutors: the agent can also communicate nonverbally using gestures, gaze, facial expressions, and locomotion. In addition, students also have more freedom; they can move around the virtual world, gaze around (via a head-mounted display), and interact with objects (e.g., via a data glove). Agents can perceive these human actions; the position and orientation data used to track the users of a virtual reality system can provide agents with each user's location, field of view, and object manipulations. Thus, virtual reality is an important application area for research on multimodal dialogues because it allows more humanlike interactions among synthetic agents and humans than typical desktop interfaces can.

To explore the use of animated agents for task-oriented collaboration in virtual worlds, we have designed such an agent: Steve (Soar Training Expert for Virtual Environments). Steve is fully implemented and integrated with the other software components on which he relies (i.e., visual interface software, a simulator, and commercial speech synthesis and recognition products). We have tested Steve on a variety of naval operating procedures; he can teach students how to operate and maintain the gas turbine engines aboard naval ships, including both individual tasks and team tasks. Steve is not limited to this domain; he can provide instruction in a new domain when given only the appropriate declarative domain knowledge. Despite the growing number of animated agents that converse with human users (André 1999; Johnson, Rickel, and Lester 2000; Lester et al., chap. 5), Steve is unique in having domain-independent capabilities to support task-oriented dialogues situated in three-dimensional virtual worlds.

This chapter focuses on Steve's ability to integrate verbal and nonverbal communication to collaborate with students. Section 4.2 discusses the important roles that nonverbal communication plays in task-oriented collaboration. Section 4.3 illustrates Steve's current capabilities through an example interaction with a student. Sections 4.4 and 4.5 briefly review our architecture for virtual worlds and Steve's architecture; details are available in earlier papers (Johnson et al. 1998; Rickel and Johnson 1999a). Finally, section 4.6 describes the methods that govern Steve's communicative behavior, and section 4.7 provides conclusions and directions for future work.

4.2 Roles for Nonverbal Communication

While most of the previous research on task-oriented dialogues has focused on verbal interactions, an animated agent that cohabits the virtual world with students permits other types of interactions that play important roles in human task-oriented dialogues. These roles for nonverbal communication provide the primary motivation for using animated agents for task-oriented collaboration.

4.2.1 Interactive Demonstrations

An animated agent can demonstrate physical tasks, such as operation and repair of equipment. Demonstrating a task may be far more effective than trying to describe how to perform it, especially when the task involves motor skills and spatial relations, and the experience of seeing a task performed is likely to lead to better retention (Najjar 1998). Moreover, an interactive demonstration given by an agent offers several advantages over showing students a videotape. First, students are free to move around in the environment and view the demonstration from different perspectives. Second, they can interrupt with questions or even a request to finish the task themselves. Third, the agent can adapt the demonstration to different situations. For example, Steve is able to construct and revise plans for completing a task in response to changes in the virtual world, so he can demonstrate tasks under different initial states and failure modes, as well as help the student recover from errors.

4.2.2 Navigational Guidance

When a student's work environment is large and complex, such as a ship, one of the primary advantages of a virtual mock-up is to teach the student where things are and how to get around. In this context, animated agents can serve as navigational guides, leading students around and preventing them from becoming lost. For example, Steve inhabits a complex shipboard environment, including multiple rooms. The engine room alone is quite complex, with the large turbine engines that propel the ship, several platforms and pathways around and into the engines, a console, and a variety of different parts of the engines that must be manipulated, such as valves.

As Steve demonstrates tasks, he leads students around this environment, showing them where relevant objects are and how to get to them. Leading someone down a hallway, up a flight of stairs, around a corner, and through some pipes to the valve they must turn is likely to be more effective than trying to tell them where the valve is located. Our experience in training people using immersive virtual reality has shown that students can easily become disoriented and lost in complex environments, so animated agents that can serve as guides are an important instructional aid.

4.2.3 Gaze, Gesture, and Body Orientation as Attentional Guides

To draw a student's attention to a specific aspect of the virtual world, tutoring systems make use of many devices, including arrows, highlighting by color, and verbal referring expressions. An animated agent, however, can guide a student's attention with the most common and natural methods: gaze and deictic (pointing) gestures. Steve uses both methods to guide students' attention to objects in the virtual world, as well as to connect his verbal referring expressions to objects so that students learn their names. Argyle and Cook (1976) discuss the use of deictic gaze in human conversation, and the prevalence of deictic gestures in human task-oriented dialogues was noted in the earliest studies (Deutsch 1974).

Steve also uses his body orientation as a cue to his attentional focus. When he moves to an object to perform an action on it, he ends his locomotion with his body facing the object. Steve's immediate attention (indicated by his gaze) subsequently shifts back and forth between the student and the object as Steve describes the action, performs it, and finally discusses its results. During that time, however, the lower trunk of Steve's body remains oriented toward the object; Steve looks at the student when appropriate by turning his upper body, neck, and head. Thus, Steve's lower body orientation indicates to the student his focus on the object, and the orientation changes only as the focus of the task shifts to a new object, providing a cue to help the student recognize such focus shifts. Kendon (1972) observed a similar hierarchy of body movements in human speakers; while the head and hands tend to move during each sentence, shifts in the trunk and lower limbs occur primarily at topic shifts.

4.2.4 Nonverbal Tutorial Feedback

The primary role of a tutor is to provide feedback on a student's actions. In addition to providing verbal feedback, an animated agent can also use nonverbal communication to influence the student. Nonverbal feedback can reinforce a verbal comment. For example, Steve shakes his head when telling students that they made an error. However, nonverbal feedback can also provide more varied degrees of feedback than verbal comments alone. For example, nonverbal feedback may often be preferable because it is less obtrusive than a verbal comment. Steve uses a simple nod of approval when students perform correct actions to reassure them without interrupting. Similarly, human tutors often display a look of concern or puzzlement to make a student think twice about their actions, especially in cases where either they are unsure that the student has actually made a mistake or they do not want to interrupt with a verbal correction yet. Graesser and his colleagues even found that human tutors often respond to student errors with a positive, polite verbal comment accompanied by a puzzled expression; the tutor, out of politeness, avoids directly criticizing the student but still communicates disapproval by nonverbal means (Graesser et al. n.d.).

4.2.5 Conversational Signals

When people carry on face-to-face dialogues, they employ a wide variety of nonverbal signals to complement their utterances and regulate the conversation. While tutorial dialogue in most previous tutoring systems resembles Internet chat or a telephone conversation, animated agents allow us to more closely model the face-to-face interactions to which people are most accustomed. Some nonverbal signals help regulate the flow of conversation, and would be most valuable in tutoring systems that support speech recognition as well as speech output, such as Steve or the Circuit Fix-It Shop (Smith and Hipp 1994). This includes back-channel feedback, such as head nods to acknowledge understanding of a spoken utterance (Duncan 1974). It also includes the use of eye contact to regulate turn taking in mixed-initiative dialogue (Argyle and Cook 1976). Steve employs these types of conversational signals.

Other nonverbal signals are closely tied to spoken utterances and could be used by any animated agent that produces speech output. For example, intonational pitch accents indicate the degree and type of salience of words and phrases in an utterance, including rhematic (i.e., new) elements of utterances and contrastive elements (Pierrehumbert and Hirschberg 1990); to further highlight such utterance elements, a pitch accent is often accompanied by a short movement of the eyebrows or a beat gesture (i.e., a short batonlike movement of the hands) (Ekman 1979). Steve does not currently employ such nonverbal signals. However, Cassell and her colleagues have developed agents that do (Cassell et al. 1994; Cassell et al. 1999), and we are working in that direction. Although people can clearly communicate in the absence of nonverbal signals (e.g., by telephone), communication and collaboration proceed most comfortably and smoothly when they are available.

4.2.6 Activities of Virtual Teammates

Complex tasks often require the coordinated actions of multiple team members. Team tasks are ubiquitous in today's society; for example, teamwork is critical in manufacturing, in an emergency room, and in rescue operations. To perform effectively as a team, members must master their individual roles and learn to coordinate actions with their teammates.

Distributed virtual reality provides a promising vehicle for training teams; students, possibly at different locations, cohabit a virtual mock-up of their work environment, where they can practice together in realistic situations. In such training, animated agents can play two valuable roles: they can serve as instructors for individual students, and they can substitute for missing team members, allowing students to practice team tasks when some or all human instructors and teammates are unavailable. While verbal communication is often required for team coordination, the ability to track visually the activities of teammates is often indispensable. Although this chapter focuses on one-on-one interaction between Steve and a student, we have extended Steve to support team training, as described in an earlier paper (Rickel and Johnson 1999b).

4.3 Example

To illustrate Steve's capabilities, let us suppose that Steve is demonstrating how to inspect a high-pressure air compressor aboard a ship. The student's head-mounted display gives her a three-dimensional view of her shipboard sur-roundings, which include the compressor in front of her and Steve at her side. As she moves or turns her head, her view changes accordingly. Her head-mounted display is equipped with a microphone (to allow her to speak to Steve) and earphones (through which Steve speaks to her).

After introducing the task, Steve begins the demonstration. "I will now check the oil level," Steve says, and he leads her over to the dipstick. Steve looks down at the dipstick, points at it, looks back at the student, and says, "First, pull out the dipstick." Steve pulls it out (fig. 4.1). Pointing at the level indicator, Steve says, "Now we can check the oil level on the dipstick. As you can see, the oil level is normal." To finish the subtask, Steve says, "Next, insert the dipstick," and he pushes it back in.

Continuing the demonstration, Steve says, "Make sure all the cutout valves are open." Looking at the cutout valves, Steve sees that all of them are already open except one. Pointing to it, he says, "Open cutout valve three," and he opens it.

Next, Steve says, "I will now perform a functional test of the drain alarm light. First, check that the drain monitor is on." Steve looks at the power light and back at the student. "As you can see, the power light is illuminated, so the monitor is on" (fig. 4.2). The student, realizing that she has seen this procedure before, says, "Let me finish." Steve acknowledges that she can finish the task, and he shifts to monitoring her performance.

The student steps forward to the relevant part of the compressor but is suddenly unsure of what to do first. "What should I do?" she asks. Steve replies, "I suggest that you press the function test button." The student asks, "Why?" Steve replies, "That action is relevant because we want the drain monitor in test mode." The student, wondering why the drain monitor should be in test mode, asks, "Why?" again. Steve replies, "That goal is relevant because it will allow us

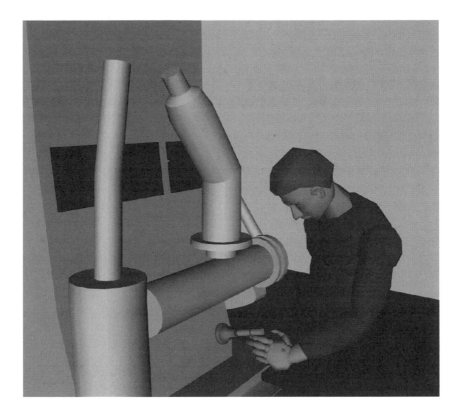

Figure 4.1
Steve pulling out a dipstick.

to check the alarm light." Finally, the student understands, but she is unsure which button is the function test button. "Show me how to do it," she requests. Steve moves to the function test button and pushes it (fig. 4.3). The alarm light comes on, indicating to Steve and the student that it is functioning properly. Now the student recalls that she must extinguish the alarm light, but she pushes the wrong button, causing a different alarm light to illuminate. "No," Steve responds as he shakes his head. Flustered, she asks Steve, "What should I do next?" Steve replies, "I suggest that you press the reset button on the temperature monitor." She presses the reset button to extinguish the second alarm light, causing Steve to nod in approval, and then she presses the correct button

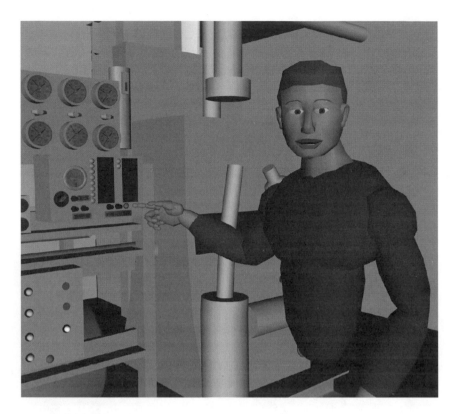

Figure 4.2
Steve describing a power light.

to extinguish the first alarm light. Steve looks at her and says, "That completes the task. Nice job."

4.4 Creating Virtual Worlds for People and Agents

Before we can discuss Steve's architecture, we must introduce a software architecture for creating virtual worlds that people and agents can cohabit (fig. 4.4). With our colleagues from Lockheed Martin Corporation and the USC Behavioral Technologies Laboratory, we have designed and implemented such an architecture (Johnson et al. 1998). For purposes of modularity and efficiency, the architecture consists of separate components running in parallel as

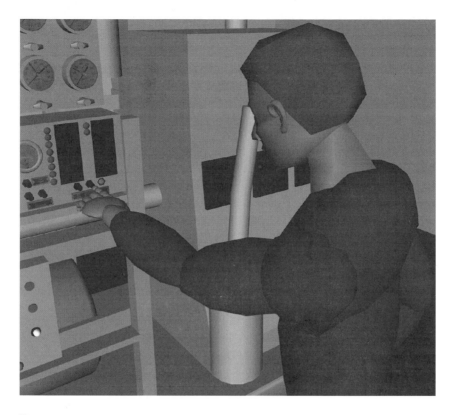

Figure 4.3
Steve pressing a button.

separate processes, possibly on different machines. The components communicate by exchanging messages. Our architecture includes the following types
of components.

- *Simulator:* A simulator controls the behavior of the virtual world. Our current
  implementation uses the VIVIDS simulation engine (Munro et al. 1997) developed at the USC Behavioral Technologies Laboratory.

- *Visual Interface:* Each human participant has a visual interface component
  that allows him or her to view and manipulate the virtual world. Several

hardware devices connect participants to this component: a head-mounted display provides their view into the world, position sensors on their head and hands track their movements, and they interact with the world by "touching" virtual objects using a data glove. The visual interface component plays two primary roles. First, it receives messages from the other components (primarily the simulator) describing changes in the appearance of the world, and it outputs a three-dimensional graphical representation through each person's head-mounted display. Second, it informs the other components when each person interacts with objects. Our current implementation uses Lockheed Martin's Vista Viewer (Stiles, McCarthy, and Pontecorvo 1995) as the visual interface component.

- *Audio:* Each human participant has an audio component. This component receives messages from the simulator describing the location and audible radius of various sounds, and it broadcasts appropriate sounds to the headphones on the person's head-mounted display.

- *Speech generation:* Each human participant has a speech generation component that receives text messages from other components (primarily agents), converts the text to speech, and broadcasts the speech to the person's headphones. Our current implementation uses Entropic's TrueTalk text-to-speech product.

- *Speech recognition:* Each human participant has a speech recognition component that receives speech signals via the person's microphone, recognizes the speech as a path through its grammar, and outputs a semantic token representing the speech to the other components. (Steve agents do not have any natural language understanding capabilities, so they have no need for the recognized sentence.) Our current implementation uses Entropic's Graphvite product.

- *Agent:* Each Steve agent runs as a separate component. The remainder of the chapter focuses on the architecture of these agents and their capabilities.

The various components do not communicate with one another directly. Instead, all messages are sent to a central message dispatcher. Each component tells the dispatcher the types of messages in which it is interested. Then, when a message arrives, the dispatcher forwards it to all interested components. For

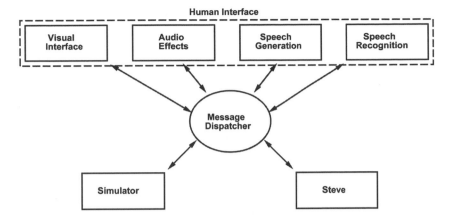

Figure 4.4
An architecture for virtual worlds. Although the figure only shows components for one agent and one human, other agents and humans can be added simply by connecting them to the message dispatcher in the same way.

example, each visual interface component registers interest in messages that specify changes in the appearance of the virtual world (e.g., a change in the color or location of an object). When the simulator sends such a message, the dispatcher broadcasts it to every visual interface component. This approach increases modularity, since one component need not know the interface to other components. It also increases extensibility, since new components can be added without affecting existing ones. It has been especially valuable in supporting team training, since it allows any number of students and agents to be connected to the virtual world. Our current implementation uses Sun's ToolTalk as the message dispatcher.

4.5 Steve's Architecture

Steve consists of three main modules: perception, cognition, and motor control (fig. 4.5). The perception module monitors messages from the message dispatcher and identifies events that are relevant to Steve, such as actions taken in the virtual world by people and agents and changes in the state of the virtual world. Its main job is to provide a coherent view of the state of the virtual world to the cognition module. The cognition module interprets the input it

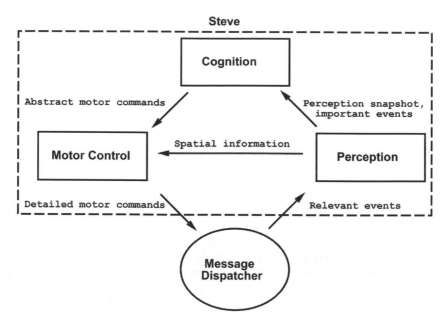

Figure 4.5
The three main modules in Steve and the types of information they send and receive.

receives from the perception module, chooses Steve's next actions, and sends out high-level motor commands to control the agent's voice and body. The motor control module decomposes these motor commands into a sequence of lower-level commands that are sent to other components via the message dispatcher. In our current implementation, cognition runs as one process, and perception and motor control run as a separate, parallel process. This chapter will focus primarily on Steve's cognition module; for details on the perception and motor control modules, see Rickel and Johnson (1999a).

The cognition module is organized into three main layers. The lowest layer is Soar (Laird, Newell, and Rosenbloom 1987; Newell 1990). Soar was designed as a general model of human cognition, so it provides a number of features that support the construction of intelligent agents. Soar's decision cycle is the feature most relevant to this chapter; we describe it below.

The next layer provides a set of domain-independent capabilities to support task-oriented collaboration. Soar is a general cognitive architecture, but it does not provide built-in support for particular cognitive skills such as demonstration and conversation. Our main task in building Steve was to design a set of domain-independent capabilities such as these and layer them on top of the Soar architecture.

The final layer of the cognition module provides Steve's domain-specific knowledge. To teach students how to perform procedural tasks in a particular domain, Steve needs a representation of the tasks. A course author must provide such knowledge to Steve. Given appropriate task knowledge for a particular domain, Steve uses his domain-independent capabilities to teach that knowledge to students. Our layered approach to Steve's cognition module allows Steve to be used in a variety of domains; each new domain requires only new task knowledge, without any modification of Steve's abilities as a teacher.

The cognition module operates by looping continually through a decision cycle. During each decision cycle, it receives new input from the perception module, it executes the *operator* that was selected at the end of the previous decision cycle, and it selects the operator to apply during the next decision cycle. Each operator is represented by a set of production rules that implement one of Steve's capabilities, such as answering a question or demonstrating an action. These serve as the building blocks for his behavior, and the process of operator selection serves as an arbitration mechanism for sequencing them. The timing of each decision cycle depends on the hardware on which Steve is running, and each decision cycle varies slightly in duration depending on Steve's cognitive activities. Steve typically executes about five to ten decision cycles per second on our current hardware (an SGI Onyx).

Low-level animation of Steve's body runs as software that is linked into the Visual Interface software (Vista Viewer) rather than into Steve. Before each graphical frame is rendered (about 15 to 30 times per second), Vista calls the animation code to update Steve's body position. The animation code is controlled by messages it receives from Steve's motor control module. Because the animation code controls the dynamics of all body motions, the motor control module need only specify the type of motion it wants. The animation code currently supports locomotion (movement of the entire body from one location to another), facial movements (eyes, eyebrows, eyelids, and mouth), gaze (dynamic tracking of objects and people), head movements (nodding and shaking the head), and arm and hand movements (including grasping, pressing, and pointing), all subject to motion limits. It generates all movements dynamically; there are no keyframes or canned animations. Movements involving different parts of the body can be performed simultaneously, and a new command to a body part interrupts any existing motion for that part. Steve's motor control module isolates the details of how to control the animation code, allowing the cognition module to send higher-level motor commands that do not depend on those details.

4.6 Task-Oriented Collaboration

Having discussed Steve's architecture and its interface to the other software components that make up the virtual world, we now focus on the domain-independent layer of Steve's cognition module, which provides his capabilities for task-oriented collaboration. First, we describe the actions that serve as the building blocks from which his dynamic behavior is constructed. Next, we discuss Steve's representation of the task and dialogue context. Finally, we examine how Steve uses the current context to choose his next action.

4.6.1 Behavioral Building Blocks

The cognition module generates Steve's communicative behavior by dynamically selecting his next action from a repertoire of behavioral primitives. To support the needs of task-oriented collaboration and exploit the roles for nonverbal communication outlined in section 4.2, we currently generate Steve's behavior from the following building blocks.

- *Speak:* Steve can produce a verbal utterance directed at the student (or a teammate in team training). To make it clear to whom the utterance is directed, the motor control module automatically shifts Steve's gaze to the hearer just prior to the utterance. (Task-related events can cause gaze to shift to something else before the utterance is complete.) To make it clear that Steve is speaking, the motor control module automatically maintains a "speaking face" (eyebrows slightly raised and mouth moving) throughout the utterance. Steve has a wide range of utterances, all generated from text templates, ranging from a simple "OK" or "no" to descriptions of domain actions and goals. A message from the speech synthesis component indicates to Steve's perception module when the utterance is complete.

- *Move to an object:* To guide the student to a new object, Steve can plan the shortest path from his current location and move along that path (Rickel and

Johnson 1999a). To guide the student's attention, the motor control module automatically shifts Steve's gaze to his next destination on each leg of the path. In contrast, to simply follow the student around (e.g., when monitoring the student's activities), Steve shrinks and attaches himself to the corner of the student's field of view, so that he can provide visual feedback on his or her actions.

- *Manipulate an object:* To demonstrate domain task steps, Steve can manipulate objects in a variety of ways. Currently, this includes manipulations that can be done by grasping the object (e.g., moving, pulling, inserting, turning) or using his fingers (e.g., pressing a button, flipping a switch). To guide the student's attention, the motor control module automatically shifts Steve's gaze to the object just prior to the manipulation. State change messages from the simulator indicate to Steve's perception module when the manipulation is complete (e.g., a button's state attribute changing to "depressed").

- *Visually check an object:* Steve can also demonstrate domain task steps that simply require visually checking an object (e.g., checking the oil level on a dipstick or checking whether an indicator light is illuminated). This requires Steve to shift gaze to the object and make a mental note of the relevant property of that object.

- *Point at an object:* To draw a student's attention to an object, or connect a verbal referring expression to the object it denotes, Steve can point at the object. To further guide the student's attention, the motor control module automatically shifts Steve's gaze to the object just prior to pointing at it.

- *Give tutorial feedback:* To provide tutorial feedback on a student's action, Steve indicates a student error by shaking his head as he says "no," and he indicates a correct action by simply looking at the student and nodding. As discussed earlier, the motivation for shaking the head is to complement and reinforce the verbal evaluation, and the motivation for the head nod is to provide the least obtrusive possible feedback to the student.

- *Offer turn:* Since our goal is to make Steve's demonstrations interactive, we allow students to interrupt with questions (currently just "What next?" and "Why?") or to request to abort the task or finish it themselves. Although they can talk during Steve's utterances or demonstrations, Steve explicitly offers the conversational turn to them after each speech act (which could be several sentences) or performance of a domain action. He does this by shifting his gaze to them and pausing one second. Not only does this give students convenient openings for interruptions, but it also helps to structure Steve's presentations. (Prior to adding this feature, users complained that Steve's presentations were hard to follow because he never paused to take a breath.)

- *Listen to student:* When the student is speaking, Steve can choose to quietly listen. This simply involves shifting gaze to the student to indicate attention.

- *Wait for someone:* When Steve is waiting for someone to take an action (either the student or a teammate in a team training scenario), he can shift gaze to that person (or agent) to indicate his expectation.

- *Acknowledge an utterance:* When a student or teammate says something to Steve, he can choose to explicitly acknowledge his understanding of their utterance by looking at them and nodding. The speech recognizer does not provide recognition of intermediate clauses, so Steve is currently limited to acknowledging understanding of entire utterances.

- *Drop hands:* When Steve is not using his arms and hands, he can drop them back down to hang loosely at his sides. Although there is evidence that such a move can convey a conversational signal (e.g., end of turn) (Duncan 1974), Steve does not currently use this behavior for that purpose; it simply means he has nothing else to do with his hands (such as pointing or manipulating).

- *Attend to action:* When someone other than Steve manipulates an object in his environment, Steve automatically shifts his gaze to the object to indicate his awareness. Unlike all the above behaviors, which are chosen deliberately by the cognition module, this behavior is a sort of knee-jerk reaction invoked directly by the perception module. Because an object manipulation is a very transient event, our design rationale was to have Steve react as quickly as possible.

4.6.2 Representation of Context

If Steve's environment were predictable, his behavior could be carefully scripted to ensure coherence. However, our goal is to support dynamic environments where Steve is not in complete control. To make the training experience as interactive as possible, the student has the freedom to speak or act on the environment at any time. To expose the student to a wide range of situations he or she might face, the simulator will create unexpected circumstances such as equipment failures. Rather than script Steve for each possible training scenario, our approach has been to give him a more general model of tasks that allows him to adapt dynamically to many variations in the task context. Team training provides additional dynamics to Steve's environment; the presence of other students and autonomous agents makes the possibility of scripting his behavior impractical.

The key to maintaining coherent behavior in a dynamic environment is to maintain a rich representation of context. The ability to react to unexpected events and handle interruptions is crucial for task-oriented collaboration in virtual worlds, yet it threatens the coherence of the agent's behavior. A good representation of context allows the agent to be responsive while maintaining its overall focus. For task-oriented collaboration, an agent must maintain two separate but complementary types of context: the task context and the dialogue context.

4.6.2.1 *Task Context*   The task context represents the state of the task on which the student and Steve are collaborating. It must specify which task goals are already satisfied and how the remaining task goals can be achieved.

Steve is given knowledge of domain tasks represented as hierarchical plans. Each task consists of a set of steps, ordering constraints, and causal links. Each step is either a primitive action (e.g., press a button) or a composite action (i.e., itself a task). Composite actions give tasks a hierarchical structure. Each ordering constraint specifies that one step must be performed before another. These constraints define a partial order over the steps. Finally, the causal links specify the role of each step in the task. Each causal link specifies that one step achieves a goal that is a precondition for another step (or for completion of the task). This basic task representation has proven effective in a wide variety of research on task-oriented collaboration and generation of procedural instructions (Delin et al. 1994; Mellish and Evans 1989; Young 1997).

Steve represents the task context as an annotated task model for the current task on which he and the student are collaborating. When he and the student begin collaborating on a task, he creates the task model through simple top-down decomposition (Sacerdoti 1977). That is, starting with his representation for that task, he recursively expands each composite action with its task definition until he has a complete hierarchical model of the task. Then, on each subsequent decision cycle, he uses input from his perception module that specifies the current state of the virtual world to annotate the task model.

While the task model provides general information about how to perform the task, the annotations specify how to complete it from the current state of the virtual world. Using the input from the perception module, Steve marks each goal in the task model as currently satisfied or not. This includes the end goals of the task as well as all intermediate goals.

Using this information about the state of the task goals, Steve uses a partial-order planning algorithm (Weld 1994) to determine which steps are relevant to completing the task (i.e., which subset of the task model constitutes his current plan), as described in Rickel and Johnson (1999a). This allows him to revise his plan dynamically when the state of the virtual world changes, perhaps unexpectedly. The planner runs as a set of background production rules (i.e., not requiring deliberate operator selection). Because the planning algorithm is linear in the size of the task model, it is predictably fast, preventing the planner from slowing down Steve's decision cycle and threatening his responsiveness.

4.6.2.2 Dialogue Context The dialogue context represents the state of the interaction between the student and Steve. It includes the following information:

- Each decision cycle, the perception module tells the cognition module whether the student is currently speaking, based on messages from the speech recognition component.

- Steve keeps track of whether he is currently speaking. When he outputs a speak command, he records his current speech act. When his utterance is complete, the speech synthesis component sends a message to Steve's perception module, which informs his cognition module.

- Steve keeps track of which objects are currently in the student's field of view, using messages from the visual interface software.

- He records who currently has the task initiative. When he has the task initiative, he teaches the student how to complete the task. When the student has the task initiative, Steve watches as the student performs the task, evaluating the student's actions and answering her questions when she needs help.

Students currently control the task initiative by asking Steve to demonstrate a task or asking to finish the task themselves. In the future, we plan to use the approach used in TOTS (Rickel 1988) to allow Steve to initiate shifts in task initiative based on a model of the student's knowledge.

- Steve keeps track of the steps he and the student have executed. For his own steps, he maintains an episodic memory that records the state of the world when each step was executed, so that he can explain later why he performed the step (Rickel and Johnson 1999a). Keeping track of prior steps also allows Steve to recognize when a step is being repeated, and it lets him use cue phrases (Grosz and Sidner 1986) to indicate the relation between the previous step and the current one (Rickel and Johnson 1999a).

- When he answers a student's question (currently just "What next?" or "Why?"), he records his answer in case the student asks a follow-up question (e.g., "Why?").

- To represent the attentional state of the collaboration, Steve uses a discourse focus stack (Grosz and Sidner 1986). Each element of the stack is a task step, either a primitive or composite action. Initially, the stack contains one element, the task on which Steve and the student are collaborating. When they begin collaborating on a new step, whether it is a step in the task definition of the current focus or an interruption (e.g., a step being executed out of its normal order), the step is pushed onto the focus stack. When the step currently in focus is completed, it is popped off the stack. This helps ensure a systematic, coherent execution of the task, and it allows Steve to recognize digressions and resume the prior demonstration when unexpected events require a temporary deviation from the usual order of task steps.

- For the step currently in focus, Steve records the status of his collaboration with the student on that step (e.g., whether he proposed the step, whether he explained it, whether he or the student performed it, whether they discussed the results).

- When the student makes a request, Steve records it until he responds. This is needed when Steve chooses to finish his current activity (e.g., utterance or demonstration) before responding.

4.6.3 Controlling Steve's Behavior

Given Steve's repertoire of behaviors and his representation of the current context, the cognition module must repeatedly choose his next action. His behavioral building blocks are implemented as Soar operators. Each decision cycle, the cognition module must choose to continue the current operator in the next decision cycle or select a new one. The representation of the current context gives it the information to make this decision.

Soar provides architectural support for action selection. To program an agent in Soar, one writes three types of production rules: operator proposal rules suggest an operator for selection in the next decision cycle, operator comparison rules assert preferences among the proposed operators, and operator application rules execute an operator after it has been selected. At the end of each decision cycle, Soar considers the proposed operators and the preferences among them, and it chooses one operator for application during the next decision cycle.

Thus, the behavioral building blocks for Steve are implemented as operator application rules, and their sequencing comes from operator proposal and comparison rules. Since Steve typically executes five to ten decision cycles per second, he can be very responsive to the environment.

Steve can choose his next action to fill one of three roles. First, he can respond to the student. This includes responding to a student's request, giving them tutorial feedback on their action, or simply listening when they are talking. Second, Steve can choose for himself how to advance the collaborative dialogue. This includes things like suggesting the next task step, describing it, or demonstrating it in cases where the student did not explicitly request such help. Third, Steve can choose a turn-taking or grounding act (Traum and Hinkelman 1992) that helps regulate the dialogue between the student and himself without advancing the task. This includes offering the student the conversational turn or acknowledging understanding of an utterance with a head nod.

While operator proposal rules may suggest several such actions, operator comparison rules give these three types of actions different priorities. The highest priority is to respond to the student. If no such operators are proposed, the next priority is to perform any relevant conversational regulation action. However, if an opportunity for a conversational regulation action is missed due to a higher priority operator for responding to the student, it will not be deferred and displayed later. Only when neither of these types of operators is proposed will Steve take the initiative to advance the task collaboration, and he only does that when he has the task initiative. Traum proposed a similar priority scheme in his model of spoken task-oriented dialogue (Traum 1994).

Because of their importance in conversation, grounding acts deserve special mention. Research has shown that listeners frequently provide some combination of verbal and nonverbal cues to indicate understanding or lack thereof (Clark and Schaefer 1989). The cue can be explicit, as with back-channel feedback (e.g., a brief "Mmm hmm" or head nod), or it can be implicit if the listener simply follows the speaker's utterance with an appropriate response (e.g., an answer to a question). Steve uses the implicit approach (i.e., no separate grounding act) when responding to student requests and task actions. When possible, his response is chosen to indicate what he understood, in case of faulty speech recognition. For example, when he thinks the student just asked to finish the task, he responds with "OK, you finish"; if he misunderstood the student's utterance and simply responded with "OK," the student could be confused when he subsequently watches the student and waits for the student's next action.

Steve uses an explicit grounding act in only two cases. First, he uses a head nod to acknowledge his understanding of an utterance when someone informs him of some condition, which only occurs during team tasks. In this case, the teammate may not watch his subsequent activity, so a clear acknowledgment of understanding is helpful. Since speech recognizers cannot indicate to whom an utterance is directed, the acknowledgment also indicates that the agent has determined from the current context that the speech was directed to him. Second, Steve asks the student to repeat an utterance when the speech recognizer cannot understand it.

Some operator proposal productions trigger other operator proposals. When Steve proposes an operator whose execution would require a particular location for Steve (e.g., demonstrating a task step), that precondition appears on the structure for the proposed operator. If Steve is not currently at the location, another production rule will propose a higher priority operator for moving Steve to it. Similarly, an operator for an utterance whose focus is a particular object may, depending on context, be annotated with a deictic precondition. The deictic precondition will trigger a proposal rule for Steve to point at the object first. Our criteria for choosing when to accompany a verbal referring expression with locomotion or a deictic gesture are currently simple; before demonstrating an action on an object, Steve first moves to it, and then he points at it while describing what he is about to do. Work by Lester and his colleagues (Lester et al. 1999) offers more sophisticated criteria that could be incorporated easily into Steve. Finally, some operators (e.g., an action demonstration) have a precondition that requires the student to be looking at a particular object (e.g., to see the action). If the operator is proposed and the object is not in the student's field of view, Steve will propose an operator to get their attention (e.g., by saying "Look over here!").

Since task steps may be only partially ordered, there may be multiple steps that could be performed next. From the standpoint of completing the task, any of them could be chosen. However, research has shown that collaborators shift focus from one task step or subtask to another only with good reason (Grosz and Sidner 1986). To maximize the coherence of his actions, Steve uses the discourse focus stack. As long as the current task step or subtask in focus is still appropriate, all his proposed operators will relate to it. When Steve has the task initiative, and several task steps could be performed next, he chooses one and pushes it onto the focus stack before performing any operators for one of the steps (e.g., move, point, explain, demonstrate). This does not prevent Steve from pushing a new step or subtask onto the stack to interrupt the current one (e.g., to handle an unexpected emergency) or from popping the current focus if it suddenly becomes irrelevant; he handles such cases by explaining the unexpected (but required) focus shift to the student. However, the focus stack prevents Steve from shifting focus in cases where it is not required.

The sequence of operators that Steve applies when teaching the student a new task step (e.g., describe step, perform step, explain result) depends on the type of action the step requires. Steve has a class hierarchy of action types (e.g., manipulate an object, move an object, check a condition), and each type of action is associated with a suite of communicative acts. Each suite is essentially a finite-state machine represented as Soar productions. Each node represents an operator, such as describing the step or performing it, and arcs represent the conditions for terminating one operator and beginning another. Each action type in the class hierarchy inherits from the action types above it, so the communicative suite for an action type can be represented compactly as the deviations from its parent's suite. Currently, all action types inherit their communicative suite from one of a few general action types. However, our approach allows us to extend Steve's behavior if these suites prove inadequate for new types of actions encountered in new domains. The communicative suites need only specify the next contribution to the dialogue needed to advance the task collaboration; operators for responding to the student, moving and pointing, and regulating the conversation (i.e., turn-taking and grounding acts) are proposed independently as described above.

Steve's communicative suites are similar to the schemata approach to explanation generation pioneered by McKeown (1985). In contrast, André and her colleagues employ a top-down discourse planning approach to generating the communicative behavior of their animated agent, and they compile the resulting plans into finite-state machines for efficient execution (André, Rist, and Müller 1999). The trade-offs between these two approaches are well known (Moore 1995).

Many of Steve's behavioral building blocks take several decision cycles to execute, and some (speech and locomotion) can take many decision cycles. During this period, Steve's perception and cognition modules remain active, monitoring the state of the virtual world and deciding whether to react. In principle, any of the building blocks could be aborted at any time. In practice, Steve does not abort most actions. A notable exception is that Steve halts his demonstration of a task immediately, even in midsentence, when students interrupt and ask to abort the task or to finish it themselves. Steve's reluctance to abort his actions rarely seems unusual, since, for example, people often finish what they are saying before acknowledging an interruption. Nonetheless, our current work is focusing on cases where Steve should be more responsive to interruptions.

4.7 Conclusions and Future Work

We have tested Steve on a variety of naval operating procedures. He can perform tasks on several of the consoles that are used to control the gas turbine engines that propel naval ships, he can check and manipulate some of the valves that surround these engines, and he can perform a handful of procedures on the high-pressure air compressors that are part of these engines. A student in the USC School of Education recently completed an evaluation of users interacting with Steve in a variety of circumstances. The student is currently analyzing the data and formulating conclusions, which will appear in his dissertation (Kroetz n.d.).

Our work has focused more on multimodal behavior generation than multimodal input. To model face-to-face communication, we must extend the range of nonverbal communicative acts that students can use. To handle multimodal input in virtual reality, the techniques of Billinghurst and Savage (1996) neatly complement Steve's current capabilities. Their agent, which is designed to train medical students to perform sinus surgery, combines natural language understanding and simple gesture recognition. The work of Thórisson and Cassell on the Gandalf agent (Cassell and Thórisson 1999; Thórisson 1996) is even more ambitious; people talking with Gandalf wear a suit that tracks their upper body movement, an eye tracker that tracks their gaze, and a microphone that allows Gandalf to hear their words and intonation. More recent work by Cassell and her colleagues on their Rea agent is exploring the use of a vision system for tracking the user's nonverbal communication (Cassell et al. 1999). Although Gandalf and Rea were not developed for conversation in virtual reality, many of the techniques used for multimodal input apply.

Our work on Steve complements the long line of research on verbal task-oriented dialogues in the computational linguistics community. Steve currently has no natural language understanding capabilities; he can only understand phrases that we add to the grammar for the speech recognition program. Steve's natural language generation capabilities are also simple; all of Steve's utterances are generated from text templates, although more sophisticated methods could be added without affecting other aspects of Steve's behavior. We are particularly interested in integrating Steve with recent work on spoken dialogue systems. For example, the TRAINS system (Allen et al. 1996; Ferguson, Allen, and Miller 1996) supports a robust spoken dialogue between a computer agent and a person working together on a task. However, their agent has no animated form and does not cohabit a virtual world with users. Because TRAINS and Steve carry on similar types of dialogues with users, yet focus on different aspects of such conversations, a combination of the two systems seems promising.

Our work also complements research on sophisticated control of human figures (Badler, Phillips, and Webber 1993). That research targets more generality in human figure motion. Our human figure control is efficient and predictable, and it results in smooth animation. However, it does not provide sophisticated object manipulation (Douville, Levison, and Badler 1996), and it would not suffice for movements such as reaching around objects or through tight spaces. Our architecture is carefully designed so that a new body, along with its associated control code, can be integrated easily into Steve; a well-defined API separates Steve's control over his body from the detailed motion control code.

Steve illustrates the enormous potential for face-to-face, task-oriented collaboration between students and synthetic agents in virtual environments. Although verbal exchanges may be sufficient for some tasks, we expect that many domains will benefit from an agent that can additionally use gestures, gaze, facial expressions, and locomotion. Although Steve has only been tested on a virtual shipboard environment for naval training, he can be used for other domains when given only a description of the domain tasks and minimal knowledge of the spatial environment; none of the capabilities described in this chapter are specific to our naval domain. Moreover, Steve's architecture is designed to accommodate advances in related research areas, such as natural language processing and human figure control. This makes Steve an extensible foundation for further research on task-oriented collaboration in virtual worlds.

Acknowledgments

This work was funded by the Office of Naval Research under grant N00014-95-C-0179 and AASERT grant N00014-97-1-0598. We are grateful to our collaborators who developed the other software components on which Steve relies. Randy Stiles and his colleagues at Lockheed Martin developed the visual interface component (Vista Viewer). Allen Munro and his colleagues at the Behavioral Technologies Laboratory developed the simulator (VIVIDS). Ben Moore at ISI developed the speech recognition and audio components. Finally, Marcus Thiébaux at ISI developed the 3-D model of Steve's current body and the code in the visual interface component that controls its animation.

References

Allen, J. F., B. W. Miller, E. K. Ringger, and T. Sikorski. 1996. Robust understanding in a dialogue system. In *Proceedings of the 34th Annual Meeting of the Association for Computational Linguistics*, 62–70. San Francisco, Calif.: Morgan Kaufmann.

André, E., ed. 1999. Special issue on Animated interface agents: Making them intelligent. *Applied Artificial Intelligence* 13(4–5).

André, E., T. Rist, and J. Müller. 1999. Employing AI methods to control the behavior of animated interface agents. *Applied Artificial Intelligence* 13:415–448.

Argyle, M., and M. Cook. 1976. *Gaze and mutual gaze*. Cambridge: Cambridge University Press.

Badler, N. I., C. B. Phillips, and B. L. Webber. 1993. *Simulating humans*. New York: Oxford University Press.

Billinghurst, M., and J. Savage. 1996. Adding intelligence to the interface. In *Proceedings of the IEEE Virtual Reality Annual International Symposium (VRAIS '96)*, 168–175. Los Alamitos, Calif.: IEEE Computer Society Press.

Cassell, J., and K. R. Thórisson. 1999. The power of a nod and a glance: Envelope vs. emotional feedback in animated conversational agents. *Applied Artificial Intelligence* 13:519–538.

Cassell, J., T. Bickmore, L. Campbell, K. Chang, H. Vilhjálmsson, and H. Yan. 1999. Requirements for an architecture for embodied conversational characters. In *Proceedings of Computer Animation and Simulation '99*, 109–120. Berlin: Springer-Verlag.

Cassell, J., C. Pelachaud, N. Badler, M. Steedman, B. Achorn, T. Becket, B. Douville, S. Prevost, and M. Stone. 1994. Animated conversation: Rule-based generation of facial expression, gesture and spoken intonation for multiple conversational agents. In *Computer Graphics*, 413–420. New York: ACM SIGGRAPH.

Clark, H. H., and E. F. Schaefer. 1989. Contributing to discourse. *Cognitive Science* 13:259–294.

Delin, J., A. Hartley, C. Paris, D. Scott, and K. V. Linden. 1994. Expressing procedural relationships in multilingual instructions. In *Proceedings of the Seventh International Workshop on Natural Language Generation* (Kennebunkport, Me.), 61–70.

Deutsch, B. G. 1974. The structure of task oriented dialogs. In *Proceedings of the IEEE Symposium on Speech Recognition*. Pittsburgh, Penn.: Carnegie Mellon University. (Also available as Stanford Research Institute Technical Note 90, Menlo Park, Calif.)

Douville, B., L. Levison, and N. I. Badler. 1996. Task-level object grasping for simulated agents. *Presence: Teleoperators and Virtual Environments* 5(4):416–430.

Duncan Jr., S. 1974. Some signals and rules for taking speaking turns in conversations. In S. Weitz, ed., *Nonverbal communication*, 298–311. New York: Oxford University Press.

Durlach, N. I., and A. S. Mavor, eds. 1995. *Virtual reality: Scientific and technological challenges*. Washington, D.C.: National Academy Press.

Ekman, P. 1979. About brows: Emotional and conversational signals. In M. von Cranach, K. Foppa, W. Lepenies, and D. Ploog, eds., *Human ethology*. Cambridge: Cambridge University Press.

Ferguson, G., J. Allen, and B. Miller. 1996. TRAINS-95: Towards a mixed-initiative planning assistant. In *Proceedings of the Third Conference on AI Planning Systems*, 70–77. Menlo Park, Calif.: AAAI Press.

Graesser, A. C., K. Wiemer-Hastings, P. Wiemer-Hastings, R. Kreuz, and the Tutoring Research Group. N.d. AutoTutor: A simulation of a human tutor. *Journal of Cognitive Systems Research*. Forthcoming.

Grosz, B. J., and C. L. Sidner. 1986. Attention, intentions, and the structure of discourse. *Computational Linguistics* 12(3):175–204.

Johnson, W. L., J. W. Rickel, and J. C. Lester. 2000. Animated pedagogical agents: Face-to-face interaction in interactive learning environments. *International Journal of Artificial Intelligence in Education*. Forthcoming.

Johnson, W. L., J. Rickel, R. Stiles, and A. Munro. 1998. Integrating pedagogical agents into virtual environments. *Presence: Teleoperators and Virtual Environments* 7(6):523–546.

Kendon, A. 1972. Some relationships between body motion and speech. In A. W. Siegman and B. Pope, eds., *Studies in dyadic communication*, 177–210. New York: Pergamon Press.

Kroetz, A. N.d. The role of intelligent agency in synthetic instructor and human student dialogue. Ph.D. diss., University of Southern California, Los Angeles. Forthcoming.

Laird, J. E., A. Newell, and P. S. Rosenbloom. 1987. Soar: An architecture for general intelligence. *Artificial Intelligence* 33(1):1–64.

Lester, J. C., J. L. Voerman, S. G. Towns, and C. B. Callaway. 1999. Deictic believability: Coordinating gesture, locomotion, and speech in lifelike pedagogical agents. *Applied Artificial Intelligence* 13:383–414.

Lochbaum, K. E. 1994. Using collaborative plans to model the intentional structure of discourse. Ph.D. diss., Harvard University. Technical Report TR-25-94, Center for Research in Computing Technology.

McKeown, K. R. 1985. *Text generation*. Cambridge: Cambridge University Press.

Mellish, C., and R. Evans. 1989. Natural language generation from plans. *Computational Linguistics* 15(4):233–249.

Moore, J. D. 1995. *Participating in explanatory dialogues*. Cambridge, Mass.: The MIT Press.

Munro, A., M. C. Johnson, Q. A. Pizzini, D. S. Surmon, and D. M. Towne. 1997. Authoring simulation-centered tutors with RIDES. *International Journal of Artificial Intelligence in Education* 8:284–316.

Najjar, L. J. 1998. Principles of educational multimedia user interface design. *Human Factors* 40(2):311–323.

Newell, A. 1990. *Unified theories of cognition*. Cambridge, Mass.: Harvard University Press.

Pierrehumbert, J., and J. Hirschberg. 1990. The meaning of intonational contours in the interpretation of discourse. In P. Cohen, J. Morgan, and M. Pollack, eds., *Intentions in communication*, 271–311. Cambridge, Mass.: The MIT Press.

Rickel, J. 1988. An intelligent tutoring framework for task-oriented domains. In *Proceedings of the International Conference on Intelligent Tutoring Systems*, 109–115. Montréal, Canada: Université de Montréal.

Rickel, J., and W. L. Johnson. 1999a. Animated agents for procedural training in virtual reality: Perception, cognition, and motor control. *Applied Artificial Intelligence* 13:343–382.

———. 1999b. Virtual humans for team training in virtual reality. In *Proceedings of the Ninth International Conference on Artificial Intelligence in Education*, 578–585. Amsterdam: IOS Press.

Sacerdoti, E. 1977. *A structure for plans and behavior*. New York: Elsevier/North-Holland.

Smith, R. W., and D. R. Hipp. 1994. *Spoken natural language dialog systems*. New York: Oxford University Press.

Stiles, R., L. McCarthy, and M. Pontecorvo. 1995. Training studio: A virtual environment for training. In *Workshop on Simulation and Interaction in Virtual Environments (SIVE-95)*. New York: ACM Press.

Thórisson, K. R. 1996. Communicative humanoids: A computational model of psychosocial dialogue skills. Ph.D. diss., Massachusetts Institute of Technology, Cambridge, Mass.

Traum, D. R. 1994. A computational theory of grounding in natural language conversation. Ph.D. diss., Department of Computer Science, University of Rochester, Rochester, N.Y.

Traum, D. R., and E. A. Hinkelman. 1992. Conversation acts in task-oriented dialogue. *Computational Intelligence* 8(3):575–599.

Walker, M. A. 1996. The effect of resource limits and task complexity on collaborative planning in dialogue. *Artificial Intelligence* 85:181–243.

Weld, D. S. 1994. An introduction to least commitment planning. *AI Magazine* 15(4):27–61.

Young, R. M. 1997. Generating descriptions of complex activities. Ph.D. diss., University of Pittsburgh, Pittsburgh, Pennsylvania.

5

Deictic and Emotive Communication in Animated Pedagogical Agents

James C. Lester, Stuart G. Towns, Charles B. Callaway,

Jennifer L. Voerman, and Patrick J. FitzGerald

5.1 Introduction

Lifelike animated agents offer great promise for knowledge-based learning environments. Because of the immediate and deep affinity that children seem to develop for these agents, the potential pedagogical benefits they provide may perhaps even be exceeded by their motivational benefits. By creating the illusion of life, animated agents may significantly increase the time that children seek to spend with educational software. Recent advances in affordable graphics hardware are beginning to make the widespread distribution of real-time animation technology a reality, so children across the socioeconomic spectrum will reap its benefits. Endowing animated agents with believable, lifelike qualities has been the subject of a growing body of research (André et al., chap. 8; Badler et al., chap. 9; Bates 1994; Blumberg and Galyean 1995; Cassell et al. 1994; Kurlander and Ling 1995). Researchers have begun to examine the incorporation of gesture and facial expression in embodied conversational agents (Cassell et al., chap. 2; Poggi and Pelachaud, chap. 6), and the social aspects of human-computer interaction and users' anthropomorphization of software (Isbister and Nass 1998) has been the subject of increasing interest in recent years.

Animated pedagogical agents (Rickel and Johnson, chap. 4; Lester, Stone, and Stelling 1999; Paiva and Machado 1998) constitute an important category of animated agents whose intended use is educational applications. A recent large-scale, formal empirical study suggests that these agents can be pedagogically effective (Lester et al. 1997b), and it was determined that students perceived the agent as being very helpful, credible, and entertaining (Lester et al. 1997a). Although these results are preliminary and precise measures of agents' pedagogical contributions will begin to appear as the technologies mature and longitudinal studies are undertaken, we believe the *potential* for animated pedagogical agents is significant. The work described here is part of a long-term research program to bring about fundamental improvements in learning environments by broadening the bandwidth of "face-to-face" tutorial communication (Johnson, Rickel, and Lester n.d.).

Designing engaging animated pedagogical agents that communicate effectively involves a broad and complex matrix of psycholinguistic and engineering phenomena, many of which are discussed in this book. Two of these issues, *deictic believability* and *emotive believability*, are particularly important for animated pedagogical agents that are (1) situated in (virtual representations of) physical worlds that they immersively co-inhabit with students and (2) designed to engage students affectively.

In the same manner that humans refer to objects in their environment through combinations of speech, locomotion, and gesture, animated agents should be able to move through their environment, point to objects, and refer to them appropriately as they provide problem-solving advice. Deictic believability in animated agents requires the design of an agent behavior planner that considers the physical properties of the world inhabited by the agent. The agent must exploit its knowledge of the positions of objects in the world, its relative location with respect to these objects, as well as its prior explanations to create deictic gestures, motions, and utterances that are both natural and unambiguous.

In addition to deictic believability, animated pedagogical agents should also exhibit emotive believability. Engaging lifelike pedagogical agents that are visually expressive can clearly communicate problem-solving advice and simultaneously have a strong motivating effect on students. Drawing on a rich repertoire of emotive behaviors to exhibit contextually appropriate facial expressions and expressive gestures, they can exploit the visual channel to advise, encourage, and empathize with students. However, enabling lifelike pedagogical agents to communicate the affective content of problem-solving advice poses serious challenges. Agents' full-body emotive behaviors must support expressive movements and visually complement the problem-solving advice they deliver. Moreover, these behaviors must be planned and coordinated in real time in response to students' progress. In short, to create the illusion of emotional life typified by well-crafted animated characters, animated pedagogical agents must be able to communicate through both visual and aural channels.

To address these issues, we have developed the *spatial deixis* framework for achieving deictic believability and the *emotive-kinesthetic behavior sequencing* framework for dynamically sequencing lifelike pedagogical agents' full-body emotive expression. In the spatial deixis framework, a deictic behavior planner exploits a world model and the evolving explanation plan as it selects and coordinates locomotive, gestural, and speech behaviors. In the emotive-kinesthetic behavior sequencing framework, a behavior space is populated by emotive behaviors with full-body movements, including facial expressions featuring eye, eyebrow, and mouth movements as well as gestures with arms and hands; these behaviors are produced in real time by sequencing pedagogical speech acts and their associated emotional intent and kinesthetic expression. These frameworks have been used to implement Cosmo (fig. 5.1), a lifelike pedagogical agent with real-time deictic planning and full-body emotive expression. Cosmo inhabits the Internet Advisor, a learning environment for the domain of Internet packet routing. An impish, antenna-bearing creature who hovers about the virtual world of routers and networks, he provides advice to students as they decide how to ship packets through the network to specified destinations.

5.2 Deictic Behavior Sequencing

In the course of communicating with one another, interlocutors employ deictic techniques to create context-specific references. Hearers interpret linguistic events in concrete contexts. To understand a speaker's utterance, hearers must consider the physical and temporal contexts in which the utterance is spoken, as well as the identities of the speaker and hearer. Referred to as the *deictic center* of an utterance, the trio of location, time, and identities also plays an important role in generating linguistic events (Fillmore 1975). The first of these, location, is critical for achieving *spatial deixis*, a much-studied phenomenon in linguistics that is used to create references in the physical world (Jarvella and Klein 1982). Speakers use spatial deixis to narrow hearers' attention to particular entities. In one popular framework for analyzing spatial deixis, the *figure-ground* model (Roberts 1993), the world is categorized into *ground*, which is the common physical environment shared by the speaker and hearer, and the *referent*, the aspect of the ground to which the speaker wishes to refer. Through carefully constructed referring expressions and well-chosen gestures, the speaker assists the hearer in focusing on the particular referent of interest.

The ability to handle spatial deixis effectively is especially critical for animated pedagogical agents that inhabit virtual worlds. To provide problem-solving advice to students who are interacting with objects in the world, the agent must be able to refer to objects in the world to explain their function clearly and to assist students in performing their tasks. Deictic mechanisms for animated pedagogical agents should satisfy three criteria:

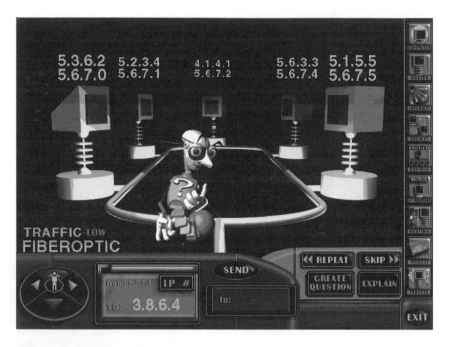

Figure 5.1
Cosmo and the Internet Advisor world.

1. *Lack of Ambiguity:* In a learning environment, an animated agent's clarity of expression is of the utmost importance. To effectively communicate advice and explanations to students, the agent must be able to create deictic references that are unambiguous. Avoiding ambiguity is critical in virtual environments, where an ambiguous deictic reference can cause mistakes in problem solving and foster misconceptions. Ambiguity is particularly challenging in virtual environments housing a multitude of objects, especially when many of the objects are visually similar.

2. *Immersivity:* An agent's explanatory behaviors should be situated (Suchman 1987), that is, all of its actions—not merely its advisory actions but also its communication of conceptual knowledge—should take place in concrete problem-solving contexts. Frequently, these are (virtual) physical contexts.

For example, in the course of delivering problem-solving advice, an agent frequently needs to refer to a particular object; it should be able to combine speech, gesture, and locomotion immersively (i.e., within a 2-D or 3-D environment) to do so, for example, by walking across a scene to a cluster of objects and pointing to one of them as it makes a verbal reference to the object.

3. *Pedagogical Soundness*: Deictic mechanisms for agents that inhabit learning environments must support their central pedagogical intent. Rather than operating in a communicative vacuum, spatial deixis must support the ongoing advisory discourse and be situated appropriately in the problem-solving context.

The lack-of-ambiguity requirement implies that deictic planning mechanisms must make use of an expressive representation of the world. While unambiguous deictic references can be created with object highlighting or by employing a relatively stationary agent with a long pointer (André and Rist 1996), the immersivity requirement implies that lifelike agents should artfully combine speech, gesture, and locomotion. Finally, the pedagogical soundness requirement implies that all deictic utterances, speech, and movements must be integrated with explanation plans that are generated in response to student questions and problem-solving impasses.

Following the lead of Bates (1994), we refer to the *believability* of lifelike agents as the extent to which users interacting with them come to believe that they are observing a sentient being with its own beliefs, desires, intentions, and personality. It has been shown that believable pedagogical agents in interactive learning environments can produce *the persona effect*, in which the very presence of a lifelike character in a learning environment can have a strong positive effect on students' perception of their learning experience (Lester et al. 1997a). A study involving one hundred middle school students revealed that when they interact with a lifelike agent that is expressive—namely, an agent that exhibits both animated and verbal advisory behaviors—students perceive it to be encouraging and useful.

A critical but largely unexplored aspect of agents' believability for learning environments is deictic believability. We say that lifelike agents making deictic references in a manner that achieves a lack of ambiguity, that does so in an immersive setting, and that is pedagogically sound exhibit *deictic believability*.

5.2.1 Related Work in Deictic Generation

The natural language generation and intelligent multimedia communities have addressed several aspects of spatial deixis. Natural language researchers have studied reference generation, for example, Dale's classic work on referring expressions (Dale 1992), scene description generation (Novak 1987), and spatial layout description generation (Sibun 1992). Work on intelligent multimedia systems (André et al. 1993; Feiner and McKeown 1990; Maybury 1991; Mittal et al. 1995; Roth, Mattis, and Mesnard 1991) has produced techniques for dynamically incorporating highlights, underlines, and blinking (Neal and Shapiro 1991). However, none of these consider the orchestration of an agent's communicative behaviors in an environment.

Work on lifelike agents has yielded more sophisticated techniques for referring to on-screen entities. The Edward system (Claassen 1992) employs a stationary persona that "grows" a pointer to a particular object in the interface, and the PPP agent (André and Rist 1996) is able to dynamically indicate various on-screen objects with a long pointer. While these techniques are effective for many tasks and domains, they do not provide a general solution for achieving deictic believability that deals explicitly with ambiguity both by selecting appropriate referring expressions and by producing lifelike gestures and locomotion.

Begun at the University of Pennsylvania's Jack project and continued at MIT, the work of Cassell and colleagues on conversational agents is perhaps the most advanced to date on agents that combine gesture, speech, and facial expression (Cassell et al. 1994). In addition to deictics, their agents also exhibit iconic, metaphoric, and beat gestures. However, this work neither provides a solution to the intricacies of detecting ambiguity in complex physical environments (and then addressing it with integrated speech, gesture, and locomotion) nor focuses on pedagogical interactions.

Despite the promise of lifelike pedagogical agents, with the exception of work on the Design-A-Plant project (Lester, Stone, and Stelling 1999) and the Soar Training Expert for Virtual Environments (Steve) (Rickel and Johnson, chap. 4), in which agents provide instruction about procedural tasks in a virtual reality environment, lifelike agents for pedagogy have received little attention. Neither the Steve nor the Design-A-Plant projects address deictic believability.

5.2.2 A Deictic Believability Test Bed

Features of environments, agents, and tasks that force spatial deixis issues to the forefront are threefold: (1) A world populated by a multitude of objects, many of which are similar, will require agents to plan speech, gesture, and locomotion carefully to avoid ambiguity. (2) We can select a domain and a problem-solving task for students that require agents to provide advice and explanations that frequently refer to different objects in the world. (3) Problem-solving tasks that require students to make decisions based on factors physically present in the environment will impose clarity requirements on agents' communicative capabilities. In contrast to a more abstract domain such as algebra, we can select a domain that can be represented graphically with objects in perhaps idiosyncratic and complex spatial layouts, thereby requiring the agent to produce clear problem-solving advice that integrates spatial deixis with explanations of concepts and problem-solving strategies.

To investigate deictic believability in lifelike pedagogical agents, we have developed a test bed in the form of an interactive learning environment. Because it has each of the features outlined above, the Internet Advisor provides a "laboratory" in which to study the coordination of deictic speech, gesture, and locomotion. Designed to foster exploration of computational mechanisms for animation behavior sequencing of lifelike characters and real-time human-agent problem-solving interaction, the Internet Advisor consists of a virtual world populated by many routers and networks.

Students interact with Cosmo as they learn about network routing mechanisms by navigating through a series of subnets. Given a packet to escort through the Internet, they direct it through networks of connected routers. At each subnet, they may send their packet to a specified router or view adjacent subnets. By making decisions about factors such as address resolution and traffic congestion, they learn the fundamentals of network topology and routing mechanisms. Helpful, encouraging, and with a bit of attitude, Cosmo explains how computers are connected, how routing is performed, what types of networks have different physical characteristics, how Internet address schemes work, and how network outages and traffic considerations come into play. Students' journeys are complete when they have navigated the network successfully and delivered their packet to its proper destination. The learning environment serves as an excellent test bed for exercising spatial deixis because each subnet has a variety of routers attached to it and the agent must refer unambiguously to them as it advises students about their problem-solving activities.

5.2.3 Coordinating Deictic Gesture, Locomotion, and Speech

The primary role of lifelike pedagogical agents is to serve as an engaging vehicle for communication. Hence, in the course of observing a student attempt different solutions in a learning environment, a lifelike pedagogical agent should clearly explain concepts and convey problem-solving strategies. It is in this context that spatial deixis arises. The spatial deixis framework guides the operation of the *deictic planner*, a key component of the agent behavior planning architecture. The interaction manager provides an interface between the learning environment and the agent that inhabits it. By monitoring a student's problem-solving activities in the learning environment, the interaction manager invokes the agent behavior planner in two situations: (1) when a student pauses for an extended period of time, which may signal a problem-solving impasse, and (2) when a student commits an error, which indicates a possible misconception.

The agent behavior planner consists of an explanation planner and a deictic planner. The explanation planner serves an analogous function to that of the discourse planner of natural language generation systems (Hovy 1993; Lester and Porter 1997; Moore 1995; Suthers 1991). Natural language generation systems typically consist of a discourse planner that determines the content and structure of multisentential texts and a realization system that plans the surface structure of the resulting prose. Analogously, given a communicative goal, the explanation planner of the agent behavior planner determines the content and structure of an agent's explanations and then passes these specifications to the deictic planner, which realizes these specifications in speech, gesture, and locomotion. The explanation planner invokes the deictic planner by specifying a communicative act, a topic, and a referent.

To accomplish its task, the deictic behavior planner examines the representational structures in a world model, a curriculum information network, a user model, the current problem state (which includes both the student's most recently proposed solution and the learning environment's analysis of that solution), and two focus histories, one for gesture and one for speech. (Algorithmic details of the deictic behavior planner can be found in Lester et al. 1999.) It then constructs a sequence of physical behaviors and verbal explanations that will collectively constitute the advice that the agent will deliver. For example, given a communicative goal, the explanation planner for Cosmo typically produces an explanation plan that calls for the agent to speak from six to ten utterances and perform several locomotive and gestural behaviors. These are then passed to the presentation manager that manipulates the agent persona in the learning environment. Problem-solving actions performed by the student are therefore punctuated by customized explanations provided by the agent in a manner reminiscent of classic task-oriented dialogues.

Deictic planning comes into play when the behavior planner determines that an explanation must refer to an object in the environment. For each utterance that makes a reference to an environmental object, the explanation planner invokes the deictic system and supplies it with the intended referent. The deictic system operates in the following phases to plan the agent's gestures, locomotion, and speech:

1. *Ambiguity Appraisal:* The deictic system first assesses the situation by determining whether a reference may be ambiguous. By examining the evolving *explanation plan*, which contains a record of the objects the agent has referred to during utterances spoken so far in the current explanation sequence, the deictic planner evaluates the initial potential for ambiguity. This assessment will contribute to gesture, locomotion, and speech planning decisions.

2. *Gesture and Locomotion Planning:* The deictic system uses the specification of the relative positions of the objects in the scene of the world model, as well as the previously made ambiguity assessment, to plan the agent's deictic gestures and movement. By considering the proximity of objects in the world, the deictic system determines whether the agent should point to the referent and, if so, whether it should move to it.

3. *Utterance Planning and Coordination:* To determine what the agent should say to refer to the referent, the deictic system considers focus information, the ambiguity assessment, and the world model. Utterance planning pays particular attention to the relative locations of the referent and the agent, taking into account its planned locomotion from the previous phase. The result of utterance planning is a referring expression consisting of the appropriate proximal/nonproximal demonstratives and pronouns. Finally, the behavior planner coordinates the agent's spoken, gestural, and locomotive behaviors, orchestrates their exhibition by the agent in the learning environment, and returns control to the student.

The computational methods underlying ambiguity appraisal, gesture and locomotion planning, and deictic referring expression planning are described below.

5.2.3.1 *Ambiguity Appraisal*   The first phase of deictic planning consists of evaluating the potential for ambiguity. For each utterance in the evolving explanation plan that makes a reference to an object in the environment, the explanation planner invokes the deictic system. Deictic decisions depend critically on an accurate assessment of the discourse context in which the reference will be communicated. To plan the agent's gestures, movements, and utterances correctly, the deictic system determines whether the situation has the potential for ambiguity within the current explanation. This initial phase of ambiguity assessment considers only discourse issues; spatial considerations are handled in the two phases that follow. Because focus indicates the prominence of the referent at the current juncture in the explanation, the deictic system uses focus as the primary predictor of ambiguity: potentially ambiguous situations can be combated by combinations of gesture and locomotion.

A referent R has the potential for ambiguity if it is currently not in focus or if it is in focus but is one of multiple objects in focus. To determine if the referent is in focus, the deictic system examines the evolving explanation plan and inspects it for previous deictic references to R. Suppose the explanation planner is currently planning utterance U_i. It examines utterances U_{i-1} and U_{i-2} for preceding deictic references to R. There are three cases to consider:

1. *Novel Reference:* If the explanation planner locates no deictic reference to R in U_{i-1} or U_{i-2}, then R is ambiguous and is therefore deserving of greater deictic emphasis. For example, if a student interacting with the Internet Advisor chooses to send a packet to a particular router that does not lie along the optimal path to the packet's destination, Cosmo interrupts the student and makes an initial reference to that router. He should therefore introduce the referent into the discourse.

2. *Unique Focus:* If the explanation planner locates a reference to R in U_{i-1} and U_{i-2} but not to other entities, then R has already been introduced and the potential for ambiguity is less. For example, when Cosmo's explanation consists of multiple utterances about a particular router, a reference to that router will be in unique focus. Consequently, the need for special deictic treatment is reduced.

3. *Multiple Foci:* If the explanation planner locates a reference to R but also to other entities in U_{i-1} and U_{i-2}, then the situation is potentially ambiguous. For example, if Cosmo points to one router and subsequently points to another that the student has just selected, but he now needs to refer to the first router

again for purposes of comparison, multiple referents are in focus and he must therefore take precautions against making an ambiguous reference.

The result of this determination is recorded for use in the following two phases of gesture and locomotion planning and referring expression planning.

5.2.3.2 *Gesture and Locomotion Planning* When potential ambiguities arise, endowing the agent with the ability to point and move to objects to which it will be referring enables it to increase its clarity of reference. The deictic system plans two types of physical behaviors: gestures and locomotion. In each case, it first determines whether a behavior of that type is warranted. If so, it then computes the behavior.

To determine whether the agent should exhibit a pointing gesture to physically designate the referent within the environment, the behavior planner inspects the conclusion of the ambiguity computation in the previous phase. If the referent was deemed ambiguous or potentially ambiguous, the system will plan a pointing gesture for the agent.

In addition to pointing, the agent can also move from one location to another to clarify a deictic reference that might otherwise be ambiguous. If the referent has been determined to be unambiguous—namely, it is in a unique focus—the agent will remain stationary. (More precisely, the agent will not perform a locomotive behavior; in fact, for purposes of believability, the agent is always in subtle but constant motion, for example, Cosmo typically performs "antigravity bobbing" and blinking behaviors.) In contrast, if the referent is ambiguous—that is, if it is a novel reference—the deictic system instructs the agent to move toward the object specified by the referent as the agent points at it. For example, if Cosmo is discussing a router that has not been previously mentioned in the last two utterances, he will move to that router as he points to it. If the referent is potentially ambiguous, that is, it is a reference to one of the concurrently active foci, then the deictic planner must decide if locomotion is needed. If no locomotion is needed, the agent will point at R without moving toward it. In contrast, if any of the following three conditions hold, the agent will move toward R as it points:

1. *Multiple Proximal Foci:* If the object specified by R is near another object that is also in focus, the agent will move to the object specified by R. For example, if two nearby routers are being compared, Cosmo will move to the router to which he is referring to ensure that his reference is clear.

2. *Multiple Proximal Similarity:* Associated with each object is an ontological category. If the object specified by R is near other objects of the same category, the agent will move to the object specified by R. For example, if Cosmo is referring to a computer and there are several computers nearby, he would move to the intended computer.

3. *Diminutiveness:* If the object specified by R is unusually small, the agent will move to the object specified by R. Small objects are labeled as such in the world model. For example, many interface control buttons are relatively small compared to objects in the environment. If Cosmo needs to make a clear reference to one of them, he will move toward that button.

After a sequence of high-level gestures and locomotive behaviors are computed, they must be interpreted within the learning environment. For example, the current implementation of Cosmo provides for six basic pointing gestures: left-up, left-across, left-down, right-up, right-across, and right-down. To enable the agent to point correctly to the object specified by the referent, the behavior planner first consults the world model. It obtains the location of the agent (L_A) and the referent (L_R) in the environment. It then determines the relative orientation of the vector from (L_A) to (L_R). For example, Cosmo might be hovering in the lower-left corner of the environment and need to point to a router in the upper-right corner. In this case, he will point up and to his left toward the router using his left-up gesture.

The behavior planner must then determine whether or not the agent really needs to move based on his current location. If it determines that locomotion is called for, the interaction manager must first determine if the agent is already near the object, which would obviate the need to move toward it. Nearness of two objects is computed by measuring the distance between them and ascertaining whether it is less than a *proximity bound*. If the distance between the agent and the intended object is less than the proximity bound, then there is no need for the agent to move because it can already point clearly to the object, and so it will remain in its current position.

If locomotion is appropriate, the behavior planner computes a direct motion path from the agent's current location to the object specified by R. To do so, it first determines the *deictic target*, which is the precise location in the world at which the agent will point. To avoid ambiguity, the agent will move its finger (or, more generally, its deictic pointer) toward the center of the referent. It then computes the direction of the vector defining the agent's direction of travel from L_A and to the deictic target. To do so, it first determines the position of its finger if it were extended in the direction computed in step 2 with the agent in L_A. It then determines the ideal location of the agent's body position if its outstretched finger were to touch the deictic target in the final position. Finally, it traverses the resulting motion path connecting L_A and its final body position and location.

5.2.3.3 Deictic Referring Expression Planning and Coordination To effectively communicate the intended reference, the deictic system must combine gesture, locomotion, and speech. Having completed gesture and locomotion planning, the deictic planner turns to speech. To determine an appropriate referring expression for the agent to speak as it performs the deictic gestures and locomotion, the deictic system first examines the results of the ambiguity appraisal. If it was determined that R is in unique focus, there is no potential for ambiguity because R has already been introduced and no other entities are competing for the student's attention. It is therefore introduced with a simple referring expression using techniques similar to those outlined in Dale (1992). For example, "the router" will be pronominalized to "it."

In contrast, if R is ambiguous or potentially ambiguous—namely, R is a novel reference or is one of multiple foci—the deictic planner makes three assessments: (1) it determines the demonstrative category called for by the current situation; (2) it examines the ontological type of R and the other active foci; and (3) it considers the number of R. It first categorizes the situation into one of two deictic families:

1. *Proximal Demonstratives*: If the deictic planner has determined that the agent must move to R or that it would have moved to R if it were not already near R, then employ a proximal demonstrative such as "this" or "these."
2. *Nonproximal Demonstratives*: If the deictic planner has determined that R was not nearby but that the agent did not need to move to R, then employ a nonproximal demonstrative such as "that" or "those."

After it has determined which of the demonstrative categories to use, the deictic planner narrows its selection further by considering the ontological type of R and the previous two utterances in the evolving explanation plan. If R belongs to the same ontological type as the other entities that are in focus, then the deictic planner selects the phrase "This one . . ." For example, suppose the system has determined that a proximal demonstrative should be used and that the preceding utterance referred to one router, for example, "This router has more traffic." To refer to a second router in the current utterance, rather than saying, "This router has less traffic," it will say, "This one has less traffic." Finally, it uses the number of R to make the final lexical choice. If R is singular, it uses "this" for proximal demonstratives and "that" for nonproximals. If R is plural, it uses "these" and "those." The resulting referring expression is then passed onto the behavior planner for the final phase.

To integrate the agent's physical behaviors and speech, the behavior planner then coordinates the selected utterances, gestures, and locomotion. Three types of coordination must be achieved. First, each utterance may be accompanied by a deictic gesture, and it is critical that the agent's referring expressions be tightly coupled to its corresponding pointing movements. Second, pointing and locomotion should be carefully coordinated so that they occur in a natural manner, where "natural" suggests that the agent should perform its pointing gesture *en route* to the referent and arrive at the referent at precisely the same time that it reaches the apex of the pointing gesture. Third, when the agent exhibits a sequence of speech, gestural, and locomotive behaviors to communicate an explanation, the behavior planner must ensure that each cluster of utterances, gestures, and possible agent movements are completed before the next is initiated. The behavior planner enacts the coordination by specifying that the utterance be initiated when the agent reaches the apex of its pointing gesture. In contrast, if the speech were initiated at the same time as the gesture and locomotion, the utterance would seem to be completed prematurely, thereby producing both ambiguity and the appearance of incongruous behavior.

Finally, to underscore the deictic gestures, the behavior planner introduces gaze into the final behavior. As demonstrated by Cassell's incorporation of a gaze generator in her conversational agents (Cassell et al. 1994), gaze offers an important communication medium for acknowledgments and turn taking. In addition, gaze can play an important role in deixis. For example, when Cosmo refers to a particular computer on a subnet by moving toward it and pointing at it as he speaks about it, he should also look at it. The behavior planner enacts gaze via specifications for the agent to "look" at the referent by moving its head in precisely the direction in which it is pointing. In the implementation, the behavior planner accomplishes this not through run-time inference of eye control but by exploiting agent head rendering in which the eyes were crafted by the animators to look in the direction in which the head is pointing, for example, if the head is turned toward the right, the eyes look toward the right. The USC/ISI animated agents group has been successfully experimenting with similar gaze techniques such as "leading with the eyes" (Johnson and Rickel 1997).

The behavior planner combines the speech, gesture, locomotion, and gaze specifications and directs the agent to perform them in the order dictated by the explanation plan. The agent's behaviors are then assembled and sequenced in the learning environment in real time to provide students with clear advice that couples full deictic expression with integrated lifelike locomotion, gesture, speech, and gaze. Currently, although the resulting behaviors are coordinated after they have been constructed, limited (and ad hoc) communication occurs between the modules that individually plan speech, gesture, and locomotion. An important direction for future work, which is currently being pursued in the Rea project (Cassell and Stone 1999), is a principled model of media allocation in which the individual modules can communicate bidirectionally with one another to carefully plan the content to be conveyed in each modality.

5.3 Emotive Behavior Sequencing

In the same manner that human-human communication is characterized by affective multimodal interaction utilizing both the visual and aural channels, agent-human communication can be achieved in a similar fashion. As master animators have discovered repeatedly over the past century, the quality, overall clarity, and dramatic impact of communication can be increased through the creation of emotive movement that underscores the affective content of the message to be communicated: by carefully orchestrating facial expression, full-body behaviors, arm movements, and hand gestures, animated pedagogical agents could visually augment verbal problem-solving advice, give encouragement, convey empathy, and perhaps increase motivation. Although initial forays have begun on emotion generation in pedagogical environments (Abou-Jaoude and Frasson 1998) and reasoning about students' emotions (de Vicente and Pain 1998), emotive behavior sequencing in pedagogical agents remains unexplored.

Creating lifelike pedagogical agents that are endowed with facilities for exhibiting student-appropriate emotive behaviors potentially provides four important educational benefits (Elliott, Rickel, and Lester 1999). First, a pedagogical agent that appears to care about a student's progress may convey to the student that it and she are "in things together" and may encourage the student to care more about her own progress. Second, an emotive pedagogical agent that is in some way sensitive to the student's progress may intervene when she becomes frustrated and before she begins to lose interest. Third, an emotive pedagogical agent may convey enthusiasm for the subject matter at hand and may foster similar levels of enthusiasm in the student. Finally, a pedagogical agent with a rich and interesting personality may simply make learning more fun. A student who enjoys interacting with a pedagogical agent may have a more positive perception of the overall learning experience and may consequently opt to spend more time in the learning environment.

5.3.1 The Emotive-Kinesthetic Behavior Framework

To enable a lifelike pedagogical agent to play an active role in facilitating students' progress, its behavior sequencing engine must be driven by students' problem-solving activities. As students solve problems, an explanation system monitors their actions in the learning environment (fig. 5.2). When they reach an impasse, as indicated by extended periods of inactivity or suboptimal problem-solving actions, the explanation system is invoked to construct an explanation plan that will address potential misconceptions. By examining the problem state, a curriculum information network, and a user model, the explanation system determines the sequence of pedagogical speech acts that can repair the misconception and passes the types of the speech acts to the emotive-kinesthetic behavior sequencing engine. By assessing the speech act categories and then selecting full-body emotive behaviors that the agent can perform to communicate the affective impact appropriate for those speech act categories, the behavior sequencing engine identifies relevant behaviors and binds them to the verbal utterances determined by the explanation system. The behaviors and utterances are then performed by the agent in the environment and control is returned to the student who continues her problem-solving activities.

The techniques for designing emotive-kinesthetic behavior spaces, the representations for structuring them with pedagogical speech act categories, and the computational mechanisms that drive the emotive behavior sequencing engine are described below.

5.3.2 Emotive-Kinesthetic Behavior Space Design

To exhibit full-body emotive behaviors, a pedagogical agent's behavior sequencing engine must draw on a large repertoire of behaviors that span a broad emotional spectrum. For many domains, tasks, and target student populations, fully expressive agents are very desirable. To this end, the first phase in creating a lifelike pedagogical agent is to design an *emotive-kinesthetic behavior space* that is populated with physical behaviors that the agent can perform

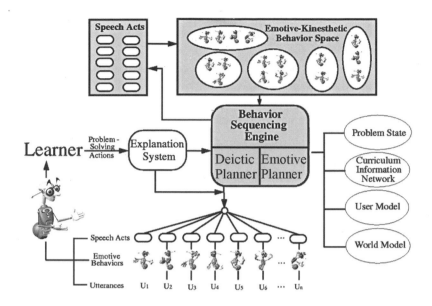

Figure 5.2
The lifelike pedagogical agent behavior planning architecture.

when called upon to do so. Because of the aesthetics involved, an agent's behaviors are perhaps best designed by a team that includes character animators. Creating a behavior space entails setting forth precise visual and audio specifications that describe in great detail the agent's actions and speech, rendering the actions, and creating the descriptive utterances. By exploiting the character behavior canon of the animated film (Jones 1989; Noake 1988) (which itself draws on movement in theater) and then adapting it to the specific demands posed by learning environments, we can extract general emotive animation techniques that artists in this medium have developed over the past hundred years.

5.3.2.1 *Stylized Emotive Behaviors*   It is important to draw the critical distinction between two approaches to animated character realization, life-quality versus stylized (Culhane 1988). In the *life-quality* approach, character designers and animators follow a strict adherence to the laws of physics. Characters' musculature and kinesthetics are defined entirely by the physical principles that govern the structure and movement of human (and animal) bodies. For example, when a character becomes excited, it raises its eyebrows and its eyes widen. In the *stylized* approach, the laws of physics (and frequently the laws of human anatomy and physiology) are broken at every turn. When a character animated with the stylized approach becomes excited, for example, as in the animated films of Tex Avery (Lenburg 1993), it may express this emotion in an exaggerated fashion by rising from the ground, inducing significant changes to the musculature of the face, and bulging out its eyes. Not all stylized animation features such exaggerated emotive overstatement—for learning environments, a more restrained approach is called for—but its ability to communicate with dramatic visual cues can be put to good use in the real-time animation of pedagogical agents. For example, when a student solves a complex problem in the Internet Advisor environment, Cosmo smiles broadly and uses his entire body to applaud the student's success.

5.3.2.2 *Expressive Range*   To be socially engaging, animated characters must be able to express many different kinds of emotion. As different social situations arise, they must be able to convey emotions such as happiness, elation, sadness, fear, envy, shame, and gloating. In a similar fashion, because lifelike pedagogical agents should be able to communicate with a broad range of speech acts, they should be able to support these speech acts visually with an equally broad range of emotive behaviors. However, because their role is primarily to facilitate positive learning experiences, only a critical subset of the full range of emotive expression is useful for pedagogical agents. For example, they should be able to exhibit body language that expresses joy and excitement when students do well, inquisitiveness for uncertain situations (such as when rhetorical questions are posed), and disappointment when problem-solving progress is less than optimal. For example, the Cosmo agent can scratch his head in wonderment when he poses a rhetorical question.

5.3.2.3 *Anatomical Emotive Information Carriers*   Years of experimentation in animation demonstrate that specific anatomical components communicate emotion more than others. By focusing on the more expressive components, we can create lifelike agents that convey emotive content more effectively. For example, longtime Disney animators stress the critical importance of the hands (Thomas and Johnston 1981). It is for this reason that great attention is paid to hand movement and that hands are often rendered much larger than would be

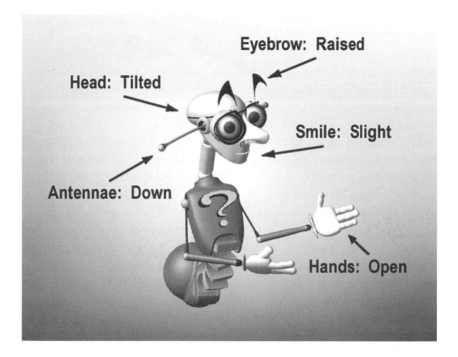

Figure 5.3
Sample Cosmo posture.

anatomically correct. Although literally every body part can be used to convey emotion, the principle carriers of emotive information are the eyes, eyebrows, face, mouth, head tilt, posture, and gesturing with the arms and hands. For example, figure 5.3 depicts a frame of Cosmo taken from a behavior in which he appears quizzically friendly. His eyebrows are raised, his head is slightly askew, his mouth forms a smile, and his hands are raised. Moreover, stylized characters can have additional appendages to further convey emotion. For example, in the frame of Cosmo shown in figure 5.3, his antennae droop slightly.

5.3.3 Behavior Space Structuring with Pedagogical Speech Acts
An agent's behaviors will be dictated by design decisions in the previous phase, which to a significant extent determine its personality characteristics.

Critically, however, its run-time emotive behaviors must be somehow modulated to a large degree by ongoing problem-solving events driven by the student's activities. Consequently, after the behavior space has been populated with expressive behaviors, it must then be structured to assist the sequencing engine in selecting and assembling behaviors that are appropriate for the agent's communicative goals. Although, in principle, behavior spaces could be structured along any number of dimensions such as degree of exaggeration of movement or by the type of anatomical components involved in movements, experience with the implemented agent suggests that the most effective means for imposing a structure is based on *speech acts*. While it could be indexed by a full theory of speech acts, our research to date leverages a highly specialized collection of speech acts that occur in pedagogical dialogue with great frequency.

Given the primacy of the speech act in this approach, the question then arises about the connection between rhetorical goals, on the one hand, and physical behaviors, on the other. Emotive categories inspired by foundational research on affective reasoning supply this linkage. Work on the Affective Reasoner (AR) (Elliott 1992) uses Ortony's computational model of emotion (Ortony, Clore, and Collins 1988) to design agents that can respond emotionally. In the AR framework, agents are given unique pseudopersonalities modeled as both an elaborate set of *appraisal frames* representing their individual goals (with respect to events that arise), *principles* (with respect to perceived intentional actions of agents), *preferences* (with respect to objects), *moods* (temporary changes to the appraisal mechanism), and as a set of about 440 differentially activated *channels* for the expression of emotions (Elliott 1992; Elliott and Ortony 1992). Situations that arise in the agents' world may map to twenty-six different emotion types (e.g., *pride*, as approving of one's own intentional action), twenty-two of which were originally theoretically specified by Ortony and his colleagues (Ortony, Clore, and Collins 1988). Quality and intensity of emotion instances in each category are partially determined by some subset of roughly twenty-two different *emotion intensity variables* (Elliott and Siegle 1993). To communicate with users, Elliott's implementation of the AR framework uses line-drawn facial expressions, which are morphed in real time.

The emotive-kinesthetic behavior sequencing framework exploits the fundamental intuition behind the AR—namely, that the emotive states and communication are intimately interrelated. Rather than employing the full computational apparatus of the AR, the emotive-kinesthetic framework uses highly simplified emotive annotations that connect pedagogical speech acts to relevant physical behaviors. Computationally, this is accomplished by employing a model of communication that places pedagogical speech acts in a *one-to-one* mapping to emotive states: each speech act type points to the behavior type that expresses it. To illustrate, in creating the Cosmo agent, the design team focused on the speech acts (and their associated emotions) that are prominent in problem-solving tutorial dialogues. The Cosmo agent deals with cause and effect, background, assistance, rhetorical links, and congratulatory acts as follows:

- *Congratulatory act:* When a student experiences success, a congratulatory speech act triggers an admiration emotive intent that will be expressed with behaviors such as applause, which, depending on the complexity of the problem, will be either restrained or exaggerated. The desired effect is to encourage the student.
- *Causal act:* When a student requires problem-solving advice, a causal speech act is performed in which the agent communicates an interrogative emotive intent that will be expressed with behaviors such as head scratching or shrugging. The desired effect is to underscore questioning.
- *Deleterious effect:* When a student experiences problem-solving difficulties or when the agent needs to pose a rhetorical question with unfortunate consequences, disappointment is triggered that will be expressed with facial characteristics and body language that indicate sadness. The desired effect is to build empathy.
- *Background* and *assistance:* In the course of delivering advice, background or assistance speech acts trigger inquisitive intent that will be expressed with "thoughtful" restrained manipulators such as finger drumming or hand waving. The desired effect is to emphasize active cognitive processing on the part of the agent.

The one-to-one mapping is used to enact a threefold adaptation of the AR framework. First, while the AR framework is intended to be generic, the emotive-kinesthetic behavior framework is designed specifically to support problem-solving advisory communication. Second, while the AR framework is enormously complex, the emotive-kinesthetic framework employs only the speech acts and only the emotive intentions that arise frequently in tutorial situations. Third, while work on computational models of social linguistics indicates that the combination of speech and gesture in human-human communication is enormously complex (Cassell, chap. 1), the one-to-one mapping approach turns out in practice to be a reasonable starting point for real-time emotive behavior sequencing.

To create a fully operational lifelike agent, the behavior space includes auxiliary structuring to accommodate important emotive but non-speech-oriented behaviors such as dramatic entries into and exits from the learning environment. Moreover, sometimes the agent must connect two behaviors induced by multiple utterances that are generated by two speech acts. To achieve these rhetorical link behaviors, it employs subtle "micromovements" such as slight head nods or blinking.

5.3.4 Dynamic Emotive Behavior Sequencing

To dynamically orchestrate full-body emotive behaviors that achieve situated emotive communication, complement problem-solving advice, and exhibit real-time visual continuity, the emotive behavior sequencing engine selects and assembles behaviors in real time. By exploiting the pedagogical speech act structuring, the sequencing engine navigates coherent paths through the emotive behavior space to weave the small local behaviors into continuous global behaviors. Given a communicative goal G, such as explaining a particular misconception that arose during problem solving, a simple overlay user model, a curriculum information network, and the current problem state, it employs the following algorithm to select and assemble emotive behaviors in real time:

1. Determine the pedagogical speech acts $A_1 \ldots A_n$ used to achieve G. When the explanation system is invoked, employ a top-down goal decomposition planner to determine a set of relevant speech acts. For each speech act A_i, perform steps (2)–(5).
2. Identify a family of emotive behaviors F_i to exhibit when performing A_i. Using the emotive annotations in the behavior speech act structuring, index into the behavior space to determine a relevant family of emotive behaviors F_i.
3. Select an emotive behavior B_i that belongs to F_i. Either by using additional contextual knowledge, for example, the level of complexity of the current problem, or by choosing randomly when all elements of F_i are relevant, select an element of F_i.
4. Select a verbal utterance U_i from the library of utterances that is appropriate for performing A_i. Using an audio library of voice clips that is analogous to physical behaviors, extract a relevant voice clip.

5. Coordinate the exhibition of B_i with the speaking of U_i. Couple B_i with U_i on the evolving timeline schedule.

6. Establish visual continuity between $B_1 \ldots B_n$. Examine the final frame of each B_i, compare it with the initial frame of each B_{i+1}, and if they differ, introduce transition frames between them.

For each speech act A_i identified in step 1, the sequencing engine performs the following actions. During step 2, it identifies a family of emotive behaviors F_i that can be exhibited while the agent is performing A_i. It accomplishes this by employing pedagogical speech act indices that have been used to index the agent's physical behavior space. For example, a congratulatory speech act created during top-down planning will cause the sequencing engine to identify the admiration emotive behavior family.

Next, during step 3, it selects one of the physical behaviors in F_i. By design, all of the behaviors have the same emotive intent, so they are all legitimate candidates. However, because a key aspect of agent believability is exhibiting a variety of behaviors, the behavior space was constructed so as to enable the agent to perform a broad range of facial expression and gestures. Hence, the sequencing engine selects from a collection of behaviors, any of which will effectively communicate the relevant emotive content. For example, in the current implementation of the Cosmo agent, the behavior sequencing engine makes this decision pseudorandomly with elimination—that is, it randomly selects from among the behaviors in F_i that have not already been marked as having been performed. After all behaviors in a given F_i have been performed, they are unmarked, and the process repeats. Empirical evidence suggests that this pseudorandom element contributes significantly to believability.

During the final three steps, the behavior sequencing engine determines the narrative utterances to accompany the physical behaviors and assembles the specifications on an evolving timeline. In step 4, it selects the narrative utterances U_i, which are of three types: *connective* (e.g., "but" or "and"), *phrasal* (e.g., "this subnet is fast"), or *sentential* (i.e., a full sentence). Because each instantiated speech act specifies the verbal content to be communicated, narrative utterance selection is straightforward. In step 5, it lays out the physical behaviors and verbal utterances in tandem on a timeline. Because the emotive physical behaviors were determined by the same computational mechanism that determined the utterances, the sequencing engine can couple their exhibition to achieve a coherent overall behavior.

Finally, in step 6, it ensures that the visual continuity is achieved by introducing appropriate transition frames. To do so, for each of the visual behaviors selected above, it inspects the first and final frames. If adjacent behaviors are not visually identical, it splices in visual transition behaviors and installs them, properly sequenced, into the timeline.

The sequencing engine passes all behaviors and utterances to the learning environment, which cues them up and orchestrates the agent's actions and speech in real time. The net effect of the sequencing engine's activities is the student's perception that an expressive lifelike character is carefully observing their problem-solving activities and behaving in a visually compelling manner. The resulting behaviors are then exhibited by the agent in the learning environment, and control is immediately returned to the student who continues her problem-solving activities.

5.4 An Implemented, Full-Body Emotive Pedagogical Agent

The spatial deixis framework and the emotive-kinesthetic framework have been implemented in Cosmo, the lifelike (stylized) pedagogical agent that inhabits the Internet Advisor learning environment. Cosmo and the Internet Advisor environment are implemented in C++, employ the Microsoft Game Software Developer's Kit (SDK), and run on a PC at 15 frames/second. Cosmo's deictic planner is implemented in the CLIPS production system language (NASA 1993).

Cosmo has a head with movable antennae and expressive blinking eyes, arms with bendable elbows, hands with a large number of independent joints, and a body with an accordionlike torso. His speech was supplied by a voice actor. Cosmo was modeled and rendered in 3-D on SGIs with Alias/Wavefront. The resulting bitmaps were subsequently postedited and transferred to PCs where users interacted with them in a 2½-D environment. Cosmo can perform a variety of behaviors including locomotion, pointing, blinking, leaning, clapping, and raising and bending his antennae. His speech was created by a trained voice actor and an audio engineer. His verbal behaviors include 240 utterances ranging in duration from one to twenty seconds.

Cosmo's behaviors are assembled in real time as directed by the behavior planner. Each action is annotated with the number of frames and transition methods. Actions are of two types: *full-body* behaviors, in which the agent's entire body is depicted, and *compositional* behaviors that represent various body parts individually. To sequence nondeictic behaviors such as clapping and leaning, the behavior planner employs the full-body images. To sequence deictic

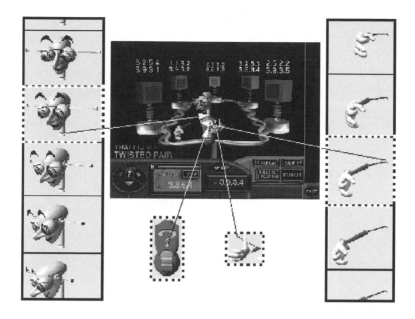

Figure 5.4
Real-time composition of deictic gestural and gaze components.

behaviors, including both the gesture and gaze, the behavior planner combines compositional behaviors of torsos, left and right arms, and heads (fig. 5.4).

As the student attempts to route her packet to a given destination, she makes a series of routing decisions to direct the packet's hops through the network. At each router, she is given four different subnets, each with five possible computers with multiple unique addresses from which to choose. She is also provided information about the type of the subnet and the amount of traffic on the subnet. In the lower left-hand corner of the interface, she can click on different quadrants of a spinner to navigate among the four possible attached subnets. When she has found what she believes to be a reasonable computer toward which to send her packet, she clicks on the address of the computer. Cosmo then comments on the correctness and optimality of her decision. If it is either incorrect or suboptimal, he provides assistance on how to improve it. If her decision was deemed optimal, he congratulates her, and she clicks on the "Send" button to send her packet to the next subnet in the network.

To illustrate the behavior planner's behavior, suppose a student has just routed her packet to a fiber optic subnet with low traffic. She surveys the connected subnets and selects a router that she believes will advance it one step closer to the packet's intended destination. Although she has chosen a reasonable subnet, it is suboptimal because of nonmatching addresses, which will slow her packet's progress. She has made two mistakes on address resolution already, so the explanation is somewhat detailed. Working in conjunction, the deictic and emotive behavior planners select and sequence the following communicative acts and orchestrate the agent's gestural, locomotive, and speech behaviors (fig. 5.5):

- State-Correct(Subnet-Type): The explanation planner determines that the agent should interject advice and invokes the deictic planner. Since nothing is in focus because this is the first utterance to be planned for a new explanation, and Cosmo currently occupies a position on the screen far from information about the subnet—namely, the distance from his current location to the subnet information exceeds the proximity bound—he moves toward and points at the onscreen subnet information and says, "You chose the fastest subnet."

- State-Correct(Traffic): Cosmo then tells the student that the choice of a low traffic subnet was also a good one. The focus history indicates that while the type of subnet has already been the subject of a deictic reference, the traffic information has not. Cosmo therefore moves to the on-screen congestion information and points to it. However, the focus history indicates that he has mentioned the subnet in a recent utterance, so he pronominalizes the subnet as "it" and says, "Also, it has low traffic."

- Congratulatory(Generic): Responding to a congratulatory speech act, the sequencing engine selects an admiration emotive intent that is realized with an enthusiastic applauding behavior as Cosmo exclaims, "Fabulous!"

- Causal(Generic): The sequencing engine's planner selects a *causal* speech act, which causes the interrogative emotive behavior family to be selected. These include actions such as head scratching and shrugging, for which the desired effects are to emphasize a questioning attitude. Hence, because Cosmo wants the student to rethink her choice, he scratches his head and poses the question, "But more importantly, if we sent the packet here, what will happen?"

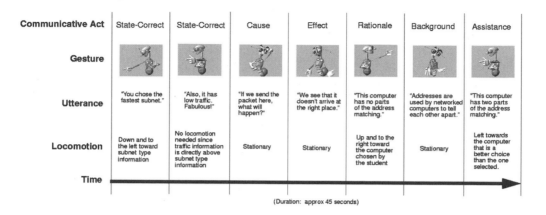

Communicative Act	State-Correct	State-Correct	Cause	Effect	Rationale	Background	Assistance
Gesture							
Utterance	"You chose the fastest subnet."	"Also, it has low traffic. Fabulous!"	"If we send the packet here, what will happen?"	"We see that it doesn't arrive at the right place."	"This computer has no parts of the address matching."	"Addresses are used by networked computers to tell each other apart."	"This computer has two parts of the address matching."
Locomotion	Down and to the left toward subnet type information	No locomotion needed since traffic information is directly above subnet type information	Stationary	Stationary	Up and to the right toward the computer chosen by the student	Stationary	Left towards the computer that is a better choice than the one selected.
Time							

(Duration: approx 45 seconds)

Figure 5.5
Sample behavior sequencing.

- Deleterious-Effect(Address-Resolution): After the causal act, the sequencing engine's planner now selects a deleterious-effect speech act, which causes it to index into the disappointment behavior family. It includes behaviors that indicate sadness, which is intended to build empathy with the learner. Cosmo therefore informs the learner of the ill effect of choosing that router as he takes on a sad facial expression, slumping body language, and dropping his hands, and says, "If that were the case, we see it doesn't arrive at the right place."

- Rationale(Address-Resolution): To explain why the packet won't arrive at the correct destination, Cosmo adds, "This computer has no parts of the address matching." Because the computer that serves as the referent is currently not in the focus histories and Cosmo is far from that computer, the behavior planner sequences deictic locomotion and a gesture to accompany the utterance.

- Background(Address-Resolution): The sequencing engine has selected a background speech act. Because all background and assistance speech acts cause the sequencing engine to index into the inquisitive behavior family, it obtains one of several "thoughtful" restrained manipulators such as hand waving. In this case, it selects a form of finger tapping that he performs as he explains, "Addresses are used by networked computers to tell each other apart."

- Assistance(Address-Resolution): Finally, Cosmo assists the student by making a suggestion about the next course of action to take. Because the student has committed several mistakes on address resolution problems, Cosmo provides advice about correcting her decision by pointing to the location of the optimal computer—it has not been in focus—and stating, "This router has two parts of the address matching."

5.5 Conclusions

We have discussed two characteristics of embodied conversational agents that are critical for learning environments, deictic believability and full-body emotive expression. To dynamically sequence lifelike pedagogical agents in a manner that promotes deictic believability, agent behavior planners can employ the spatial deixis framework to coordinate gesture, locomotion, and speech. To sequence full-body emotive expression, agent behavior planners can employ the emotive-kinesthetic behavior sequencing framework, which exploits the structure provided by pedagogical speech act categories to weave small emotive behaviors into larger, visually continuous ones that are responsive to students' problem-solving activities.

The spatial deixis framework and the emotive-kinesthetic framework have been informally "stress tested" in a focus group study in which ten subjects interacted with Cosmo in the Internet Protocol learning environment. Subjects unanimously expressed delight in interacting with him. Most found him fun, engaging, interesting, and charismatic. In one phase of the study in which subjects compared an "agent-free" version of the learning environment with the one inhabited by Cosmo, subjects unanimously preferred the one with Cosmo. It appeared that the learning environment with the agent clearly communicated advice with deictic speech, gesture, and locomotion, though not necessarily more clearly than did the agent-free version. Although some subjects voiced the opinion that Cosmo was overly dramatic, almost all exhibited particularly strong positive responses when he performed exaggerated congratulatory behaviors. In short, they found his deictic advice to be clear and helpful and his emotive to be entertaining.

This work represents a small step toward the larger goal of creating interactive, fully expressive lifelike pedagogical agents. To make significant progress in this direction, it will be important to leverage increasingly sophisticated models of human-human communication and affective reasoning. We will be pursuing these lines of investigation in our future work.

Acknowledgments

Thanks to Dorje Bellbrook, Tim Buie, Mike Cuales, Jim Dautremont, Amanda Davis, Rob Gray, Mary Hoffman, Alex Levy, Will Murray, and Roberta Osborne of the North Carolina State University IntelliMedia Initiative for their work on the behavior sequencing engine implementation and the 3-D modeling, animation, sound, and environment design for the Internet Advisor. Thanks also to Bradford Mott for comments on an earlier draft of this chapter. Support for this work was provided by the following organizations: the National Science Foundation under grants CDA-9720395 (Learning and Intelligent Systems Initiative) and IRI-9701503 (CAREER Award Program); the North Carolina State University IntelliMedia Initiative; Novell, Inc.; and equipment donations from Apple and IBM.

References

Abou-Jaoude, S., and C. Frasson. 1998. Emotion computing in competitive learning environments. In *Working Notes of the ITS '98 Workshop on Pedagogical Agents*, 33–39.

André, E., and T. Rist. 1996. Coping with temporal constraints in multimedia presentation planning. In *Proceedings of the Thirteenth National Conference on Artificial Intelligence*, 142–147. Menlo Park, Calif.: AAAI Press.

André, E., W. Finkler, W. Graf, T. Rist, A. Schauder, and W. Wahlster. 1993. WIP: The automatic synthesis of multi-modal presentations. In M. Maybury, ed., *Intelligent multimedia interfaces*, 75–93. Menlo Park, Calif.: AAAI Press.

Bates, J. 1994. The role of emotion in believable agents. *Communications of the ACM* 37(7):122–125.

Blumberg, B., and T. Galyean. 1995. Multi-level direction of autonomous creatures for real-time virtual environments. In *SIGGRAPH '95*, 47–54. New York: ACM.

Cassell, J., and M. Stone. 1999. Living hand to mouth: Psychological theories about speech and gesture in interactive dialogue systems. In *Proceedings of the AAAI Fall Symposium on Psychological Models of Communication in Collaborative Systems*. Menlo Park, Calif.: AAAI Press.

Cassell, J., C. Pelachaud, N. Badler, M. Steedman, B. Achorn, T. Becket, B. Douville, S. Prevost, and M. Stone. 1994. Animated conversation: Rule-based generation of facial expression, gesture and spoken intonation for multiple conversational agents. In *Computer Graphics*, 413–420. New York: ACM SIGGRAPH.

Claassen, W. 1992. Generating referring expressions in a multimodal environment. In R. Dale, E. Hovy, D. Rosner, and O. Stock, eds., *Aspects of automated natural language generation*, 247–262. Berlin: Springer-Verlag.

Culhane, S. 1988. *Animation from script to screen*. New York: St. Martin's Press.

Dale, R. 1992. *Generating referring expressions*. Cambridge, Mass.: The MIT Press.

de Vicente, A., and H. Pain. 1998. Motivation Diagnosis in Intelligent Tutoring Systems. In *Proceedings of the Fourth International Conference on Intelligent Tutoring Systems*, 86–95. Berlin: Springer-Verlag.

Elliott, C. 1992. The affective reasoner: A process model of emotions in a multi-agent system. Ph.D diss., Institute for the Learning Sciences, Northwestern University.

Elliott, C., and A. Ortony. 1992. Point of view: Reasoning about the concerns of others. In *Proceedings of the Fourteenth Annual Conference of the Cognitive Science Society*, 809–814. Hillsdale, N.J.: Lawrence Erlbaum.

Elliott, C., and G. Siegle. 1993. Variables influencing the intensity of simulated affective states. In *AAAI Spring Symposium on Reasoning about Mental States: Formal Theories and Applications*, 58–67. Menlo Park, Calif.: AAAI Press.

Elliott, C., J. Rickel, and J. Lester. 1999. Lifelike pedagogical agents and affective computing: An exploratory synthesis. In M. Wooldridge and M. Veloso, eds., *Artificial intelligence today*, 195–212. Berlin: Springer-Verlag.

Feiner, S., and K. McKeown. 1990. Coordinating text and graphics in explanation generation. In *Proceedings of the Eighth National Conference on Artificial Intelligence*, 442–449. Menlo Park, Calif.: AAAI Press.

Fillmore, C. 1975. Santa Cruz Lectures on Deixis 1971. Indiana University Linguistics Club, Bloomington, Indiana.

Hovy, E. H. 1993. Automated discourse generation using discourse structure relations. *Artificial Intelligence* 63:341–385.

Isbister, K., and C. Nass. 1998. Personality in conversational characters: Building better digital interaction partners using knowledge about human personality preferences and perceptions. In *Notes from the Workshop on Embodied Conversational Characters* (Tahoe City, Calif.), 103–111.

Jarvella, R., and W. Klein. 1982. *Speech, place, and action: Studies in deixis and related topics*. New York: John Wiley and Sons.

Johnson, W. L., and J. Rickel. 1997. Personal communication.

Johnson, W. L., J. Rickel, and J. Lester. N.d. Animated pedagogical agents: Face-to-face interaction in interactive learning environments. In *The International Journal of Artificial Intelligence in Education*. Forthcoming.

Jones, C. 1989. *Chuck amuck: The life and times of an animated cartoonist.* New York: Avon.

Kurlander, D., and D. T. Ling. 1995. Planning-based control of interface animation. In *Proceedings of CHI '95,* 472–479. New York: ACM Press.

Lenburg, J. 1993. *The great cartoon directors.* New York: Da Capo Press.

Lester, J. C., and B. W. Porter. 1997. Developing and empirically evaluating robust explanation generators: The Knight Experiments. *Computational Linguistics* 23(1):65–101.

Lester, J. C., S. A. Converse, S. E. Kahler, S. T. Barlow, B. A. Stone, and R. Bhogal. 1997a. The persona effect: Affective impact of animated pedagogical agents. In *Proceedings of CHI '97 Human Factors in Computing Systems,* 359–366. New York: ACM.

Lester, J. C., S. A. Converse, B. A. Stone, S. E. Kahler, and S. T. Barlow. 1997b. Animated pedagogical agents and problem-solving effectiveness: A large-scale empirical evaluation. In *Proceedings of Eighth World Conference on Artificial Intelligence in Education,* 23–30. Amsterdam: IOS Press.

Lester, J., B. Stone, and G. Stelling. 1999. Lifelike pedagogical agents for mixed-initiative problem solving in constructivist learning environments. *User Modeling and User-Adapted Interaction* 9(1–2):1–44.

Lester, J., Voerman, J., Towns, S., and C. Callaway. 1999. Deictic believability: Coordinating gesture, locomotion, and speech in lifelike pedagogical gents. *Applied Artificial Intelligence* 13(4–5):383–414.

Maybury, M. 1991. Planning multimedia explanations using communicative acts. In *Proceedings of the Ninth National Conference on Artificial Intelligence,* 61–66. Menlo Park, Calif.: AAAI Press.

Mittal, V., S. Roth, J. Moore, J. Mattis, and G. Carenini. 1995. Generating explanatory captions for information graphics. In *Proceedings of the International Joint Conference on Artificial Intelligence,* 1276–1283. San Francisco: Morgan Kaufmann.

Moore, J. D. 1995. *Participating in explanatory dialogues.* Cambridge, Mass.: The MIT Press.

NASA. 1993. CLIPS reference manual. Technical report, Software Technology Branch, Lyndon B. Johnson Space Center.

Neal, J., and S. Shapiro. 1991. Intelligent multi-media interface technology. In J. Sullivan and S. Tyler, eds., *Intelligent user interfaces,* 11–43. Reading, Mass.: Addison-Wesley.

Noake, R. 1988. *Animation techniques.* London: Chartwell.

Novak, H. 1987. Strategies for generating coherent descriptions of object movements in street scenes. In G. Kempen, ed., *Natural language generation*, 117–132. Dordrecht, The Netherlands: Martinus Nijhoff.

Ortony, A., G. L. Clore, and A. Collins. 1988. *The cognitive structure of emotion*. New York: Cambridge University Press.

Paiva, A., and I. Machado. 1998. Vincent, an autonomous pedagogical agent for on-the-job training. In *Proceedings of the Fourth International Conference on Intelligent Tutoring Systems*, 584–593. Berlin: Springer-Verlag.

Roberts, L. 1993. *How reference works: Explanatory models for indexicals, descriptions and opacity*. New York: SUNY Press.

Roth, S., J. Mattis, and X. Mesnard. 1991. Graphics and natural language as components of automatic explanation. In J. Sullivan and S. Tyler, eds., *Intelligent user interfaces*, 207–239. Reading, Mass.: Addison-Wesley.

Sibun, P. 1992. Generating text without trees. *Computational Intelligence* 8(1):102–122.

Suchman, L. 1987. *Plans and situated actions: The problem of human machine communication*. New York: Cambridge University Press.

Suthers, D. 1991. A task-appropriate hybrid architecture for explanation. *Computational Intelligence* 7(4):315–333.

Thomas, F., and O. Johnston. 1981. *The illusion of life: Disney animation*. New York: Walt Disney Productions.

6

Performative Facial Expressions in Animated Faces

Isabella Poggi and Catherine Pelachaud

6.1 Introduction

In face-to-face interaction, multimodal signals are at work. We communicate not only through words, but also by intonation, body posture, hand gestures, gaze patterns, facial expressions, and so on. All these signals, verbal and nonverbal, do have a role in the communicative process. They add to/modify/substitute for information in discourse and are highly linked with one another. This is why facial and bodily animation is becoming relevant in the construction of embodied conversational agents.

In building autonomous agents with talking faces, agents capable of expressive and communicative behavior, we consider it important that the agent express his communicative intentions. Suppose an agent has the goal of communicating something to some particular interlocutor in a particular situation and context: he has to decide which words to utter, which intonation to use, and which facial expression to display. In this work, we restrict ourselves to the visual display of communicative intentions, leaving aside the auditory ones. We focus on facial expressions and propose a meaning-to-face approach, aiming at a face simulation automatically driven by semantic data.

After reviewing the literature on face communication and presenting some existing systems that simulate synthetic agents with talking faces, we focus on the structure of the communicative act and on the notion of the performative. Next, we introduce our model of context and we show how to express the performative by facial expression. Finally, an overview of our system and some examples are provided.

6.2 The Relevance of Nonverbal Signals in Communication

When talking, we all move our hands, we nod, we glance at our interlocutor, we smile, we turn our head away . . . Gesture, gaze, facial expression, and body orientation all give information about what we are saying and help the interlocutor understand our attitude toward her, our emotion, and our relation to what we are saying (for instance, in emphasis or irony). They may also act as syntax markers: if a person punctuates the end of her statement with a raised eyebrow, her statement could be interpreted as a question. For example, if a person says *Peter is going to Boston,* and she raises her eyebrow at the word *Boston* and sustains the raised eyebrow during the pause following her utterance; the sentence will be interpreted as the nonsyntactically marked question *Peter is going to Boston?* rather than the affirmation *Peter is going to Boston.* Intonation may also serve as syntactic markers: high pitch at the end of an utterance may mark a question while a statement may be indicated by a low pitch (Bolinger 1989; Pierrehumbert and Hirschberg 1987; Prevost 1996).

Several studies (Argyle and Cook 1976; Ekman 1979; Kendon 1993; McNeill 1992) have shown the importance of nonverbal signals within a conversation. They have reported the different functions of these signals. The meaning of such signals may complement the meaning of what is being said (e.g., showing a direction with the index finger while saying *He went in this street*); they may substitute for words (shaking the index finger to a child to say *no*); they may modify the conversation (making a mocking face while saying *You look nice tonight*).

In particular, Bolinger (1989, 211) demonstrates how nonverbal signals may vary the sense of what is being said by interpreting a very common sentence such as *I don't know* when accompanied by different gestures:

Lips pursed: "No comment."
Eyebrows arched: "I'm wondering too."
Shoulders raised: Same.

Head tilted sideways: "Evasion."
Hands held slightly forward, palms up: "Empty, no information."

This very simple sentence may receive a number of varied interpretations. The slightest head movement or eyebrow raising may modify the sense of the utterance. The interpretation of the meaning conveyed by the speaker does need to consider both sets of signals: verbal and nonverbal.

Verbal and nonverbal signals are highly synchronized. They do not occur in a random way; most gestures occur during speech (McNeill 1992). Gestures tend to end with our speech: our hands come to a stop, and we often look at our interlocutor to signal to her that she can take the speaking floor. The timing relationship between both sets of signals occurs at different levels of the discourse: change of body orientation and leg posture often happen at a change of topic discussion, while blink is often synchronized at the phoneme level. A microanalysis of an interaction (Condon 1988) shows the organizational structure of all signals. In the microanalysis of the word *sam* (Condon 1988), it was found that several gestures happen in parallel, and gesture and speech follow the same timing pattern; during the /s/ sound, the head goes down and the eyes close; during the /ae/ sound, the head goes right and the eyes remain closed; and during the /m/ sound, the head goes up and the eyes open.

If, during a conversation, your interlocutor moves only her lips to talk but uses no other signals (no intonation to mark an accent or the end of an utterance, no facial expression, no change in the gaze direction, no hand gesture, and so on), you might soon have the impression of dialoguing with a humanoid rather than a human. Moreover, you might have a hard time understanding what she is saying, since neither new and important information nor end of turn is clearly marked in her discourse. Furthermore, no change in the direction of her gaze may soon become embarrassing. Having a person either always fixing her gaze on you or always avoiding looking at you can inspire a very awkward feeling.

For a sentence such as *I asked Mary to take the brown pot and put it over there*, various interpretations are possible: if no accent is indicated, the sentence could be interpreted either as *I asked Mary and not Charles to take the brown pot and put it over there* or as *I asked Mary to take the brown pot and not the black pot and put it over there*. If no pointing gesture or head direction accompanies the word *there*, it has no meaning: *there* could be anywhere. In the same way, if a listener does not give you any feedback during your speech, you will not know his reactions to what you are saying; you will not know if he understands, agrees, or is interested. It will be like talking to a wall!

Again, not displaying the correct facial expression at the right moment can be a source of misunderstanding and convey the wrong message. Marking a nonaccented word with a head nod can put the focus of the conversation on the wrong information. Suppose that in the sentence *David went to New York by car*, the voice is stressing the word *car* but a head nod occurs on the word *David*: two very different interpretations are possible, depending on which sign (verbal or nonverbal) dominates. If the verbal signal (accent on *car*) prevails, the sentence can be understood as *David went to New York by car and not by train*; but in the case where the head nod on *David* has more weight, the interpretation could be *David and not Peter went to New York by car*. In the former, the new information is the means of transportation David is using to go to New York, while in the latter it is who went to New York. Identically stressing a word and raising the eyebrow at another, one creates asynchrony between verbal and facial channels and causes difficulties in understanding the message conveyed.

These examples show the importance and the role of multimodal signals in a conversation. Signals in different modalities are intersynchronized, and their meanings need to be evaluated in the context in which they are emitted. We can add that deliberately stressing such a dichotomy of the channels as well as using the wrong signals is extremely difficult to do in a normal conversation.

6.3 The Role of Face in Multimodal Communication

The face plays an important role in the communication process. A smile can express happiness, be a polite greeting, or be a back-channel signal. Some facial expressions are linked to the syntax structure of the utterance: eyebrows may raise on an accent and on nonsyntactically marked questions. Gaze and head movements are also part of the communicative process (Argyle and Cook 1976; Collett and Contarello 1987; Poggi, Pezzato, and Pelachaud 1999). The sequence of looking at the addressee and of breaking the gaze reflects the social status of the two interlocutors, their degree of intimacy, their culture, and so on. Gaze also helps regulate the flow of speech and the exchange of turns. As the literature on face communication has shown, all these facial signals can be decomposed in the following clusters based on their communicative functions (Duncan 1974; Ekman 1979; Fridlund 1994; Scherer 1980).

6.3.1 Affective Display

Different studies have investigated the facial expression of emotions. The facial expressions of seven universal prototypes of emotions have been specified: anger, disgust, fear, happiness, sadness, surprise (Ekman 1982), and embarrassment (Castelfranchi and Poggi 1990; Keltner 1995). The expressive patterns of these emotions may well be universal; yet each different culture has a set of norms, called "display rules" (Ekman 1982), which prescribe if and when, out of contextual convenience, an emotion is supposed to be utterly expressed, or else masked, lowered, or intensified.

6.3.2 Syntactic Function

Frowning and eyebrow raising co-occur with accents, emphasis, pauses, questions, and so on. Nods may punctuate an emphatic discourse (Ekman 1979).

6.3.3 Dialogic Function

Facial expressions and gaze are part of the signals involved during the exchange of speaking turn when sender and addressee change roles in the conversation (Cassell, Torres, and Prevost 1999; Duncan 1974). They help in regulating who takes the floor, who keeps it, or who asks for it. They provide cues to the addressee on when to ask for the turn, thus avoiding the addressee interrupting the sender without waiting for his speaking turn. Turn-taking system refers to how people negotiate speaking turns (Duncan 1974). When taking the floor, the sender turns his head away from the addressee to concentrate on what she is going to say. At some particular moments of her speech (co-occurring often with the completion of a grammatical clause), the sender might check how the addressee might show his involvement in the conversation by gazing at the sender, nodding, smiling, emitting a vocalization of agreement such as /mhm/, or asking for clarification. The sender may signal her desire to handle the speaking turn by turning her head toward the addressee, finishing any arm gestures, and assuming a more relaxed position (Duncan 1974).

6.3.4 Social Attitude Function

Facial expression conveys the sender's social attitude or relationship to the addressee. A raised chin is a signal of dominance, while a bent head is one of submission.

But there is a function of facial expression that has not yet been systematically investigated in research on face communication and that we are going to deal with in our work: it has something to do with attitude expression, but it is, more precisely, the facial expression of the performative of a speech act or of any communicative (not necessarily verbal) act. Anytime we communicate something to other people, we perform a communicative act, which includes something we are speaking of (its propositional content) and why we are speaking of that (our performative or communicative intention) (see sec. 6.6). Our question is how the communicative intention of a speaker in performing communicative acts is communicated through facial expression, and how this can be simulated in animated faces.

6.4 Multimodal Systems

As with human-human communication, it seems that human-computer communication benefits from the use of multimodality. Humans use facial expressions as well as gaze, head, arm, and hand gestures to communicate. Computers may use pen, speech recognition, speech synthesizer, facial feature tracking, 3-D agents, graphics, video, and so on. All these different cues coming from different modalities should be integrated to improve the interaction.

6.4.1 Multimodal Systems in Human Communication

Several reasons exist for human communication to be multimodal.

6.4.1.1 *Modality Synergy*   Different studies have shown that the redundancy of audio and visual signals can improve speech intelligibility and speech perception (Bolinger 1989; Hadar et al. 1983; Magno Caldognetto and Poggi 1997; Schwippert and Benoit 1997). For example, an accent can be marked by any one of the following signals: the voice pitch, a raised eyebrow, a head movement or a gesture, or a combination of these signals. At the same time, looking at a face while talking improves human perception (Benoit 1990; Massaro and Cohen 1990; Summerfield 1992). People, especially those who are hard of hearing, make use of gesture information to perceive speech. Similarly, speech recognition performance when combining the audio and visual channels is higher than when using only one channel (Risberg and Lubker 1978).

6.4.1.2 *Different Modalities, Different Benefits*   Signals from visual and audio channels complement each other. The complementary relation between audio and visual cues helps in ambiguous situations. Indeed, some phonemes can be difficult to distinguish on the basis of sound alone (e.g., /m/ and /n/) but easily differentiated visually (/m/ is done by lip closure while /n/ is not) (Jeffers and Barley 1971).

6.4.1.3 *Adaptability*   Speech is the product of several activities: the configuration of the vocal cords, larynx, and lungs as well as the movement of the lips and tongue. That is, the visual and audio channels are associated in speech: the ear hears the sound while the eye sees the lip and tongue movements. These channels are the most common ones. Hearing impaired and blind people may use other speech channels (visual and audio) such as the tactile one to get information (Benoit et al. n.d.) to compensate for the loss of information from the other channels. Blind people use their sense of touch to understand spoken or written language, relying on, for example, the Braille or the Tadoma methods (users feel with their hands the speaker's articulators).

6.4.1.4 *Naturalness* Speech is a very natural means of communication among humans; we have been using it since we were young. We learn to speak but also to express our emotions, beliefs, attitudes, and so on with our body, eyes, face, and voice. Every day we converse with others using verbal and nonverbal signals to exchange our ideas, give orders, provide directions, and so on.

6.4.2 Multimodal Artificial Systems

Artificial systems may take advantage of multimodality just as human communication does (Benoit et al. n.d.; Blattner and Dannenberg 1990; Suhm 1998).

6.4.2.1 *Modality Synergy Interfaces* Interfaces can benefit from modality synergy on both the input and output sides of the system since an interface will integrate the different strengths and contributions of each modality. Information on both the input and output sides may be conveyed redundantly across modalities and/or in a complementary way (with some information conveyed in one modality and other information conveyed in the other modality) to increase the chances of interpretation and to represent information accurately, respectively. For example, lately, automatic speech recognition systems combine information from acoustic and visual channels to augment their recognition rate (Adjoudani and Benoit 1996; Meier, Stiefelhagen, and Yang 1997). Recognition results for normal audio condition (no noise added) may reach a 99.5 percent success rate when information from both channels is integrated, while the results for the visual channel reach only 55 percent and for the acoustic channel reach only 98.4 percent (Meier, Stiefelhagen, and Yang 1997).

6.4.2.2 *Different Modalities, Different Benefits* Combining modalities enables the interface to take advantage of the combination of benefits from each modality. For example, in some applications, having the choice of using different modalities as input such as speech, pointing gestures, and menu may help the interaction. It is easier and faster to speak a command than to choose it from a menu, while it is easier to select an object directly by pointing at it on the screen than to describe it verbally.

6.4.2.3 *Adaptability* The user may have the choice of performing the same task through several modalities (keyboard, speech, pointing gestures) and then select the modality that is best adapted to her at the moment of the action. For example, in car navigation, speech input is more suitable for asking for a particular direction since the hands must be on the wheel and may not be used to select a direction on a menu. Interfaces may offer different modalities to users with disabilities, adapting modalities to suit each person's needs.

6.4.2.4 *Naturalness*   Much effort has been made to make computer interaction more natural and less constraining to the user, thereby making her more at ease. This is especially critical in the case where human-human communication aspects are transmitted to human-computer interfaces. Several interfaces have been built where a user can dialogue with a 3-D synthetic agent (Cassell et al. 1994; Cassell et al. 1999; Nagao and Takeuchi 1994; Thórisson 1997), which aims at creating a natural conversation setting.

In the case of speech multimodal systems—that is, multimodal systems with speech as one of their components—several studies have been undertaken. In this chapter, we concentrate on interfaces using speech associated with a conversational agent.

6.5 Animated Faces

Multimodal speech systems and animated agents have been created for the personalization of user interfaces (Cassell et al. 1994; Chopra-Khullar and Badler 1999; Pelachaud and Prevost 1994; Rist, André, and Müller 1997) and for pedagogical tasks (Badler et al., chap. 9; Lester et al., chap. 5; Rickel and Johnson, chap. 4), exhibiting nonverbal behaviors such as pointing gestures, gaze, and communicative facial expressions. The links between facial expression and intonation (Pelachaud and Prevost 1994) and between facial expression and dialogue situation (Cassell et al. 1994; Cassell et al. 1999; Thórisson 1997) have been studied, and a method to compute automatically some of the facial expressions and head movements performing syntactic and dialogic functions has been proposed. This has made it possible to create faces exhibiting natural facial expressions to communicate emphasis, topic, and comment through eyes and eyebrow movements, while also performing these functions through voice modulation (Cahn 1989; Pelachaud and Prevost 1994; Prevost 1996).

In particular, to simulate face-to-face conversation with a user in real time, Nagao and Takeuchi (1994) categorize facial expressions based on their communicative meaning, following Chovil's (1991) work. The system is able to understand what the user is saying (within the limits of a small vocabulary) and to answer the user. The synthetic agent speaks with the appropriate facial expression: for example, the head is nodding in concert with *Yes* and a facial shrug is used as an *I don't know* signal. *Ymir* (Thórisson 1997) is an architecture to simulate face-to-face conversation between the agent *Gandalf* and a user. The system takes as sensory input hand gesture, eye direction, intonation, and body position of the user. Gandalf's behavior is computed automatically in real time. He can exhibit context-sensitive facial expressions, eye movement, and pointing gestures as well as generate turn-taking signals. Nevertheless, Gandalf has limited capacity to analyze the discourse at a semantic level and therefore to generate semantically driven nonverbal signals. *Rea*, the real estate agent (Cassell et al. 1999), is capable of multimodal conversation: she can understand and answer in real time. She moves her arms to indicate a particular element in the image, to take the turn. She uses gaze, head movements, and facial expressions for functions such as turn taking, emphasis, and greetings as well as for back channels to give feedback to the user speaking to her. Even though Rea is able to do very sophisticated behaviors, she does not exhibit nonverbal behaviors for performatives.

PPP Persona (André, Rist, and Müller 1998), a 2-D animated agent, has been created for the personalization of user interfaces. This agent is able to present and explain multimedia documents and to select which material to present to the user. He or she exhibits nonverbal behaviors such as deictic gestures and communicative facial expressions. In this work, the emphasis is on the discourse generation that also includes information on the relation between text and the images that illustrate it. Later on, the authors enhanced their system to include animated characters that present multimedia information to the user (André et al., chap. 8).

Noma and Badler (1997) developed tools to create a virtual human presenter based on *Jack*, an animated agent system. The tools allow the user to specify gesture, head movement, and other nonverbal behaviors within the text that the presenter should make. A set of markup elements was developed to describe the different gestures accompanying the presenter's speech. The animation is then performed synchronized to speech in real time. The specification of the markup within the text is done manually, not automatically.

The *Olga* project (Beskow 1997) integrates conversational spoken dialogue (i.e., speech recognition and natural language understanding), 3-D animated facial expressions, gestures, lip-synchronized audiovisual speech synthesis, and a direct manipulation interface. In the human-human communicative process, verbal and nonverbal signals are active. One chooses the appropriate signal to display from an internal state, goal to achieve, and mental state but also from the context where the conversation is taking place, the interlocutors, and the relationship with the interlocutor.

Takeuchi and Naito (1995) introduced the notion of "situated facial displays." Situatedness means that the system not only follows its internal logic but is also affected by external events. External events include reactions of users, arrival of a new user interacting with the system, actions done by one of the users, and so forth. These events are perceived using a vision module that detects when users enter its field of view and track users' gaze and head behavior. As in Nagao and Takeuchi's system (1994), facial displays, called "actions" here, are computed based on their communicative meaning, and their choice depends on the internal logic of the system. On the other hand, "reactions" correspond to behaviors invoked by the system as a reaction to a new external event: the 3-D agent will turn his head fast to look at the user moving in front of him. The facial animation module outputs the 3-D face model.

In their system, Takeuchi and Naito consider only external events (users' movement and position). As we show below, our method differs from their system. Indeed, in our definition of context, we propose to take into account the social relationship of the interlocutors (here, machine/human) and their personality, along with the goal the speaker intends to communicate. We think that the choice of words, body postures, facial displays, and gaze behaviors is highly dependent on who our interlocutor is and what our relationship is to him or her.

Another difference from other systems is that in most of the mentioned agents, face simulation is triggered by written or intonational input: for instance, if a part of a written sentence is marked "comment," or a spoken phrase carries an emphatic stress, the system triggers a synchronized eyebrow raising; the visual signal is therefore directly connected with an audio or graphic output. The challenge of the system we designed (see also Poggi and Pelachaud 1998) is to generate a complex message that coordinates auditory and visual signals on the basis of underlying cognitive/semantic information. Our aim is to construct an expressive face starting with a meaning-to-face approach rather than a voice-to-face approach—that is, a face simulation directly driven by semantic data.

6.6 The Notion of the Performative in Speech Act Theory

The notion of the performative dates back to the very beginning of speech act theory. Ever since his first formulation, Austin (1962) stressed that every sentence has a performative aspect, since it performs some action. In fact, any sentence performs a locutionary, an illocutionary, and a perlocutionary act: it is an act of doing something physically, but *in* being uttered (*in* locution), it also performs a social action, and through this (*per* locution), it may also have some effects on the other. The illocutionary force of the sentence (the type of action it performs) is its performative, and it can be made explicit verbally by performative verbs (such as *I assure, I promise,* or *I command* . . .) or performative formulas (such as *thanks* or *please*). Searle (1969) clearly states the notion of the speech act as an act including a propositional attitude and a propositional content, one formed in its turn by the act of referring to and the act of predicating.

Among the theoretical models in the line of speech act theory, the view of performatives we present here is based on a model of social action and communication in terms of goals and beliefs (Castelfranchi and Parisi 1980; Conte and Castelfranchi 1995; Parisi and Castelfranchi 1976). By matching Austin's intuition that a sentence is an action with Miller, Galanter, and Pribram's (1960) cybernetic model of action, which holds that any action is regulated by a goal, Parisi and Castelfranchi (1976) claim that every sentence has a goal—that is, in every sentence, the speaker aims at having the hearer do some action, or answer some question, or assume some information. The goal of the sentence is its meaning, and it is made up of a performative and a propositional content.

Moreover, sentences as well as actions may be hierarchically ordered in plans; any sentence has a goal but it may also have one or more supergoals, goals superordinate to the literal goal of the sentence and inferable from it; and the supergoal may be either idiomatized or not. In the former case, the inference to understand is automatic, as in Searle's (1975) indirect speech acts: *Can you pass the salt?* is no more a question but a request. In the latter, the supergoal is to be inferred anew from context and shared knowledge, somehow as a Grician implicature (Grice 1975): if I tell you *Pass me the salt*, it may mean "Please help me to cook fast" or "Don't put too much salt in your dish; watch your blood pressure." Finally, the goals and supergoals of sentences in sequence may be hierarchically ordered and make discourses: a discourse is a plan of speech acts that all, directly or indirectly, aim at a final communicative goal (Parisi and Castelfranchi 1976).

6.7 Communicative Act Theory

In the model we present here (Poggi 1991, n.d; Poggi and Magno Caldognetto 1997), communication holds any time that an agent S (a sender) has the goal of having another agent A (an addressee) get some belief *b* (a belief about S's beliefs and goals); in order to reach this goal, S produces a signal *s* that S supposes is or may be linked in both S's and A's minds to some meaning m (the belief about one's goals and beliefs which S has the goal of communicating).[1]

To produce a signal in order to achieve the goal of communicating some meaning is to perform a communicative act. A communicative act is then the minimal unit of communication, and it can be performed via linguistic devices (thus being a speech act proper), or via gestural, bodily, facial devices. Communicative acts are then a superset of speech acts: speech acts are those communicative acts that are performed through verbal language, while communicative acts in general may be performed through any kind of signal: a dress, a perfume, a strike, a slap, a kiss, a drawing.

A communicative act is an action performed (but also, sometimes, a morphological feature exhibited) by a sender through any (biological or technological) device apt to produce some stimulus perceivable by an addressee, with the goal that the addressee acquire some belief about the sender's beliefs and goals. Therefore, by saying that communication holds only with a goal of letting the other know something, we do not mean that a communicative goal is necessarily a conscious intention, that is, a goal one is aware of. Given our general cybernetic notion of a goal as a regulatory state (as any state that determines behavior), among communicative goals we include also unconscious goals—say, a neurotic symptom that tries to "tell" me there is something wrong with me—or even biological goals—say, blushing—that may be viewed (Castelfranchi and Poggi 1990) as an involuntary apology for transgressing a social norm or value, aimed at preventing the group's aggression. Various levels of intentionality are then possible in communication, and all have to be included in a notion that encompasses even animal communication. Within human communicative behavior, the existence of different levels of intentionality is particularly clear in nonverbal communication. Some types of gestures or facial expressions are produced at a high level of awareness, so much that subsequently one can remember the specific gesture or expression produced, while others, especially those produced in the flow of discourse, are often not self-aware gestures or expressions, and one could not remember them precisely. This is also the case because these communicative signals are produced and perceived in a modality other than the acoustic one; that is why, as we have seen, they may occur at the same time as the verbal signal.

A communicative act has two faces: a *signal* (the muscular actions performed or the morphological features displayed—say, vocal articulation for speech acts, and facial expression, hand movements, or gaze for nonverbal communicative acts) and a *meaning* (the set of goals and beliefs that Ai has the goal to transfer to Aj's mind). The signal part of a communicative act may be represented formally by facial actions, phonetic articulations, intonation contours, and so on; the meaning part may be represented in terms of logical propositions that we call "cognitive units," declarative representations of semantic primitives, by which all kinds of semantic content, including communicative intentions, word meanings, and emotions, may be expressed (see below).

6.8 The Meaning Side of a Communicative Act

The meaning of a communicative act includes a *performative* and a *propositional content*. In the sentence "Put on your raincoat," the propositional content includes what the sender S is referring to (the addressee and the raincoat) and what the sender is predicating about the referents (the action of putting on); the performative is the type of social action that S is performing toward A in mentioning the propositional content (fig. 6.1). Here the performative is one of advice—that is, the goal of having the addressee do some action that is good for him or her.

That a communicative act is made up of both a performative and a propositional content is shown by the fact that we may have different communicative acts that share the same performative but have different propositional contents, as well as different communicative acts where the same propositional content is the object of different performatives. Thus, I may advise you to put on your raincoat or to study artificial intelligence; moreover, I may suggest to you, order you, or implore you to put on your raincoat.

As Austin and Searle have shown, different classes of performatives can be distinguished; in our model, we distinguish three "general types of goal," very broad classes of performatives that differ for the type of action they request from the addressee. Performatives like *order, command, implore, propose, offer,* and *advise* all have the goal that the addressee do some action, and we class them as requests; *ask, interrogate,* and the like make up the class of questions; *inform, warn,* and *announce* belong to the class of informative acts.

6.9 The Signal Side of a Communicative Act

In performing our communicative acts, we can use verbal or nonverbal signals, or a mix of the two. Suppose I want to advise my friend to put on his raincoat and provide the justification that it's raining. I can convey both communicative acts using only verbal signals and say *Put on your raincoat. It's raining* (see fig. 6.2, line 1). But I could also use a mixed (verbal and nonverbal) discourse: for

Communicative Act

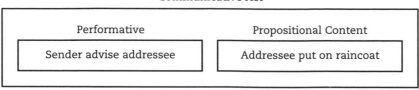

Performative	Propositional Content
Sender advise addressee	Addressee put on raincoat

Figure 6.1
The structure of a communicative act.

instance, tell him to put on his raincoat and at the same time point out the window and show him the rain, using a gesture or simply a head nod or gaze (line 2). Finally, I could rely completely on nonverbal discourse: hand him the raincoat and point out the window (line 3).

In fact, when we perform communicative acts through different modalities, we have to "decide" (meaning a decision usually not at a high level of consciousness and intentionality) what to communicate by verbal and nonverbal signals; moreover, since signals may use different modalities and may then be simultaneous, we may have to decide whether to use the two modalities sequentially or simultaneously, and in this case whether to convey the same message by two signals in the different modalities (hence being redundant) or to provide different information in the two modalities.

For instance, by using the two modalities simultaneously, I could convey the same communicative act by both the verbal and the nonverbal signal, at the same time saying "it's raining" and pointing out the window (line 4). Or else, I could simultaneously convey different but congruent communicative acts: say "*Put on your raincoat*" and point at the rain (line 5).

Now, this division of labor among verbal and nonverbal signals may hold not only at the level of combinations of communicative acts, like discourse or conversation, but also at the level of a single communicative act.

Take again the advise to a friend to put on his raincoat: within this single communicative act, I may convey the performative verbally, by a performative verb or formula, or else simply through intonation or facial expression (fig. 6.3); and in this case, since the signals use different modalities, performative and propositional content may be conveyed at the same time.

	CA1 S ADVISE A THAT A PUT ON RAINCOAT	CA2 S INFORM A THAT IT RAINS	
v nv	*Put on your raincoat*	*It's raining*	(1) sequential
v nv	*Put on your raincoat*	.... Point window	(2) sequential
v nv	.... Hand raincoat	.... Point window	(3) sequential
v nv	.... 	*It's raining* .... Point window	(4) simultaneous
v nv	*Put on your raincoat*	.... Point window	(5) simultaneous

Figure 6.2
Verbal and nonverbal sequential and simultaneous communicative acts.

	Performative S ADVISE A	Propositional Content A PUT ON RAINCOAT	
v nv	*I advise you*	*To put on your raincoat*	(1) sequential
v nv	.... Advice expression	*Put on your raincoat*	(2) simultaneous

Figure 6.3
Verbal and nonverbal sequential and simultaneous performative and propositional content in the same communicative act.

The decision of how to distribute the verbal and the nonverbal will depend not only on a consideration of the available modality but also on the cognitive ease of production and processing of signals (in describing an object, a gesture may be more expressive than a word), on the fact that some signals may be more easily devoted to communicate some kinds of meanings than others (emotions are better conveyed by facial expression than by words), and on their different appropriateness to different social situations (an insulting word may be less easily persecuted than a scornful gaze). Moreover, there may be metacommunicative constraints that, say, lead to the use of redundancy (both the verbal and nonverbal signals) when information to convey is particularly important or when it needs to be particularly clear.

6.10 The Generation of Performatives in Communicative Acts

How can we simulate the generation of a performative of a communicative act?[2] Our idea is that the performative is not generated all at once, but through subsequent specification of the general type of goal of the communicative act, whose cognitive structure is combined with contextual information.

According to this hypothesis, then, first comes the goal, a very general goal (I want the other simply to do something, or tell me something, or believe something). But since the way I can lead the other to perform actions, tell me, or assume beliefs varies according to who the other is, what our social relationship is, and so on, I have to take all this "contextual" information into account and specify my communicative goal more narrowly, ending up with a very specific goal (a performative) tailored to the actual addressee and the social situation at hand.

In this view, the performative of a communicative act is a "context-situated interaction goal," a communicative goal where information is specified about a number of relevant interactional features. Suppose I have the general type of goal of requesting somebody to put on his raincoat because it's raining outside. I can *order* my four-year-old child to do so, but if he is sixteen I may have to *implore* him; to my boss, I may perhaps *suggest* it, while I may *warn* a friend of mine because I am worried about him. In all these cases, the sentence may be the same but my performative facial expression will be different from case to case.

In fact, in real interaction the goal of our communicative act is not only a general type of goal, but a very specific goal: for requests, we distinguish among orders, advice, implorations, proposals, suggestions; for information, we distinguish among warning, swearing, criticism, and so on. These more specific goals of communicative acts are their performatives, and they are different from each other in that each of them is semantically richer; each contains more information than the plain general type of goal. As Austin pointed out, a performative is always present in a speech act, and, we add, in a communicative act; but different from what he held, it is also always explicit, not only as it is stated through performative verbs or formulas: often, in both speech acts and communicative nonverbal acts, it is not expressed through words but through intonation or facial expression. As we request that somebody do something, we may do it in a very bossy, polite, or empathic way, depending on the context in which the conversation takes place; and our bossiness, politeness, or empathy is made explicit, either jointly or alternatively, by words, voice, or face.

In this chapter, we investigate two points related to the generation and expression of performatives. First, we have to show how it happens that from a general goal a particular performative is specified: how it is, for instance, that from the general goal of requesting an addressee to do some action, the sender comes to specify it as a performative of, say, commanding, imploring, advising, and so forth. Second, we will see how the specified performative is exhibited through facial expression.

6.11 General Types Of Goals

Take these sentences:

(1) *John, put on your raincoat.*
(2) *John is putting on his raincoat.*
(3) *Is John putting on his raincoat?*

These sentences exemplify the three general types of goal—request, information, and question—where, respectively, a sender wants an addressee to do some action, or to believe some belief, or to provide some information. Moreover, two types of questions can be distinguished:

(4) *What is John putting on?*
(5) *Is John putting on his raincoat?*

The former is a Wh-Question, where S wants A to let S know some new information: the latter is a Yes/No Question, where S wants A to tell whether some hypothesized information is true or not.

Below, we represent formally these four general types of goals of communicative acts in cognitive units. In our formalism, which follows Castelfranchi et al. (1998), S is called Ai and A, Aj; x is a variable, a constant or a function denoting a domain "object": specifically, a denotes a domain "action," b a domain "fact."

1. Request:

Goal Ai (Do Aj a)

Ai has the goal that Aj do some action a.

2. Inform:

Goal Ai (Bel Aj b)

Ai has the goal that Aj believe some belief *b*.
3. Ask (two types):
Wh-Question

Goal Ai (Goal Aj (Bel Ai b))

Ai has the goal that Aj do something in order to have Ai believe some belief *b*.
Yes/No Question

Goal Ai (BW Ai (Bel Aj b))

Ai has the goal that Aj do something in order to have Ai know whether some belief *b* is true or not.[3]

6.12 From the General Type of Goal to the Performative

As we mentioned, in different communicative acts all having the same general type of goal, the different performatives are semantically richer than the general type of goal itself in that they contain additional cognitive units; therefore, the performatives can be distinguished from each other in terms of specific features, all representable in terms of cognitive units. Some of these cognitive units are particularly relevant for distinguishing within requests, some within informations, and so on. Here are the features that distinguish performatives from each other.

6.12.1 In Whose Interest Is the Action Requested or Information Provided?

In a command as opposed to a piece of advice, a relevant difference can be seen in the answers to these questions: Whose goal does the requested action serve? In whose interest is it? If I command you *Go and get me the newspaper*, then you getting the newspaper is a goal of mine. But if I offer you the advice *Take the umbrella when you go out*, I am suggesting that taking the umbrella will prevent you from getting damp, which is a goal of yours—more precisely, an interest of yours or a goal you may not be aware of (Conte and Castelfranchi 1995). So,

- in a command, Ai wants Aj to do a, where a, the requested action, is in Ai's interest. This means that Ai wants to achieve the goal g and believes that the action a will be useful in achieving it:

Goal Ai (Do Aj a),
(Goal Ai g) $\wedge$ (Bel Ai (Achieve a g))

- in advice, Ai also wants Aj to do a, but the difference from a command is that the requested action is in Aj's interest. Ai believes that Aj wants to achieve the goal g and that the action a will allow Aj to achieve it:

Goal Ai (Do Aj a),
(Goal Aj g) $\wedge$ (Bel Ai (Achieve a g))

6.12.2 Degree of Certainty

Among performatives of information, a relevant difference is the degree of certainty with which the provided information is assumed by the sender: this distinguishes, for instance, claiming from suggesting (in its reading as information). Uncertainty is represented by the mental atom "uncertain."[4]
4. Suggest:

Bel Ai (Uncertain (Achieve a g))

Ai is not certain that the action a may help to achieve the goal g.

6.12.3 Power Relationship

One more difference among requests—particularly clear when comparing, say, commands, advice, and implorations—is the power relationship holding between sender and addressee. In a command, Ai calls up to one's power on Aj and shows a willingness to take advantage of it; this implies that if Aj does not fulfill the request, then Ai could retaliate. In imploring, Ai acknowledges Aj's power over Ai; while in advising, even if having power over Aj, Ai claims that he or she does not want to take advantage of it, thus leaving Aj free to do the requested action or not.
5. Command:

(Goal Ai (Do Aj a)) $\wedge$ (Goal Ai (Bel Aj (Power-on Ai Aj)))

6. Implore:

(Goal Ai (Do Aj a)) ∧ *(Goal Ai (Bel Aj (Power-on Aj Ai)))*

6.12.4 Type of Social Encounter
Our talk is different in a familiar context (say, to a friend) than in a service encounter (say, to a clerk); hence, performatives differ in how formal or informal the relationship between sender and addressee is and, more generally, according to the kind of social relationship they have with each other, whether motivated by instrumental or affective goals. *Forgive* and *excuse*, for instance, seem to be more linked to forgetting a person's faults against, respectively, ethics versus etiquette rules; in the same vein, *inform* seems more formal than *tell*.

6.12.5 Affective State
Many performatives contain information about some actual or potential affective state of Ai's. In a peremptory order, Ai shows that he or she might be angry if Aj did not fulfill Ai's request; in a warning, Ai reveals worrying about Aj's good.

In the system we present here, information that specifies the general type of goal as a performative, and then outputs it through expressive devices, comes in at two different stages. Information about interest, certainty, power relationship, and social encounter (degree of formality) determines the mental state of the specific performative, while affective state only comes in at the expressive stage, resulting in enhancement or deintensification of the expression, or in the addition of affect displays to it.

Our hypothesis is, in fact, that information that specifies the general type of goal of a communicative act is not part of our communicative goal from the beginning, but it comes from consideration of context. A sender "decides" which specific performative to use in his or her sentence (or other nonverbal communicative act) on the basis of the social situation, the social relationship to the addressee, and the addressee's cognitive, affective, and personality factors.

6.13 A Model of Context
As any action of our life, communicative behavior is determined by both our goals and the world conditions at hand—that is, by the context (see fig. 6.4). So, at the start, a sender has a global idea of a communicative act in mind, but he or she has to specify how to convey it by taking into account the communicative possibilities at hand (Poggi and Pelachaud 1998). On the one hand, the

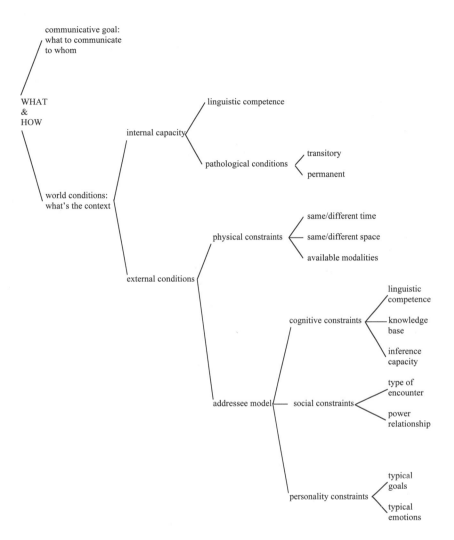

Figure 6.4
A model of context.

sender has to consider her internal capacities, which include her linguistic competence (say, she may be a foreigner who has not mastered the language completely) and possible transitory or permanent pathological conditions (such as slips of the tongue or aphasia). On the other hand, external conditions exist: physical constraints and the sender's model of the addressee.

As for physical constraints, the sender will take into account whether communication is face to face or at a distance, whether the addressee is simultaneously present in the same spatiotemporal situation, and what the available modalities are: only acoustic (say, on the phone), only visual (through a window or across a road), or both. This may determine, for instance, whether to communicate a performative through intonation and words or facial expression. Finally, the model the sender has of the addressee includes his or her cognitive, social, and personality constraints. Cognitive constraints are the addressee's linguistic competence, knowledge base, and inference capacity: they account for why, for instance, we speak slowly to a tourist, because we think he does not understand our language well; why we explain things more at length to students lacking background knowledge; or why we explicate obvious causal links to children or dull people, assuming them to be inferentially slower. Among the social constraints we consider are the type of social encounter we are engaged in, our power and status relationship to the addressee, and personality factors (see Ball and Breese, chap. 7; Nass, Isbister, and Lee, chap. 13).

Now, the physical constraints and the constraints of the addressee's linguistic competence and inference capacity are particularly relevant in deciding whether to communicate in a visual or acoustic modality and in choosing the level of explicitness in sentences; but since we are now dealing with the facial expression of performatives, here we focus only on the contextual constraints that are relevant in choosing facial actions.

These include:

6.13.1 Type Of Social Encounter (Formal vs. Informal)

Suppose I ask someone to pass me the salt: if I am at the same table with a friend I may simply say *Salt*, or even only point at the salt with gaze or a chin tilt. But if I ask unknown people at another table, I may say *Could you please give me the salt?* with a shy, smiling expression. A more formal situation, in fact, determines the triggering of politeness rules that may for instance generate a smile as an equivalent of polite forms in sentences (the use of *please* or indirect requests).

6.13.2 Power Relationship between Sender and Addressee

This is what determines the difference among, say, command, advice, and imploration. I may decide to display a straight and serious face if I think that the addressee is obliged to do what I want—that is, if I think I have some power over him or her.

6.13.3 Personality Factors of Both Sender and Addressee

Personality factors, in our model, can be seen especially in terms of the two following elements:

6.13.3.1 *Typical Goals* In our model (Conte and Castelfranchi 1995; Poggi 1998), personality may be viewed, at least in part, as the different importance that different people attribute to the same goal. For instance, a bossy person is one who always has the goal to impose his or her will; a very autonomous person attributes a high value to the goal of choosing one's goals freely and of not being helped by others, so he or she will not give advice; to a generous one, the goal of helping others is particularly worthy; for a proud one, the goal of not submitting to other people is very important.

6.13.3.2 *Typical Emotions* We often describe people's personalities linguistically, with adjectives such as *shy* or *touchy*. This means that we also classify people in terms of their higher or lower tendency to feel some emotions. So a shy person is one quite likely to feel shame; a touchy person is one who has a low threshold for feeling offended, that is, wounded in one's own image or self-image.

Now, these personality factors of both Ai and Aj determine the choice of a performative. If Ai is proud, he or she will never implore; if Aj is very touchy, Ai will be very soft in disagreeing.

6.14 Some Performatives of Request

Let us now see how some performatives can be represented in terms of cognitive units. We start from the performative of peremptory order.

- Peremptory order:

(1) *Goal Ai (Do Aj a)*
(2) *(Goal Ai g) $\wedge$ (Bel Ai (Achieve a g))*
(3) *Goal Ai (Bel Aj (Power-on Ai Aj a))*
(4) *If (Not (Do Aj a)) then (Feel Ai (Angry Ai))*

The first cognitive unit (1) characterizes the peremptory order as a request; the second (2) mentions the feature "in whose interest" the requested action is made. Action a is useful to achieve goal g, which is a goal of Ai. In fact, when I order you something, it is for a goal of mine, not for yours. The third cognitive unit (3) remarks the power relationship between Ai and Aj: I order when I want you to think I have power over you. The fourth cognitive unit (4) mentions the potential affective state of the peremptory order: if you are not doing what I request, I will be angry at you.

- Advice:

(1) *Goal Ai (Do Aj a)*
(2) *(Goal Aj g) ∧ (Bel Ai (Achieve a g))*
(3) *Goal Ai (Not (Bel Aj (Power-on Ai Aj a)))*
(4) *Goal Ai (Bel Aj (Can Aj (Not (Do Aj a))))*

In advice, the action requested is in the interest of Aj (2), and in making the request Ai remarks that he or does not assume to have, or at least does not evoke, power over Aj (3), so that Aj is free to do the requested action or not (4).

- Imploration:

(1) *Goal Ai (Do Aj a)*
(2) *(Goal Ai g) ∧ (Bel Ai (Achieve a g))*
(3) *Goal Ai (Bel Aj (Power-on Aj Ai a))*
(4) *If (Not (Do Aj a)) then (Feel Ai (Sad Ai))*

When Ai implores, the action Aj is requested is in Ai's interest (2), Ai claims (3) that Aj has power over Ai (hence, Aj would be free to not do a), but if Aj should not do a, Ai would be sad (4).

- Proposal:

(1) *Goal Ai (Do Aj a)*
(2) *(Bel Ai (Goal Ai g)) ∧ (Goal Aj g)*
(3) *Bel Ai (Uncertain (Achieve a g))*
(4) *Goal Ai (Not (Bel Aj (Power-on Ai Aj a)))*
(5) *Goal Ai (Bel Aj (Can Aj (Not (Do Aj a))))*

In a proposal, like in advice, Ai claims to be in a peer relationship with Aj (4) and therefore leaves Aj free not to do the requested action (5). The two most distinctive units are that the goal the action serves is supposed to be a goal of both Ai and Aj (2) and that Ai shows uncertainty about whether the proposed action is useful to that shared goal or not (3).

- Suggestion:

(1) *Goal Ai (Do Aj a)*
(2) *Bel Ai (Goal Aj g)*
(3) *Bel Ai (Uncertain (Achieve a g))*

Suggestion is like an advice in that the requested action is in the interest of Aj (2), and it is like a proposal in that Ai is not completely sure that the suggested action is useful to Aj's goal (3).

6.15 The Expression of Performatives

Let us now come to the signal part of a performative: how we can compute facial expression. Our hypothesis is that to each cognitive unit or cluster of them defining a performative is associated one or more nonverbal behaviors. For example, performatives whose general type of goal is request are signalled by "keep head right." Power relationships will be marked by a "bend head aside" when the addressee has power over the sender (ethologically, the sender displays a weak position showing her neck as a demonstration that she is not in attacking position); but in the opposite case, when the sender has power over the addressee, the sender will look down at the addressee (typical behavior of domination). Moreover, many performatives contain information about a particular affective state and may therefore be associated with a facial expression. For example, since in a peremptory order the sender shows she could be angry at the addressee in case she should not perform the requested action, this potential anger will be expressed by frowning, a typical eyebrow expression of anger. On the other hand, since in imploring the sender is potentially sad in the event that the addressee does not do *a*, potential sadness is expressed by raising the inner parts of eyebrows.

In our computer graphics system, facial expression is computed in terms of Ekman and Friesen's (1978) FACS (Facial Action Coding System), a notational system to describe visible facial actions. FACS is derived from an analysis of the anatomical basis of facial movement. Muscular actions (contraction or relaxation) are the underlying basis for changes in facial expression, and single muscular actions (or groups of related muscular actions) of the face are denoted as action units. An action unit (AU) corresponds to the minimal visible facial action. The facial model we are using is a hierarchically structured, regionally defined object (Platt 1985). The face is decomposed into regions (forehead, brow, cheek, nose, lip, for example) and subregions (upper-lip, lower-lip, left lip corner, upper lip corner). The model uses FACS to encode any basic action, so that each region corresponds to the application of particular AUs. For each facial expression, we compute the corresponding set of AUs. The final expression is obtained by adding each signal and therefore by adding each set of AUs.

6.16 System Overview

In this section, we present an overview of our system (see fig. 6.5) and a detailed example.

The system does not have a vision module that is able to detect the user's presence and movements. It assumes the user is in front of it ready to communicate with it. The input to the system includes a propositional content and a general type of goal (GTG) (request, inform, or ask). The system takes this information as input and combines it with context information (CI). Within the model of context outlined above, the relevant information for the generation and expression of the performative includes the social constraints (type of encounter and power relationship) and the addressee's personality (typical goals and typical emotions).

In order to generate the complete cognitive structure of a specific performative—that is, to specify the single cognitive units that form the final representation of a specific performative—the system uses the GOLEM resolution engine (Castelfranchi et al. 1998) to infer specific cognitive units to complete the final performative representation. For example, suppose the social encounter Ai is engaged in is a formal encounter with his boss, one who attributes great importance to status relationships and who is very selfish and quite touchy. Here are the inferences that can be drawn:

- *if Aj is my boss, then Aj has power over Ai (power relationship);*
- *if Aj attributes great importance to status relationship, then the goal of looking powerful is an important goal of his (typical goals);*
- *if Aj is selfish, then an important goal of his is that actions he does are in his interest (typical goals);*

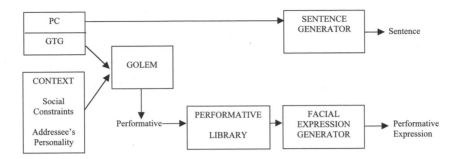

Figure 6.5
System overview.

- *if he is touchy, then he is particularly likely to feel offended if people don't acknowledge his status (typical emotions).*

From these inferences, the system decides that the specific performative to express, the kind of attitude and social relationship Ai should express to Aj with its cognitive units must (a) imply that the action Ai is requesting from Aj is useful to Aj's goals, and (b) show uncertainty about whether the requested action is really the best for Aj's goal, and present it as just one of different possible actions.

In other words, the system concludes that the most convenient performative to express contains the following cognitive units:

(a)   Bel Ai (Goal Aj g)
(b)   Bel Ai (Uncertain (Achieve a g))

The system then goes to a performative library, looks for the performative that matches these requirements (whose representation contains the required cognitive units), and outputs the resulting performative.

In this example, the system concludes that the most adequate performative is *suggest*

(1)   Goal Ai (Do Aj a)
(2)   Bel Ai (Goal Aj g)
(3)   Bel Ai (Uncertain (Achieve a g)) (see fig. 6.6)

Figure 6.6
The suggesting expression, the imploring expression, the ordering expression.

Of course, different contextual information would trigger other inferences, and the system would choose another performative. Taking the same example as before, but with only one cognitive unit changed, we get a different result: for instance, if power relationship is

Power-on Ai Aj

(Ai has power over Aj), then Ai could show potential anger in case of nonfulfillment, and the resulting performative would be one of peremptory order.

Last, the outputted performative is dispatched to the facial expression generator, while the propositional content is sent to the sentence generator: they finally give as outputs, respectively, a facial expression in terms of AUs and a sentence taken from a library of prestored sentences. The facial expression for a given performative is obtained by combining all nonverbal signals specified for each cognitive unit. For the moment, the combination is simply obtained by adding the nonverbal signal. Currently, personality traits are not yet implemented in our system, but in the future we foresee implementing both generators (facial expression generator and sentence generator) so they may again receive information on the context as an input.

Thus, type of encounter and power relationship as well as the addressee's personality traits may also motivate enhancement or intensification of facial expression. For instance, in imploring, I may show sadness because if I ask you something very important to me and I am in your power, I can anticipate that I will be sad if you do not fulfill my request. Moreover, in this case, if Ai thinks that Aj is particularly eager to be moved, an imploring face may be loaded with a more intense expression of sadness, provided by inner parts of eyebrows particularly raised. The intensity of facial expression is computed by changing either the intensity of each AU of the facial expression or the basic facial expression itself. For example, in *suggest* the eyebrows may be more or less raised, or they may be accompanied by a wide eye opening. These modulations may function as Ekman's display rules (Ekman 1982).[5]

6.17 Conclusion

We have proposed a way to construct an artificial agent that can express one's communicative intentions through facial expression. The agent computes the appropriate performative of one's communicative acts through consideration of the context of communication, particularly of the addressee, and then makes it explicit through facial expression.

Acknowledgments

We are very indebted to Fiorella de Rosis for her comments and discussion of our work. We are very thankful to Justine Cassell and the reviewers for their precious detailed criticism.

Notes

1. Our notion of communication and of communicative act differs from information theory (Shannon and Weaver 1949) and semiotic models (Eco 1975; Jakobson 1963; Pierce 1931–35) in that it is basically defined in terms of the goal of communicating. This is why we speak of a sender and an addressee instead of an emitter and a receiver: only if the sender has the goal of having the addressee know something is it the case that not simply a transfer of information, but a communicative process holds: we would not call communication, for instance, a case in which someone (say, a spy) comes to get some information that someone else had not the goal to let him or her know. Therefore, we speak of a sender and an addressee because these are intrinsically goal-based notions: a sender is defined as one who has the goal of transferring beliefs to someone else; an addressee is the one to whom some sender has the goal to transfer some beliefs (Poggi n.d.).

2. In this chapter, we do not discuss other important views of performatives and communicative actions in AI, such as Cohen and Levesque (1990; 1995) and Posner (1993).

3. *Belief-Whether (BW): (Bel A b)* $\lor$ *(Bel A not b).*

4. For computational simplicity, we consider at the moment only three degrees of certainty: *Bel*, *BelNot*, *Uncertain* (Castelfranchi et al. 1998).

5. One thing we did not deal with in this work is the computation of intonation. In principle, we think that it should be possible to build a system that, starting from a given cognitive material, is able to generate, not only a verbal output through a natural language sentence generator, but also the appropriate intonation and an adequate facial expression. In this work, we focused only on the visual output. On the other hand, as we mentioned, intonation is an acoustic device that, to a great extent, is equivalent to facial expression as far as the function of communicating the performative of sentences goes; in addition, it is an even more sophisticated device than the face itself in expressing performatives: in everyday communication, we can distinguish very subtly between a suggestion and an advice, a prayer and an imploration, a warning and an announcement, and we do this thanks to the subtle intonational differences in our voice (Ladd, Scherer, and Silverman 1986). Unfortunately, the nature of such a sophisticated device has not yet been determined by researchers, neither by auditory nor by acoustic instrumental analysis (Scherer 1988); intonational differences have been identified among, for instance, interrogative and informative sentences in general (Bolinger 1989; Pierrehumbert and Hirschberg 1987), but research is at its first steps in distinguishing the intonational differences within each general class of sentence (Cahn 1989; Prevost 1996): within the class of informative sentences, how does one phonetically distinguish an announcement from a warning? Once research has filled in this gap, it will also be possible to construct synthetic talking faces that can mark these differences from an intonational point of view.

References

Adjoudani, A., and C. Benoit. 1996. On the integration of auditory and visual parameters in an HMM-based ASR. In D. G. Stork and M. E. Hennecke, eds., *Speechreading by humans and machines: Models, systems, and applications*, 461–472. Berlin: Springer-Verlag.

André, E., T. Rist, and J. Müller. 1998. Webpersona: A lifelike presentation agent for the world-wide web. *Knowledge-Based Systems* 11(1):25–36.

Argyle, M., and M. Cook. 1976. *Gaze and mutual gaze*. Cambridge: Cambridge University Press.

Austin, J. L. 1962. *How to do things with words*. London: Oxford University Press.

Benoit, C. 1990. Why synthesize talking faces? In *Proceedings of the ESCA Workshop on Speech Synthesis* (Autrans, France), 253–256.

Benoit, C., J. C. Martin, C. Pelachaud, L. Schomaker, and B. Suhm. N.d. Audio-visual and multimodal speech systems. In *Handbook of standards and resources for spoken language systems*. The Hague: Kluwer. Forthcoming.

Beskow, J. 1997. A conversational agent with gestures. In *Proceedings of IJCAI '97 Workshop on Animated Interface Agents—Making Them Intelligent* (Nagoya, Japan, August).

Blattner, M. M., and R. Dannenberg. 1990. CHI '90 workshop on multimedia and multimodal interface design. *SIGCHI Bulletin* 22(2):54–57.

Bolinger, D. 1989. *Intonation and its uses*. Stanford: Stanford University Press.

Cahn, J. 1989. Generating expression in synthesized speech. Ph.D. diss., Media Lab, Massachusetts Institute of Technology, Cambridge, Massachusetts.

Cassell, J., J. Bickmore, M. Billinghurst, L. Campbell, K. Chang, H. Vilhjálmsson, and H. Yan. 1999. Embodiment in conversational interfaces: Rea. In *CHI '99 Conference Proceedings* (Pittsburgh, Pennsylvania), 520–527.

Cassell, J., C. Pelachaud, N. Badler, M. Steedman, B. Achorn, T. Becket, B. Douville, S. Prevost, and M. Stone. 1994. Animated conversation: Rule-based generation of facial expression, gesture and spoken intonation for multiple conversational agents. In *Computer Graphics*, 413–420. New York: ACM SIGGRAPH.

Cassell, J., O. Torres, and S. Prevost. 1999. Turn taking vs. discourse structure: How best to model multimodal conversation. In Y. Wilks, ed., *Machine conversation*. The Hague: Kluwer.

Castelfranchi, C., and D. Parisi. 1980. *Linguaggio, conoscenze e scopi*. Bologna: Il Mulino.

Castelfranchi, C., and I. Poggi. 1990. Blushing as a discourse: Was Darwin wrong? In R. Crozier, ed., *Shyness and embarrassment: Perspectives from social psychology*, 230–251. Cambridge: Cambridge University Press.

Castelfranchi, C., F. de Rosis, R. Falcone, and S. Pizzutilo. 1998. Personality traits and social attitudes in multiagent cooperation. *Applied Artificial Intelligence* 12(7–8): 649–675.

Chopra-Khullar, S., and N. I. Badler. 1999. Where to look? Automating attending behaviors of virtual human characters. In *Proceedings of Autonomous Agents '99* (Seattle, Washington, May).

Chovil, N. 1991. Social determinants of facial display. *Journal of Nonverbal Behavior* 15(3):141–154.

Cohen, P. R., and H. J. Levesque. 1990. Performatives in a rationally based speech act theory. In *Proceedings of the 28th Annual Meeting of the Association for Computational Linguistics*, 79–88.

———. 1995. Communicative actions for artificial agents. In *Proceedings of the International Conference on Multi-Agent Systems*. San Francisco: AAAI Press.

Collett, P., and A. Contarello. 1987. Gesti di assenso e di dissenso. In P. E. Ricci Bitti, ed., *Comunicazione e gestualità*. Milan: Franco Angeli.

Condon, W. S. 1988. An analysis of behavioral organization. *Sign Language Studies* 58:55–88.

Conte, R., and C. Castelfranchi. 1995. *Cognitive and social action*. London: University College.

Duncan, S. 1974. On the structure of speaker-auditor interaction during speaking turns. *Language in Society* 3:161–180.

Eco, U. 1975. *Trattato di semiotica generale*. Milan: Bompiani.

Ekman, P. 1979. About brows: Emotional and conversational signals. In M. von Cranach, K. Foppa, W. Lepenies, and D. Ploog, eds., *Human ethology: Claims and limits of a new discipline. Contributions to the Colloquium*. Cambridge: Cambridge University Press.

———. 1982. *Emotion in the human face*. Cambridge: Cambridge University Press.

Ekman, P., and W. Friesen. 1978. *Facial Action Coding System*. Palo Alto, Calif.: Consulting Psychologists Press.

Fridlund, A. 1994. *Human facial expression: An evolutionary view*. New York: Academic Press.

Grice, H. P. 1975. Logic and conversation. In P. Cole and J. L. Morgan, eds., *Syntax and semantics: Speech acts*. New York: Academic Press.

Hadar, U., T. J. Steiner, E. C. Grant, and F. Clifford Rose. 1983. Kinematics of head movements accompanying speech during conversation. *Human Movement Science* 2:35–46.

Jakobson, R. 1963. *Essais de Linguistique générale*. Paris: Minuit.

Jeffers, J., and M. Barley. 1971. *Speechreading (lipreading)*. Springfield, Ill.: C. C. Thomas.

Keltner, D. 1995. Signs of appeasement: Evidence for the distinct displays of embarrassment, amusement, and shame. *Journal of Personality and Social Psychology* 68(3):441–454.

Kendon, A. 1993. Human gesture. In T. Ingold and K. Gibson, eds., *Tools, language and intelligence*. Cambridge: Cambridge University Press.

Ladd, D. R., K. Scherer, and K. E. A. Silverman. 1986. An integrated approach to studying intonation and attitude. In C. Johns-Lewis, ed., *Intonation in discourse*. London: Crom Helm.

Magno Caldognetto, E., and I. Poggi. 1997. Micro- and macro-bimodality. In C. Benoit and R. Campbell, eds., *Proceedings of the Workshop on Audio-Visual Speech Processing. Cognitive and Computational Approaches* (Rhodes, Greece, September 26–27).

Massaro, D. W., and M. M. Cohen. 1990. Perception of synthesized audible and visible speech. *Psychological Science* 1(1):55–63.

McNeill, D. 1992. *Hand and mind*. Chicago: University of Chicago Press.

Meier, U., R. Stiefelhagen, and J. Yang. 1997. Preprocessing of visual speech under real world conditions. In C. Benoit and R. Campbell, eds., *Proceedings of the ESCA Workshop on Audio Visual Speech Processing. Cognitive and Computational Approaches* (Rhodes, Greece), 113–116.

Miller, G. A., E. Galanter, and K. H. Pribram. 1960. *Plans and the structure of behavior.* New York: Holt, Rinehart & Winston.

Nagao, K., and A. Takeuchi. 1994. Speech dialogue with facial displays: Multimodal human-computer conversation. In *Proceedings of the 32nd ACL '94*, 102–109.

Noma, T., and N. Badler. 1997. A virtual human presenter. In *Proceedings of the IJCAI '97 Workshop on Animated Interface Agents—Making Them Intelligent* (Nagoya, Japan). San Francisco: Morgan Kaufmann.

Parisi, D., and C. Castelfranchi. 1976. Discourse as a hierarchy of goals. Working chapters, Università di Urbino.

Pelachaud, C., and S. Prevost. 1994. Sight and sound: Generating facial expressions and spoken intonation from context. In *Proceedings of the 2nd ESCA/AAAI/IEEE Workshop on Speech Synthesis* (New Paltz, New York), 216–219.

Pelachaud, C., N. I. Badler, and M. Steedman. 1996. Generating facial expressions for speech. *Cognitive Science* 20(1):1–46.

Pierce, C. C. 1931–35. *Collected chapters.* Cambridge: Harvard University Press.

Pierrehumbert, J., and J. Hirschberg. 1987. The meaning of intonational contours in the interpretation of discourse. Technical memorandum, AT&T Bell Laboratories.

Platt, S. M. 1985. *A structural model of the human face.* Ph.D. diss., Dept. of Computer and Information Science, University of Pennsylvania, Philadelphia, Pennsylvania.

Poggi, I. 1991. La comunicazione. In R. Asquini and P. Lucisano, eds., *L'italiano nella scuola elementare. Aspetti linguistici.* Florence: La Nuova Italia.

———. 1998. A goal and belief model of persuasion. Paper presented at *The 6th International Pragmatics Conference*, Reims, France, July 19–24.

———. N.d. *Multimodal communication. Hands, face and body.* Forthcoming.

Poggi, I., and E. Magno Caldognetto. 1997. *Mani che parlano. Gesti e Psicologia della comunicazione.* Padova: Unipress.

Poggi, I., and C. Pelachaud. 1998. Performative faces. *Speech Communication* 26:5–21.

Poggi, I., N. Pezzato, and C. Pelachaud. 1999. Gaze and its meanings in animated faces. In P. McKevitt, ed., *Language, Vision and Music. Proceedings of the CSNLP-8* (Galway, Ireland, August 9–11).

Posner, R. 1993. Believing, causing, intending: The basis for a hierarchy of sign concepts in the reconstruction of communication. In R. J. Jorna, B. van Heusden, and R. Posner, eds., *Signs, search, and communication: Semiotic aspects of artificial intelligence*. Berlin: De Gruyter.

Prevost, S. 1996. Modeling contrast in the generation and synthesis of spoken language. In *Proceedings of ICSLP '96: The Fourth International Conference on Spoken Language Processing* (Philadelphia, Pennsylvania).

Risberg, A., and J. L. Lubker. 1978. Prosody and speechreading. *Technical Report Quarterly Progress and Status Report 4, Speech Transmission Laboratory*. KTH, Stockholm, Sweden.

Rist, T., E. André, and J. Müller. 1997. Adding animated presentation agents to the interface. In *Proceedings of Intelligent User Interface*, 79–86.

Scherer, K. R. 1980. The functions of nonverbal signs in conversation. In R. St. Clair and H. Giles, eds., *The social and physiological contexts of language*, 225–243. Hillsdale, N.J.: Erlbaum.

———. 1988. *Facets of emotion: Recent research*. Hillsdale, N.J.: Erlbaum.

Schwippert, C., and C. Benoit. 1997. Audiovisual intellegibility of an androgynous speaker. In C. Benoit and R. Campbell, eds., *Proceedings of the ESCA Workshop on Audio Visual Speech Processing. Cognitive and Computational Approaches* (Rhodes, Greece), 81–84.

Searle, J. R. 1969. *Speech acts*. Cambridge: Cambridge University Press.

———. 1975. Indirect speech acts. In P. Cole and J. L. Morgan, eds., *Syntax and semantics: Speech acts*. New York: Academic Press.

Shannon, C. E., and W. Weaver. 1949. *The mathematical theory of communication*. Urbana: Illinois University Press.

Suhm, B. 1998. Multimodal interactive error recovery for non-conversational speech user interfaces. Ph.D. diss., Dept. of Computer Science, Karlsruhe University, Germany.

Summerfield, Q. 1992. Lipreading and audio-visual speech perception. *Philosophical Transactions of the Royal Society of London* 335:71–78.

Takeuchi, A., and T. Naito. 1995. Situated facial displays: Towards social interaction. In *Proceedings of ACM CHI '95—Conference on Human Factors in Computing Systems*, 1:450–455.

Thórisson, K. R. 1997. Layered modular action control for communicative humanoids. In *Computer Animation '97*. Geneva: IEEE Computer Society Press.

7

Emotion and Personality in a Conversational Agent

Gene Ball and Jack Breese

7.1 Introduction

Within a decade or two, computers are likely to be the constant companions of most people in the industrialized world. Many of our interactions with them will continue to be like those with simpler machines: we push a button and the machine takes a limited and well-defined action, like zapping our food or washing the dishes.

However, within the human-computer interaction community, a growing consensus exists that traditional WIMP (windows, icons, mouse, and pointer) interfaces need to become more flexible, adaptive, and human-oriented (Flanagan et al. 1997). One path to such interfaces is the creation of embodied interface agents, animated computer characters that converse with the user in a natural spoken dialogue. Once such technology is available, many situations will occur where spoken conversation will be the preferred means of communicating with a computer: perhaps to ask what the weather is likely to be in Boston next week, or to select a good book to read on the plane.

Huge technical challenges must still be overcome before conversational computers will be competent and reliable enough to use in this fashion, but there is little doubt that we will get there in twenty years (possibly much sooner). An embodied computer with which we engage in casual conversation (even if limited to narrow domains) will inevitably become a significant social presence (at least as affecting as a human ticket agent with whom we carry out a brief transaction). For many people, such a system will eventually become a long-term companion with which (whom?) they share much of their day-to-day activity.

To be *useful*, conversational interfaces must be competent to provide some desired service; to be *usable*, they must be efficient and robust communicators; and to be *comfortable*, they will have to fulfill our deeply ingrained expectations about how human conversations take place.

One subtle aspect of those expectations involves the emotional sensitivity of our conversational partners. We would be surprised if an outburst of anger toward someone produced a completely deadpan response, and we might even be further angered by failure to acknowledge our own emotional state. If we laugh in response to someone's joke, we expect the person to laugh (or at least smile) along with us; to do otherwise would be disconcerting.

We also expect our conversational partners to exhibit a consistent personality: unexpected and unpredictable swings between shy and authoritarian behavior, for example, will leave us with a strong sense of discomfort, even wariness. Moreover, sensitive speakers can adapt to the personality type of their partners in order to produce a more comfortable and satisfying interaction.

Our work on the computational modeling of emotion and personality is intended as a first step toward a psychologically sensitive conversational interface: one that can recognize the emotional state and personality type of the human user and respond in a fashion that adds to the naturalness of the overall interaction. After further discussion of the motivation for agents with emotional awareness (sec. 7.1), related work (sec. 7.2), and our application domain (sec. 7.3), we describe our chosen representation of emotion and personality in section 7.4. Section 7.5 introduces Bayesian networks, which we use to represent the connection between internal psychological states and externally observable behavior. We discuss the reasons for choosing this approach, especially the ability to use the same network to both interpret the psychological significance of observations of the user's behavior and also to generate realistic affective behavior in our embodied agent. Section 7.6 describes the architecture of the psychological subsystem for an agent and presents several examples of the detailed structure of the Bayesian network that connects internal state to both verbal and nonverbal behaviors.

7.1.1 Communicating with Computers

People frequently find spoken conversation to be the most efficient and comfortable way to conduct interactions with others. Particularly for tasks requiring many back-and-forth steps, written communication (even e-mail) can be tedious and suffers from the loss of working context between steps of the interaction. Graphical computer interfaces have been quite successful as a medium for conducting many well-specified tasks of this sort. For example, common requests to a travel agent (long a favorite target application of the spoken language research community) can be carried out quite efficiently as an interaction with a Web server. However, if a request is unusual, it may be difficult to build a graphical user interface to handle it without unduly complicating the interface for more common cases. "Hidden commands" can provide less common capabilities without complicating simple ones, but they require that the user know both that they exist and how to find them.

One likely path for computer interface design is to augment graphical user interfaces gradually with linguistic capabilities. An "assistant" would accept flexible descriptions of commands or objects outside the immediately visible workspace: "I'd like to reserve a group of fifty seats for travel from Minneapolis to Seattle next December" or "Check which movies are showing on flights from London to Seattle." The ability to respond properly to powerful natural language requests (whether typed or spoken) would be a welcome addition to current interfaces. While natural language may first be introduced as an "escape" for uncommon requests, its role is likely to expand steadily as it becomes more capable and as speech recognition becomes more reliable.

Natural language requests of the sort suggested above are convenient and powerful but often result in ambiguities that require clarification: "Do you want round trip tickets?" As a consequence, spoken interactions won't usually consist of just isolated commands but will quickly become conversational dialogues.

Although many of the capabilities of a conversational agent could be delivered if the agent were disembodied (e.g., in a telephone-based service), a visible animated character on a computer screen helps provide a comfortable representation of the agent. Evidence is accumulating that interfaces with embodied characters are often preferred over similar applications without the character (André, Rist, and Müller 1998; Lester et al. 1999). Anecdotal reports also suggest that people are often much more comfortable speaking to a computer if their conversational partner has a visible presence.

7.1.2 Social Aspects of Human-Computer Interaction

In many fundamental ways, people respond psychologically to interactive computers as if they were human. Reeves and Nass (1995) have demonstrated that strong social responses are evoked even if the computer isn't presented as an explicitly anthropomorphic embodied agent. They suggest that humans have evolved to accord special significance to the movement and language produced by other people and, at some deeply ingrained level, cannot avoid responding to the communication of twentieth-century technology as if it were coming from another person.

As user interface designers, we have a responsibility to try to understand the psychological reality and significance of these effects and to adapt our computer systems to the needs of our users. In addition, we should recognize that this social response is likely to become much stronger when the user is having a spoken conversation with a computer. It is clear that our social responses do not disappear while we are interacting with machines of all types: we get annoyed when they do not work properly, we respond with joy when a difficult task is completed smoothly, we even attribute human motives to their inanimate behaviors on occasion. Thus it will not be surprising to see even stronger responses to embodied agents that can speak, including expectations for appropriate emotional responses and personality traits in the agent itself.

7.1.3 Psychologically Aware Computing

Explicit attention to the social aspects of computer interaction will be necessary in order to avoid degrading the user's experience by generating unnatural and disconcerting behaviors. For example, early text-to-speech systems generated nearly monotonic speech, which conveyed a distinctly depressed (and depressing) emotional tone. Similarly, conversational systems that always wait for the user to initiate an interaction but then insist on controlling every subsequent step may be disconcerting because they portray an inconsistent personality type. The initial goal for psychological interfaces should be to simulate appropriate social responses by demonstrating an awareness of the psychological content of an interaction.

We can illustrate the sort of social reactivity that might appropriately be demonstrated by an embodied agent by considering some plausible (but imaginary) responses from the agent to a user. Each example is labeled with an emotion or personality label suggesting the nonlinguistic signals that should accompany the words, giving them a more natural feel and a greater communicative potency.

When the agent is reporting the results of an assigned search task:

- I was unable to find anything meeting that description. (sad)
- This is just what you were looking for. (proud)
- I'm not sure, but one of these might suit your needs. (hesitant)
- Gee, and it only took me **twelve** minutes to find it! (embarrassed)

When the assistant is reacting to difficulties with the conversation itself:

- I'm afraid I don't understand what you mean by that. (confused)
- I believe I just told you that I don't know anything about that topic. (irritated)
- This doesn't seem to be going so well . . . shall we try again? (friendly)
- I'm really sorry, but could you repeat that one more time? (solicitous)

When the assistant has detected a strong emotional reaction from the user:

- Whoa . . . Can we calm down and try again? (soothing)
- Gee, that was pretty frustrating, wasn't it? (empathetic)
- Great! Glad to be of help. (joyful)

When the assistant is trying to fulfill a user's request to help them modify their own behavior:

- You'd better get back to work now. (arrogant)
- If you don't leave now, you'll be late. (fearful)
- Take a break now, if you want your wrists to get better! (authoritarian)

In these examples, the agent's linguistic expression is the clearest indicator of emotion and personality, but if that expression is to seem natural and believable, it needs to be accompanied by appropriate nonlinguistic signals as well. Whether generated by preauthored scripts or from strong AI first principles, such utterances will seem false if the vocal prosody, hand gestures, facial expressions, and posture of the character do not match the psychological state expressed linguistically.

In order to produce responses demonstrating as much social sensitivity as these examples suggest, a system must be able to (1) evaluate the personality and emotional state of the user and then (2) synthesize and communicate an appropriate social response from the computer.

In this chapter, we describe a simple model of emotion and personality that can be used to adjust the expressive style of a talking computer. While the motivation for this work is strongest for conversational systems, its application may be appropriate more generally. As computer use becomes ever more widespread in our culture, it is likely that we will see greatly increased attention to the subjective experiences of computer users, including the aesthetic and psychological impact of computer use. Our expectation is that the experience gained from modeling the social dynamics of spoken interfaces will also be used to inform the design (and possibly the adaptive behavior) of conventional graphical interfaces, in order to improve user satisfaction.

7.2 Work in Social Computing

A number of efforts have been made in recent years to create computer programs that incorporate some aspects of emotion and, to a lesser degree, personality. The largest group is concerned with computational simulations of the (theorized) human processes that produce emotion. Other research has focused on the believable expression of emotion and personality and on methods for detecting the emotional state of humans. We are not aware of any user interface systems that attempt to recognize explicitly the personality types of their users.

7.2.1 Computational Models of Emotion

Elliott's Affective Reasoner (Elliott 1992) implemented a simulated environment containing multiple agents, each with emotional states based on the cognitive theory of emotion of Ortony, Clore, and Collins (1988). Elliott's agents model their own goals and expectations, as well as those of other agents within the environment, and reason about the possible emotional causes of the observed behaviors of other agents.

In the Oz project at Carnegie Mellon University, Bates, Loyall, and Reilly (Bates 1994; Bates, Loyall, and Reilly 1994; Reilly 1996) created an architecture for the control of dramatic characters within simulated worlds. The characters experience emotional reactions to events based on an OCC-style cognitive model of their own goals and expectations.

Several other research efforts have also developed agents that exhibit some degree of emotional behavior as a way to gain insights into the functioning or evolutionary value of emotions in people. Martinho and Paiva (1999) describe a simulation of virtual dolphins that also uses the OCC cognitive theory of emotions to control their response to user input. El-Nasr, Ioerger, and Yen (1999) simulate an agent that learns associations between events and outcomes in order to stimulate emotional responses. Emotions are modeled as cognitive responses (based on OCC) or as direct Pavlovian conditioning.

Elsewhere, Velásquez, Fujita, and Kitano (1998) describe a computational framework that integrates perception, behavior, and motor control with drives and both primary and learned emotions. The framework is inspired by neuropsychological theories of human emotion and has been used to control reactive behaviors in an emotional robot. Kitamura (1998) controls small mobile robots with a six-level consciousness-based architecture, including memoryless emotion, stable emotion, and symbolic responses. Higher levels are activated when behavior is obstructed at the previous level. Cañamero (1997) simulates "newborn" creatures within a virtual environment, using developmental principles suggested by Minsky's Society of Mind (Minsky 1985). Emotions are modeled as modifiers of the creatures' motivational state that are activated by external events or patterns of physiological states.

In contrast to these efforts, we have not attempted to create a deep psychological model of emotion and personality. Instead, we use a very simple representation of their most significant aspects and relate them directly to observable behaviors.

7.2.2 Expression of Emotion and Personality

While many animated systems have been authored to convey both emotion and personality through predefined animation or audio effects, there have been only a few attempts to systematically synthesize emotionally expressive behavior. Cahn (1989) has demonstrated the feasibility of communicating emotional state in artificial speech by controlling the parameters of a vocal tract synthesizer (see sec. 7.6.4).

In a number of recent systems, explicit emotional models have been used to dynamically control the activation of small, emotionally expressive animation fragments. Examples include the directed improvisation system of Hayes-Roth and van Gent (1997), which selects from among animation and audio sequences based on a character's happy-sad emotional state; the improvisational dialogue of Walker, Cahn, and Whittaker (1996), which controls the synthesis of speech according to a character's emotional disposition; and Perlin and Goldberg's Improv animation system (Perlin 1997; Perlin and Goldberg 1996), which layers small animations (including emotionally expressive ones) under the control of scripts and state variables including mood and personality.

André et al. (chap. 8) in work described in this volume have constructed agents with explicit personality traits and emotional states (based on our representation) that are used to select among linguistic (and some limited nonlinguistic) behaviors in a rule-based fashion. While quite close to some aspects of our approach, our Bayesian network also enables recognition (from observed behaviors to internal state) which would be very difficult to do from behavior synthesis rules.

The Petz products by PF.Magic (Stern, Frank, and Resner 1998) are some of the most psychologically expressive systems yet developed. Their animated characters have distinct personality profiles and maintain an internal model of emotion that pervasively affects the choice of behaviors and their associated facial expression, posture, and vocalizations. The simulated animals are sufficiently psychologically believable (with only nonlinguistic interaction) that their owners regularly develop strong emotional bonds with them.

Nass et al. (1995) demonstrated that the personality attribute of dominance can be communicated efficiently in a textual interaction by using strong assertions and commands, displaying a high confidence level, and always initiating the conversation. The same study showed that when subjects interacted with a computer that was similar in personality to themselves, they rated it as friendlier and more competent and felt the interaction was more satisfying. As Nass, Isbister, and Lee (chap. 13) discuss, the factors leading to a preference for a particular personality type are unclear, but personality certainly plays a role in establishing the comfort level of any interaction. Klein, Moon, and Picard (1999) have performed experiments that demonstrate that the behavior of users can be significantly modified by social-affective feedback (statements of empathy and sympathy) from a computer following a frustrating experience.

All of these research efforts are combining to establish the significance of affective attributes in computer systems. Since the perceived psychological attributes of an embodied agent have a demonstrable influence on the user's response to an interactive experience, it follows that we need to develop methods for constructing agent personalities that will evoke desirable reactions.

7.2.3 Recognizing Human Emotion

Recently, several groups have begun efforts to diagnose the emotional state of a user based on interactively sensed attributes. Picard has demonstrated confusion-sensing glasses and has investigated other physiological sensors including blood pressure, galvanic skin response, and electromyogram (Picard 1997, 1998). Ark, Dryer, and Lu (1999) report promising results from their initial efforts to discriminate among emotions based on general somatic activity, galvanic skin response, pulse rate, and finger temperature. They plan to incorporate sensors for these measures in a computer mouse.

Elsewhere, Essa and Pentland (1995) have reported highly accurate recognition of facial expressions (on a small data set), using motion energy templates created from a detailed analysis of optical flow in a library of training videos. Kobayashi and Hara (1994) also achieved high expression recognition accuracy by training a neural network with displacement data for thirty key facial locations. Lisetti, Rumelhart, and Holler (1998) also used a neural network to distinguish between smiles and neutral expressions.

Research into the recognition of emotional state from acoustic analysis of vocal expression has been very limited. Roy and Pentland (1996) have shown some ability to distinguish between positive and negative spoken sentences (discussed further in sec. 7.6.4). In an informal demonstration of new work, Petrushin (1999) has also shown some success in recognizing the emotional content of vocal expression.

These efforts are all attempts to recognize salient features from the behavior of users. While these features may be useful independently, our work attempts to combine information from a variety of such features into a coherent picture of the user's emotional state.

7.3 A Personal Time Management Companion

The creation of a model of emotion and personality was inspired by our experiences in developing an embodied conversational agent that communicates by means of a free-form spoken dialogue. The interface presents itself as an on-screen animated character (using Microsoft Agent, Trower 1997) called Peedy the Parrot. Peedy is based upon the animated character in an earlier prototype system (Ball et al. 1997) at Microsoft Research.

Peedy is intended to act as a personal assistant on the computer desktop: scheduling events, generating reminders, informing the user of breaking news, and generally acting as an entertaining companion. Peedy can respond to spoken input that is captured by a large vocabulary continuous speech recognition engine (Huang et al. 1995) as well as to typed natural language input. The agent's interaction is controlled by a script authored in SpeakEasy (Ball 1997), described below. Peedy's conversational content is updated periodically by downloading additional scripts from a network server, which makes it possible for users to encounter fresh information and novel capabilities whenever they converse with the agent.

7.3.1 The SpeakEasy Scripting Language

The SpeakEasy dialogue controller interprets conversational scripts that determine how Peedy will interact with a user. These scripts are written in a simple imperative programming language that was designed to make authoring interactive dialogues as easy as possible.

```
*[What time is it?]
  say "It is $(daytime)."
  return

*[Is there anything new about the hurricane?]
say "Do you want a news story or the weather
forecast?"
  if [the news story]
    say "Ok, there's an update on MSNBC."
    show "http://msnbc.com/..."
  elseif [the weather forecast]
    say "Dennis is still stalled just off the coast."
    show "http://msnbc.com/weather/..."
  endif
```

Figure 7.1

A fragment of a SpeakEasy dialogue script.

The starting place for the design of a human-computer dialogue is often a scenario that defines a typical interaction. A SpeakEasy script is built directly from that scenario, then augmented to allow conditional branching and the handling of exceptional situations.

In the script fragment in figure 7.1, an interaction can be initiated when the user asks, "Is there anything new about the hurricane?" The user's utterance (in square brackets) actually is an input pattern that represents an exemplar of the class of natural language utterances that the script is intended to handle—consequently, user inputs that are paraphrases of the exemplar but convey essentially the same meaning will also match the input pattern.

At a specific point in a conversational thread, the interface designer will usually be able to enumerate contextually appropriate responses without too much trouble. User inputs that do not fit directly into the immediate context are another matter. When a user "changes the subject," the script must be able to respond accordingly. Utterances that begin a new conversation (or a subdialogue) can occur at virtually any time. SpeakEasy allows input patterns to be designated as conversation starters, which are always valid as input. When a conversation starter is recognized, a new conversational context is created—an independent flow of control activated at that point in the SpeakEasy script.

For example, in figure 7.1, the conversation starter "What time is it?" will result in a new context that responds to the question (note that "$(daytime)" is replaced with the value of the variable "daytime," which holds the current time of day) and then immediately terminates. Thus, a time request can be handled at any point without interfering with the active conversation.

7.3.2 Automatic Script Construction

A major problem with scripted conversational agents is that they have a limited repertoire, and as soon as an interaction becomes obviously repetitive it becomes boring. Worse, even a small amount of repetition can destroy the illusion of an intelligent conversational partner.

The best Web sites avoid staleness by constantly updating their content, so that loyal customers can return frequently and still find new material of interest. Peedy adopts this principle by periodically retrieving new scripts from the Web. Ideally, "What's new?" will get a different response every time you ask.

The scripts on the Web server can be created in two ways. As with other popular sites, the content can be updated by a staff of authors (this is the only way to get a steady supply of clever quips, which is the most effective way to maintain user interest).

In addition, existing Web sites can be mined (with permission, of course) for content that is automatically reformatted into Peedy scripts. With a small (but perpetual) amount of maintenance to deal with page restructurings, many Web sites can be reformatted automatically into informative dialogues like the one in figure 7.1.

7.4 Modeling Emotions and Personality

7.4.1 Emotion

The understanding of emotion is the focus of an extensive psychology literature. Much of this work is based upon a deep understanding of an individual's beliefs about how events will affect him or her, and then predicts how those beliefs lead to an emotional response (Ortony, Clore, and Collins 1988; Scherer 1984). As discussed in section 7.2.1, most attempts to build computer models of emotion have attempted to represent an agent's goals and expectations with enough detail to support the direct application of these cognitive models.

We have chosen to adopt a much simpler model of emotion; one that corresponds more directly to the universal responses (including physical responses) that people have to the events that affect them. Although this approach is unable to model many subtle emotional distinctions, it seems like a good match to conversational interfaces that communicate with people (within specific domains) using only a limited understanding of language and the user's goals.

The term *emotion* is used in psychology to describe short-term (often lasting only a few seconds) variations in internal mental state, including both largely physical responses like fear and cognitive responses like jealousy. We focus on two basic dimensions of emotional response (Lang 1995) that can usefully characterize nearly any experience: (1) Valence represents the positive or negative dimension of feeling, and (2) Arousal represents the degree of intensity of the emotional response.

Figure 7.2 shows the emotional space defined by these dimensions and indicates where a few named emotions fit within that space. In our model, these two continuous dimensions are further simplified by encoding them as a small number of discrete values. Valence is considered to be negative, neutral, or positive; similarly, Arousal is judged to be excited, neutral, or calm.

7.4.2 Personality

Psychologists also recognize that individuals have long-term traits that guide their attitudes and responses to events. The term *personality* is used to describe permanent (or very slowly changing) patterns of thought, emotion, and behavior associated with an individual. McCrae and Costa (1989) analyzed Wiggins's five basic dimensions of personality, which form the basis of commonly used personality tests. They found that this interpersonal circumplex can be characterized usefully within a two-dimensional space.

Taking an approach similar to our representation of emotion, we have incorporated into our model a representation of personality, based upon the dimensions of (1) Dominance, indicating an individual's relative disposition toward controlling (or being controlled by) others, and (2) Friendliness, measuring the tendency to be warm and sympathetic. Dominance is encoded in our model as dominant, neutral, or submissive; and Friendliness is represented as friendly, neutral, or unfriendly.

7.4.3 Relating Internal State to Behavior

Given this quite simple, but highly descriptive, model of an individual's internal emotional state and personality type, we wish to relate it to behaviors that help communicate that state to others. The behaviors to be considered can include any observable variable that might be caused by these internal states. In laboratory settings, some of the most reliable measures of emotional state involve physiological sensing such as galvanic skin response and heart rate. Self-assess-

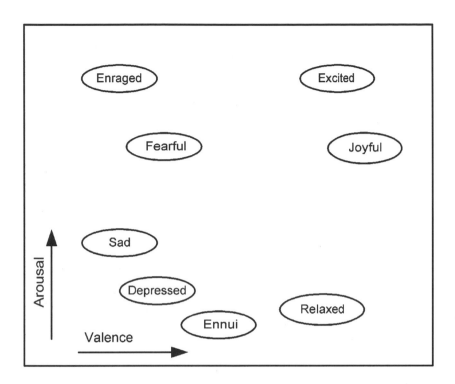

Figure 7.2
Position of some named emotions within the Valence-Arousal space.

ment surveys are also frequently used to get subjects' personal impressions of their emotional state. Personality type can be reliably measured by questionnaires such as the Myers-Briggs Type Indicator (Myers and McCaulley 1985). However, in normal human interaction, we rely primarily on visual and auditory observation to judge the emotional state and personality type of others.

A computer-based agent might be able to use direct sensors of physiological changes, but if those measures require the attachment of unusual devices, they would be likely to have an adverse effect on the user's perception of a natural interaction. For that reason, we have been most interested in observing behavior unobtrusively, either through audio and video channels, or possibly by using information (especially timing) that is available from traditional input

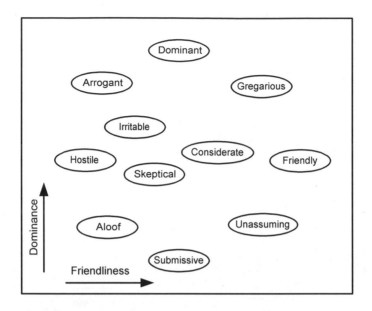

Figure 7.3
Position of some named personality types within the Dominance-Friendliness space.

devices such as keyboards and mice but might be a good indicator of the user's internal state. More specialized devices such as a GSR sensing mouse or pressure-sensitive keyboard might be worth investigating as well, although unless they turned out to be extraordinarily useful, they are unlikely to make it into widespread use.

7.5 Bayesian Networks

Bayesian networks (Jensen 1996; Pearl 1991) are a formalism for representing networks of probabilistic causal interactions that have been effectively applied to medical diagnosis (Horvitz and Shwe 1995), troubleshooting tasks (Heckerman, Breese, and Rommelse 1995), and many other domains.

We have chosen to use a Bayesian network to model the relationships between emotion and personality and their behavioral expression. The remainder of this section discusses the reasons for this choice, and it is followed by a detailed description of the model itself in the next section.

7.5.1 Advantages for Psychological Modeling

Bayesian networks have a number of properties that make them an especially attractive mechanism for modeling emotion and personality. First, they deal explicitly with uncertainty at every stage, which is a necessity for modeling anything as inherently nondeterministic as the connections between emotion/personality and behavior. For example, an approach using explicit rules (if behavior B is observed, then deduce the presence of emotional state E) would have great difficulty accounting for inconsistent reactions to the same events. However, a Bayesian network is able to make predictions about the relative likelihood of different outcomes, which can naturally capture the inherent uncertainty in human responses.

Second, the links in a Bayesian network are intuitively meaningful, since they directly represent the connections between causes and their effects. For example, a link between emotional arousal and the base pitch of speech can be used to represent the theoretical effect that arousal (and the resulting increased muscular tension) has on the vocal tract. It is quite easy to encode the expectation that with increasing arousal the base pitch of speech is likely to increase as well. The exact probabilities involved can still be difficult to determine, but if the network is designed so that the parameters represent relatively isolated effects, relevant quantitative information from psychological studies is sometimes available. Interactions between causes can be minimized by representing only the most significant factors. Moreover, *any* representation that can model even simple emotional responses is likely to have a large number of parameters that have to be determined, and in a Bayesian network these parameters at least have clearly understandable meanings.

Within the framework of a Bayesian network, it is a simple matter to introduce a new source of information to the model. For example, suppose we got a new speech recognition engine that reported the pitch range of the fundamental frequencies in each utterance (normalized for a given speaker). We could add a new network node that represents PitchRange with a few discrete values, and then construct causal links from any emotion or personality nodes that we expect to affect this aspect of expression. In this case, a single link from Arousal to PitchRange would capture the significant dependency. Then the model designer would estimate the distribution of pitch ranges for each level of emotional arousal, to capture the expectation that increased arousal leads to generally raised pitch. The augmented model would then be used both to recognize that increased pitch may indicate emotional arousal in the user and to add to the expressiveness of a computer character by enabling it to communicate heightened arousal by adjusting the base pitch of its synthesized speech.

Finally, and especially relevant to the twin requirements of psychologically aware computing (recognizing emotion and personality in the user and simulating social responses by the computer), Bayesian networks can be used both to calculate the likely consequences of changes to their causal nodes and also to diagnose the likely causes of a collection of observed values at the dependent nodes. This means that a single network (and all of its parameters) can be used for both the recognition and simulation tasks.

7.5.2 Symmetry of Recognition and Simulation

When used to simulate psychologically realistic behavior by the embodied agent, the states of the internal nodes representing dimensions of emotion and personality can be set to the values that we wish the agent to portray. The evaluation of the Bayesian network will then predict a probability distribution for each possible category of behavior. This has the extra advantage that by sampling this distribution over time, we can generate very naturally a sequence of computer behaviors that are consistent with the desired emotional state but are not completely deterministic. Since excessively deterministic behavior is a strong clue of mechanistic origins, observers frequently judge that such behavior appears unnatural. By introducing some random (but consistent) variability, that source of unnaturalness can be avoided.

When user behavior is observed by the computer (through cameras, microphones, etc.), the observations can be used to set the values of the corresponding leaf (or dependent) nodes in the network. Evaluation of the network then results in estimated values for the internal dimensions of the user's emotional state and personality type. The most probable value can be taken as the user's state (as perceived by the computer). If multiple values have similar probabilities, the diagnosis can be treated as uncertain.

7.6 Emotion and Personality in an Embodied Agent

The Bayesian model that we have built (fig. 7.4) contains internal states for emotional Valence and Arousal and for the Dominance and Friendliness aspects of personality. These nodes are treated as unobservable variables in the Bayesian formalism, with links connecting them to nodes representing aspects of behavior that are judged to be influenced by that hidden state. The behavior nodes currently represented include linguistic behavior (paraphrase selection), vocal expression (base pitch and pitch variability, speech speed and energy),

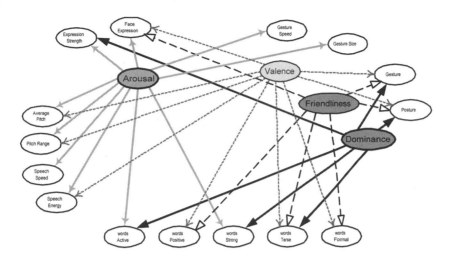

Figure 7.4
A Bayesian network relating emotion and personality to various classes of observable behavior.

posture, and facial expressions.

Our Bayesian network therefore integrates information from a variety of observable linguistic and nonlinguistic behaviors. We have carefully adjusted the probability assessments for only a few of these behaviors; in other cases, such as vocal expression, the probability distributions have been defined to fit the trend relationships reported in the psychology literature (see sec. 7.6.4).

7.6.1 Psychological Subsystem Architecture

In a psychologically aware interactive system, the recognition and simulation of emotion and personality will play an auxiliary and probably quite subtle role. Our goal is to provide an additional channel of communication alongside the spoken or graphical exchanges that carry the main content of the interaction. If the social aspects of the system call attention to themselves, the primary motivation of producing natural interactions will have been defeated. In fact, users who get the feeling that the system is monitoring them too closely may begin to feel anxious or resentful (of course, the system, upon detecting that emotional reaction, could always turn itself off!).

Since developing technology to recognize and control psychological attributes is likely to require considerable effort and produce only subtle benefits, it will be important to share that effort among many applications. Therefore, another attraction of adopting simple two-dimensional models of emotion and personality is that they do not require detailed knowledge of the cognitive structure of the application. If we observe and simulate psychological behaviors that are expressed automatically and unconsciously, then the recognition and interpretation of those behaviors can take place in an independent psychological subsystem.

This module will be responsible for receiving sensory input, making judgments about the personality type of the user, and estimating the current emotional state of the user. It will select a socially appropriate attitude for the agent to adopt, and then adjust the speech and animated behaviors of the system in order to express that attitude in a natural way.

The system architecture that we have experimented with is demonstrated in figure 7.5. In our agent, we maintain two copies of the emotion/personality model. One is used to diagnose the user, the other to generate behavior for the agent. The model operates in a cycle, continuously repeating the following steps:

1. Observation. First, the available sensory input is analyzed to identify the value of any relevant input nodes. For example, a phrase spoken by the user might be recognized as one possible paraphrase among a group of semantically equivalent, but emotionally distinct, ways of expressing a concept. (The modeling of such alternatives is discussed in sec. 7.6.3.) In parallel, the vision subsystem might report its analysis that the user is currently producing large and fast gestures along with their speech. For each such perception, the corresponding node in the diagnostic copy of the Bayesian network is set to the appropriate value.

2. Assessment. Next, we use a standard probabilistic inference algorithm (Jensen, Lauritzen, and Olesen 1989; Jensen 1996) to update the emotion and personality nodes in the diagnostic network so that they reflect the new evidence.

3. Policy. The linkage between the models is captured in the policy component. This component makes the judgment of what emotional response from the computer is desirable, given the new estimate of the user's psychological state, and it sets the emotion and personality nodes of the second copy of

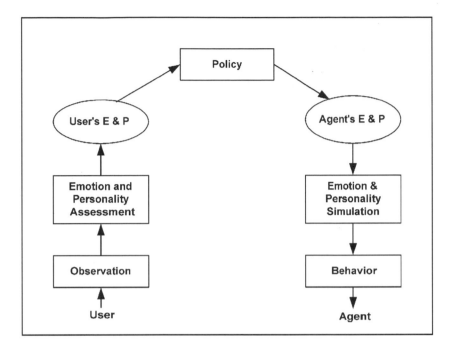

Figure 7.5

An architecture for psychological assessment and subsequent behavior generation by an embodied conversational agent.

the network accordingly. Possible approaches to the policy component are discussed in section 7.6.2.

4. Simulation. Next, a probabilistic inference algorithm is applied to the second copy of the Bayes network. This time, the consequences of the new states of the emotion and personality nodes are propagated to generate probability distributions over the available behaviors of the agent. These distributions indicate which paraphrases, animations, speech characteristics, and so forth would be most consistent with the agent's emotional state and personality (as determined by the policy module).

5. Behavior. Some agent behaviors can be expressed immediately; for example, instructions for changes in posture or facial expression can be transmitted

directly to the animation routines and generate appropriate background movement. Other behavior nodes act as modifiers on application commands to the agent. At a given stage of the dialogue, the application may dictate that the agent should express a particular concept, such as a greeting or apology. The current distribution for the node corresponding to that concept is then sampled to select a paraphrase to use in the spoken message.

7.6.2 Policy

In a fully developed conversational application, the policy module will necessarily be quite complex. It must select the agent's psychological state based on all aspects of the conversational context. The application will typically specify the agent's basic emotional state to reflect progress on a task. The policy module may then need to make adjustments based on the psychological history of the dialogue and its own model of the user's conversational preferences. The estimates of personality and emotion from the diagnostic network provide an additional source of information for the policy decision.

The imagined responses in section 7.1.3 illustrate a few of the difficulties. For example, at what point should a computer agent express irritation toward a user? Conversational systems frequently encounter explicit attempts to "break the demo." These attacks are sometimes sufficiently predictable that a clever response can be generated in an attempt to deflect the attack. If the user then persists in generating additional antagonistic input, perhaps an expression of irritation is actually the appropriate response.

Thus far, we have only considered two very simplistic policies. The *empathetic* agent tries to match the user's emotion and personality. Evidence exists that people prefer to deal with an agent personality that is similar to their own (Nass et al. 1995), so this might be a good starting point. However, emotional empathy needs to be moderated to avoid positive feedback loops, particularly if the user becomes angry!

We have also experimented briefly with a contrary agent, whose emotions and personality try to be the exact opposite of the user. While there are particular contexts in which this may produce interesting results (e.g., when the user becomes bored or sad), it obviously is too simplistic to be a general policy.

7.6.3 Linguistic Behavior

A key method of communicating emotional state is by choosing among semantically equivalent, but emotionally diverse paraphrases—for example, the differences between responding to a request with "sure thing," "ok," or "if you

Table 7.1 Alternative paraphrases for three concepts from agent utterances

Concept	Paraphrases	
greeting	Hello hi there Howdy	greetings hey
yes	Yes Yeah I think so	absolutely I guess so for sure
suggest	I suggest that you perhaps you would like to maybe you could	you should let's

insist." Similarly, an individual's personality type will frequently influence his or her choice of phrasing—for example, "you should definitely" versus "perhaps you might like to."

Our approach to differentiating the emotional content of language is based on behavior nodes that represent "concepts" having a set of alternative expressions or paraphrases. Some examples are shown in table 7.1.

We model the influence of emotion and personality on word choice in two stages, only the first of which is shown in the network of figure 7.1. Because the choice of a phrase can have a complex relationship with both emotion and personality, the problem of directly assessing probabilities that depend on all four dimensions rapidly becomes burdensome. However, inspired by Osgood's work on meaning (Osgood, Suci, and Tannenbaum 1967), in which he identified several key dimensions that characterize the connotation of a word, we first capture the relationship between personality and emotion and several "expressive styles." The current model has nodes representing positive, strong, and active styles of expression (similar to Osgood's Evaluative, Potent, and Active), as well as measures of terseness and formality.

These nodes appear in the network of figure 7.4 as dependents of the emotion and personality nodes, and they capture the likelihood that an individual will choose to speak in a positive (judgmental), strong, active, terse, and/or formal manner. Each of these nodes is binary valued, true or false. Thus, this stage

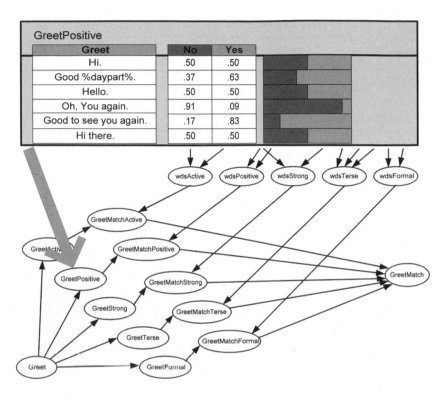

Figure 7.6
A belief network fragment relating expressive styles to paraphrases of the concept "Greet" and showing the assessment of each paraphrase as a "Positive" expression.

captures the degree to which an individual with a given personality and in a particular emotional state will tend to communicate in a particular style.

The second stage, an example of which is shown in figure 7.6, captures the degree to which each paraphrase of a concept actually is positive, strong, active, and terse. This stage says nothing about the individual but rather reflects a general cultural interpretation of the paraphrase—namely, the likelihood that a phrase will be interpreted as positive, active, and so forth by a speaker of American English. A node such as "GreetPositive" is also binary valued, and is true if the paraphrase would be interpreted as "Positive" but false otherwise.

Finally, a set of nodes evaluates whether the selected paraphrase of a concept actually matches the chosen value of the corresponding expressive style. A node such as "GreetMatchPositive" has value true if and only if the values of "GreetPositive" and "wdsPositive" are the same. The node "GreetMatch" is simply a Boolean that has value true when all of its parents (the match nodes for each expressive style) are true. When using the network, we set "GreetMatch" to have an observed value of true. This causes the Bayesian inference algorithm to force the values of the nodes in the concept and style stages to be consistent. For example, when simulating the behavior of an agent, each style node (like "wdsPositive") will have a value distribution implied by the agent's personality and emotional state. The likelihood of alternative phrasings of a concept node (like "Greet") will then be adjusted in order to produce the best possible match between its attributes and the style nodes. In this fashion a negative emotional state will greatly increase the chance that the agent will select "Oh, You again." as a greeting.

In developing a version of this Bayesian network for a particular application, we need to generate a network fragment such as that shown in figure 7.6 for each conceptual element for which we want to select paraphrases based on emotion and personality. These fragments are merged into a global Bayesian network capturing the dependencies between the emotional state, personality, natural language, and other behavioral components of the model.

The various fragments differ only in the assessment of the paraphrase scorings—namely, the probability that each paraphrase will be interpreted as active, strong, and so forth. Five assessments are needed for each alternative paraphrase of a concept. Figure 7.6 shows the estimated probabilities that each paraphrase of "Greet" will be interpreted as "Positive." Note that the size of the belief network representation grows linearly in the number of paraphrases (the number of concepts modeled times the number of paraphrases per concept).

A more direct representation, in which each concept node has all five expressive nodes as parents, would produce a much more difficult assessment problem. The probability of each paraphrase would have to be estimated separately for each of the thirty-two combinations of styles, since a causal independence assumption such as noisy-or is not appropriate (Heckerman 1993). The current structure greatly reduces the assessment burden, since each style attribute is considered independently (as seen in figure 7.6). In addition, the network can be extended much more easily. If we add a new expressive style node to the network (such as "cynical"), then the only additional assessments we need to generate are the "cynical" interpretation nodes for each concept. These features of the Bayesian network structure make it easy to extend the model for new concepts and dimensions of expressive style.

7.6.4 Vocal Expression

As summarized by Murray and Arnott (1993), considerable (but fragmented) literature exists on the vocal expression of emotion. Research has been complicated by the lack of agreement on the fundamental question of what constitutes emotion and how it should be measured. Most work is based upon either self-reporting of emotional state or upon an actor's performance of a named emotion. In both cases, a short list of "basic emotions" is generally used; however, the categories used vary among studies.

A number of early studies—using very short fragments of speech, meaningless or constant carrier phrases, or speech modified to make it unintelligible—demonstrated that vocal expression carries an emotional message independent of its verbal content (see, e.g., Scherer, Koivumaki, and Rosenthal 1972). These studies generally found that listeners can recognize the intended emotional message, although confusions between emotions with a similar arousal level are relatively frequent. Using synthesized speech, Cahn (1989) showed that the acoustic parameters of the vocal tract model in the DECtalk speech synthesizer could be modified to express emotion and that listeners could correctly identify the intended emotional message in most cases.

Studies done by the Geneva Emotion Research Group (Banse and Scherer 1996; Johnstone, Banse, and Scherer 1995) have looked at some of the emotional states that seem to be most easily confused in vocal expression. They suggest, for example, that the communication of disgust may not depend on acoustic parameters of the speech itself but on short sounds generated between utterances. In more recent work (Johnstone and Scherer 1999), they have collected both vocal and physiological data from computer users expressing authentic emotional responses to interactive tasks.

The body of experimental work on vocal expression indicates that arousal, or emotional intensity, is encoded fairly reliably in the average pitch and energy level of speech. This is consistent with the theoretical expectations of increased muscle tension in high arousal situations. Pitch range and speech rate also show correlations with emotional arousal, but these are less reliable indicators.

The communication of emotional valence through speech is a more complicated matter. While there are some interesting correlations with easily measured acoustic properties, particularly pitch range, complex variations in rhythm seem to play an important role in transmitting positive/negative distinctions. In spite of the widely recognized ability to "hear a smile," which Tartter (1980) related to formant shifts and speaker-dependent amplitude and duration changes, no reliable acoustic measurements of valence have been found. Roy and Pentland (1996) more recently performed a small study in which a discrimination network trained with samples from three speakers expressing imagined approval or disapproval was able to distinguish those cases with reliability comparable to human listeners. Thus, recognition of emotional valence from acoustic cues remains a possibility, but supplementary evidence from other modalities (especially observation of facial expression) will probably be necessary to achieve reliable results.

Our Bayesian subnetwork representing the effects of emotional valence and arousal on vocal expression therefore captures the trends that increasing arousal tends to generate higher average pitch, wider pitch range, faster speech, and higher speech energy. Similarly, as a speaker feels more positive valence, his or her speech will move toward a higher average pitch, with slightly wider pitch range, and higher speech energy.

7.6.5 Facial Expressions

As indicated in section 7.2.1, algorithms for the automatic recognition of facial expressions from visual input are under development in several research labs. Generally, these algorithms attempt to classify an expression into one of a small number of "standard" expressions: happiness, surprise, anger, and so forth. Our current network contains an "Expression" node relating Arousal, Valence, and Friendliness to seven expression types. The probability assessment for this node (7 by 27) is the most complex in our current network. Recent work by Kaiser and Wehrle (Kaiser, Wehrle, and Schmidt 1998; personal communication) suggests that relating individual facial features to emotional appraisal dimensions (e.g., brow height and novelty) may enable a decomposition of facial expressions in a fashion similar to our use of expressive styles for language.

7.6.6 Gesture and Posture

Our observations of body movements tell us a great deal about the personality and emotional state of others (Collier 1985). Emotional arousal is reflected in more frequent and faster body movements, although the highest levels of arousal can be immobilizing. Increasing arousal also produces less relaxed body posture.

Postures and gestures that increase accessibility to a conversational partner, such as leaning forward, directly orienting the body, and placing arms in an open position, tend to express a positive emotional state or friendly personality. A dominant personality is communicated by an upright ("confident") posture or by a relaxed, asymmetrical ("fearless") positioning of the body. Submissive personalities tend to adopt postures that minimize size, such as slouching or sitting.

These observations are sufficient to define the general trends of relationships between emotion and personality and between specific postures and gestures, such as slouching, folding the arms across the chest, and so forth. We have therefore included behavior nodes for gesture speed and size and for enumerations of specific psychologically significant gestures and postures. The resulting network can generate sequences of agent behaviors that convey the desired psychological state.

However, human conversations include a variety of face, hand, and body movements that play specific and significant roles in communication and in the maintenance and synchronization of the communication channel itself (Cassell, chap. 1). A conversational agent cannot produce a natural and comfortable interaction without properly generating these signals. The emotion and personality dimensions of body movement are best viewed as subtle background behaviors behind the gestures that carry more specific meaning.

This discussion suggests the difficulties that will confront attempts to decode gesture and posture from visual input. Indications of arousal based on the size, frequency, and speed of body movements will be the most approachable, with the recognition of more specific postures and gestures only becoming feasible as part of a system to comprehend nonverbal communicative behaviors.

7.7 Conclusion

We have constructed a Bayesian network that relates emotion and personality to observable behaviors, and have experimented informally with it to produce sequences of background behavior for an embodied agent. The sequences produced are intuitively plausible—for example, asserting that the agent is angry will produce adjusted distributions of behaviors that are more agitated and negative.

The choice of a Bayesian network representation has allowed us to create a highly intuitive and comprehensible model of a very complex collection of phenomena. Although we have only experimented with the recognition capabilities of the model using artificial sensory inputs, the symmetry between the generation and recognition processes leads us to believe that it will be a useful tool for synthesizing a coherent view of the user's emotions and personality.

One problem with the model as described above is that the simulated behaviors change immediately (and can vary widely) in response to changes in the agent's internal state. In order to produce more believable emotional transitions, we have designed an extended version of the network in which earlier states of the emotional nodes are represented explicitly. Thus the agent's level of excitement can depend on the previous arousal level as well as on the direct effects of external events. This modification promises to produce more gradual state changes in response to small events, while still allowing quick reactions to extreme stimuli.

Many challenges remain in the construction of embodied conversational agents that are both useful and communicatively competent. Once those challenges have been met and spoken interaction with an embodied agent becomes commonplace, we believe that the computer's social competence will be seen as a major factor influencing user satisfaction with conversational systems. The ability of an agent to recognize and respond appropriately to the personality and emotional state of the user will be a crucial prerequisite to building socially competent systems. We have shown that a single Bayesian network can represent a rich probabilistic model of many different behavioral manifestations of emotion and personality that is suitable for both recognition and synthesis of natural social interaction.

References

André, E., T. Rist, and J. Müller. 1998. Guiding the user through dynamically generated hypermedia presentations with a life-like character. In *Proceedings of the 1998 International Conference on Intelligent User Interfaces*, 21–28. New York: ACM Press.

Ark, W., D. C. Dryer, and D. J. Lu. 1999. The emotion mouse. In *Proceedings of the Eighth International Conference on Human Computer Interaction*. Stuttgart: University of Stuttgart.

Ball, G. 1997. The SpeakEasy dialogue controller. In *First International Workshop on Human-Computer Conversation*. Sheffield: University of Sheffield.

Ball, G., D. Ling, D. Kurlander, J. Miller, D. Pugh, et al. 1997. Lifelike computer characters: The persona project at Microsoft Research. In J. M. Bradshaw, ed., *Software agents*, 191–222. Menlo Park, Calif.: AAAI Press/The MIT Press.

Banse, R., and K. Scherer. 1996. Acoustic profiles in vocal emotion expression. *Journal of Personality and Social Psychology* 70(3):614–636.

Bates, J. 1994. The role of emotion in believable agents. *Communications of the ACM, Special Issue on Agents* 37(7):122–125.

Bates, J., A. B. Loyall, and W. S. Reilly. 1994. An architecture for action, emotion, and social behavior. In *Artificial Social Systems: Fourth European Workshop on Modeling Autonomous Agents in a Multi-Agent World*. Berlin: Springer-Verlag.

Cahn, J. E. 1989. *Generating expression in synthesized speech*. Master's thesis, Massachusetts Institute of Technology, Cambridge, Massachusetts.

Cañamero, D. 1997. Modeling motivations and emotions as a basis for intelligent behavior. In *Proceedings of the Conference on Autonomous Agents, AGENTS97*, 148–155. New York: ACM Press.

Collier, G. 1985. *Emotional expression*. Hillsdale, N.J.: Lawrence Erlbaum Associates.

Elliott, C. D. 1992. *The affective reasoner: A process model of emotions in a multi-agent system*. Ph.D. diss., Northwestern University, Evanston, Illinois.

El-Nasr, M. S., T. R. Ioerger, and J. Yen. 1999. In *Proceedings of the Third Annual Conference on Autonomous Agents, AGENTS99*, 9–15. New York: ACM Press.

Essa, I., and A. Pentland. 1995. Facial expression recognition using a dynamic model and motion energy. In *Proceedings of the International Conference on Computer Vision*, 360–367. Los Alamitos, Calif.: IEEE Computer Society.

Flanagan, J., T. Huang, P. Jones, and S. Kasif. 1997. *Final Report of the NSF Workshop on Human-Centered Systems: Information, interactivity, and intelligence*. Washington, D.C.: National Science Foundation.

Hayes-Roth, B., and R. van Gent. 1997. Story-making with improvisational puppets. In *Proceedings of the Conference on Autonomous Agents, AGENTS97*, 1–7. New York: ACM Press.

Heckerman, D. 1993. Causal independence for knowledge acquisition and inference. In *Proceedings of the 9th Conference on Uncertainty in Artificial Intelligence*, 122–127. San Francisco: Morgan Kaufmann.

Heckerman, D., J. Breese, and K. Rommelse. 1995. Troubleshooting under uncertainty. *Communications of the ACM* 38(3):49–57.

Horvitz, E., and M. Shwe. 1995. Melding Bayesian inference, speech recognition, and user models for effective handsfree decision support. In *Proceedings of the Symposium on Computer Applications in Medical Care*. Los Alamitos, Calif.: IEEE Computer Society.

Huang, X., A. Acero, F. Alleva, M. Y. Hwang, L. Jiang, et al. 1995. Microsoft Windows highly intelligent speech recognizer: Whisper. In *Proceedings of the IEEE International Conference on Acoustics, Speech, and Signal Processing*. Los Alamitos, Calif.: IEEE Computer Society.

Jensen, F. V. 1996. *An introduction to Bayesian networks*. New York: Springer-Verlag.

Jensen, F. V., S. L. Lauritzen, and K. G. Olesen. 1989. Bayesian updating in recursive graphical models by local computations. Report R89-15, Institute for Electronic Systems, Department of Mathematics and Computer Science, University of Aalborg, Denmark.

Johnstone, T., R. Banse, and K. R. Scherer. 1995. Acoustic profiles from prototypical vocal expressions of emotion. In *Proceedings of the 13th International Congress of Phonetic Sciences*, 4:2–5. Stockholm, Sweden: Royal Institute of Technology.

Johnstone, T., and K. R. Scherer. 1999. The effects of emotions on voice quality. In *Proceedings of the 14th International Congress of Phonetic Sciences*. Berkeley, Calif.: University of California.

Kaiser, S., T. Wehrle, and S. Schmidt. 1998. Emotional episodes, facial expression, and reported feelings in human-computer interactions. In A. H. Fischer, ed., *Proceedings of the 10th Conference of the International Society for Research on Emotions* (ISRE '98), 82–86. Würzburg: ISRE Publications.

Kitamura, T. 1998. An architecture of behavior selection grounding emotions. In *Grounding Emotions in Adaptive Systems*. Papers presented at a workshop held during the Fifth International Conference of the Society for Adaptive Behavior (SAB '98). Zurich, Switzerland: University of Zurich.

Klein, J., Y. Moon, and R. W. Picard. 1999. This computer responds to user frustration: Theory, design, results, and implications. TR-501, MIT Media Laboratory, Vision and Modeling Technical Group.

Kobayashi, H., and F. Hara. 1994. Analysis of the neural network recognition characteristics of 6 basic facial expressions. In *Proceedings of the IEEE International Workshop on Human and Robot Communication*, 222–227. Los Alamitos, Calif.: IEEE Computer Society.

Lang, P. 1995. The emotion probe: Studies of motivation and attention. *American Psychologist* 50(5):372–385.

Lester, J. C., L. S. Zettlemoyer, J. P. Grégoire, and W. H. Bares. 1999. Explanatory lifelike avatars: Performing user-centered tasks in 3D learning environments. In *Proceedings of the Third Annual Conference on Autonomous Agents*, AGENTS99, 24–31. New York: ACM Press.

Lisetti, C., D. Rumelhart, and M. Holler. 1998. An environment to acknowledge the interface between affect and cognition. In *Working Notes of the AAAI Spring Symposium Series: Intelligent Environments (SSS '98)*. Menlo Park, Calif.: AAAI Press.

Martinho, C., and A. Paiva. 1999. Pathematic agents: Rapid development of believable emotional agents in intelligent virtual environments. In *Proceedings of the Third Annual Conference on Autonomous Agents*, AGENTS99, 1–8. New York: ACM Press.

McCrae, R., and P. T. Costa. 1989. The structure of interpersonal traits: Wiggins's circumplex and the five factor model. *Journal of Personality and Social Psychology* 56(5):586–595.

Minsky, M. 1985. *The society of mind*. New York: Simon & Schuster.

Murray, I. R., and J. L. Arnott. 1993. Toward the simulation of emotion in synthetic speech: A review of the literature on human vocal emotion. *Journal of the Acoustical Society of America* 93(2):1097–1108.

Myers, I. B., and M. H. McCaulley. 1985. *Manual: A guide to the development and use of the Myers-Briggs Type Indicator*. Palo Alto, Calif.: Consulting Psychologists Press.

Nass, C., Y. Moon, B. Reeves, and C. Dryer. 1995. Can computer personalities be human personalities? *Journal of Human-Computer Studies* 43:223–239.

Ortony, A., G. L. Clore, and A. Collins. 1988. *The cognitive structure of emotions*. Cambridge: Cambridge University Press.

Osgood, C. E., G. J. Suci, and P. H. Tannenbaum. 1967. *The measurement of meaning*. Urbana: University of Illinois Press.

Pearl, J. 1991. *Probabilistic reasoning in intelligent systems: Networks of plausible inference*. Rev. 2d ed. San Mateo, Calif.: Morgan Kaufmann.

Perlin, K. 1997. Layered compositing of facial expression. SIGGRAPH'97 Technical Sketch. New York University Media Research Lab. Available: <http://mrl.nyu.edu/improv/sig97-sketch/>.

Perlin, K., and A. Goldberg. 1996. Improv: A system for scripting interactive actors in virtual worlds. In *SIGGRAPH '96. Proceedings of the 23rd Annual Conference on Computer Graphics*, 205–216. New York: ACM Press.

Petrushin, V. 1999. Informal software demonstration. User Modeling, UM99. Banff, Canada.

Picard, R. W. 1997. *Affective computing*. Cambridge, Mass.: The MIT Press.

———. 1998. Panel on affect and emotion in the user interface. In *Proceedings of the 1998 International Conference on Intelligent User Interfaces*, 91–94. New York: ACM Press.

Reeves, B., and C. Nass. 1995. *The media equation*. New York: CSLI Publications/Cambridge University Press.

Reilly, W. S. N. 1996. Believable social and emotional agents. Ph.D. diss., CMU-CS-96-138, School of Computer Science, Carnegie Mellon University, Pittsburgh, Pennsylvania.

Roy, D., and A. Pentland. 1996. Automatic spoken affect analysis and classification. In *Proceedings of the Second International Conference on Automatic Face and Gesture Recognition*, 363–367. Los Alamitos, Calif.: IEEE Computer Society.

Scherer, K. R. 1984. Emotion as a multicomponent process: A model and some cross-cultural data. *Review of Personality and Social Psychology* 5:37–63.

———. 1986. Vocal affect expression: A review and a model for future research. *Psychological Bulletin* 99(2):143–165.

Scherer, K. R., J. Koivumaki, and R. Rosenthal. 1972. Minimal cues in the vocal communication of affect: Judging emotions from content-masked speech. *Journal of Psycholinguistic Research* 1(3):269–285.

Stern, A., A. Frank, and B. Resner. 1998. Virtual Petz: A hybrid approach to creating autonomous, lifelike Dogz and Catz. In *Proceedings of the Second International Conference on Autonomous Agents, AGENTS98,* 334–335. New York: ACM Press.

Tartter, V. 1980. Happy talk: Perceptual and acoustic effects of smiling on speech. *Perception and Psychophysics* 27(1):24–27.

Trower, T. 1997. Microsoft Agent. Redmond, Wash.: Microsoft Corporation. Available: <http://www.microsoft.com/msagent>.

Velásquez, J., M. Fujita, and H. Kitano. 1998. An open architecture for emotion and behavior control of autonomous agents. In *Proceedings of the Second International Conference on Autonomous Agents, AGENTS98,* 473–474. New York: ACM Press.

Walker, M. A., J. E. Cahn, and S. J. Whittaker. 1996. Linguistic style improvisation for lifelike computer characters. In *Proceedings of the Conference on Autonomous Agents, AGENTS97,* 96–105. New York: ACM Press.

The Automated Design of Believable Dialogues for Animated Presentation Teams

Elisabeth André, Thomas Rist, Susanne van Mulken,

Martin Klesen, and Stephan Baldes

8.1 Introduction

During the last few years, an increasing number of attempts have been made to develop systems that are able to generate presentations automatically. The aim to generate presentation variants on the fly to accommodate for different purposes and user needs is a driving force behind these developments. The availability of multiple media offers the choice between media as well as the possibility to compose media combinations that convey information in a more intelligible and appealing way. The output of such presentation systems comprises mere replications of illustrated texts laid out on a computer screen, but also multimedia documents with timed media, such as video and audio clips, and hypertext-style documents.

Trying to deploy the repertoire of skills of human presenters, some R&D projects have begun to use animated characters (or agents) in presentation tasks. Based on either cartoon drawings, recorded video images of persons, or 3-D body models, presentation agents enrich the repertoire of available presentation styles. For instance, consider the presentation of research results at a conference. Even though a slide show, a video clip, or a poster may contain all the relevant information, the presence of a skilled speaker in addition to well-prepared presentation material is usually much more appealing. A potential strength of animated characters is their ability to convey nonverbal conversational signals that are difficult to communicate in traditional media.

In this chapter, we investigate a new style for presenting information. We introduce the notion of presentation teams which—rather than addressing the user directly—convey information in the style of performances to be observed by the user. The chapter is organized as follows. First, we report on our experience with two single animated presentation agents and explain how to evaluate their success. After that, we move to presentation teams and discuss their potential benefits for presentation tasks. In section 8.2, we describe the basic steps of our approach to the automated generation of performances with multiple characters. This approach has been applied to two different scenarios: sales dialogues and soccer commentary that are presented in sections 8.3 and 8.4, respectively. Section 8.5 discusses early impressions gained from informal tests that have been conducted for the two applications. A comparison to related work is given in section 8.6. Section 8.7 provides a conclusion and an outlook on future research.

8.1.1 Animated Presentations with Embodied Conversational Characters

Our work has concentrated on the development of animated presenters that show, explain, and verbally comment on textual and graphical output on a window-based interface. The first project we conducted in this area was the PPP (Personalized Plan-Based Presenter) project that generated multimedia help instructions presented by an animated agent, the so-called PPP persona (André and Rist 1996). The overall behavior of the presentation agent is determined partly by a *script* and partly by the agent's *self behavior*. Presentation scripts specify the presentation acts to be carried out as well as their temporal coordination. For example, a script may instruct the character to point to an object in an illustration and explain its function. While a script is an external behavior determinant that is specified outside the character, our characters also have an internal behavior determinant resulting in what we call self behavior. A character's self behavior comprises not only gestures that are necessary to execute the script but also navigation acts, idle time gestures, and immediate reactions to events occurring in the user interface. Note that the borderline between scripted behavior and self behavior is a matter of the degree of abstraction. The more detailed a script is in prescribing what a character should do, the less need there is to equip a character with a rich repertoire of reasonable self behaviors.

In the AiA project (Adaptive Communication Assistant for Effective Infobahn Access), we developed a number of personalized information assistants that facilitate user access to the Web (André, Rist, and Müller 1999) by providing orientation assistance in a dynamically expanding navigation space. These assistants are characterized by their ability to retrieve relevant information, reorganize it, encode it in different media (such as text, graphics, and animation), and present it to the user as a multimedia presentation. The novelty of PPP and AiA are that the presentation scripts for the characters and the hyperlinks between the single presentation parts are not stored in advance but generated automatically from preauthored document fragments and items stored in a knowledge base.

Reasons to embody the assistants were, among others, (1) that it might ease conveying particular types of information in an unobtrusive way (e.g., gestures; conversational and emotional signals) and (2) that it might have the conjectured *persona effect* (Lester et al. 1997)—that is, the presence of a *persona* might have a positive effect on the user's attitudes and experience of the interaction (for a critical review, see Dehn and van Mulken 1999).

To investigate whether this effect indeed holds if we compare persona conditions with no-persona conditions and to see whether it extends to objective measures rather than just subjective measures, we performed a psychological experiment. In this experiment, we tested the effect of the presence of our PPP persona with respect to the user's understanding, recall, and attitudes. Twenty-eight subjects were shown Web-based presentations with two different types of content. In the experimental condition, a speaking and gesturing PPP persona made the presentations. In the control condition, the (audiovisual) information presented was exactly the same, except that there was no persona and pointing arrows replaced all gesturing. After the presentations, the subjects were asked comprehension and recall questions and subsequently provided with a questionnaire that measured their attitudes regarding the system and PPP persona. Statistical analyses of the results showed that there was no effect on comprehension or recall. However, analysis of the data on the subjects' attitudes indeed revealed a significant positive effect of persona. Subjects who had seen presentations guided by persona indicated on a questionnaire that they found the presentations themselves and the corresponding tests less difficult than subjects who had seen presentations without persona. In addition, subjects found these presentations significantly more entertaining (van Mulken, André, and Müller 1998).

In a follow-up study, we investigated whether the subjective persona-effect could be found to extend even toward an increased trustworthiness of the information presented by a lifelike character. In this study, subjects had to perform a navigation task. Subjects were in turn assisted in navigation by one of four agents: one was invisible and merely gave textual recommendations as to how to proceed with the task; the second presented these recommendations acoustically; the third was a speaking cartoon-style agent; and the fourth was a speaking agent based on video images of a real person. In the text and audio conditions, reference to a recommended path was accompanied by a highlighting of the corresponding parts of the navigation tree. In the conditions with an agent, such a reference was accompanied by pointing gestures. We hypothesized that the embodied agents would appear more convincing or believable and that the subjects would therefore follow the agents' recommendations more readily.

This hypothesis, however, was not supported by the data. We found numerical differences only in the expected direction: the proportion of recommendations actually followed by the subjects dropped off going from video-based to cartoon-style, audio, and text agents (for further details, see van Mulken, André, and Müller 1999). These findings suggest, among other things, that merely embodying an interface agent may not be enough: to come across as trustworthy, one may need to model the agent more deeply—for instance, by giving it personality. We return to this issue later.

8.1.2 From a Single Presenter to Presentation Teams

Often, systems that use presentation agents rely on settings in which the agent addresses the user directly, as if it were a face-to-face conversation between human beings. For example, an agent may serve as a personal guide or assistant in information spaces (as in AiA), it can be a user's personal consultant or tutor, or it may represent a virtual shop assistant who tries to convince an individual customer. Such a setting seems appropriate for a number of applications that draw on a distinguished agent-user relationship. However, other situations exist in which the emulation of direct agent-to-user communication is not necessarily the most effective way to present information. Empirical evidence suggests that, at least in some situations, indirect interaction can have a positive effect on the user's performance. For example, Craig and colleagues found that, in tutoring sessions, users who overheard dialogues between virtual tutors and tutees, subsequently asked significantly more questions and also memorized the information significantly better (Craig et al. 1999, experiment 1).

Along the lines of Alpert, Singley, and Caroll (1999), who use multiple agents to impose a visible and enacted structure on the instructional material presented, we hypothesize that placing such a structure on the presentation may help users organize the information conveyed. Imposing an organizational structure on the material presented has been shown to facilitate the assimilation of new information with related prior knowledge (Bower et al. 1969). In addition, such organization deepens processing and makes the information easier to remember (Ornstein and Trabasso 1974). The individual personified members of a presentation team could serve as visual indices that might help the user in a sort of cued recall.

With regard to presentation design, a team of presenters enriches the repertoire of possible communication strategies. For example, they allow the conveyance of certain relationships among information units in a more canonical way. Among other things, this benefits decision support systems where the user has to be informed about different and incompatible points of view, pairs of arguments and counterarguments, or alternative conclusions and suggestions. For solving such presentation tasks, it seems natural to structure presentations according to argumentative and rhetorical strategies common in real dialogues with two or more conversational partners. For instance, a debate between two characters representing contrary opinions is an effective means of informing an audience of the pros and cons of an issue.

In addition, embodied presentation teams can serve as rhetorical devices that allow for a reinforcement of beliefs. For example, they enable us to repeat the same piece of information in a less monotonous and perhaps more convincing manner simply by employing different agents to convey it. Furthermore, in an empirical study, Nass and colleagues showed that subjects who watched news and entertainment segments on different TVs rated them higher in quality than news and entertainment segments shown on just one TV (Nass, Reeves, and Leshner 1996). We suppose that such effects may even be reinforced if information is distributed onto several agents that represent different specialists.

Finally, programs on TV demonstrate how information can be conveyed in an appealing manner by multiple presenters with complementary characters and role castings. This presentation style is used heavily in advertisement clips and infotainment/edutainment that try to combine information presentation with entertainment. In contrast to TV presentations, however, the generation of performances on a computer system allows to take into account particular information needs and preferences of the individual user.

The observations above encouraged us to investigate scenarios in which the user observes (or overhears) a dialogue between several lifelike characters. A necessary requirement for the success of such presentations is that the agents come across as socially believable individuals with their own distinct personalities and emotions (cf. Bates 1994). The manual scripting of such dialogues is, however, not flexible enough to adapt presentations to the specific needs of an audience on the fly. Therefore, our work concentrates on the development of a generative mechanism that allows for the automated design of believable dialogues.

8.2 Designing Presentation Dialogues: Basic Steps

Given a certain discourse purpose and a set of information units to be presented, we determine an appropriate dialogue type, define roles for the characters involved, recruit concrete characters with personality profiles that go together with the assigned roles, and, finally, work out the details of the individual dialogue turns and have the characters perform them.

8.2.1 Dialogue Types and Character Roles

The structure of a performance is predetermined by the choice of a certain dialogue type. Various types of dialogues exist including debates, panel discussions, chats, interviews, consultation, sales, brokering, and tutoring dialogues. Which one to adopt depends on the overall presentation goal. In this chapter, we concentrate on scenarios common in TV transmissions: sales dialogues and chats about jointly watched sport events.

Once a certain dialogue type has been chosen, we need to define the roles to be occupied by the characters. Most dialogue types induce certain constraints on the required roles. For instance, in a debate on a certain subject matter, there is at least a proponent and an opponent role to be filled. In a sales scenario, we need at least a seller and a customer.

The next step is the casting of the designated roles. To generate effective performances with believable dialogues, we cannot simply copy an existing character. Rather, characters have to be realized as distinguishable individuals with their own areas of expertise, interest profiles, personalities, and audiovisual appearance, taking into account their specific task in a given context.

When talking about a character's personality and affective state, we adopt the view of Moffat, who contends that "personality is consistent reactive bias within the fringe of functionality" (1997, 134). Psychologists have attempted to characterize personality by traits, relying on the statistical method of factor analysis to group words, commonly used to describe people, into chief organizing themes. The use of this technique has led to the consensus that five major factors or dimensions account for most of the variation in human personality. Although different researchers use slightly different terms for them, they can be summarized as *open, conscientious, extrovert, agreeable,* and *neurotic* (McCrae and John 1992).

Closely related to personality is the concept of emotion. Emotions are often characterized as "valenced reactions to events, agents, or objects, with their particular nature being determined by the way in which the eliciting situation is construed" (Ortony, Clore, and Collins 1988, 13). Moffat differentiates between personality and emotion by using the two dimensions *duration* and *focus*. Whereas personality remains stable over a long period of time, emotions are short-lived. Moreover, while emotions are focused on particular events or objects, factors determining personality are more diffuse and indirect.

A further important component of a character's profile is its audiovisual appearance. Empirical evidence for this is, for instance, provided by Dryer who presented subjects with a set of animated characters to measure their perception of the characters' personality. He found that characters perceived as extroverted and agreeable tend to be represented by rounder shapes, bigger faces, and happier expressions while characters perceived as extroverted and disagreeable were typically represented through bold colors, big bodies, and erect postures (Dryer 1999).

8.2.2 Generation of Dialogue Contributions

After a team of presenters has been recruited, a performance is generated. As in our earlier work on presentation planning, we follow a communication-theoretic view and consider the generation of simulated dialogues a plan-based activity. However, to account for presentations given by a character team, a number of extensions have become necessary.

In André and Rist (1996), we argued that a presentation system should clearly distinguish between the creation of material and its presentation. Consequently, we refined the notion of a communicative act by differentiating between *acquisition* and *presentation* acts. While acquisition acts, such as designing a graphical illustration or retrieving it from a database, contribute to the contents of a conversation, presentation acts, such as showing the illustration to an audience, refer to its communicative function. In the scenarios presented in this chapter, the user is not addressed directly. Instead, information is conveyed implicitly by a dialogue between several characters to be observed by the user. To account for the new communicative situation, we have to extend our previous communication model by introducing dialogue acts, such as *responding to a question* or *making a turn*, which refer to the interaction between the individual agents.

A further level of complexity arises from the fact that information is no longer simply allocated to just one agent, but instead distributed over the members of a presentation team whose activities have to be coordinated. To accomplish this task, we are investigating the following two approaches:

- *Agents with Scripted Behaviors:* In this approach, the system takes the role of a producer that generates a script for the agents that become the actors of a play. The script specifies the dialogue and presentation acts to be carried out as well as their temporal coordination. Since the script writer has almost complete control over all actors, this approach facilitates the generation of coherent dialogues. On the other hand, it requires that all the information to be communicated is a priori known by the script writer. Consequently, it is less suitable in situations where the actors have to immediately respond to events at presentation runtime, such as reactions from the audience. From a technical point of view, this approach may be realized by a central planning component that decomposes a complex presentation goal into elementary dialogue and presentation acts that are allocated to the individual agents. Knowledge concerning the decomposition process is then realized by operators of the planning component.

- *Autonomous Actors:* In this approach, the individual agents have their own communicative goals that they try to achieve. That is, there is no external script for the agents. Rather, both the determination and assignment of dialogue contributions is handled by the agents themselves. To accomplish this task, each agent has a repertoire of dialogue strategies at its disposal. However, since the agents have only limited knowledge concerning what other agents may do or say next, this approach puts much higher demands on the agents' reactive capabilities. Furthermore, it is much more difficult to ensure the coherence of the dialogue. Think of two people giving a talk together without clarifying in advance who is going to explain what. From a technical point of view, this approach may be realized by a distributed system with multiple reactive planners. The agents' dialogue strategies are then realized as operators of the individual planners.

Depending on their role and personality, characters may pursue completely different goals. For instance, a customer in a sales situation usually tries to get information on a certain product in order to make a decision, while the seller aims at presenting this product in a positive light. To generate believable dialogues, we have to ensure that the assigned dialogue contributions do not conflict with the character's goal. Furthermore, characters may apply very different dialogue strategies to achieve their goals depending on their personality and emotions. For instance, in contrast to an extrovert agent, an introvert agent will be less likely to take the initiative in a dialogue and exhibit a more passive behavior. Finally, what an agent is able to say depends on its area of expertise. Both the central and the distributed planning approach allow us to consider the character's profile by treating it as an additional filter during the selection and instantiation of dialogue strategies. For instance, we may define specific dialogue strategies for characters of a certain personality and formulate constraints that restrict their applicability.

Even if the agents have to strictly follow a script as in the script-based approach, there is still room for improvisation at performance time. In particular, a script leaves open how to render the dialogue contributions. Here, we have to consider both the contents and the communicative function of an utterance. For instance, utterances would be rendered differently depending on whether they are statements or warnings. To come across as believable, agents with a different personality should not only differ in their high-level dialogue behaviors but also perform elementary dialogue acts in a character-specific way. According to empirical studies, extrovert characters use more direct and powerful phrases than do introvert characters (Furnham 1990), speak louder and faster (Scherer 1979), and use more expansive gestures (Gallaher 1992). Furthermore, the rendering of dialogue acts depends on an agent's emotional state. Effective means of conveying a character's emotions include body gestures, acoustic realization, and facial expressions (see Collier 1985 for an overview of studies on emotive expression).

To consider these factors, the planner(s) enhances the input of the animation module and the speech synthesizer with additional instructions, for instance, in an XML-based markup language.

8.3 Inhabited Marketplace

As a first example, we address the generation of animated sales dialogues that was inspired by Jameson et al. (1995) and Mehlmann et al. (1998). For the graphical realization of this scenario, we use the Microsoft Agent™ package (Microsoft 1999) that includes a programmable interface to four predefined characters: Genie, Robby, Peedy, and Merlin. Since the use of these characters might lead to wrong implications in car sales scenarios, we are currently designing our own characters whose visual appearance better fits the agents' role in such scenarios.

Figure 8.1 shows a dialogue between Merlin as a car seller and Genie and Robby as buyers. Genie has uttered some concerns about the high running costs, which Merlin tries to play down. From the point of view of the system, the presentation goal is to provide the observer with facts about a certain car.

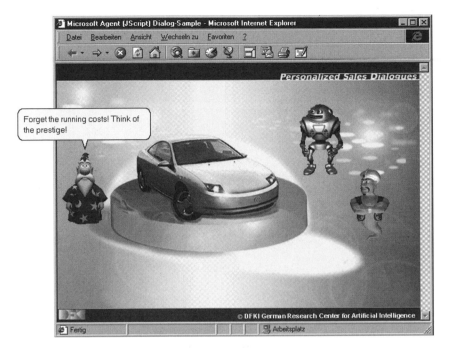

Figure 8.1
Screen shot of the inhabited marketplace.

However, the presentation is not just a mere enumeration of the plain facts about the car. Rather, the facts are presented along with an evaluation under consideration of the observer's interest profile in value dimensions, such as safety, sportiness, comfort, and economy, that are important to him or her (see sec. 8.3.2). Our system is neutral in so far that it presents positive as well as negative facts about the product.

8.3.1 Character Profiles

To enable experiments with different character settings, the user has the possibility of choosing three out of the four characters and assigning roles to them. For instance, he or she may have Merlin appear in the role of a seller or buyer. Furthermore, he or she may assign to each character certain interests in value dimensions which may reflect his or her own interests (see fig. 8.2). Our system

Select the agents and their personality:

Genie

Merlin

Peedy

Robby

SELLER Genie ▾		BUYER1 Peedy ▾		BUYER2 Merlin ▾	
Agreeableness	**Extraversion**	**Agreeableness**	**Extraversion**	**Agreeableness**	**Extraversion**
⦿ agreeable	○ extravert	○ agreeable	○ extravert	⦿ agreeable	⦿ extravert
○ neutral	○ neutral	○ neutral	○ neutral	○ neutral	○ neutral
○ disagreeable	⦿ introvert	⦿ disagreeable	⦿ introvert	○ disagreeable	○ introvert

Figure 8.2
Role casting interface for the car sales scenario.

allows for two operating modes. In the first mode, the system (or a human author) chooses the appropriate character settings for an audience. In the second mode, it allows the audience to test various character settings itself. The potential benefits of this mode will be discussed further in section 8.5.

Personality dimensions may be set by the user as well. As mentioned in section 8.2.1, personality traits can be reduced to five big dimensions. Two of them seem to be most important for social interaction (cf. Nass, Isbister, and Lee, chap. 13). Therefore, we have decided to model these two personality factors:

- *Extroversion* with these possible values: extrovert, neutral, or introvert
- *Agreeableness* with these possible values: agreeable, neutral, or disagreeable

In this version of the sales scenario, we concentrated on one dimension of emotive response, namely valence (Lang 1995). It has the following values: positive, neutral, and negative. In our scenarios, emotions are essentially driven by the occurrence of events. The events in the sales scenario are the speech acts of the dialogue participants that are evaluated by the characters in terms of their role, personality traits, and individual goals (see sec. 8.2.1). The goals, in particular, determine the desirability of events; for example, a buyer will be displeased if he is told that a relevant attribute of a car (e.g., electric window lifters) is missing for a dimension that is important to him (e.g., comfort). In this scenario, we do not deal with emotion structures and emotion generating rules explicitly (e.g., see Elliott 1992) but rather connect the scenario-specific dialogue acts (e.g., DiscussValue, PositiveResponse, InformIf) to the relevant animation sequences and utterance templates by using the current internal state of the character as an additional constraint in the behavior selection mechanism, as described in the next section. This approach is similar to that of Lester and colleagues (Lester et al., chap. 5), where pedagogical speech acts drive the selection and sequencing of emotive behaviors.

8.3.2 Source, Structure, and Representation of the Information to Be Communicated

Part of the domain knowledge is an ordinary product database, organized in the form of an n-dimensional attribute vector per product. In this scenario, the products are cars with attributes, such as model type, maximum speed, horsepower, fuel consumption, price, air conditioning, electric window lifters, and airbag type. Thus, to a large extent, the contents of the database determine what an agent can say about a product. However, the mere enumeration of product attributes would not make an appealing sales presentation, especially if it gets long-winded, as in the case of complex products like cars. Furthermore, products and their attributes described in a technical language run the risk of sounding unfamiliar to the user. It seems much more appropriate to have a further description of the products that reflects the impact of the product attributes on the value dimensions of potential customers.

Such an approach can be modeled in the framework of multi-attribute utility theory (von Winterfeldt and Edwards 1986) and has already been used for the identification of customer profiles in an electronic marketplace for used cars (Mehlmann et al. 1998). In this project, a large German/American car producer and retailer provided the car database, whereas the value dimensions for the product "car" were adopted from a study of the German car market (Spiegel-Verlag 1993) that suggests that safety, economy, comfort, sportiness, prestige, and family and environmental friendliness are the most relevant. In addition, we represent how difficult it is to infer such implications. For instance, high gas consumption has a negative impact on economy, and this relationship is relatively easy to infer.

In this chapter, however, we do not address the question of how to build up and refine profiles based on the dialogue contributions of real customers interacting with the system. Rather, for the sake of simplicity, we assign to the characters a particular interest in one or several value dimensions before the planning of the agent's dialogue contributions starts, or we ask the user to do so. The user's assignments are interpreted by the system as an indication of his or her own interests. Furthermore, we use a more simplified model representing the implications of attribute values on the agent's value dimensions and for representing how difficult it is to infer them. Figure 8.3 shows an excerpt of the represented domain knowledge used for the generation of the car sales performances. It lists the value and the implications of the attribute "consumption." For instance, the attribute "consumption" of "car-1" has a negative impact on the dimensions "environment" and "running costs," an implication that is not difficult to infer. The impact on the dimension "prestige" is positive, but this relationship is less obvious.

8.3.3 Design of Product Information Dialogues

To automatically generate product information dialogues, we use a central planning component that decomposes a complex goal into more elementary goals. The result of this process is a dialogue script that represents the dialogue acts to be executed by the individual agents as well as their temporal order. Knowledge concerning the generation of scripts is represented by means of plan operators. An example is listed in figure 8.4.

The operator represents a scenario where two agents discuss a feature of an object. It only applies if the feature has a negative impact on any dimension and if this relationship can be easily inferred. According to the operator, any disagreeable buyer produces a negative comment referring to this dimension (NegativeResponse). The negative comment is followed by a response from the seller (ResponseNegativeResp).

One possible response is listed in figure 8.5. It only applies if there is an attribute that has a positive impact on the dimension under discussion. In this case, the seller first tells the buyer(s) that it disagrees and then lists attributes with a positive impact on the dimension. Note that our plan operators include both the propositional contents of an utterance and its communicative function. This is in line with Cassell and colleagues, who regard conversational behaviors as fulfilling propositional and interactional conversational functions (Cassell et al., chap. 2). For instance, we explicitly represent that "Bad for the" $dimension "?" is a response to a negative comment.

```
FACT attribute "car-1" "ccar1";

FACT type "ccar1" "consumption";

FACT value "ccar1" 8;

FACT polarity "ccar1" "environment" "neg";

FACT difficulty "ccar1" "environment" "low";

FACT polarity "ccar1" "prestige" "pos";

FACT difficulty "ccar1" "prestige" "medium";

FACT polarity "ccar1" "running costs" "neg";

FACT difficulty "ccar1" "running costs" "low";
```

Figure 8.3

Excerpt of the domain knowledge: Value and implications of the attribute "consumption" (coded as "ccar1").

```
NAME: "DiscussValue1"

GOAL: PERFORM DiscussValue $attribute;

PRECONDITION:

FACT polarity $attribute $dimension "neg";

FACT difficulty $attribute $dimension "low";

FACT Buyer $buyer;

FACT Disagreeable $buyer;

FACT Seller $seller;

BODY:

PERFORM NegativeResponse $buyer $dimension;

PERFORM ResponseNegativeResp $seller $attribute $dimension;
```

Figure 8.4

Example of a plan operator for discussing an attribute value.

The Automated Design of Believable Dialogues for Animated Presentation Teams

```
NAME: "ResponseNegativeResponse2"

GOAL:

PERFORM ResponseNegativeResp $agent $attribute $dimension;

PRECONDITION:

FACT Polarity $attribute $dimension "pos";

BODY:

PERFORM Respond $agent (+ "Bad for the " $dimension "?");

PERFORM EnumeratePos $agent $dimension;
```

Figure 8.5
Example of a plan operator for responding to a negative comment.

Our approach allows us to interleave character and dialogue act selection. For instance, in the operator in figure 8.4, characters are selected by instantiating the variable bindings with characters that satisfy the constraints.

The implementation of the planning approach is based on the Java™-based JAM agent architecture (Huber 1999). The outcome of the planning process is an HTML file that includes control sequences for the Microsoft characters. The performances can be played in the Microsoft Internet Explorer. Since the Microsoft Agent™ Programming tool does not allow for detailed intonational markups, we do not convey emotions by acoustic realization in this scenario.

8.3.4 What About This Car? Two Generation Examples
In what follows, we present two examples that illustrate how the agents' personality and interest profiles influence the contents and the structure of the sales dialogue. For expository reasons, we use extreme parameter settings here, so that differences in behavior are readily distinguishable.

```
Genie:
    Role: seller;
    Personality factors: agreeable, extrovert;
    Interests: environmental issues
```

```
Peedy:
    Role: customer;
    Personality factors: disagreeable, extrovert;
    Interests: economy
Merlin:
    Role: customer;
    Personality factors: agreeable, introvert;
    Interests: comfort
```

The conversations are based on just a few dialogue strategies. Essentially, each agent asks about the values of features that might have an impact—positive or negative—on a dimension it is interested in. After that, the value of this attribute is discussed.

```
Genie:
Hello, I'm Genie. What can I do for you?
    ;;; starts the conversation because it is
    ;;; extrovert
Peedy:
We're interested in this car.
    ;;; responds to the question because it is
    ;;; extrovert
Genie:
This is a very environment-friendly car.
    ;;; provides a summary by emphasizing the
    ;;; dimension "environment" that is most
    ;;; important to him. here, the default assumption
    ;;; is that the buyers have the same interests
    ;;; as the seller
It has a catalytic converter. It is made of recyclable material.
    ;;; provides evidence by listing all features
    ;;; which have a positive impact on the dimension
    ;;; "environment"
Peedy:
How much gas does it consume?
    ;;; starts asking a question because it is
    ;;; extrovert, wants to know more about gas
```

    ;;; consumption because this feature has an impact
    ;;; on the dimension "economy," which is important
    ;;; to him
Genie:
It consumes 8 liters per 100 km.
    ;;; retrieves the value from the car database
Peedy:
I'm worrying about the running costs.
    ;;; the value of the attribute "gas consumption"
    ;;; has a negative impact on "economy"
    ;;; Peedy is disagreeable and therefore makes a
    ;;; negative comment
Genie:
Forget the running costs. Think of the prestige.
    ;;; tries to distract the buyers by mentioning any
    ;;; positive implication. "prestige" has been
    ;;; chosen since there is no other easier-to-
    ;;; infer positive implication
Peedy:
How much does it cost?
    ;;; requests more information on a second
    ;;; attribute that has an impact on "economy"
Genie:
It costs 50000 dollars.
    ;;; retrieves the value of the attribute "cost of
    ;;; purchase" from the database
Peedy:
That's rather expensive.
    ;;; negative impact on "economy"
Genie:
Consider what a nice car you get for it.
    ;;; tries to play down the negative comment
Merlin:
Does it have electric window lifters?
    ;;; Merlin is interested in the dimension
    ;;; "comfort" and the attribute "electric window
    ;;; lifters" has an impact on this dimension

```
Genie:
```
No.
```
   ;;; retrieves the value of the attribute "electric
   ;;; window lifters" from the database
Peedy:
```
Well, a bit more comfort wouldn't hurt.
```
   ;;; the value of the attribute "electric window
   ;;; lifters" has a negative impact on the
   ;;; dimension "comfort"
Merlin:
```
Could you please tell me more about its interior?
```
   ;;; asks after the interior because this attribute
   ;;; has an impact on comfort which is important to
   ;;; him
Genie:
```
It has a spacious interior.
```
   ;;; retrieves the value of the attribute
   ;;; "interior" from the database
Peedy:
```
<scratches its head>.
```
   ;;; would like to say something negative, but
   ;;; there is no dimension on which the attribute
   ;;; "interior" has a negative impact
Merlin:
```
Good!
```
   ;;; the value of the attribute "interior" has a
   ;;; positive impact on comfort, Merlin is
   ;;; introvert, but since Peedy doesn't say
   ;;; anything, Merlin makes a comment
   ...
```

The second dialogue is based on the same dialogue strategies and knowledge bases. However, we assign the roles for the seller and the buyers to different agents. Furthermore, we modify the agents' interest profile and personality.

```
Robby:
   Role: seller;
```

```
     Personality factors: agreeable, extrovert;
     Interests: sportiness
Peedy:
     Role: customer;
     Personality factors: disagreeable, introvert;
     Interests: environmental issues
Merlin:
     Role: customer;
     Personality factors: agreeable, extrovert;
     Interests: safety
```

Robby:

Hello, I'm Robby. What can I do for you?

```
   ;;; starts the conversation because it is
   ;;; extrovert
```

Merlin:

We're interested in this car.

```
   ;;; responds to the question because it is
   ;;; extrovert
```

Robby:

This is a very sporty car.

```
   ;;; provides a summary by emphasizing
   ;;; "sportiness," which is most important to him
```

It can drive 100 miles per hour.

```
   ;;; provides evidence by listing features which
   ;;; have a positive impact on "sportiness"
```

Merlin:

Does it have air bags?

```
   ;;; starts asking questions because it is
   ;;; extrovert and requests more information on an
   ;;; attribute that has an impact on safety
```

Robby:

Sure!

```
   ;;; retrieves the value of the attribute "air
   ;;; bags" from the database
```

Merlin:

Excellent!

```
;;; positive impact on the dimension "safety"
```
Does it have anti-lock brakes?
```
    ;;; requests more information on a second
    ;;; attribute with impact on safety
```
Robby:
Of course!
```
    ;;; retrieves the value of the attribute "anti-
    ;;; lock brakes" from the database
```
Merlin:
Wonderful!
```
    ;;; positive impact on the dimension "safety"
```
Peedy:
How much gas does it consume?
```
    ;;; wants to know more about gas consumption
    ;;; because this feature has an impact on
    ;;; "environment," which is important to him
```
Robby:
It consumes 8 liters per 100 km.
```
    ;;; retrieves the value from the car database
```
Peedy:
Isn't that bad for the environment?
```
    ;;; the value of the attribute "gas consumption"
    ;;; has a negative impact on "environment,"
    ;;; less direct speech since it is introvert
```
Robby:
Bad for the environment?
```
    ;;; questions negative impact
```
It has a catalytic converter. It is made of recyclable material.
```
    ;;; provides counterarguments
    ...
```

The two dialogues partially discuss the same car attributes, but from different points of view. For instance, in both cases, one of the buyers criticizes the high gas consumption of the car. But in the first case, it is concerned about the high costs, while, in the second case, it is thinking of the environment. According to the applied strategies, the dialogues terminate after all relevant attributes of the car under consideration have been discussed.

The Automated Design of Believable Dialogues for Animated Presentation Teams

8.4 Gerd and Matze Commenting on RoboCup Soccer Games

The second application for our work on multiple presentation agents is Rocco II, an automated live report system for the simulator league of RoboCup, the Robot World-Cup Soccer. Figure 8.6 shows a screen shot of the system that was taken during a typical session. In the upper window, a previously recorded game is played back while being commented on by two soccer fans: Gerd and Matze sitting on a sofa. Unlike the agents of our sales scenario, Gerd and Matze have been designed specially for soccer commentary. Furthermore, this application is based on our own Java™-based Persona Engine (André, Rist, and Müller 1999).

8.4.1 Character Profiles

Apart from being smokers and beer drinkers, Gerd and Matze are characterized by their sympathy for a certain team, their level of extroversion (extrovert, neutral, or introvert) and openness (open, neutral, not open). As in the previous application, these values may be interactively changed. Following Ball and Breese (chap. 7), we decided to focus on the following two emotional dispositions: arousal with the values calm, neutral, and excited and valence with the values positive, neutral, and negative. Both seem useful in characterizing important aspects of a soccer spectator's emotional state.

Emotions are influenced by the current state of the game. For instance, both agents get excited if the ball approaches one of the goals and calm down again in phases of little activity on the field. An agent is pleased if the team it supports performs a successful action and displeased if it fails.

8.4.2 Source, Structure, and Representation of the Information to Be Communicated

Rocco II concentrates on the RoboCup simulator league, which involves software agents only (as opposed to the real robot leagues). Thus, the soccer games being commented on are not observed visually. Rather, the system obtains its basic input from the Soccer Server (Kitano et al. 1997), which delivers player location and orientation (for all players), ball location, game score, and play modes (such as throw-ins and goal kicks). Based on these data, Rocco's incremental event recognition component performs a higher-level analysis of the scene in order to recognize conceptual units at a higher level of abstraction, such as spatial relations or typical motion patterns. Recognized events are internally represented by instantiations of case frames which indicate the event type, the involved objects as well as time and location of the occurrence. The

Figure 8.6
Commentator team Gerd and Matze.

interpretation results of the time-varying scene, together with the original input data, provide the required basic material for Gerd's and Matze's commentary (André, Herzog, and Rist 1997).

8.4.3 Generation of Live Reports for Commentator Teams
Since Gerd and Matze comment on a rapidly changing environment, they have to produce speech utterances on the fly. In such situations, no global organization of the presentation is possible. Instead, the commentators need to respond immediately to incoming data. Furthermore, they have to meet severe time

constraints imposed by the flow of the game. They have to decide whether to utter short telegram-style phrases or provide more detailed descriptions according to the situation. In some cases, it might even be necessary for the commentators to interrupt themselves. For example, if an important event (e.g., a goal kick) occurs, utterances should be interrupted to communicate the new event as soon as possible.

Unlike the agents in the car sales scenario, Gerd and Matze have been realized as (semi-)autonomous agents. That is, each agent is triggered by events occurring in the scene or by dialogue contributions of the other agent. Interactions in this scenario are based on less complex dialogue strategies than the sales scenario. In most cases, the goal of the commentators is to inform the viewer about ongoing events which can be usually realized by a sequence of event descriptions.

As in the previous application, we rely on a template-based natural language generator. That is, language is generated by selecting templates consisting of strings and variables that will be instantiated with natural language references to objects retrieved from the domain knowledge base or delivered by a nominal phrase generator. To obtain a rich repertoire of templates, extensive studies of the soccer language have been necessary. Since most studies of the soccer terminology concentrate on newspaper reports (Frank 1997), we decided to perform our own corpus analysis and transcribed and annotated 13.5 hours of TV soccer reports in English. Inspired by Hovy (1987), we associate with each template the following linguistic features:

- *Verbosity:* The verbosity of a template depends on the number of words it contains.
- *Specificity:* The specificity of a template depends on the number of verbalized slots of the case frames and the specificity of the natural language expression chosen for the event type.
- *Force:* We distinguish between forceful, normal, and hesitant language. Forceful language is energetic and contains strong and confident phrases. Hesitant language is characterized by an increased number of linguistic hedges.
- *Formality:* We distinguish between formal, normal, and colloquial language. Templates marked as formal refer to grammatically correct sentences that are more common in newspaper reports. Colloquial templates, such as "ball played toward ?y," are simple phrases characteristic of informal language. Spoken soccer commentary especially is

characterized by unfinished or ill-formed sentences and nonverbal utterances, such as "Ooh!" or "Aah!" (e.g., see Rosenbaum 1969). Nonverbal utterances will be considered in a future version of the system.

- *Floridity:* We distinguish between dry, normal, and flowery language. Flowery language is composed of unusual ad hoc coinages, such as "a lovely ball." Templates marked as flowery may contain metaphors, such as "squeezes the ball through," while templates marked as dry, such as "plays the ball toward ?y" just convey the plain facts.
- *Bias:* Biased templates, such as "well done" contain an evaluation of an action or event. Bias may be positive, negative, or neutral.

Since the generation of live reports has to meet hard time constraints, we decided to use a four-phase filtering mechanism to prune the search space for template selection. Only the best templates of each filtering phase will be considered for the next evaluation step. The first filtering phase tries to accommodate the specific needs of a real-time live report. If time pressure is high, only short templates will pass this filtering phase where more specific templates will be given preference over less specific ones. In the second phase, templates that have been used only recently will be eliminated in order to avoid monotonous repetitions. The third phase serves to communicate the speaker's personality. For instance, if the speaker is strongly in favor of a certain team, templates with a positive bias will be preferred for describing the activities of this team. As in the sales scenario, forceful language is used primarily for extrovert commentators, while hesitant language is used for introvert ones. We are not aware of any empirical studies concerning the use of flowery phrases. However, we assume that such phrases are used primarily by open individuals who are characterized as being creative and imaginative. If several templates remain for selection, verbose and specific templates are preferred for extrovert characters, and terse and less specific ones for introvert characters. To increase the fluency of the commentary, the selected templates still allow for various modifications considering contextual constraints. For instance, "Now X" should not be uttered if X is already in focus.

Another important way of conveying personality is acoustic realization. We have not yet addressed this issue but simply designed two voices that may be distinguished easily by the user. Acoustic realization is, however, used for the expression of emotions. Drawing upon Cahn (1990), we have been examining how we can generate affective speech by parameterizing the TrueTalk™ speech synthesizer. Currently, we mainly vary pitch, accent, pitch range, and speed.

For instance, arousal is expressed by a higher talking speed and pitch range. Unfortunately, the TrueTalk speech synthesizer only allows a few parameters to be set. Consequently, we can only simulate a small subset of the effects investigated by Cahn.

8.4.4 Kasuga against Andhill: Commented on by Gerd and Matze

In the car sales example, personality is essentially conveyed by the choice of dialogue acts. Gerd and Matze portray their personality and emotions by linguistic style, which is characterized by the choice of semantic content, syntactic form, and acoustical realization (Walker, Cahn, and Whittaker 1997). In addition, they make use of body gestures, such as jumping up and down and raising their arms. In the current version of Rocco II, each commentator concentrates on the activities of a certain team. That is, there is an implicit agreement between the characters concerning the distribution of dialogue contributions. Responses to the dialogue contributions of the other commentator are possible, provided that the speed of the game allows for it. Furthermore, the commentators may provide background information on the game and the involved teams. This information is simply retrieved from a database. In what follows, we present a protocol of a system run. We start from these parameter settings:

```
Gerd:
    Attitude: in favor of the Kasuga team;
    Personality factors: extrovert, open
Matze:
    Attitude: neutral;
    Personality factors: introvert, not open


Gerd:
Kasuga kicks off
  ;;; recognized event: kick off
Matze:
Andhill 5
  ;;; recognized event: ball possession, time
  ;;; pressure
Gerd:
we are live from an exciting game, team Andhill in red versus
Kasuga in yellow
```

```
;;; time for background information
Matze:
now Andhill 9
   ;;; recognized event: ball possession
Gerd:
super interception by yellow 4
   ;;; recognized event: loss of ball, attitude: pro
   ;;; Kasuga, forceful language because it is
   ;;; extrovert
still number 4
   ;;; recognized event: ball possession, number 4 is
   ;;; topicalized
Matze:
Andhill 9 is arriving
   ;;; recognized event: approach
Gerd:
ball hacked away by Kasuga 4
   ;;; recognized event: shot, flowery language
   ;;; because it is creative
Matze:
red 5, shot towards the goal
   ;;; recognized event: shot
Gerd:
brilliant save by Kasuga's goal keeper
   ;;; recognized event: ball possession, attitude:
   ;;; pro Kasuga, forceful language because it
   ;;; it is extrovert
   ...
```

8.5 Early Feedback from Users

So far, we have only conducted some informal tests with our two prototype system demonstrators. Based on these observations, we got a clearer idea about appropriate role castings and the way people may interact with the two systems.

Although we have so far implemented our system with only simple models of personality and emotion, an interesting issue is whether the audience of a performance is able to recognize the character's personality if it has been set by someone else.

We have tried this out in a small informal system test with ten subjects. The results suggested that, generally, if asked to describe the agents in terms of given personality dimensions, subjects are indeed able to recognize the personalities. However, if the assigned personalities mismatched the character's look and voice, they had much more trouble identifying the agent's personality. For example, Merlin's soft voice was judged to conflict with a disagreeable personality.

In addition, although perhaps not being necessary conditions for eliciting personality and interest ascriptions (cf. Nass et al. 1995), subjects' comments suggested that the look and voice of a character are indeed important cues concerning its personality and interest profile. In our test, subjects tended to believe that Merlin was more interested in comfort and safety, while they expected that Robby was more interested in the technical details of a car. This suggests that reusing the look and voice of characters for different roles is only possible to a certain extent.

Finally, we observed that our subjects were very eager to "play around" with the system and try setting the personalities for the different agents to see what effect this had on the way the presentation team conveyed the information. This may be seen as an indication that users want to understand the relationship between personality and behavior. This, in turn, encourages and provides support for applications that, for instance, address the development of person perception skills (Huard and Hayes-Roth 1997).

Comments revealing that the use of presentation teams has to follow careful consideration came from some subjects with respect to the soccer scenario. They remarked that they felt that Gerd and Matze had distracted them from watching the soccer game. A reason for this may be that in this scenario the soccer game was presented in a rather abstract way (e.g., soccer players were represented as circles). Compared to this, the agents themselves and their idle time gestures (which were not only functional as in our previous empirical studies) may have been much more attractive to watch, even though they were only shown from behind. This suggests that we need to take care that the attractiveness of presentation teams per se and that of the information they comment on are appropriately set and also that idle time gestures require more careful selection on our part. For instance, if something unexpected or important happens, then the idle time movements should not be visually distracting.

In the future, as soon as the system's implementation status allows, we would like to perform more formal evaluations. It might be interesting to investigate the effects of indirect interaction with presentation teams on variables such as recall and understanding. Moreover, in everyday work situations, it is often important to recall not only what was said but also who said it and when (source monitoring, cf. Schachter, Harbluk, and McLachlan 1984). It may be interesting to investigate to what extent presentation teams with perceptually easily distinguishable agents foster this kind of source monitoring (see also Craig et al. 1999, experiment 2).

8.6 Related Work

The generation of dialogues between multiple virtual presenters is a complex endeavor that requires research in a variety of disciplines including computer science, sociology, psychology, dramaturgy, and art and design. In this section, we will restrict ourselves to related work done in the intelligent user interfaces and natural language communities.

8.6.1 Animated Presenters

A number of research projects have explored lifelike agents as a new means of computer-based presentation. Applications similar to PPP and AiA were described by Noma and Badler who developed a virtual humanlike presenter (Noma and Badler 1997) based on the Jack Software (Badler, Phillips, and Webber 1993), and by Thalmann and Kalra, who produced some animation sequences for a virtual character acting as a television presenter (Thalmann and Kalra 1995). While the production of animation sequences for the TV presenter requires a lot of manual effort, the Jack presenter receives input at a higher level of abstraction. Essentially, this input consists of text to be uttered by the presenter and commands such as *pointing* and *rejecting*, which refer to the presenter's body language. Nevertheless, here, the human author still has to specify the presentation script, while in the PPP and AiA systems, this process was automated. In addition, in contrast to the approach presented here, both systems employ just one agent for presenting information.

Byrne (Binsted and Luke 1999) and Mike (Matsubara et al. 1999) are two other systems that generate real-time natural language commentary on the RoboCup simulation league. A comparison between these systems and Rocco I, the predecessor of the commentator system described here, can be found in André, Rist, and Müller (1999). Mike and the previous Rocco system address the generation of expressive speech, but do not rely on animated characters. Most similar to our new commentary system is Byrne, since it makes use of an embodied commentator that is represented by a talking head. However, in order not to distract the audience too much, we decided not to show our agents from the front as is the case with Byrne.

The Agneta and Frida system (Höök et al. 1999) incorporates narratives into a Web environment by placing two characters on the user's desktop. These characters watch the user during the browsing process and make comments on the visited Web pages. Unlike our approach, the system relies on preauthored scripts, and no generative mechanism is employed. Consequently, the system operates on predefined Web pages only.

The system by Cassell and colleagues automatically generates and animates dialogues between a bank teller and a bank employee with appropriate synchronized speech, intonation, facial expressions, and hand gestures (Cassell et al. 1994). However, their focus is on the communicative function of an utterance and not on the personality and the emotions of the single speakers. Furthermore, they do not aim to convey information from different points of view but restrict themselves to a question-answering dialogue between the two animated agents.

Mr. Bengo (Nitta et al. 1997) is a system for the resolution of disputes with three agents: a judge, a prosecutor, and an attorney that is controlled by the user. The prosecutor and the attorney discuss the interpretation of legal rules. Finally, the judge decides who the winner is. The system is noteworthy because it includes a full multimodal interface consisting of components for the recognition and synthesis of speech and facial displays. The virtual agents are able to exhibit some basic emotions, such as anger, sadness, and surprise, by means of facial expressions. However, they do not rely on any other means, such as linguistic style, to convey personality or emotions.

Hayes-Roth and colleagues have implemented several scenarios following the metaphor of a virtual theater (Hayes-Roth, van Gent, and Huber 1997). Their characters are not directly associated with a specific personality. Instead, they are assigned a role and have to express a personality that is in agreement with this role. A key concept of their approach is improvisation. That is, characters spontaneously and cooperatively work out the details of a story at performance time, taking into account the constraints of directions either coming from the system or a human user. Even though the communication of information by means of performances was not the main focus of the work by Hayes-Roth and colleagues, the metaphor of a virtual theater can be employed in presentation scenarios as well.

The benefit of agent teams has also been recognized by developers of tutoring systems. For instance, Rickel and Johnson extended their one-on-one learning environment with additional virtual humans that may serve as instructors or substitute missing team members (Rickel and Johnson 1999). The main difference between their work and ours is that their agents directly address the user while in our case information is conveyed implicitly by means of a simulated dialogue between the agents.

8.6.2 Generation of Argumentative Discourse

Much work has been done on formal frameworks of argumentation and the generation of argumentative discourse. Most related to our work is the approach by Jameson and colleagues who developed a dialogue system that models noncooperative dialogues between a used car seller and a buyer (Jameson et al. 1995). The system is able to take on the role of both the seller and the buyer. In the role of the seller, the system tries to build up a usable model of the buyer's interests, in order to anticipate her reactions to the system's future dialogue contributions. In the role of the buyer, the system tries to arrive at a realistic estimation of the car's quality. However, while the objective of Jameson and colleagues is the generation of dialogue contributions that meet the goals of the single agents, our focus is on the development of animated agents that convey information by giving performances. Furthermore, Jameson and colleagues do not animate their agents and just produce written text. Consequently, they are not able to express human and social qualities, such as emotion and personality, through facial expressions and speech.

8.6.3 Conveying Emotions and Personality

Hovy describes one of the first natural language generators that not only is driven by the goal of information delivery but also considers pragmatic goals, such as conveying the social relationship between speaker and listener, during the generation process (Hovy 1987). His generation system PAULINE is able to produce a number of linguistic variants in dependency of parameters, such as the tone of interaction, the speaker's opinion, and the available time.

While Hovy focuses on the generation of text, Walker and colleagues examine how social factors influence the semantic content, the syntactic form and the acoustic realization of conversations (Walker, Cahn, and Whittaker 1997). The generation of their dialogues is essentially influenced by the power the listener has on the speaker and the social distance between them. Such factors could be considered in our approach by treating them as additional filters during the generation process.

Recent work in the area of animated agents considers the full range of communicative behaviors including not only linguistic style but also body gestures and facial expressions. Ball and Breese present a bidirectional model of personality and emotion represented by Bayesian networks (Ball and Breese, chap. 7). The idea is to treat personality and emotion as unobservable variables in such networks and to define model dependencies between these unobservable variables and observable ones, such as linguistic style and facial expressions. The approach is noteworthy since it makes use of a uniform mechanism for both the diagnosis and the expression of emotions and personality that can be easily extended and modified. Furthermore, it accounts for the uncertainty that is characteristic of this domain.

Our own approach has been very much inspired by Cassell and colleagues, who follow a communication-theoretic approach and present an architecture based on discourse functions (Cassell et al., chap. 2). The goal of their approach is to interpret and generate conversational behaviors in terms of the conversational functions they have to fulfill in a dialogue. Poggi and Pelachaud have taken a similar approach, but they have concentrated mainly on the generation of facial displays (Poggi and Pelachaud, chap. 6).

8.7 Conclusion

In this chapter, we proposed performances given by a team of characters as a new form of presentation. The basic idea is to communicate information by means of simulated dialogues that are observed by an audience. This new generation task comprises content selection/organization, character allocation, and content rendering. Character allocation bears much resemblance to the media coordination problem in multimedia interfaces. Here, the basic idea is to decompose a complex goal into atomic information units that are then forwarded to several media-specific generators, for instance, for text and graphics in WIP (André and Rist 1995), or speech and gestures in REA (Cassell and Stone 1999). In a similar way, dialogue contributions may be allocated to the individual agents. However, while systems like WIP may start from a set of available media, in our case, new characters first have to be designed for each application, taking into account their specific task.

We have investigated these issues in two different application scenarios and implemented demonstrator systems for each of them. In the first application, a sales scenario, the dialogue contributions of the involved characters are determined by a central planning component. In contrast, in the second application, we use a distributed planning approach to have two characters jointly watch and comment on soccer games. A main feature of the generated presentations is that the characters not only communicate plain facts about a certain subject matter but present them from a point of view that reflects their specific personality traits and interest profiles.

The purpose of our demonstration systems was not to implement a more or less complete model of personality for characters, such as a seller, a customer, or a soccer fan. Rather, the systems have been designed as test beds that allow for experiments with various personalities and roles. First informal system tests were quite encouraging but have also revealed some interesting aspects as to the importance of the matching of personality traits and surface characteristics, such as pitch of voice.

Currently, both systems are based on a small set of dialogue strategies and personality traits. It was, in fact, our intention to rely on rather simplified models to represent the characters' knowledge of the domain and interest profiles. One of the reasons was to show that recognizable effects can also be obtained by varying a small set of parameters. Furthermore, we wanted to demonstrate that the generation of appealing presentation dialogues requires only a minimal amount of additional knowledge modeling. For instance, in the sales scenario, we had to augment the car database by propositions that represent the impact of attributes on value dimensions. Of course, more fine-grained models may be used as well. Since our approach provides a declarative representation formalism for character and dialogue modeling, new dialogue strategies and personality traits may be added easily.

Our test beds provide a good point of departure for further research. In particular, we would like to systematically investigate further dialogue types to shed light on questions such as the following: What is the optimal number of roles, and what should an optimal casting look like? Which personalities do users prefer in which situations (see also Nass et al. 1995 and Nass, Isbister, and Lee, chap. 13, for experiments devoted to this issue). Currently, these tasks are performed by a human user. From a technical point of view, it is also interesting to investigate to what extent the role casting and the assignment of personalities can be automated.

Acknowledgments

We are grateful to Marc Huber for his excellent support concerning the JAM framework. Many thanks also to Sabine Bein and Peter Rist for providing us with the Gerd and Matze cartoons and to Jochen Müller and Dirk Völz for technical support. We are also grateful to Justine Cassell for many useful and insightful comments. Part of this research was supported by the German

Ministry for Education, Science, Research and Technology (BMBF) under contract 01 IW 806 and by the European Community under contracts ERB 4061 PL 97-0808 and EP-29335.

References

Alpert, S. R., M. K. Singley, and J. M. Caroll. 1999 Intelligent virtual agents in an intelligent tutoring system. In *AIED-Workshop on Animated and Personified Pedagogical Agents* (Le Mans, France), 10–17.

André, E., and T. Rist. 1995. Generating coherent presentations employing textual and visual material. *Artificial Intelligence Review* 9(2–3):147–165. (Special issue on the Integration of Natural Language and Vision Processing.)

———. 1996. Coping with temporal constraints in multimedia presentation planning. In *Proceedings of the AAAI '96*, vol. 1, 142–147. Menlo Park and Cambridge: AAAI Press/The MIT Press.

André, E., G. Herzog, and T. Rist. 1997. Generating multimedia presentations for RoboCup soccer games. In H. Kitano, ed., *RoboCup '97: Robot Soccer World Cup I*, 200–215. New York: Springer-Verlag.

André, E., T. Rist, and J. Müller. 1999. Employing AI methods to control the behavior of animated interface agents. *Applied Artificial Intelligence* 13:415–448.

Badler, N. I., C. B. Phillips, and B. L. Webber. 1993. *Simulating humans: Computer graphics, animation and control.* New York: Oxford University Press.

Bates, J. 1994. The role of emotion in believable agents. *Communications of the ACM* 37:122–125.

Binsted, K., and S. Luke. 1999. Character design for soccer commentary. In M. Asada and H. Kitano, eds., *RoboCup-98: Robot Soccer World Cup II*, 22–33. New York: Springer-Verlag.

Bower, G. H., M. C. Clark, A. M. Lesgold, and D. Winzenz. 1969. Hierarchical retrieval schemes in recall of categorized word lists. *Journal of Verbal Learning and Verbal Behavior* 8:323–343.

Cahn, J. 1990. The generation of affect in synthesized speech. *Journal of the American Voice I/O Society* 8:1–19.

Cassell, J., and H. Stone. 1999. Living hand to mouth: Psychological theories about speech and gesture in interactive dialogue systems. In *AAAI 1999 Fall Symposium on Narrative Intelligence,* 34–42. Menlo Park, Calif.: AAAI Press.

Cassell, J., C. Pelachaud, N. Badler, M. Steedman, B. Achorn, T. Becket, B. Douville, S. Prevost, and M. Stone. 1994. Animated conversation: Rule-based generation of facial expression, gesture and spoken intonation for multiple conversational agents. In *Computer Graphics*, 413–420. New York: ACM SIGGRAPH.

Collier, G. 1985. *Emotional expression.* Hillsdale, N.J.: Lawrence Erlbaum.

Craig, S. D., B. Gholson, M. H. Garzon, X. Hu, W. Marks, P. Wiemer-Hastings, and Z. Lu. 1999. Auto Tutor and Otto Tudor. In *AIED-Workshop on Animated and Personified Pedagogical Agents* (Le Mans, France), 25–30.

Dehn, D. M., and S. van Mulken. 1999. The impact of animated interface agents: A review of empirical research. *Journal of Human-Computer Studies.* Forthcoming.

Dryer, D. C. 1999. Getting personal with computers: How to design personalities for agents. *Applied Artificial Intelligence* 13:273–296.

Elliott, C. 1992. The affective reasoner: A process model of emotions in a multi-agent system. Ph.D. diss. Northwestern University, The Institute for the Learning Sciences, Technical Report No. 32.

Frank, I. 1997. Football in recent times: What we can learn from the newspapers. In H. Kitano, ed., *RoboCup '97: Robot Soccer World Cup I*, 216–230. New York: Springer-Verlag.

Furnham, A. 1990. Language and personality. In H. Giles and W. P. Robinson, eds., *Handbook of language and social psychology*, 73–95. Chichester, U.K.: John Wiley & Sons.

Gallaher, P. E. 1992. Individual differences in nonverbal behavior: Dimensions of style. *Journal of Personality and Social Psychology* 63(1):133–145.

Hayes-Roth, B., R. van Gent, and D. Huber. 1997. Acting in character. In R. Trappl and P. Petta, eds., *Creating personalities for synthetic actors*, 92–112. New York: Springer.

Höök, K., M. Sjölinder, A.-L. Ereback, and P. Persson. 1999. Dealing with the lurking Lutheran view on interfaces: Evaluation of the Agneta and Frida System. In *Proceedings of the i3 Spring Days Workshop on Behavior Planning for Lifelike Characters and Avatars* (Sitges, Spain), 125–136.

Hovy, E. 1987. Some pragmatic decision criteria in generation. In G. Kempen, ed., *Natural language generation*, 3–17. Dordrecht: Martinus Nijhoff Publishers.

Huard, R., and B. Hayes-Roth. 1997. Character mastery with improvisational puppets. In *Proceedings of the IJCAI-97 Workshop on Animated Interface Agents—Making Them Intelligent* (Nagoya, Japan), 85–89.

Huber, M. 1999. JAM: A BDI-theoretic mobile agent architecture. In *Proceedings of Autonomous Agents '99*, 236–243. New York: ACM Press.

Jameson, A., R. Schäfer, J. Simons, and T. Weis. 1995. Adaptive provision of evaluation-oriented information: Tasks and techniques. In C. S. Mellish, ed., *Proceedings of IJCAI '95*, 1886–1893. San Mateo, Calif.: Morgan Kaufmann.

Kitano, H., M. Asada, Y. Kuniyoshi, I. Noda, E. Osawa, and H. Matsubara. 1997. RoboCup: A challenging problem for AI. *AI Magazine* 18(1):73–85.

Lang, P. 1995. The emotion probe: Studies of motivation and attention. *American Psychologist* 50(5):372–385.

Lester, J. C., S. A. Converse, S. E. Kahler, S. T. Barlow, B. A. Stone, and R. S. Bhogal. 1997. The persona effect: Affective impact of animated pedagogical agents. In S. Pemberton, ed., *Human factors in computing systems, CHI '97 conference proceedings*, 359–366. New York: ACM Press.

Matsubara, H., I. Frank, K. Tanaka-Ishii, I. Noda, H. Nakashima, and K. Hasida. 1999. Character design for soccer commentary. In M. Asada and H. Kitano, eds., *RoboCup-98: Robot Soccer World Cup II*, 34–49. New York: Springer-Verlag.

McCrae, R. R., and O. P. John. 1992. An introduction to the five-factor model and its implications. *Journal of Personality* 60:175–215.

Mehlmann, O., L. Landvogt, A. Jameson, T. Rist, and R. Schäfer. 1998. Einsatz Bayes'scher Netze zur Identifikation von Kundenwünschen im Internet. *Künstliche Intelligenz* 3(98):43–48.

Microsoft. 1999. Microsoft Agent: Software Development Kit. Redmond, Wash.: Microsoft Press. Available: <http://microsoft.public.msagent>.

Moffat, D. 1997. Personality parameters and programs. In R. Trappl and P. Petta, eds., *Creating personalities for synthetic actors*, 120–165. New York: Springer-Verlag.

Nass, C., Y. Moon, B. J. Fogg, B. Reeves, and D. C. Dryer. 1995. Can computer personalities be human personalities? *International Journal of Human-Computer Studies* 43:223–239.

Nass, C., B. Reeves, and G. Leshner. 1996. Technology and roles: A tale of two TVs. *Journal of Communication* 46(2):121–128.

Nitta, K., O. Hasegawa, T. Akiba, T. Kamishima, T. Kurita, S. Hayamizu, K. Itoh, M. Ishizuka, H. Dohi, and M. Okamura. 1997. An experimental multimodal disputation system. In *Proceedings of the IJCAI '97 Workshop on Intelligent Multimodal Systems*.

Noma, T., and N. Badler. 1997. A virtual human presenter. In *Proceedings of the IJCAI '97 Workshop on Animated Interface Agents—Making Them Intelligent*, 45–51.

Ornstein, P. A., and T. Trabasso. 1974. To organize is to remember: The effects of instructions to organize and to recall. *Journal of Experimental Psychology* 103(5):1014–1018.

Ortony, A., G. Clore, and A. Collins. 1988. *The cognitive structure of emotions*. Cambridge: Cambridge University Press.

Rickel, J., and W. L. Johnson. 1999. Virtual humans for team training in virtual reality. *In Proceedings of the Ninth International Conference on Artificial Intelligence in Education*, 578–585. Amsterdam: IOS Press.

Rosenbaum, D. 1969. Die Sprache der Fußballreportage im Hörfunk. Ph.D. diss., Universität des Saarlandes. Philosophische Fakultät.

Schachter, D. L., J. L. Harbluk, and D. R. McLachlan. 1984. Retrieval without recollection: An experimental analysis of source amnesia. *Journal of Verbal Learning and Verbal Behavior* 23:593–611.

Scherer, K. R. 1979. Personality markers in speech. In K. R. Scherer and H. Giles, eds., *Social markers in speech*, 147–209. Cambridge: Cambridge University Press.

Spiegel-Verlag. 1993. SPIEGEL-Dokumentation: Auto, Verkehr und Umwelt. Hamburg: Augstein.

Thalmann, N. M., and P. Kalra. 1995. The simulation of a virtual TV presenter. In *Computer graphics and applications*, 9–21. Singapore: World Scientific Press.

van Mulken, S., E. André, and J. Müller. 1998. The persona effect: How substantial is it? In H. Johnson, L. Nigay and C. Roast, eds., *People and Computers XIII* (Proceedings of HCI-98), 53–66. Berlin: Springer.

———. 1999. An empirical study on the trustworthiness of lifelike interface agents. In H.-J. Bullinger and J. Ziegler, eds., *Human-computer interaction* (Proceedings of HCI-International 1999), 152–156. Mahwah, N.J.: Lawrence Erlbaum Associates.

von Winterfeldt, D., and W. Edwards. 1986. *Decision analysis and behavioral research*. Cambridge: Cambridge University Press.

Walker, M., J. Cahn, and S. J. Whittaker. 1997. Improving linguistic style: Social and affective bases for agent personality. In *Proceedings of Autonomous Agents '97*, 96–105. Marina del Ray, Calif.: ACM Press.

9

Parameterized Action Representation for Virtual Human Agents

Norman I. Badler, Rama Bindiganavale, Jan Allbeck,

William Schuler, Liwei Zhao, and Martha Palmer

9.1 Introduction

Conversation among people serves many purposes: to share experiences, provide information, elicit responses, negotiate agreements, and modify behaviors. Instructions form an important conversational subspace that addresses physical or behavioral actions performed by or with other people. Conversational acts involving instructions provide a rich environment in which people must understand and carry out meaningful actions. Naturally, those actions must be done in a physical context and may vary across people or across situations. When we substitute embodied, humanlike characters—virtual humans—as conversational partners in instruction interpretation, a suitable computational framework must be used to transform language commands into visualized actions.

By studying and understanding person-to-person instructions, we can create analogous communications between people and embodied agents. This approach has benefits not only for guiding system design, but also for increasing understanding of our own interpersonal communication mechanisms: for example, how instruction interpretation is dependent on the spatial context in which the agent is situated. Eventually, we can use this identical mechanism for agent-to-agent conversations as well. Although it is a programming convenience to pass logical forms back and forth between agents (and we will in fact propose such a form here), that does require mutual agreement on the form. A language-based interaction may potentially simplify yet enhance interactions between separately designed and implemented agent systems. Moreover, many instructions already exist in textual form in instruction manuals, recipes, and job guides, so it would be convenient to use these resources as is, without preprocessing. An agent that understands instructions would be able to use these information resources by parsing and analyzing them (forming its own appropriate logical forms) in real time. A successful design and implementation of instruction understanding will open communication channels that blur the boundary between interactions with real beings and interactions with virtual beings.

This chapter therefore addresses the problem of *making virtual humans respond to verbalized commands in a context-sensitive fashion*. We first define the kinds of virtual human characters we wish to control. This leads to a focus on language-based control or instruction interpretation. To support *both* language understanding and animation, we define a *parameterized action representation* (PAR). We then give an outline of the architecture for interpreting and executing such represented actions and show how they control embodied agent models. Finally, we describe several examples to show how the characters can interact when given context-dependent instructions.

9.2 Smart Avatars

Animating virtual conversational humans involves actions like posture changes, balance adjustments, reaching, pointing, grasping, giving-taking and other arm/hand gestures, locomotion, eye gaze and head gestures, facial expressions, and speech. These animations involve controlling their parts at the graphical level via joint transformations (e.g., for limbs) or surface deformations (e.g., for face). Motion capture from live participants or procedurally synthesized motions are used to animate the 3-D model.

In real-time applications, *avatars* (Wilcox 1998) are virtual human representations driven directly by a real person. Their joint angles and other location parameters are sensed by magnetic, optical, or video methods and converted to joint rotations and body poses. Physically sensed motions look natural but may limit the performer with cumbersome equipment or movement restricted to the sensor's field of view. Moreover, directly sensed motion is difficult to modify on the fly to achieve subject or environmental sensitivity (Bindiganavale and Badler 1998; Gleicher 1998). For movements not based on live performance, computer programs have to generate the right sequences and combinations of parameters to create the movements' desired actions.

In general, an embodied (humanlike) character that acts from its own motivations is often called an *agent*. In this sense, an avatar is an agent that represents an actual person. Its actions may be portrayed through captured or synthesized motions performed in the current context. These require parameterizing and, in turn, proper specification of parameters (sec. 9.4). We call an avatar *controlled via instructions* from a live participant a *smart avatar*. Parameters for its actions may come from the instruction itself, from the local object context, and from the avatar's available capabilities and resources.

We have explored the contextual control of embodied agents, avatars, and smart avatars (with and without conversation) in a number of experiments including:

- two-person animated conversation in *Gesture Jack* (Cassell et al. 1994)
- medic interventions and patient physiological interactions in *MediSim* (Chi et al. 1995)
- multiparameter game behaviors in *Hide & Seek* (Badler et al. 1996)
- a real-time animated *Jack Presenter* (Noma and Badler 1997; Zhao and Badler 1998)
- multi-user *Jack-MOO virtual worlds* (Shi et al. 1999)
- virtual environment simulation using a parameterized action representation (Badler, Palmer, and Bindiganavale 1999)

In the last two systems, we began to explore an architecture for interacting with virtual humans that was solely language-based in order to explicitly approach a level of interaction between virtual humans comparable to that between real people. We focused on instructions for physical action to bound the problem, to enable interesting applications, and to refine a representation bridging natural language (NL) and embodied action.

9.3 Levels of Architectural Control

Building a virtual human model for conversation that admits control from sources other than direct sensing or animator manipulations requires an architecture that supports higher-level expressions of movement. Although layered architectures for autonomous beings are not new (Brooks 1989; Rickel and Johnson 1999; Zeltzer 1990), we have found that a particular set of architectural levels seems to provide efficient localization of control for both graphics and language requirements. Our multilevel architecture is grounded in typical graphical models and articulation structures, and it includes various motor skills for endowing virtual humans with useful abilities. The higher architectural levels organize these skills with parallel automata, use a conceptual representation to describe the actions a virtual human can perform, and finally create links between natural language and action animation.

9.3.1 Graphical Models

A typical virtual human model consists of a geometric skin and an articulated skeleton. Usually modeled with polygons to optimize graphical display speed, a body can be crafted manually or shaped more automatically from a digitized person. The surface may be rigid or, more realistically, deformable during movement. Deformation demands additional modeling and computational loads. Clothes are desirable, though today, loose garments still have to be animated off-line due to computational complexity (Volino, Courchesne, and Magnenat-Thalmann 1995).

The skeletal structure is usually a hierarchy of segments connected together by joint rotation transformations (Badler, Phillips, and Webber 1993; Earnshaw et al. 1998). The body is moved over time by setting various joint angles and the overall global position and location. In sophisticated models, joint angle changes induce geometric modifications that keep joint surfaces smooth and mimic human musculature within a character's body segments (Cavazza et al. 1998; Ting 1998; Wilhelms and van Gelder 1997).

9.3.2 Motion Generators

A virtual human's actions can be generated either by live motion capture directly or by motion generators—procedures for changing joint angles and body position. Motion generators should be capable of

- playing a stored motion sequence that may have been synthesized by a procedure, captured from a live person, or scripted manually
- blending one movement into another, in sequence or in parallel
- generating various motor skills such as the following:
  - changing postures and adjusting balance
  - reaching and other arm gestures
  - grasping and other hand gestures
  - locomoting, such as stepping, walking, turning, and climbing
  - looking and other eye and head gestures
  - facial expressions, such as lip and eye movements
  - physical force- and torque-induced movements, such as jumping, falling, and swinging

Numerous methods help create each of these movements including inverse kinematics, locomotion, (Badler, Phillips, and Webber 1993), physics-based simulation (Hodgins et al. 1995; Metaxas 1996), and noise functions (Perlin 1995). But we want to allow several of them to be executed simultaneously. A virtual human should be able to walk, talk, and chew gum at the same time. Simultaneous execution also leads to the next level of our architecture's organization: parallel automata.

9.3.3 Parallel Transition Networks

Almost twenty years ago, we realized that human animation would require some model of parallel movement execution (Badler and Smoliar 1979). But it was not until the 1990s that graphical workstations were finally powerful enough to support functional implementations of simulated parallelism. Our parallel programming model for virtual humans is called Parallel Transition Networks, or PaT-Nets (Badler, Phillips, and Webber 1993). Other human animation systems, including Motion Factory's Motivate and New York University's Improv (Perlin and Goldberg 1996), have adopted similar paradigms with alternative syntactic structures. In general, network nodes represent processes. Arcs connect the nodes and contain predicates, conditions, rules, and other functions that trigger transitions to other process nodes. Synchronization across processes or networks is made possible through message passing or global variable blackboards to let one process know the state of another process.

The benefits of PaT-Nets derive not only from their parallel organization and execution of low-level motion generators but also from their conditional structure. Traditional animation tools use linear timelines on which actions are placed and ordered. A PaT-Net provides a *nonlinear* animation model, since movements can be triggered, modified, and stopped by transitions to other nodes. Nonlinear animation tools represent a crucial step toward autonomous behavior, since conditional execution is key to a virtual human's interactivity, reactivity, and decision making.

Providing a virtual human with humanlike reactions and decision-making skills is more complicated than just controlling its joint motions from captured or synthesized data. Simulated humanlike actions and decisions are how we convince the viewer of the character's skill and intelligence in negotiating its environment, interacting with its spatial situation, and engaging other agents. This level of performance requires significant investment in action models that allow conditional execution.

PaT-Nets are effective programming tools but must be hand-coded in C++. No matter what artificial language we invent to describe human actions, it is not likely to represent exactly the way people conceptualize a particular situation. If we want human-like conversational-level control, then we need a higher-level representation to capture additional information, parameters, and aspects of human action. We create such representations by incorporating natural language semantics into a parameterized action representation.

9.3.4 Language-Based Control

Even with powerful motion generators and PaT-Nets to invoke them, we still have to provide effective user interfaces to control, manipulate, and animate virtual humans. We would also like to be able to instruct these virtual humans while a simulation is running, so a user could dynamically refine his or her avatar's behavior or react to simulated stimuli without having to undertake a lengthy programming session.

Interactive point-and-click tools (such as Maya from Alias/Wavefront, 3D Studio Max from Autodesk, and SoftImage from Avid) could be configured to accept instructions during runtime, but they require specialized training and animation skills and force the user's instructions for the avatar through a narrow communication channel of hand/mouse motions. This narrow channel precludes, among other things, any conditional instruction that references a hypothetical object in its condition. For example, a user could not give the instruction "if a rabbit enters the trap, pull the string" if there were no rabbit to click on when the instruction is given.

On the other hand, a programming or scripting language such as that used in Improv (Perlin and Goldberg 1996) can provide a sufficiently powerful interface for instructing characters and would be able to handle the kinds of conditional instructions discussed above. But such interfaces are generally more appropriate for off-line applications, where instructions are written in advance, than for run-time applications, where instructions are written in response to observed events in the simulation. Not only does such a scripting interface require a great deal of specialized programming expertise (even for "English-like" languages), but the required instructions can often be too complex to implement reliably in real time. A script to simply "turn off all the lights," for example, would involve at least one condition for testing whether each light was on, nested inside a loop over all the lights in the environment, in addition to the "turn off light" command itself.

One promising and relatively unexplored option for giving run-time instructions to characters is a natural language interface. After all, instructions for real humans are given in natural language, augmented with graphical diagrams, and, occasionally, live or previously generated animations. Recipes, instruction manuals, and interpersonal conversations all use natural language as a medium for conveying information about processes and actions (Badler et al. 1990; Badler, Phillips, and Webber 1993; Webber at al. 1995). A natural language interface should be powerful enough to express conditional instructions and hypothetical situations such as those described above, and it should be simple enough to use in a real-time application without substantial formal training on the part of the user.

We are not advocating that animators throw away their tools, only that natural language offers a communication medium we all know and can use to efficiently formulate run-time instructions for virtual characters. Some aspects of actions are certainly difficult to express in natural language (such as precise locations and orientations of objects), but the availability of a language interpreter can make the user interface more closely simulate real interpersonal communication. Our goal is to build smart avatars that understand what we tell them to do in the same way humans follow instructions. These smart avatars have to be able to process natural language instructions into a conceptual representation that can be used to control their actions. This representation is what we refer to as a parameterized action representation.

9.4 Parameterized Action Representation (PAR)

A PAR (Badler et al. 1997) gives a description of an action. The PAR has to specify the agent of the action as well as any relevant objects and information about path, location, manner, and purpose for a particular action. There are linguistic constraints on how this information can be conveyed by the language; agents and objects tend to be verb arguments, path is often a prepositional phrase, and manner and purpose might be in additional clauses (Palmer, Rosenzweig, and Schuler 1998). A parser and translator map the components of an instruction into the parameters or variables of the PAR, which is then linked directly to PaT-Nets executing the specified movement generators.

Natural language often describes actions at a high level, leaving out many of the details that have to be specified for animation (Narayanan 1997). The PAR bridges the gap between natural language and animations.

We use the example "Walk to the door and turn the handle slowly," to illustrate the function of the PAR. Whether or not the PAR system processes this instruction, there is nothing explicit in the linguistic representation about grasping the handle or which direction it will have to be turned, yet this information is necessary to the action's actual visible performance. The PAR has to include information about applicability, preparatory, and termination conditions in order to fill in these gaps. It also has to be parameterized, because other details of the action depend on the PAR's participants, including agents, objects, and other attributes. The representation of the "handle" object lists the actions that the object can perform and what state changes they cause (Douville, Levison, and Badler 1996; Kallmann and Thalmann 1999). The number of steps it will take to get to the door depends on the agent's size and starting location.

PAR

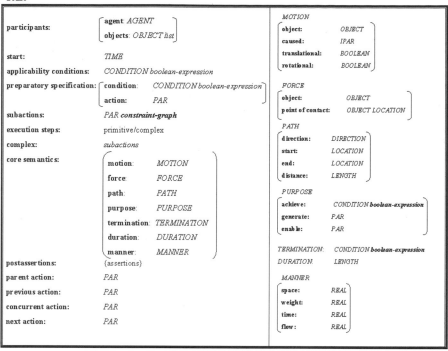

Figure 9.1
Syntactic representation of PAR.

Next, we briefly describe some of the terminology and concepts used to define a PAR and the architecture that we have designed to interpret it.

9.4.1 PAR Terminology

Some of the parameters in a PAR template are shown in figure 9.1:

9.4.1.1 Participants

- Agent: The agent executes the action. When an agent is not specifically mentioned in the instruction, the user's avatar is the implied agent. In our example, the walking and turning actions share the same agent. We assume that the agent refers to a human model, a process simulator, or physical forces like gravity (in which case the agent is understood to be causal and not volitional).

An agent has a specific personality and a set of actions it is capable of performing. The agent can also be considered to be capable of playing different roles. For each role, the agent performs different actions. So, instead of maintaining one long list of actions, we could group these actions under different roles. For example, the actions involved in driving a car, such as grasping a steering wheel, sitting with a foot on the accelerator pedal, and so forth, would be grouped under the "car-driver" role. Unlike for the objects, each action is associated with a set of preparatory conditions (tests for reachability, etc.) that check if the agent can perform the action. If not, another set of actions is generated for that agent which have to be completed before the current action can be performed.

The agent type also specifies nominal values and distribution types and ranges for some of the actions and state space descriptors. For example, the walking rate of the agent could be specified to have a nominal value of 2 steps per second with a normal distribution and standard deviation of 1. This gives a range of values over which the walking rate can be varied, say, by a manner specification.

- Objects: The object type is defined explicitly for a complete representation of a physical object and is stored hierarchically in a database (sec. 9.4.2). Each object in the environment is an instance of this type and is associated with a graphical model in a scene graph.

  The *state* field of an object describes a set of constraints on the object that leave it in a default state. The object continues in this state until a new set of constraints is imposed on the object by an action that causes a change in state. The other important fields are the reference coordinate frame, a list of grasp sites and their purposes, and intrinsic directions (top, front, etc.) defined with respect to the object.

  In our example, the walking action has an implicit floor as an object, while the turn action refers to the handle.

9.4.1.2 *Start*   This is the time at which the action begins.

9.4.1.3 *Applicability Conditions*   The applicability conditions of an action specify what needs to be true in the world in order to carry out an action. These can refer to agent capabilities, object configurations, and other unchangeable or uncontrollable aspects of the environment. The conditions in this boolean expression must be true to perform the action. For "walk," one of the applicability conditions may be "Can the agent walk?" If these conditions are not satisfied, the action cannot be executed.

In some instances, the applicability conditions may also replace an action with a more specific one: opening the door might be specialized to a sliding action if that is what this particular door calls for. The implementation details for this are discussed in section 9.4.3.

9.4.1.4 Preparatory Specifications This is a list of <CONDITION, action> statements. The conditions are evaluated first and have to be satisfied before the current action can proceed. If the conditions are not satisfied, then the corresponding action is executed; it may be a single action or a very complex combination of actions, but it has the same format as the execution steps described below. In general, actions can involve the full power of motion planning to determine, perhaps, that a handle has to be grasped before it can be turned. The instructions are essentially goal requests, and the smart avatar must then figure out how (if possible) it can achieve them. We presently specify the conditions to test for likely (but generalized) situations and execute appropriate intermediate actions. Adding more general action planners is also possible, since the PAR represents goal states and supports a full graphical model of the current world state (Trias et al. 1996).

In our example, one of the conditions to be checked could be *standing?(agent)* and the corresponding action could be *("stand",agents: ("Jack"))*. If the agent is not standing, for example, if he is sitting or prone, then the action causes him to change to the standing posture.

9.4.1.5 Subactions Each action is organized into partially ordered or parallel substeps, called subactions. Actions described by PARs are ultimately executed as PaT-Nets.

9.4.1.6 Execution Steps A PAR can describe either a primitive or a complex action. The execution steps contain the details of executing the action after all the applicability and preparatory conditions have been satisfied. If it is a primitive action, the underlying PaT-Net for the action is directly invoked. A complex action can list a number of subactions that may need to be executed in sequence, in parallel, or as a combination of both. A complex action can be considered done if all of its subactions are done or if its explicit termination conditions are satisfied.

9.4.1.7 Core Semantics   The core semantics represent an action's primary components of meaning and include motion, force, path, purpose, termination conditions, duration, and agent manner. For example, "walking" is a form of locomotion that results in a change of location. "Turning" requires a direction and an end point.

- Motion: This specifies the object that is being moved and the type of motion—rotational, translational, or both. It also specifies whether this is a causal motion.
- Force: This points to the affected object and indicates the force or torque amount and point of contact.
- Path: This contains information on the location of the object at the beginning or the end of the motion and the directional changes that model the approximate path of the motion.
- Purpose: This specifies the state or condition that will be achieved as a result of this motion. It also points to the PARs that are either generated or enabled during the course of or at the end of the motion.
- Termination Conditions: This is a list of conditions that, when satisfied, complete the action. A termination condition can be determined from the main verb or attached clauses (Bourne 1998).
- Duration: This specifies the duration of the motion.
- Manner: Manner specifications describe the way in which an agent carries out an action. We define manner as composed of *Effort* parameters that are derived from Laban Effort Notation (Bartenieff and Lewis 1980) expressing the quality of a movement. Each parameter takes on a real value in the range from -1 to 1. Effort elements are weight, space, time, and flow and can be combined and phrased to vary the dynamics of the movement (Badler, Chi, and Chopra 1999).

9.4.1.8 Post Assertions   This is a list of statements or assertions that are executed after the termination conditions of the action have been satisfied. These assertions update the database to record the changes in the environment. The changes may be due to direct or side effects of the action.

9.4.2 PAR Representations

A PAR takes on two different forms: uninstantiated (UPAR) and instantiated (IPAR). We store all instances of the UPAR, which contains *default* applicability conditions, preparatory specifications, and execution steps, in a hierarchical database called the *Actionary*. An IPAR is a UPAR instantiated with specific information on agent, physical object(s), manner, termination conditions, and other bound parameters. Any new information in an IPAR overrides the corresponding UPAR default. An IPAR can be created by a parser or by other PARs dynamically during execution.

9.4.3 PAR Architecture

Figure 9.2 shows the architecture of the PAR system:

9.4.3.1 NL2PAR This module consists of two parts: parser and translator. The parser takes a NL instruction/command and outputs a tree identifying the different components as noun, verb, adverb, preposition, and so forth. For each new instruction, the translator uses the output of the parser and information stored in the database to first determine the correct instances of the physical object and agent in the environment. It then generates the instruction as an IPAR. This is discussed in detail in section 9.5.1.

9.4.3.2 Database All instances of physical objects, UPARs, and agents are stored in a hierarchical persistent database. Currently, during the initialization phase, a world model is created that is constantly updated during the simulation with any changes in the environment or in the properties of the agents or objects. The agent processes can query the world model for the current state of the environment and for the current properties of the agents and objects in the environment.

9.4.3.3 Execution Engine The execution engine is the main controller of the system. It maintains the global timer/controller, sends commands to the visualizer to update the displayed scene, and accepts PARs from the NL2PAR module and passes them on to the correct agent process.

The execution engine also maintains a table of rules that is managed by a separate rule-manager. Each standing order (sec. 9.5.1) or instruction issued in natural language to an agent is first sent to the NL2PAR module to be parsed. The parsed rule is then stored as a *Python* script (Lutz 1996) (sec. 9.4.3) in the rule-table. The *Python* script contains a set of conditions that it tests during evaluation of the script and returns a new IPAR or a list of IPARs. At each simulation frame, the rule-manager evaluates each rule in the table and sends the resulting IPARs, if any, to the agent process for execution.

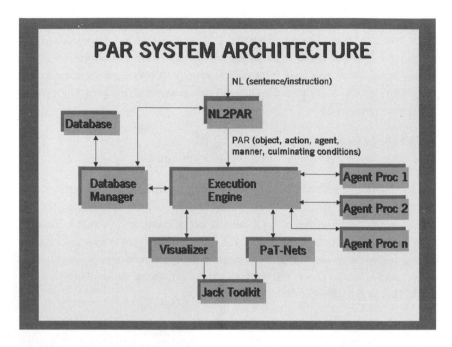

Figure 9.2
PAR architecture.

9.4.3.4 *Agent Process* A separate agent process controls each instance of an agent. Each agent process has a queue manager that manages a priority-based multilayered queue of all IPARs to be executed by the agent. The various tasks of an agent process are to

- add a given IPAR at the top level of the queue
- communicate with other agent processes through message passing
- trigger different actions for the agent based on the agent's personality, messages received from another agent process, and the existing environmental state
- return the process status (on queue, aborted/preempted, being executed, completed, etc.) of an IPAR
- ensure nonrecursive addition of IPARs resulting from rules

The queue manager in the agent process is implemented using PaT-Nets. Each UPAR is assigned a priority number by the user or by the situation. At any time, if the first action on the queue has a higher priority than the IPAR currently being executed, the queue manager preempts the current action. In general, either after preemption or completion of an action, a new action is selected and then popped from the top level of the IPAR queue of the agent and sent to a process manager. The selected new action has the highest priority in the first subset of monotonically increasing actions (with respect to priorities) at the beginning of the queue.

For each popped IPAR, a process manager first checks the applicability conditions. If they are not satisfied, the entire process is aborted after taking care of failure conditions and proper system updates. If the applicability conditions are satisfied, the preparatory conditions are then checked. If any of the corresponding preparatory actions need to be executed, an IPAR is created (using the specified information of the UPAR, agent, and the list of objects) and added to the agent's existing queue of IPARs. It should be noted that the queue of IPARs is a multilayered structure. Each new IPAR created for a preparatory action is added to a layer below the current one. The current action is continued only after the successful termination of all the preparatory actions. If the current action is very complex, more IPARs are generated and the depth of the queue structure increases. During the execution phase, a PaT-Net is created dynamically for each complex action specified in the execution steps or in the preparatory specifications. Each subaction corresponds to a subnet in the PaT-Net. The PaT-Nets ultimately ground the action in parameterized motor commands to the embodied character.

9.4.3.5 *Toolkit* We use the *Jack*® toolkit and OpenGL® to maintain and control the actual geometry, scene graphs, and human behaviors and constraints.

9.4.4 PAR Implementation

We have implemented PAR using C++ and *Python*, an interpreted object-oriented language that is quite compatible with C++. This makes it easy for both the action and object hierarchies to be visible from both *Python* and C++. It also provides serialization and persistence that is ideal for database implementation.

The system is built in two layers. The bottom layer contains the implementation of the core system and is in C++ and *Python*. The top layer has a graphical user-friendly interface (GUI) built using Python-Tk. The user needs to interact only with the top layer. This allows for the UPARs and objects to be created dynamically. The applicability conditions, preparatory specifications, and executable actions are presently written through the GUI as simple Python scripts that can be easily tested. As *Python* can be extended and embedded in C++, objects of different data types can be passed between them. The objects passed from *Python* to C++ are all perceived by C++ to be of a single *Python* object type that could later be typecast to different types. This allows conditions to return the various test results as either a Boolean type or a Python string. The agent process is capable of expanding this string into a new action and adding it to the agent's queue.

9.5 Natural Language for Instructions

Communicating between users and avatars can be done through natural language. In addition to commands for the immediate performance of actions, we would also like to use natural language input to convey conditional actions that need to persist in the avatar's memory and may be triggered by future circumstances. For example, "If the driver is hostile, draw your weapon" is a standing instruction that would be triggered whenever the driver is hostile. This requires a sophisticated natural language processing system with broad syntactic coverage and close integration of syntax and domain-specific lexical semantics that can interact with the underlying graphical world model. The predicates that make this work, for example, the determination that a driver is or is not hostile (sec. 9.6.3), are provided in advance. Generating such predicates from natural language is a tantalizing but future effort.

In order for smart avatars to respond to instructions expressed in natural language sentences, we have to be able to coordinate verbal and physical representations of actions. The basic linguistic representation of an action is a *predicate-argument structure* such as "slide(John, box)," which indicates a particular action (the predicate "slide") and its participants (the arguments "John" and "box"). Certain kinds of actions can sometimes integrate additional information and use it to enrich the action description. Motion verbs often specify details with respect to the path the object in motion will take. These can include the medium of the path (for example, down a gravel road, through the air, along the river) as well as specific locations for end-points such as sources and goals (e.g., to the store, across the room, from the beach, home). Our common sense tells us that path information is relevant to the description of actions involving motion, but more significantly from a methodological point of view, linguistic evidence points to the facility with which path prepositional phrases (e.g., through the door, across the street) can modify descriptions of motion events.

It is critical for the PAR to adequately specify any and all possible enrichments of the basic predicate-argument structure so that these types of extended meanings can be accommodated.

9.5.1 Parser and Translator

We are using the XTAG Synchronous Tree Adjoining Grammar system (Palmer, Rosenzweig, and Schuler 1998) as the basis of our NL interface. This consists of a parser for extracting the predicate-argument structure from an input sentence and a translator for generating an instruction script from this predicate-argument structure. The instruction script is written in Python and contains one or more PARs. The parser extracts a predicate-argument structure by first associating each word in an input sentence with one or more *elementary tree* fragments, which are combined into a single-phrase structure tree for the entire input sentence using the constrained operations of the Tree Adjoining Grammar formalism (Joshi 1985). These elementary tree fragments have argument positions for the subjects and objects of verbs, adjectives, and other predicates, which constrain the way the fragments can be combined and which determine the predicate-argument structure of the input sentence. The translator converts this predicate-argument structure into an instruction script.

With this architecture, a wide variety of inflections and grammatical transformations can be reduced to a much smaller set of predicates in the parser, and a variety of synonymous predicates can be further reduced to a still smaller set of PARs and scripting-language keywords in the translator. Although some parts of the translator may be domain-specific (some actions may depend on particular objects in a domain), the parser can easily be ported between domains, since its predicates are based on linguistic observations instead of on a particular programming language or virtual environment.

For ordinary instructions, the scripts generated by the translator are executed immediately and may introduce one or more PARs into the execution engine depending on the results of test conditions and the iteration of loops within a script. Users can also give the system persistent instructions, or *standing orders*, whose scripts are added to a rule-table (sec. 9.4.3) and executed at each frame of animation. But the number of PARs introduced at each frame still depends on the execution of the scripts. For example, the system might be running a script for "if a rabbit enters the trap, pull the string" at each simulation frame. But, it is only when a rabbit actually enters the trap that the script would introduce the "pull string" PAR into the execution engine. A persistent interpretation of "catch every rabbit in the park" would work the same way, even though it does not contain an *if*-clause, because at every frame the script would iterate over all the rabbits in the park. But it is only when there actually is a rabbit that the script would introduce the "catch" PAR. Note that it cannot be generally determined if a given instruction is immediate or persistent by *if*-clauses or other cues in the input sentence. So, the user must specify this information in the input dialog.

9.6 Examples

Communication includes both verbal and nonverbal channels. In our work, the verbal communication is primarily concerned with instructions between users and avatars. Nonverbal gestures augment communication in important ways (Cassell and Vilhjálmsson 1999; Cassell et al. 1994). As they are themselves actions, they can be described, triggered, and modified as PARs. Although systems such as Gandalf and Rea (Cassell et al. 1999; Thórisson 1998) include user gestural inputs, we limit our scope to nonverbal gestures of and between virtual agents.

We describe three implemented examples that demonstrate real-time interactive agent behaviors. The first example, *Jack's MOOse lodge*, is realized in the JackMOO environment (Shi et al. 1999). Here, the conversation is mainly between the users and their avatars through limited natural language. A primitive natural language parser interprets only simple sentences containing a direct object, indirect object, verb, and preposition. In JackMOO, we also show the control of autonomous and user-instructed agents with contextual behaviors. We end this example by demonstrating a dialogue with the purpose of establishing a leader-follower relationship between two virtual agents.

In the second example, *PAR for Conversational Agents,* the communication is through gestures and speech between the virtual agents themselves. The actions and style of the agents' actions and speech are context sensitive. The agents converse among themselves according to predefined scripts, but no specific NL instructions are given to them.

The third example, *PAR for Virtual Environment Training,* has been designed to demonstrate language-based control in the PAR system. The conversation here is again mainly between the users and their avatars through natural language. The simulation allows a user to give specific instructions or standing orders to the virtual agents within the environment. Here, we demonstrate the XTAG parser interpreting complex sentences and standing orders and the translator generating new PARs from the XTAG output.

Figure 9.3
Jack's MOOse Lodge.

9.6.1 JackMOO for Conversational Agents

The scene (fig. 9.3) shows the inside of a mountain lodge and includes five virtual humans: one is a semi-autonomous waiter agent and four are user-instructed "smart avatars." The waiter agent carries out a few specific tasks based on the set of rules given to him and the existing environmental conditions. The four avatars are named "Bob," "Norm," "Sarah," and "David." In a distributed environment, different users at possibly different geographical sites could control each avatar. In a nondistributed environment, the instructions can be specifically directed to an avatar: for example, "Sarah, walk to the door." The parser is capable of interpreting a small set of actions. In the following, we will use the quoted name ("Bob") to refer to the avatar and the unquoted name (Bob) to refer to the live user who is issuing commands.

The avatars can appear to hold conversations with each other. To do this, an instruction is given to the avatar to say something, for example, "Norm, say hello to Sarah." A text-to-speech converter is used to generate a synthetic voice.

The avatars can interpret the same action in different ways depending on the context and the state of the environment. In our example, the avatar "Bob" is instructed to greet the other avatars in the room. Depending on the other agent (that is, by querying attributes of the other agent model), "Bob" either greets the agent with a handshake or by bowing. From these cases, we can see that "Bob" shows his contextual behavior by executing different actions to different targets given the same command, "greet." "Norm" and "Sarah" show their contextual behaviors by returning the greeting to "Bob" in a corresponding fashion.

A leader-follower relationship can be established where one avatar follows another avatar's actions. "Norm" invites "Sarah" to go out for a walk. This is done by issuing a command: "Norm, say 'Will you go for a walk with me?' to Sarah." When "Norm" is heard saying this, Sarah can accept the invitation: "Sarah, say 'yes.'" This is an example of a conversation modifying the role of the entities in the environment, namely, to initiate a leader-follower relationship. Then as "Norm" starts walking to the door, "Sarah" is instructed to follow "Norm" by issuing the command, "Sarah, follow Norm." As "Norm" walks to the door, opens the door, and exits the room, "Sarah" trails along behind. A pursuit locomotion condition is established between "Norm" (the leader) and "Sarah" (the follower). In the leader-follower model, one temporarily yields some aspects of the control of one's avatar to another's lead. Sarah could still instruct her avatar to wave good-bye even as she follows "Norm" out the door. Explicit textual commands would have to be issued by either party to break the relationship.

9.6.2 PAR for Conversational Agents

Creating appropriate gestures for conversational agents is not easy because the range of gestures performed during speech output is much larger than a symbolic selection set used for discrete inputs. Cassell (Cassell et al. 1994) distinguished four types of gestures: Iconics, Metaphorics, Deictics, and Beats. Some of the main components of gesture performance are coarticulation, expression, spatialization, and selection. In this example, we combine and implement these components within the PAR architecture.

Our multilevel PAR architecture permits conversational agent control. A conversational agent needs most of the motor skills specified in section 9.3.2 in addition to speech. All these actions are instances of the UPAR in the Actionary database. Several motion generators such as ArmNet, HandNet, TorsoNet,

FaceNet, SeeNet, and SpeakNet (all built from PaT-Nets) are responsible for generating and synchronizing these motions.

In this example, two virtual human agents are negotiating with each other to solve technical problems in an office environment. The text (script) is annotated with gesture tags in advance but executed in context. Many, but not all tags, could be automatically triggered through keywords in text. Here is a sample of the conversation.

```
Agent2: "Hello." [waves his hand in a hurry]
Agent1: "Hello." [waves hand slowly and nods]
Agent2: "Can you help me [points at himself] to fix the copy
machine?"
Agent1: "Sure, if you fix the mail server for me." [points at
himself too]
Agent2: "Great [smiles happily]. Follow me." [follow-me gesture
hurriedly]
```

Both agents perform the same UPAR action "Say-Hello" but they do it quite differently. Agent2 waves his hand very quickly to show that he is in a hurry to find somebody to help him solve the technical problem. However, Agent1 is a little nonchalant about his trouble, so he waves his hand slowly and nods his head at the same time. Furthermore, they speak using different voices, intonation, pitch, duration, and rate. The UPAR "Say-Hello" in the Actionary database always has the same default applicability conditions, preparatory specifications, termination conditions, and execution steps. But when it is initialized with agent-specific parameters and variables such as purpose, duration, and manner, the defaults are overridden to reflect context-appropriate behaviors (Badler, Chi, and Chopra 1999). This increases believability by preventing agents from reacting in the same manner in identical contexts and gives the impression that each agent has distinct emotions and personalities. The agent-specific parameters are specified through the graphical user interface and are resolved during the execution of the primitive action.

9.6.3 PAR for Virtual Environment Training

This scenario (fig. 9.4) is centered on a military checkpoint at the edge of a town. There are three soldiers in training (further referred to as trainees) whose job is to apprehend suspected terrorists. A separate agent process controls each of the trainees. A process simulator (an autonomous agent process) generates new

Figure 9.4
VET environment.

vehicles, controls their movements, and operates traffic lights. As each vehicle approaches the checkpoint, one of the trainees checks each civilian male driver's identification. If there is a match, the trainee is supposed to draw his weapon and take the driver into custody. All others are allowed to pass through the checkpoint.

During this process, the trainees may (inadvertently) commit different errors; these may result in one of the trainees getting shot by a driver. In an effort to correct the situation, the user can give different standing orders to the trainees.

9.6.3.1 *Agents* The agents in this scenario are the three trainees, the drivers, and the process simulator. The PAR system eases the creation of autonomous virtual human agents by providing a flexible way of representing personalities, emotions, and other agent properties and also by providing fast, straightforward ways to query the environment and communicate with other agents.

In this example, the virtual human agents can currently have one of two personalities, hostile or nonhostile. The trainees are all nonhostile. Drivers are randomly chosen to be hostile or nonhostile when they are created and can be changed at any time during the simulation. The personality of the driver is expressed through his actions. A hostile driver is far more likely to be uncooperative and even attempt to shoot one of the trainees.

In PAR, one of the properties of an agent is the emotional state of the agent. The agents are capable of being emotionally neutral, angry, sad, fearful, or happy. Initially, all of the trainees are emotionally neutral, and the drivers' emotions are set randomly at the time of their creation. During the simulation, each agent's emotion is changed to correspond to the existing environmental conditions; for example, a trainee becomes angry whenever he draws his weapon.

The emotions of the agents are expressed through facial expressions (fig. 9.5). We are currently using a facial animation model (Kalra et al. 1992) from MIRALab at the University of Geneva.

In PAR, the agents externally communicate with each other using speech and gestures. Internally, they communicate through message passing. For example, when the driver hands his identification to the trainee, the trainee needs to respond by taking the identification. He knows to do this because the driver sends him a message informing him that the identification is being handed to him. This approach sidesteps questions of gesture recognition that may be addressed in the future.

9.6.3.2 *Standing Orders*   Standing orders are instructions issued to correct the erroneous situations that arise due to trainee errors.

In the first situation, the trainee forgets to take cover while drawing his weapon at the suspected terrorist driver and so gets shot by him. To correct this, the user gives the following standing order to that trainee: "When you draw your weapon at the driver, take cover from the driver behind your drum." This standing order is immediately parsed by the NL2PAR module and stored as a *Python* script in the rule-table. So, in the next trial of the simulation, as soon as the trainee draws his weapon, the standing order (now rule) forces him to also take cover behind his drum correctly. Furthermore, when one of the trainees draws his weapon, the other two trainees remain standing still, which is situationally incorrect. So, a standing order of "If Trainee1 draws his weapon at the driver, draw your weapon at the driver and take cover from the driver behind your drum" corrects this situation.

The command "take cover" takes two oblique arguments—the potential threat (in this case, the driver), and the desired cover (the steel drum). When

Figure 9.5
Angry facial expression.

this PAR is executed, the trainee moves to a place where the drum intersects the path between herself and the driver. But since the "take cover" action is parameterized at this high level, the trainee could be instructed to take cover from virtually any object (say, from one of his companions), behind any other object (say, behind the suspect's car), and the simulation would accommodate it.

After the first suspect is taken away, the scenario continues until a second suspect enters the checkpoint. This time, however, the suspect draws a gun as soon as the first trainee asks him for his identification, and shoots the trainee before he can react. Observing that the trainees on the passenger side of the car could have seen the driver reach for the gun, the user gives two additional standing orders for trainees 2 and 3:

- "When there is a driver, watch the driver."
- "If the driver reaches for a gun, warn Trainee1."

Once again the simulation is replayed and whenever there is a driver in the car at the checkpoint, the above standing orders force trainees 2 and 3 to watch the driver. Moreover, when the driver reaches for his gun, the rules force those trainees to warn the first trainee, before the driver can grab it and fire. So, the first trainee has time to draw his own weapon and take cover. Since all the previous orders are still in the rule table, trainees 2 and 3 also draw their weapons at the driver as soon as they see trainee 1 do so, and all three still take cover when they draw their weapons. The driver, outnumbered, quickly surrenders, and the trainees successfully complete the exercise.

The "watch" action is classified as a preemptive action and so its UPAR has a lower priority. This means that whenever the trainees need to execute other actions, their agent processes will preempt the "watch" from their queues and execute the other actions. But after the other actions have been completed, if there is still a driver at the checkpoint, the rule resulting from the standing order "When there is a driver, watch the driver" will again force the trainees to watch the driver. This results in a completely natural-looking correct scenario where the trainees are always cautiously watching the driver. If they are interrupted and forced to do something else, they quickly finish that task and resume watching.

9.7 Discussion

The PAR architecture and its implementation are intended to provide a test bed for real-time conversational agents who work, communicate, and manipulate objects in a synthetic 3-D world. Our goal is to make interaction with these embodied characters the same as with live individuals. We have focused on language as the medium for communicating instructions and finite state machines as the controllers for agent or object movements.

The structure described here is the basis for a new kind of dictionary we call an Actionary. A dictionary uses words to define words. Sometimes it grounds concepts in pictures and (in on-line sources) maybe even sounds and video clips. But these are canned and not *parameterized*—flexible and adaptable to new situations the way that words function in actual usage. In contrast, the Actionary uses PAR and its consequent animations to ground action terms. It may be viewed as a 3-D (spatialized) environment for animating situated actions expressed in linguistic terms. The actions are animated to show the meaning in context, that is, relative to a given 3-D environment and individual agents.

The Actionary facilitates the study of conceptual and physical aspects of verbs and their parameters that may be overlooked in conventional dictionaries. The Actionary promotes cross-linguistic translation of instructions, since the action execution part is not dependent on the surface syntax. Finally, the Actionary enables low-bandwidth communication of instructions across a distributed multiperson simulation system since only the high-level textual commands rather than low-level character movement data need to be transmitted.

Any simulation system must be supplied with procedures that implement its semantics. PAR is no exception. We have discussed how the multilevel approach lets us focus the system implementation in separable and reusable motion generators, PaT-Nets, and PARs, but these must still be manually coded. People build their internal representations through experience and learning, but these avenues are not yet open to the simulation designer. We are developing tools that may allow UPARs and some of their parameters to be learned from observation. Additionally, we may be able to use the NL interface to construct portions of a UPAR, just as a word dictionary provides some but not all of a term's semantics.

A natural language instruction interface may also be brittle: if words are used for objects or actions that are not already defined through the database or PAR semantics, instructions or standing orders may fail. By incorporating a thesaurus, word equivalents can be selected that may substitute for the terms given. Thus, for example, the standing orders about trainee reactions to the *car's driver* should not fail if the user talks about the *vehicle's operator*. Confirming that the user's intention is understood by echoing a paraphrase with the substitutions would be a helpful dialogue feature.

Finally, the actions requested may fail for any number of reasons, from failed conditions in the PAR to unanticipated confounding events to inadequate implementation. Since our agent models admit the possibility of adding action planners, some failures may be detectable and repairs initiated automatically (Cassell and Vilhjálmsson 1999; Rickel and Johnson 1999). Giving an agent the capability of observing the consequences of its actions (or inaction) and generating compensating rules is an attractive future effort.

An instruction understanding system, based on natural language inputs, an Actionary translation, and an embodied virtual human agent could provide a nonprogramming interface between real and virtual people. We can describe tasks for others and see them carried out, whether they are real or virtual participants. Thus the door is opening to novel applications for embodied agents in job training, team coordination, manufacturing and maintenance, education, and emergency drills. As the Actionary grows, new applications should become ever easier to generate. And just as our human experience lets real people take on new tasks, so too should embodied characters be adaptable to new environments, new behaviors, and new instructions.

Acknowledgments

This research is partially supported by U.S. Air Force F41624-97-D-5002, Office of Naval Research K-5-55043/3916-1552793, DURIP N0001497-1-0396, and AASERTs N00014-97-1-0603 and N0014-97-1-0605, DARPA SB-MDA-97-2951001, NSF IRI95-04372, SBR-8900230, and IIS-9900297, Army Research Office ASSERT DAA 655-981-0147, NASA NRA NAG 5-3990, and Engineering Animation Inc.

References

Badler, N., and S. Smoliar. 1979. Digital representations of human movement. *ACM Computing Surveys* 11(1):19–38.

Badler, N., D. Chi, and S. Chopra. 1999. Virtual human animation based on movement observation and cognitive behavior models. In *Proceedings of the Computer Animation 1999*, 128–137. Los Alamitos, Calif.: IEEE Computer Society.

Badler, N., M. Palmer, and R. Bindiganavale. 1999. Animation control for real-time virtual humans. *Communications of the ACM* 42(7):65–73.

Badler, N., C. Phillips, and B. Webber. 1993. *Simulating humans: Computer graphics animation and control*. New York: Oxford University Press.

Badler, N., B. Webber, W. Becket, C. Geib, M. Moore, C. Pelachaud, B. Reich, and M. Stone. 1996. Planning for animation. In N. Magnenat-Thalmann and D. Thalmann, eds., *Interactive computer animation*, 235–262. New York: Prentice-Hall.

Badler, N., B. Webber, J. Kalita, and J. Esakov. 1990. Animation from instructions. In N. Badler, B. Barsky, and D. Zeltzer, eds., *Making them move: Mechanics, control, and animation of articulated figures*, 51–93. San Francisco: Morgan Kaufmann.

Badler, N., B. Webber, M. Palmer, T. Noma, M. Stone, J. Rosenzweig, S. Chopra, K. Stanley, J. Bourne, and B. Di Eugenio. 1997. Final report to Air Force HRGA regarding feasibility of natural language text generation from task networks for use in automatic generation of Technical Orders from DEPTH simulations. Technical Report, CIS, University of Pennsylvania.

Bartenieff, I., and D. Lewis. 1980. *Body movement: Coping with the environment*. New York: Gordon and Breach Science Publishers.

Bindiganavale, R., and N. Badler. 1998. Motion abstraction and mapping with spatial constraints. In *Modelling and motion capture techniques for virtual environments*, 70–82. Heidelberg: Springer.

Bourne, J. 1998. Generating adequate instructions: Knowing when to stop. In *Proceedings of the AAAI/IAAI Conference*, 1169. Doctoral Consortium Section, Madison, Wisconsin.

Brooks, R. 1989. A robot that walks: Emergent behaviors from a carefully evolved network. *Neural Computation* 1(2):253–262.

Cassell, J., and H. Vilhjálmsson. 1999. Fully embodied conversational avatars: Making communicative behaviors autonomous. *Autonomous Agents and Multi-Agent Systems* 2(1):45–64.

Cassell, J., T. Bickmore, M. Billinghurst, L. Campbell, K. Chang, and H. Vilhjálmsson. 1999. Embodiment in conversational interfaces: Rea. In *Proceedings of CHI '99*, 520–527. New York: ACM Press.

Cassell, J., C. Pelachaud, N. Badler, M. Steedman, B. Achorn, W. Becket, B. Douville, S. Prevost, and M. Stone. 1994. Animated conversation: Rule-based generation of facial expression, gesture and spoken intonation for multiple conversational agents. In *Computer Graphics*, 413–420. New York: ACM SIGGRAPH.

Cavazza, M., R. Earnshaw, N. Magnenat-Thalmann, and D. Thalmann. 1998. Motion control of virtual humans. *IEEE Computer Graphics and Applications* 18(5):24–31.

Chi, D., B. Webber, J. Clarke, and N. Badler. 1995. Casualty modeling for real-time medical training. *Presence* 5(4):359–366.

Douville, B., L. Levison, and N. Badler. 1996. Task level object grasping for simulated agents. *Presence* 5(4):416–430.

Earnshaw, R., N. Magnenat-Thalmann, D. Terzopoulos, and D. Thalmann. 1998. Computer animation for virtual humans. *IEEE Computer Graphics and Applications* 18(5):20–23.

Gleicher, M. 1998. Retargetting motion to new characters. In *Computer Graphics*, 33–42. New York: ACM SIGGRAPH.

Hodgins, J., W. Wooten, D. Brogan, and J. O'Brien. 1995. Animating human athletics. In *Computer Graphics*, 71–78. New York: ACM SIGGRAPH.

Joshi, A. K. 1985. How much context sensitivity is necessary for characterizing structural descriptions: Tree adjoining grammars. In D. Dowty, L. Karttunen, and A. Zwicky, eds., *Natural language parsing: Psychological, computational and theoretical perspectives*, 206–250. Cambridge: Cambridge University Press.

Kallmann, M., and D. Thalmann. 1999. A behavioral interface to simulate agent-object interactions in real-time. In *Proceedings of Computer Animation*, 138–146. Los Alamitos, Calif.: IEEE Computer Society.

Kalra, P., A. Mangili, N. Magnenat-Thalmann, and D. Thalmann. 1992. Simulation of muscle actions using rational free form deformations. *Proceedings Eurographics '92, Computer Graphics Forum* 2(3):59–69.

Lutz, M. 1996. *Programming Python*. Sebastapol: O'Reilly.

Metaxas, D. 1996. *Physics-based deformable models: Applications to computer vision, graphics and medical imaging*. Boston: Kluwer.

Narayanan, S. 1997. Talking the talk is like walking the walk. In *Proceedings of the 19th Annual Conference of the Cognitive Science Society*, 548–553. Palo Alto, Calif.: Lawrence Erlbaum and Associates.

Noma, T., and N. Badler. 1997. A virtual human presenter. In *Proceedings of the IJCAI '97 Workshop on Animated Interface Agents*, 45–51. San Francisco: Morgan Kaufmann.

Palmer, M., J. Rosenzweig, and W. Schuler. 1998. Capturing motion verb generalizations with synchronous tag. In P. St. Dizier, ed., *Predicative forms in NLP*. Text, Speech, and Language Technology Series, 250–277. Dordrecht, The Netherlands: Muwer Press.

Perlin, K. 1995. Real time responsive animation with personality. *IEEE Transactions on Visualization and Computer Graphics* 1(1):5–15.

Perlin, K., and A. Goldberg. 1996. Improv: A system for scripting interactive actors in virtual worlds. In *Computer Graphics*, 205–216. New York: ACM SIGGRAPH.

Rickel J., and W. L. Johnson. 1999. Animated agents for procedural training in virtual reality: Perception, cognition and motor control. *Applied Artificial Intelligence* (13):343–382.

Shi, J., T. J. Smith, J. Granieri, and N. Badler. 1999. Smart avatars in JackMOO. In *Proceedings of the IEEE Virtual Reality Annual International Symposium*, 156–163. Los Alamitos, Calif.: IEEE Computer Society.

Thórisson, K. 1998. Decision making in multimodal real-time face-to-face communication. In *Proceedings of the Autonomous Agents Conference,* 16–23. New York: ACM.

Ting, B. J. 1998. Real time human model design. Ph.D. diss., CIS, University of Pennsylvania.

Trias, T., S. Chopra, B. Reich, M. Moore, N. Badler, B. Webber, and C. Geib. 1996. Decision networks for integrating the behaviors of virtual agents and avatars. In *Proceedings of the IEEE Virtual Reality Annual International Symposium.* Los Alamitos, Calif.: IEEE Computer Society.

Volino, P., M. Courchesne, and N. Magnenat-Thalmann. 1995. Versatile and efficient techniques for simulating cloth and other deformable objects. In *Computer Graphics,* 137–144. New York: ACM SIGGRAPH.

Webber, B., N. Badler, B. Di Eugenio, C. Geib, L. Levison, and M. Moore. 1995. Instructions, intentions and expectations. *Artificial Intelligence* 73:253–269.

Wilcox, S. K. 1998. *Web developer's guide to 3D avatars.* New York: Wiley.

Wilhelms, J., and A. van Gelder. 1997. Anatomically-based modeling. In *Computer Graphics,* 173–180. New York: ACM SIGGRAPH.

Zeltzer, D. 1990. Task-level graphical simulation: Abstraction, representation, and control. In N. Badler, B. Barsky, and D. Zeltzer, eds., *Making them move: Mechanics, control, and animation of articulated figures,* 3–33. San Francisco: Morgan Kaufmann.

Zhao, L., and N. Badler. 1998. Gesticulation behaviors for virtual humans. In *Proceedings of Pacific Graphics,* 161–168. Los Alamitos, Calif.: IEEE Computer Society.

III
Evaluation

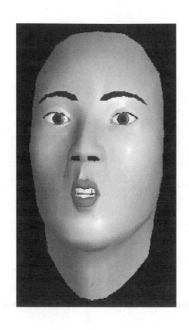

Developing and Evaluating Conversational Agents

Dominic W. Massaro, Michael M. Cohen, Jonas Beskow,

and Ronald A. Cole

10.1 Embodied Characters

The title of this book is *Embodied Conversational Agents*. Why not just "Conversational Agents"? What does embodiment add to our quest for a synthetic replication of some real human agent? Traditionally, the success of artificial intelligence was deemed to be contingent on creating a thinking machine, encompassing all of the rationality, logic, and abstract knowledge possessed by humans. The achievement of this goal doesn't appear to be much closer now than it was at the onset of the cybernetic age four decades ago. Today, an expanding cadre of cognitive scientists is offering a new image of thinking and intelligence. The functions of mind are embedded in a body, which is situated in a physical world of action. Very few of the functions of mind take place outside this embodiment. As summarized by Clark (1997, 1), "Minds are not disembodied logical reasoning devices." Newton (1996), for example, proposes that schematized sensorimotor images are the cognitive basis for understanding.

A simulacrum can be defined as a convincing rendering of a real person. Because an artificially animated simulacrum cannot experience the physical world of action, does this mean that our agent will never understand? This question touches on the infamous Chinese room scenario defended by Searle (1992). Successful dialogue can take place between an agent and a human in the Chinese room even though the artificial half has no understanding of Chinese whatsoever. His thesis is that true understanding requires a grounding in the physical and sensory world, and cannot be mimicked by artificial intelligence. Glenberg (1997), a memory and language processing researcher, has proposed an indexical hypothesis for understanding. We supposedly index words to objects or perceptual symbols. He proposes that important guides for our behavior are the relations between bodies and objects in the world.

This thesis is a variant of Gibson's (1979) notion of affordances, in which perceptual states of the world specify specific actions. These affordances necessarily change with our goals and our experiences. These various influences provide a set of constraints that must mesh appropriately for a behavioral action to occur. Glenberg's empirical behavioral experiments indicate that this framework provides a better understanding of people's meaningful judgments of sentences than do more abstract approaches such as latent semantic analysis (Landauer and Dumais 1997). Perhaps it is premature to judge how the ideas of embodiment and their implications for conversational agents will play out. One potentially valuable implication, however, is that convincing agents might be instantiated, even if or because they think less and do more. For our purposes, agents only have to give the impression of understanding, as in Weizenbaum's original Eliza therapist. The human in the Chinese room might also be fooled by the agent's ability to converse reasonably in Chinese.

In this chapter, we describe the progress we have made in the development of a conversational agent. We are currently using this agent as a classroom tutor for language training for children with hearing loss. There are several technological and psychological components to this research endeavor, and, as should be expected, some are more realized than others. We begin with a description of Baldi, a computer-animated talking head, and how it is evaluated for quality and intelligibility. Based on research with the talking head, we present evidence that people are superb pattern recognizers who exploit multiple sources of information from several modalities in parallel. We then describe its application within a speech toolkit that allows the teacher and student to develop lessons that incorporate spoken language input and output.

We believe wholeheartedly that computer users will benefit from interaction with conversational agents because of the many sources of information they can provide. Most importantly, a speaker's face provides valuable and effective information for the perception and recognition of speech and emotion. As perceivers, we naturally integrate the visible and audible cues in a variety of situations, and this ability is not easily compromised. To provide this information, we have developed a completely automated and animated synthetic talking head. With this synthetic speaker, we can control and study the informative aspects and psychological processes in face-to-face dialogues. Our talking head communicates paralinguistic as well as linguistic information, and is controlled by either a text-to-speech system or is aligned with a recording of natural speech that has been transcribed phonetically.

Our goal is to advance the development of our talking head, its design, and its accompanying technology and to create a human-computer interface centered on a virtual, conversational agent. Such agents will interact with human users in the most natural manner possible, including the ability to listen and understand as well as speak fluently. Agents that provide additional information in a natural manner should facilitate and enrich interaction between humans and machines. Even communication among humans can be improved when mediated by virtual agents. To pursue this hypothesis, our work involves the synthesis of speech and emotion by the conversational agent and the psychological evaluation of its contribution to language and emotion perception, acquisition of new knowledge, communication, and productivity.

10.2 Talking Heads in Action

Technology advocates have always hoped that natural conversational behavior would be the primary medium of communication between people and machines. Our talking head, as a conversational agent, has the potential to take us one step closer to that realization. Ideally, each of us could have our own agent (in our own image, if we wish) to handle our communications. A conversational agent does not get tired or bored, isn't waylaid by a sore throat, and (as of yet) belongs to no union—in short, it's a "talking and understanding" machine. The surely distant goal is that talking heads will be able to translate and speak in any language, at any rate of speed or level of complexity, with the culturally appropriate emotional affect. In addition to our current use of visible speech to facilitate learning and language acquisition for the hearing impaired, we envision applications of this technology in a variety of domains, including, but not limited to, education, entertainment, and human-machine interaction. For example, our talking head could serve as a useful aid in learning second languages and in improving the phonological and reading skills of dyslexic children. As we continue our research, we expect that the talking head will play an important role in the enhancement of auditory synthetic speech, an educational tool in linguistics and speech science, and a supporting agent in human-machine interactions.

In order to support the development of conversational agents for universal access and learning, research is necessary on a number of core technologies and how to integrate them successfully. These include dialogue modeling; natural language processing and information retrieval; automatic auditory, visual, and gestural recognition of a speaker's linguistic, emotional, and conversational cues; speech synthesis; and gestural and facial animation. Many of the key research challenges and potential advancements to the state of the art lie at the boundaries where these disciplines meet. Our research has made the most progress on speech synthesis and facial animation, speech recognition, and the easy implementation of spoken language dialogues.

10.3 Baldi, a Talking Head

Figure 10.1 shows our talking head, Baldi. As can be seen in the figure, not much lies behind Baldi's attractive exterior. His existence and functionality depend on computer animation and text-to-speech synthesis. With this talking head, we can control the parameters of visible speech and study its informative aspects. His speech is controlled by thirty-three parameters including jaw rotation and thrust; horizontal mouth width; lip corner and protrusion controls; lower lip f-tuck; vertical lip position; horizontal and vertical teeth offset; tongue angle, width, and length. Figure 10.2 illustrates Baldi's articulation at onset for the syllables /ba/, /va/, /ða/, /da/, /ʃa/, and /wa/.

The talking head is made of polygons that have been joined together and smooth shaded. The structure is made up of approximately nine hundred surfaces connected at the edges to create the 3-D head with eyes, pupil, iris, sclera, eyebrows, nose, skin, lips, tongue, teeth, and neck (see fig. 10.1). The polygon topology and animation are manipulated through a set of control parameters (Cohen and Massaro 1993; Parke 1974). The tongue is implemented as a parametrically controlled shaded surface made of a polygon mesh.

One of the primary objectives of our research is to identify the informative properties of the human face by evaluating the effectiveness of various properties in our synthetic face. The value of facial animation in the development of synthetic speech is analogous to the important contribution of auditory speech synthesis in speech perception research. The development of a realistic, high-quality facial display has provided a powerful tool to continue the investigation of a number of questions in auditory-visual speech perception. This visible speech synthesis permits the type of experimentation necessary to determine (1) what properties of visible speech are used, (2) how they are processed, and (3) how this information is integrated with auditory and other contextual sources of information in speech perception. In some of our research, we systematically manipulate audible and visible speech independent of each other (Massaro 1998).

Analysis of real speech articulation has guided our research in visible speech synthesis. Perception experiments have indicated how well the synthesis simulates real speakers. An understanding of visible speech perception

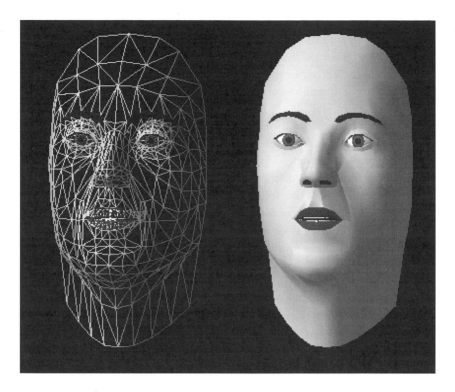

Figure 10.1
The talking head, called Baldi. As can be seen in the wire frame on the right, there is not much behind his attractive exterior on the left. [http://mambo.ucsc.edu/psl/pela/wg.jpg]

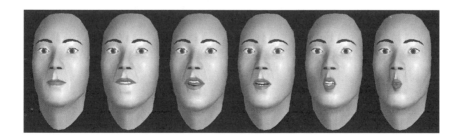

Figure 10.2
Baldi's articulation at onset for the syllables /ba/, /va/, /ða/, /da/, /ʃa/, and /wa/.

derived from these experiments has assisted in our development of visible speech. Our goal at the Perceptual Science Laboratory (PSL) has been to create a talking head whose facial motions look realistic, not to duplicate the musculature of the face. We have chosen to develop visible speech synthesis in the same manner that has proven successful with audible speech synthesis. We call this technique terminal analogue synthesis. Its goal is simply to mimic the final speech product rather than the physiological mechanisms that produce it.

One advantage of terminal analogue synthesis is that calculations for changing the surface shapes of the polygon models can be carried out much more rapidly than can calculations for muscle and tissue simulations. It also may be easier to achieve the desired facial shapes directly rather than in terms of the constituent muscle actions. The real-time animation of the synthetic head (at up to 60 frames per second) was developed on a Silicon Graphics Crimson Reality Engine with 96 megabytes of RAM and a 100MHz R4000 microprocessor using the IrisGL graphics library. Because our implementation is efficient, we have been able to port the animation algorithm to a PC platform, (an Intel® Pentium-based Windows® NT or Windows 95 platform, using the newer OpenGL graphics library). We are using this implementation for language training with profoundly deaf children at the Tucker Maxon Oral School in Portland, Oregon (Cole et al. 1999).

Our implementation of visible speech synthesis has progressed over the last three years to include additional and modified control parameters, two generations of tongues, a visual speech synthesis control strategy, text-to-speech synthesis, bimodal (auditory/visual) synthesis, and controls for paralinguistic information and affect in the face. Figure 10.3 illustrates Baldi's facial expressions for *happy, angry, surprise, fear, sadness,* and *disgust.* Most of our current parameters move points on the face geometrically by rotation (e.g., jaw rotation) or translation, in one or more dimensions (e.g., lower and upper lip height, mouth widening). Other parameters are changed by interpolation between patches on alternate faces. Examples of this type of parameter include cheek shape, neck shape, and smiling. The synthesis program, which consists of about 20,000 lines of C code, runs in real time on both SGI™ and PC.

10.4 Evaluating Talking Heads

While developing Baldi's animation and speech synthesis, we have continuously evaluated and improved its speech. It is a sobering fact that auditory speech synthesis still falls far short of natural speech after thirty years of intensive research and development (Cohen, Walker, and Massaro 1996; Massaro 1998,

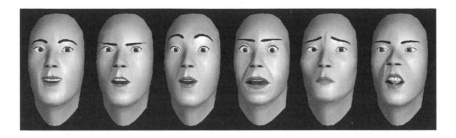

Figure 10.3
Baldi's expression of happiness, anger, surprise, fear, sadness, and disgust.

chap. 13). We have not allowed ourselves to be swayed by the subjective comments of many viewers who claim "how natural Baldi seems." Instead, we have systematically performed experiments to compare the quality of the synthetic speech to natural speech. The relative realism of Baldi's visible speech is measured in terms of its intelligibility to speech readers. The experiments measure comparative intelligibility to determine where and how Baldi falls short of natural speakers. The synthesis is then modified accordingly—bringing it more in line with natural visible speech. In a series of over a dozen such evaluation experiments, with appropriate adjustments to the synthesis, the quality of the visible speech has become almost as good as in a natural speaker (Massaro 1998).

In a typical study, we presented for identification monosyllabic English words (e.g., *sing, bin, dung, dip, seethe*) produced either by a natural speaker (Bernstein and Eberhardt 1986) or our synthetic talker randomly intermixed. The words were shown on videotape without sound. The synthetic stimuli used a specific set of parameter values and dominance functions for each phoneme and our blending function for coarticulation. The AT&T text-to-speech (TTS) module was utilized to provide the phonemic representation for each word and the durations of the speech segments, in addition to synthesizing the auditory speech (presented as feedback) (Olive 1990). Other characteristics such as speaking rate and average acoustic amplitude were equated for the natural and synthetic talker. The natural speech on the videodisk was articulated in citation form and thus had a relatively slow speaking rate.

College students who were native speakers of American English served as subjects, in two twenty-minute sessions each day for two days. Up to four at a time were tested in separate sound attenuated rooms under control of the SGI™-Crimson computer, with video from the laser disc (the human talker) or the computer being presented over 13-inch color monitors. On each trial, they were first presented with a silent word from one of the two faces and then typed in their answer on a terminal keyboard. Only actual monosyllabic English words were accepted as valid answers from a list of about 12,000 words derived mainly from the *Oxford English Dictionary*. After all subjects had responded, they received feedback by a second presentation of the word, this time with auditory speech (natural or synthetic) and with the word in written form on the left side of the video monitor. There were 264 test words, and each word was tested with both synthetic and natural speech, for a total of 2 x 264 = 528 test trials.

By comparing the overall proportion correct responses and analyzing the perceptual confusions, we can determine how closely the synthetic visual speech matches the natural visual speech. The questions to be answered are "What is the extent of confusions?" and "How similar are the patterns of confusions for the two talkers?" This analysis has been simplified by ignoring confusions that take place between visually similar phonemes. Because of the data-limited property of visible speech in comparison to audible speech, many phonemes are virtually indistinguishable by sight, even from a natural face, and so are expected to be easily confused. To eliminate these confusions from consideration, we group visually indistinguishable phonemes into categories called visemes. Some confusions do take place between viseme categories, however. This is partly because of the difficulty of speech reading. But also, as with most categories, visemes are not sharply defined (i.e., they are "fuzzy"), and any sharp definitions imposed are therefore somewhat arbitrary and inaccurate. Even so, it is worthwhile to use some standard viseme groupings in order to assess how well the more meaningful visible speech differences are perceived.

We found that the confusion matrices for natural and synthetic speech are very similar to one another. Figure 10.4 presents the word-initial consonant viseme confusions for a typical recent unpublished experiment for natural (left panel) and synthetic (right panel) speech. The area of each circle indicates the proportion of each response to a given stimulus. Of course, we don't expect perfect performance for either talker; it is the similarity of the pattern of responses that is of interest. We computed the correlation of the synthetic and natural talker data, which yielded a correlation of $r = .93$. The number of overall proportion correct responses for the natural speech (.69) was slightly higher than that for the synthetic talker (.65).

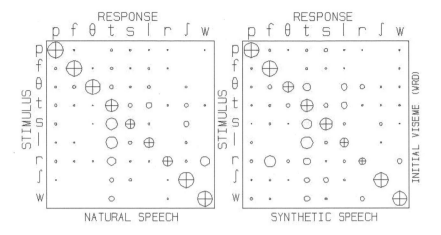

Figure 10.4

Proportion of viseme responses as a function of initial stimulus viseme of the test word. The area of the circle is proportional to the value.

An additional type of analysis carried out to compare the synthetic and natural talkers was an information transmission metric we have previously used in assessing how degrading the quality of the visual display influences the perception of visible speech (Campbell and Massaro 1997). The result of this analysis is that for initial consonant phoneme perception, the information transmitted was 44 percent for synthetic speech versus 41 percent for natural, and for initial consonant viseme, 56 percent for synthetic versus 62 percent for natural. While these findings are not exactly congruent with the identification performance statistic, they do indicate that the two talkers are roughly equivalent in terms of their informativeness. We have significantly improved the quality of our synthetic visible speech over the course of the successive modifications and tests. The overall viseme accuracy across four successive studies improved significantly. The average deficit relative to natural speech was .22, .18, .10, and .09 across the four successive experiments. Given the proposed measurement, synthesis, and evaluation studies, we are optimistic that our synthetic speech will be very close to natural speech.

Sometimes uncontrolled experiences with new technology are as informative as systematic studies. In addition to the experimental evidence, we have inadvertently obtained testimonials. Several deaf expert adult speech readers claim that Baldi is the only synthetic head that they are able to speech read.

10.5 The Importance of Talking Faces in Dialogue

Experiments in face-to-face communication have revealed conclusively that our perception and understanding are influenced by a speaker's face and accompanying gestures, as well as by the actual sound of the speech (Massaro 1998). We have convincing evidence that the perceiver's combination or integration of the auditory and visible speech is as efficient as possible (optimal). To illustrate this optimality, consider a simple syllable identification task. Synthetic visible speech and natural audible speech were used to generate the consonant-vowel (CV) syllables /ba/, /va/, /ða/, and /da/. Figure 10.2 shows a view of our talking head at the onset of articulation for each of these syllables. Using an expanded factorial design, the four syllables were presented auditorily, visually, and bimodally. Each syllable was present alone in each modality for 4 x 2 = 8 unimodal trials. For the bimodal presentation, each audible syllable was presented with each visible syllable for a total of 4 x 4 = 16 unique trials. Thus, there were twenty-four types of trials. Twelve of the bimodal syllables had inconsistent auditory and visual information.

The twenty participants in the experiment were instructed to watch and listen to the talking head and to indicate the syllable that was spoken. The subjects made their responses by pressing a key labeled "b," "v," "th," or "d" on the terminal keyboard for simple responses or pressed two keys successively for consonant cluster responses, such as the response /bda/. The experimental conditions were randomized without replacement within a block of trials. There were four experimental sessions of six blocks each for a total of twenty experimental trials for each condition. The mean observed proportion of identifications for each subject for each of the twenty-four conditions was computed by the relative frequency of response.

Figure 10.5 allows us to assess the influence of the auditory and visual speech by evaluating performance accuracy on each modality presented alone and in combination. The proportion of correct responses was .82, .94, .84, and .75 for the unimodal visible syllables /ba/, /va/, /ða/, and /da/. Thus, perceivers are fairly good at speech reading these syllables, and the more visually distinctive syllables /ba/, /va/, and /ða/ are somewhat easier than the less distinctive /da/.

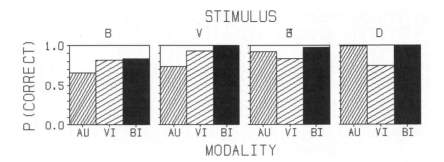

Figure 10.5

Probability correct identification of the unimodal and bimodal consistent trials for the four test syllables.

Correct identification averaged .66, .74, .92, and .99 for the unimodal auditory syllables /ba/, /va/, /ða/, and /da/. The auditory syllables /ða/ and /da/ were perceived more accurately than the syllables /ba/ and /va/. The different levels of performance on the auditory and visual syllables replicate a more general complementarity of these two modalities in speech perception. For whatever reason, several syllables that are easy to recognize in the visual modality tend to be difficult in the auditory modality and vice versa (Benoit, Mohamadi, and Kandel 1994; Summerfield 1987; Massaro 1998, chap. 14). Certainly, this is unlikely to be a rule in pattern recognition but it does occur more generally for auditory/visual speech (e.g., Robert-Ribes, Schwartz, and Escudier 1995).

Some readers might be surprised that the participants made errors on the unimodal trials. However, we are seldom expected to recognize isolated syllables and usually have the benefit of supplementary contextual cues. In addition, these auditory syllables are fairly similar to one another and, therefore, easily confused. As an example, the senior author of this chapter received a phone interview from *Tanorama*, an Italian weekly magazine. Given his Italian heritage, he was embarrassed at not knowing this magazine or even the meaning of the word. Only later did he learn that he had confused /t/ for /p/ because the magazine was actually *Panorama*. This confusion would probably not have occurred if visible speech were also available.

Accuracy is also given in figure 10.5 for bimodal trials when the two syllables are consistent with one another. Performance was more accurate when given two consistent sources of information than when given either one presented alone.

Although the results in figure 10.5 demonstrate that perceivers use both auditory and visible speech in perception, they do not indicate how the two sources are used together. The two sources might be used in many possible ways. This finer-grained analysis of the results than the one given in figure 10.5 is necessary to understand the processes involved in bimodal speech perception. The analysis involves the prototypical confusion matrix familiar to most psychophysicists. A confusion matrix gives results for all possible stimulus-response pairings. Figure 10.6 plots the confusion matrix for our results, which gives the proportion of times each stimulus event was identified as a particular alternative.

According to this theoretical framework, perception should correspond to the most reasonable alternative, given the two inputs. Figure 10.6 shows that a visual /da/ paired with an auditory /va/ was frequently identified as /ða/. Perceptual recognition will correspond to the alternative that is most similar to the conflux of audible and visible speech. A visual /da/ paired with an auditory /va/ gives one strong mismatch to each of these two alternatives. Visual /da/ is very different from a visual /va/. Similarly, auditory /va/ is very different from an auditory /da/. Thus, each of these two alternatives can be thought of as having one good match and one poor match. The alternative /ða/, however, is somewhat similar to both visual /da/ and auditory /va/. The response /ða/ is given to both unimodal auditory /va/ and unimodal visual /da/. In this case, /ða/ is a reasonable interpretation given a visual /da/ paired with an auditory /va/, as can be seen in figure 10.6.

Although we cannot analyze the confusion matrix in detail in this chapter, all of the responses can be rationalized in terms of the degree of match between the auditory and visual components of the test item and the response that is made (see Massaro 1998). We have shown that this result is predicted by an optimal integration of the two sources of information (Massaro and Stork 1998).

Information in the face is particularly effective when the auditory speech is degraded because of noise, limited bandwidth, or hearing impairment. We asked participants to report the words of short synthetic auditory test sentences presented in noise. In some trials, the auditory sentences were accompanied by our synthetic talking face, Baldi, moving in synchrony with the auditory speech. Figure 10.7 presents the proportion of words correctly reported for each subject under these two conditions. As can be seen in the figure, every person was helped by the accompaniment of our talking face.

Massaro et al.

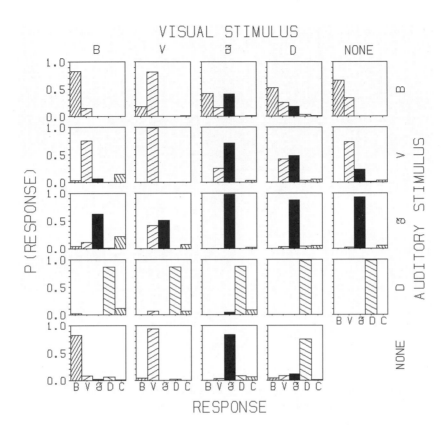

Figure 10.6

Proportion of /b/, /v/, /ð/, /d/, and consonant-cluster (C), responses as a function of the auditory and visual conditions for both the unimodal and bimodal trials.

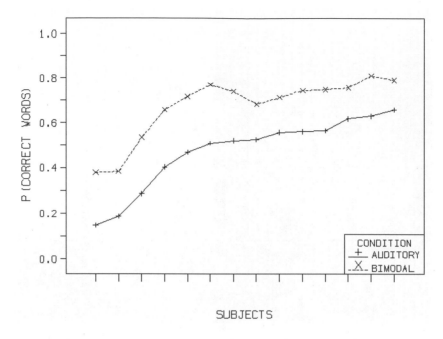

Figure 10.7

Proportion of words correctly recognized for each of the fourteen subjects indicated along the x-axis. The results are presented for the auditory and bimodal condition in which the synthetic head accompanied the auditory presentation.

The strong influence of visible speech is not limited to situations with degraded auditory input. A perceiver's recognition of an auditory-visual syllable reflects the contribution of both sound and sight. For example, if the ambiguous auditory sentence *My bab pop me poo brive* is paired with the visible sentence *My gag kok me koo grive*, the perceiver is likely to hear *My dad taught me to drive*. Two ambiguous sources of information are combined to create a meaningful interpretation (Massaro and Stork 1998).

10.6 Robustness of Bimodal Speech Perception

Several impressive properties of visible speech and bimodal speech perception exist. First, people naturally integrate visible and auditory speech in a variety of situations. Second, speech reading faces is not compromised by a number of variables. Humans are fairly good at speech reading even if they are not looking directly at the talker's lips. Furthermore, accuracy is not reduced dramatically when the facial image is blurred (because of poor vision, for example), when the image is rotated toward a profile view, when viewed from above or below, and when there is a large distance between the talker and the viewer. Another example of the robustness of the influence of visible speech is that people naturally integrate visible speech with audible speech, even when the temporal occurrence of the two sources is displaced by about one-fifth of a second. These findings indicate that speech reading is highly functional in a variety of nonoptimal situations. It follows that the pursuit of visible speech technology could be of great practical value in many spheres of communication.

10.7 The Fuzzy Logic Model of Perception

Our work has combined sophisticated experimental designs and quantitative model testing to understand not only speech perception but pattern recognition more generally. A wide variety of results have been described within a framework of a fuzzy logical model of perception (FLMP). Figure 10.8 gives a schematic representation of the three processes involved in perceptual recognition. The three processes are shown in sequence, from left to right, to illustrate their necessarily successive, but overlapping, procedures.

These processes make use of prototypes stored in long-term memory. Uppercase letters represent the sources of information. Auditory information is represented by A_i and visual information by V_j. The evaluation process transforms these sources of information into psychological values (indicated by lowercase letters a_i and v_j). These sources are then integrated to give an overall degree of support s_k, for each speech alternative k. The decision operation maps the outputs of integration into some response alternative, R_k. The response can take the form of a discrete decision or a rating of the degree to which the alternative is likely.

The assumptions central to the model are as follows: (1) each source of information is evaluated to determine the degree to which that source specifies various alternatives, (2) the sources of information are evaluated independently of one another, (3) the sources are integrated to provide an overall degree of support for each alternative, and (4) perceptual identification and interpretation follows the relative degree of support among the alternatives. In the course of our research, we have found the FLMP to be a universal principle of perceptual cognitive performance that accurately models human pattern recognition. People are influenced by multiple sources of information in a diverse set of situations.

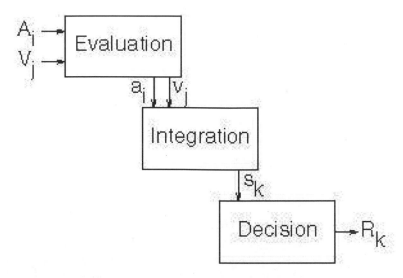

Figure 10.8
Schematic representation of the three processes involved in perceptual recognition.

In many cases, these sources of information are ambiguous, and any particular source alone does not usually completely specify the appropriate interpretation.

Outcomes from a variety of experiments are well fit by the implementation of our universal principle (Massaro 1998). The influence of one modality is greater to the extent that the other is ambiguous, a result well described by the FLMP. We have learned that people use many sources of information in perceiving and understanding speech, emotion, and other aspects of the environment. The results from many studies are consistent with the FLMP, which describes a universal law of behavior—that people naturally use both the information in the speaker's face and the sound to perceive and understand the message.

In speech perception, multiple sources of information are available to support the identification and interpretation of language. The experimental paradigm that we have developed allows us to determine which of the many potentially functional cues are actually used by human observers (Massaro 1998, chap. 1). These results show how visible speech is processed and integrated with other sources of information. The systematic variation of the properties of the speech signal and quantitative tests of models of speech perception allow the investigator to interpret the psychological validity of different cues. This paradigm has already proven effective in the study of audible, visible, and bimodal speech perception (Massaro 1987, 1998). Thus, our research strategy addresses how different sources of information are evaluated and integrated, and can identify the sources of information that are actually used.

The evidence we have harnessed for the FLMP algorithm comes from speech perception by eye and ear. Our work, in fact, began with the integration of multiple auditory cues in speech perception (Massaro and Cohen 1977; Oden and Massaro 1978). There is substantial evidence that the processes described by the FLMP in speech perception by ear and eye generalize to various modalities including electrical stimulation of cochlear implants (Massaro and Cohen 1999).

Several powerful modes of communication function very much like audio-visual speech. In addition to the widely used sign language, other forms of communication supplement rather than replace speech. Cued speech (Mohay 1983), for example, supplements lip-read information with manual hand movements for communicating with the hearing impaired. For individuals without sight as well as hearing, the Tadoma method exists, which involves the receiver placing his or her hands on the face and neck of the talker (Reed et al. 1989).

10.8 Perceiving Gestural Information

McNeill (1985) argues that manual gestures during speaking appear to have properties and functions that are strikingly similar to speech. McNeill's thesis is that manual gestures and speech are aspects of a single linguistic system. The two work together to express the same meaning. If this thesis is correct, then gestures and speech should function as two sources of information to be integrated by the perceiver. To test this hypothesis, we extended our framework to study the integration of a pointing gesture with audible speech (Thompson and Massaro 1986, 1994). Following the strategy of an expanded factorial design, preschool and fourth-grade children were presented with gesture, speech, and both sources of information together (Thompson and Massaro 1994). An auditory continuum of five levels was made between the words *ball* and *doll*. The gestural information, also with five levels, was varied between pointing to the ball or doll objects. The task was to indicate whether the talker intended a ball or a doll. "Sometimes the woman just points to the thing you should choose," the instructions went, "sometimes she just says it, and sometimes she both points and says which thing you should choose. Each time though, she wants you to choose one thing, either the 'ball' or 'doll.'"

Figure 10.9 gives the results only for the fourth-graders; the preschoolers behaved more or less equivalently except they showed a somewhat smaller influence of gesture. The children, although instructed to respond "ball" or "doll," often responded with "wall." We quickly realized that auditory "wall" is similar to the sound of "ball," and that the intermediate pointing gestures were aimed at a wall. Given this speech on the wall, we incorporated this response alternative into the data analysis and model tests. Both auditory speech and gestures influenced performance, and the form of the results were essentially identical to those found in experiments with audible and visible speech. Each source of information presented alone had some influence, and their joint influence followed the predictions of the FLMP. The top two middle panels of figure 10.9 reveal the American football trademark of the FLMP—namely, the amount of gesture influence is greatest when the auditory speech is ambiguous. These results and our interpretation are consistent with a recent finding by Cassell, McNeill, and McCullough (1999) that mismatched gestures and speech were integrated into a single representation.

10.9 Perceiving Emotional Information

One of the most frequent complaints about synthetic speech is that it is very monotonous. The stress and intonation pattern is far removed from natural speech. The presence of a talking face has the potential to improve not only the perceived quality of the segmental articulations (e.g., phonemes and visemes) but also the intonation pattern (prosody). We use facial expressions and corresponding gestures that communicate intonation. For example, in our case, we use the height of the eyebrows since there is evidence of a positive correlation between eyebrow height and voice pitch (Ohala 1994). Cave et al. (1996), for example, found that 71 percent of the fundamental frequency (F0) rises were accompanied by eyebrow rises. Some linguists have remarked that doing their transcriptions as students was made easier by surreptitiously watching their teachers' eyebrows. Along these lines, Pelachaud, Badler, and Steedman (1996) have extended the Facial Action Coding System (FACS; see Ekman and Friesen 1977) approach to simulate facial expressions, conveying information that is normally correlated with intonation of the voice.

An important dimension of communication is emotional expression, which has also been developed as an integral characteristic of our conversational agent. There is no doubt that the production of facial expressions is an effective means of communicating emotion. Although many different facial movements are possible, human facial expressions tend to be classifiable within relatively

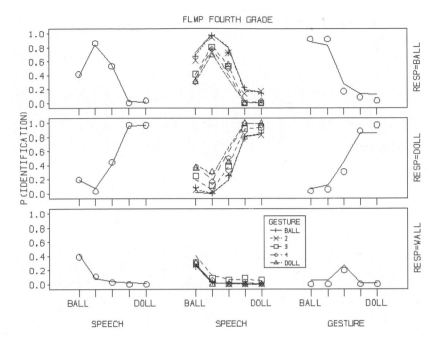

Figure 10.9

Observed (points) and predicted (lines) proportion of ball, doll, and wall identifications for speech (left panel), speech-gesture (center panel), and gesture (right panel) trials as a function of the speech and gesture levels of the speech event for fourth-grade children. The predictions are for the FLMP.

few emotional categories. Some evidence exists, based on studies of animals, as well as preliterate and isolated societies, that the production of facial expressions such as rage, surprise, startle, fear, and pleasure are fairly universal.

We have built emotional cues into our synthetic face based on empirical research. Baldi now conveys six basic emotions—*happiness, anger, fear, disgust, surprise, and sadness*—in a very realistic manner (see fig. 10.3). For example, brow displacement and mouth corner displacement are varied to create happy and angry. A slightly elevated and arched brow and a mouth fully curled up at the corner create a prototypically happy expression. A fully depressed and flattened brow and a mouth fully curled down at the corner create a prototypically angry expression. These emotional expressions are implemented to convey the appropriate emotional state of our conversational agent, tutor, or whatever role the synthetic actor happens to be playing.

We recognize and characterize facial expressions of emotion in other humans with a high degree of accuracy and consistency (Ekman 1993). The face is not unique in this regard in that we are also tuned to various nonfacial displays of emotional arousal. Hand and body gestures are well-known communicators of affective states (Archer and Silver 1991). We examined how emotion is perceived from both facial and vocal cues, analogous to the experiment we described in speech perception. Participants were presented all possible permutations of the utterance *please*, that is, visual cues alone, vocal cues alone, and visual and vocal cues together. In this experiment, we paired the synthetic face with natural audible speech. Due to the current inability of synthetic voice programs such as DECtalk to adequately portray emotion in isolated words, the vocal stimuli were produced by recording a male amateur actor speaking a semantically neutral stimulus word *please* in four different simulated emotional states: happy, angry, surprised, and fearful. Some noticeable differences across the three different emotions were the pitch contour during the vowel /i/, the word duration, and the amount of frication in the final segment /s/. To make the cues somewhat less obvious, the words were standardized for length and intensity during the vocalic (vowel) portion across the four emotions. In the bimodal condition, the auditory /p/ burst release was synchronized with the mouth opening of the /p/ articulation.

The nine participants were instructed to watch the talking head and listen to the voice on each trial and to indicate which of the four emotion categories was being communicated. The subjects made their response by pressing a labeled key. All of the experimental conditions were randomized and presented repeatedly for identification. The mean observed proportion of identifications was computed for each of the twenty-four conditions for each subject by pooling across all of the eighteen experimental trials for each condition.

The analysis of the results parallels that carried out for speech and is given in figure 10.10. Given that the participants' goal was to perceive the emotion, it is informative to evaluate performance in terms of accuracy with respect to each of the two modalities. For unimodal trials, the average correct performance given just the face was .94, .95, .73, and .64 for the emotion categories happy, angry, surprised, and fearful. Thus, perceivers are fairly good at identifying emotion from just the face even in a synthetic head.

Correct identification given just the auditory information averaged .85, .60, .82, and .96 for the auditory emotion categories happy, angry, surprised, and

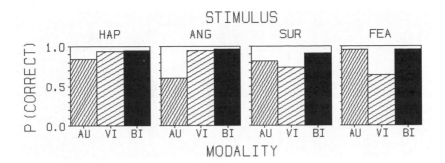

Figure 10.10

Probability correct identification of the unimodal and bimodal consistent trials for the four test emotions.

fearful. Happy, surprised, and fearful are relatively easy to identify in the voice whereas angry was somewhat more difficult.

Just as in speech recognition, we can ask whether there is a general complementarity of these two modalities in emotion perception. In speech, we found that one modality tended to be informative when the other modality was not (see also Massaro 1998, chap. 14). Several syllables that are easy to identify in the visual modality tend to be difficult in the auditory modality and vice versa. The auditory syllable /da/ is relatively easy to identify, whereas its visible counterpart is not. The syllable /ba/ shows just the opposite relationship. Angry, and to some extent happy, appears to be easier to see in the face than to hear in the voice. Surprised and fearful, on the other hand, give the opposite relationship. In agreement with our general principle of commonalities across domains, some hint of complementarity appears that is analogous to that proposed for speech. Perhaps in every domain, alternatives exist whose difficulty happens to be complementary across modalities or sources of information. For other alternatives, however, we might expect to find no correlation or even a positive correlation.

Accuracy is also given in figure 10.10 for bimodal trials. Bimodal performance was close to perfect for all four emotion categories in the consistent condition. Although the results in figure 10.10 demonstrate that both the face and the voice are used in emotion perception, they do not indicate how the two sources are used together. The two sources might be treated in many possible ways. As in the speech domain, a finer-grained analysis of the results helps reveal the underlying process. The confusion matrix in figure 10.11 plots the proportion of times each stimulus event was identified as each alternative.

308

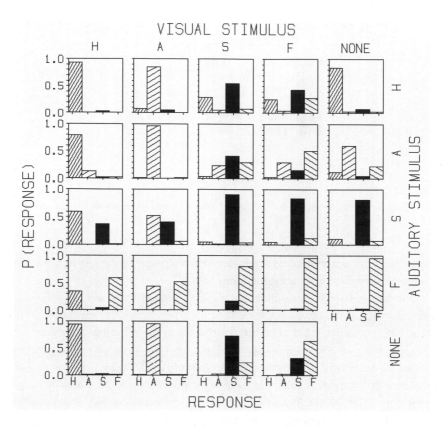

Figure 10.11

Proportion of happy (H), angry (A), surprised (S), and fearful responses as a function of the auditory and visual conditions for both the unimodal and bimodal trials.

Massaro et al.

This analysis provides a measure of what alternatives are perceived, given the different experimental conditions. Recall that a rough approximation of the FLMP prediction is that perception given two inputs will be the most reasonable alternative specified by those inputs. The bimodal emotion judgments are best understood in terms of the degree of support from each of the two modalities (as approximately estimated from the unimodal conditions). This support from the two modalities is a better predictor of bimodal performance than are other variables such as, for example, what modality is providing the support.

Surprise and fear provide an illustrative example. As can be seen in figure 10.11, when auditory surprise is paired with visual fear, surprise is the dominant judgment. On the other hand, when auditory surprise is paired with visual anger, anger is the dominant judgment. The difference between these two cases can be completely understood by the information available in the various inputs. In both cases, the dominant response is that which agrees with the least ambiguous source of information. Auditory surprise is less ambiguous than visual fear; hence, when they are combined, surprise is the dominant judgment. Auditory surprise is more ambiguous than visual anger; hence, anger is the dominant judgment. These results are qualitatively consistent with the principle that the influence of one source of information when combined with another source is related to their relative ambiguity when presented in isolation.

Of course, the true test of the influence of the two sources involves model testing. The FLMP and a variety of other models were fit to each of the nine subjects. The results of these model tests revealed that the FLMP provided the most accurate description of performance (see Massaro 1998, chap. 8).

Given that our talking head appears to convey emotions reliably, they could easily be employed in conversational dialogues. In future work, we plan to examine the hypothesis that communication dialogue is more efficient and enjoyable when emotional expression is inherently part of the message, even though it might not be as powerful as conversational process signals such as those involved in turn taking (Cassell and Thórisson 1999).

10.10 Language Tutoring

Our facial animation software is currently an integral part of a three-year project, funded by an NSF Challenge grant, now about two years old, to develop interactive learning tools for language training with profoundly deaf children. In addition to Baldi, the tools to date have combined key technologies: speech recognition, developed at the Oregon Graduate Institute (OGI); and speech synthesis, developed at the University of Edinburgh and modified at OGI. The goal of the project is to provide teachers, students, parents, and other interested individuals with state of the art tools and technologies for interactive learning and language training. These tools and technologies are integrated into the CSLU toolkit, a software environment for building and researching interactive systems (http://www.cse.ogi.edu/CSLU/toolkit/; Cole et al. 1999).

To date, many language-training applications have been developed using Baldi as a language tutor. The acoustic speech is provided by either the Festival TtS system or a natural speaker synchronized with the animated face. The speaker records an utterance and types in the words. The system then produces a time-aligned phonetic transcription that is used to drive the synthetic face. When facial animation and speech generation are combined with computer speech recognition, students are able to have limited conversations with Baldi. These educational modules are created by CSLU's toolkit developers and by educators at the Tucker-Maxon Oral School in Portland, Oregon, using the toolkit's graphical authoring environment, the Rapid Application Developer (RAD).

Language training software is being developed and tested in collaboration with the educators and deaf students at the Tucker-Maxon Oral School. The students in this school are profoundly deaf. Hearing aids, cochlear implants, or a combination of both are used to enhance their hearing. During the first year of the project, our main challenge has been to adapt and extend the toolkit to the needs of the teachers and students. To this end, we have followed principles of participatory design, in which the users of the software participate as much as possible in all phases of its design and development.

In the class of the oldest students between nine and twelve years old, instructor George Fortier has taken full advantage of the RAD to create interactive multimedia lessons. These dialogues introduce and/or review concepts and vocabulary from the social studies and science curricula. For example, he created a geography lesson by scanning in a drawing that depicted a mountain range, lake, river, stream, plateau, waterfall, coast, and ocean. When a student starts this program, one of the geographic features is selected randomly and highlighted. Baldi asks, "What landform is this?" A correct answer by the student causes the system to display another highlighted landform and ask another question. If the child does not know the answer she says, "Help." Baldi then says the word three times at a slightly slower rate and asks the question again. If the system does not recognize the student's speech, Baldi asks the student to try again. After two recognition failures, Baldi again says the word three times. This "correct speech routine" continues until the student's speech is recognized. Because of the children's varying levels of speech ability, the teacher sets the recognition threshold differently for each child. This threshold is increased daily so that the student's speech quality must improve for recognition to occur.

This program has been an effective learning tool. None of the six students knew all of these landforms before using the application. After four days of working individually, all six students knew the names of each landform and could say them with such clarity that the system accepted their answer on the first or second trial.

Fortier has created an assortment of different applications for his class. Working on a home PC in the evening, he uses the toolkit's authoring tools to create sophisticated interactive dialogues that incorporate different graphics at specific points in the dialogue. All of these applications exercise and test language comprehension, speech production, and content learning.

Alice Davis, instructor for the younger students between seven and nine years old, has created a variety of applications for different content areas to supplement her curriculum. Figure 10.12 captures a typical experience of the students being engaged by Baldi in the classroom. For example, she has built modules for the study of math, spelling, reading, listening comprehension, and writing. She has even used the toolkit as a way for the children to listen to and practice reciting their own haiku. To test math concepts, Davis created interactive math quizzes. For example, the child was shown a picture of seven bears in a forest. Baldi would then say, "There are seven bears in the forest. Three bears ran away. How many bears are left?" When the child produced the correct answer, she received the next question. Applications of this type sharpen speech reading and listening skills and speech production skills, while testing knowledge of content.

The speech therapist at Tucker-Maxon, Chris Soland, in collaboration with a graduate student researcher Tim Carmell, developed a series of listening drills based on minimal pair distinctions. For example, the screen shows a picture of "mail" and "veil." The system then says one of the words, and the student uses a mouse to select the picture that corresponds to the word that she perceived. In another task, the system produces a pair of words, for example, "veil, veil" or "mail, veil," and the student says "same" or "different" after each pair. In each application, the system produces immediate visual feedback and informs the child of her score at the end of the lesson.

Figure 10.12
Baldi engaging students in the classroom.

10.11 Current Applications and Evaluation

Our technology clearly provides an automated method of providing dedicated one-on-one language training and instruction. We learned that Baldi is highly motivating, as can be seen in figure 10.12. Children have persisted in some of the lessons until they were mastered—even though it wasn't required. We expect more than this from animated agents, however. One general expectation is to have agents do what no real person can. To this end, we have augmented the internal structures of our talking head both for improved accuracy and to pedagogically illustrate correct articulation.

Figure 10.13 shows the new palate, teeth, and tongue embedded in Baldi's mouth (Cohen, Beskow, and Massaro 1998). High-resolution models of palate and teeth were reduced to a relatively small number of polygons for real-time animation. We are using 3-D ultrasound data and electropalatography (EPG)

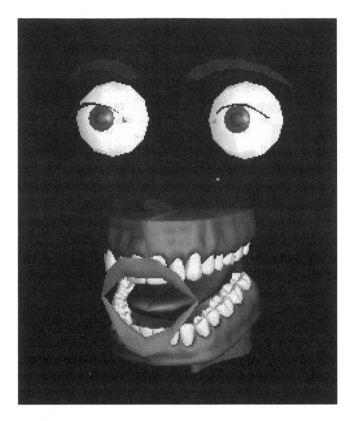

Figure 10.13
New tongue and palate embedded in the talking head.

with error minimization algorithms to educate our parametric B-spline-based tongue model to simulate realistic speech. In addition, a high-speed algorithm has been developed for detection and correction of collisions, to prevent the tongue from protruding through the palate and teeth and to enable the real-time display of synthetic EPG patterns. Figure 10.14 illustrates the tongue being highlighted in the area of contact with the palate.

One immediate motivation for developing a hard palate, teeth, and tongue is their potential utility in language training. Children with hearing impairment require guided instruction in speech perception and production. Although there

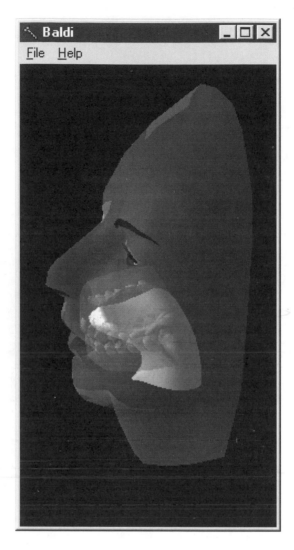

Figure 10.14

Illustration of the tongue being highlighted in the area of contact with the palate.

is a long history of using visible cues in speech training for individuals with hearing loss, such cues have usually been abstract or symbolic rather than direct representations of the vocal tract. Some of the distinctions in spoken language cannot be heard with degraded hearing—even when the hearing loss has been compensated by hearing aids or cochlear implants. To overcome this limitation, we plan to use visible speech to provide speech targets for the child with hearing loss. In addition, many of the subtle distinctions among segments are not visible on the outside of the face. The skin of our talking head can be made transparent so that the inside of the vocal track is visible, or we can present a cutaway view of the head along the sagittal plane. The goal is to instruct the child by revealing the appropriate articulation via the hard palate, teeth, and tongue.

Visible speech instruction poses many issues that must be resolved before training can be optimized. We are confident that illustration of articulation will be useful in improving the learner's speech, but it will be important to assess how well the learning transfers outside the instructional situation. Another issue is whether instruction should be focused on the visible speech or whether it should include auditory input. If speech production mirrors speech perception, then we expect that multimodal training should be beneficial. We expect that the child could learn multimodal targets, which would provide more resolution than either modality alone. Another issue concerns whether the visible speech targets should be illustrated in static or dynamic presentations. We plan to evaluate both types of presentation and expect that some combination of modes would be optimal. Last, the size of the instructional target is an issue. Should instruction focus on small phoneme and open-syllable targets, or should it be based on larger units of words and phrases? Again, we expect training with several sizes of targets would be ideal.

Finally, although we have not discussed evaluation as much as the development and application of the technology, it is an integral part of our project. Earlier we described how the quality of Baldi's speech is assessed and compared to that of a real speaker. Although more difficult, we also plan to carry out systematic evaluations of the quality of Baldi's instruction. For language training, we will provide periodic tests of both speech perception and speech production, and chart the improvement across training. This improvement will be compared to available norms and/or other types of training regiments. The outcomes of these evaluations will certainly pose new problems and challenges that will help guide our quest for an effective conversational agent.

10.12 Summary and Conclusion

We have described the development, implementation, and an application of our computer-animated synthetic talking head. Our psychological research has repeatedly demonstrated the value of talking heads in conversation. Persons benefit from having both the face and the voice in communication situations. They naturally combine the cues from the two modalities to reach a meaningful interpretation of the communicative act. Although our past effort has been on a talking head, it will be necessary to include understanding and intelligence to achieve agency. This challenging goal will maintain our engagement for many years to come.

Acknowledgments

The research reported in this chapter was supported by grants from the National Science Foundation (NSF grant ECS-9726645, NSF CHALLENGE grant CDA-9726363, NSF Grant 23818), the National Institutes of Health (PHS R01 DC00236), Intel Corporation, and the University of California Digital Media Program.

We gratefully acknowledge the contributions of Christopher Campbell, Rashid Clark, Harmony Hayes, David Jones, Michael Macon, Pamela Connors, Khaldoun Shobaki, Patrick Stone, Alice Tarachow, and Jacques H. de Villiers.

References

Archer, D. (Producer), and J. Silver (Director). 1991. *A world of gestures: Culture and nonverbal communication.* [Videorecording]. (Available from University of California Extension Media Center, Berkeley, Calif.).

Benoit, C., T. Mohamadi, and S. Kandel. 1994. Effects of phonetic context on audio-visual intelligibility of French. *Journal of Speech and Hearing Research* 37:1195–1203.

Bernstein, L. E., and S. P. Eberhardt. 1986. *Johns Hopkins lipreading corpus videodisk set.* Baltimore, Md.: Johns Hopkins University.

Campbell, C. S., and D. W. Massaro. 1997. Visible speech perception: Influence of spatial quantization. *Perception* 26:627–644.

Cave, C., I. Guaitella, R. Bertrand, S. Santi, F. Harlay, and R. Espesser. 1996. About the relationship between eye-brow movements and F0 variations. In *Proceedings of ICSLP '96,* 2175–2178. Wilmington: University of Delaware.

Cassell, J., and K. R. Thórisson. 1999. The power of a nod and a glance: Envelope vs. emotional feedback in animated conversational agents. *Applied Artificial Intelligence* 13:519–538.

Cassell, J., D. McNeill, and K. E. McCullough. 1999. Speech-gesture mismatches: Evidence for one underlying representation of linguistic and non-linguistic information. *Pragmatics and Cognition* 7(1):1–33.

Clark, A. 1997. *Being there: Putting brain, body, and world together again.* Cambridge, Mass.: The MIT Press.

Cohen, M. M., and D. W. Massaro. 1993. Modeling coarticulation in synthetic visual speech. In N. M. Thalmann and D. Thalmann, eds., *Models and techniques in computer animation,* 139–156. Tokyo: Springer-Verlag.

Cohen, M. M., J. Beskow, and D. W. Massaro. 1998. Recent developments in facial animation: An inside view. In D. Burnham, J. Robert-Ribes, and E. Vatikiotis-Bateson, eds., *Proceedings of Auditory-Visual Speech Processing '98* (Terrigal-Sydney, Australia), 201–206.

Cohen, M. M., R. L. Walker, and D. W. Massaro. 1996. Perception of synthetic visual speech. In D. G. Stork and M. E. Hennecke, eds., *Speechreading by humans and machines,* 153–168. New York: Springer-Verlag.

Cole, R., D. W. Massaro, J. de Villiers, B. Rundle, K. Shobaki, J. Wouters, M. M. Cohen, J. Beskow, P. Stone, P. Connors, A. Tarachow, and D. Solcher. 1999. New tools for interactive speech and language training: Using animated conversational agents in the classrooms of profoundly deaf children. In *Proceedings of ESCA/SOCRATES Workshop on Method and Tool Innovations for Speech Science Education,* 45–52. London: University College.

Ekman, P. 1993. Facial expression and emotion. *American Psychologist* 48:384–392.

Ekman, P., and W. V. Friesen. 1977. *Manual for the Facial Action Coding System.* Palo Alto, Calif.: Consulting Psychologists Press.

Gibson, J. J. 1979. *The ecological approach to visual perception.* Boston: Houghton Mifflin.

Glenberg, A. M. 1997. Mental models, space, and embodied cognition. In T. B. Ward, S. M. Smith, and J. Vaid, eds., *Creative thought: An investigation of conceptual structures and processes,* 495–522. Washington, D.C.: American Psychological Association.

Landauer, T. K., and S. T. Dumais. 1997. A solution to Plato's problem: The latent semantic analysis theory of acquisition, induction, and representation of knowledge. *Psychological Review* 104:211–240.

Massaro, D. W. 1987. *Speech perception by ear and eye: A paradigm for psychological inquiry.* Hillsdale, N.J.: Lawrence Erlbaum Associates.

———. 1998. *Perceiving talking faces: From speech perception to a behavioral principle.* Cambridge, Mass.: The MIT Press.

Massaro, D. W., and M. M. Cohen. 1977. Voice onset time and fundamental frequency as cues to the /zi/-/si/ distinction. *Perception and Psychophysics* 22:373–382.

———. 1999. Speech perception in hearing-impaired perceivers: Synergy of multiple modalities. *Journal of Speech, Language, and Hearing Science* 42:21–41.

Massaro, D. W., and D. G. Stork. 1998. Speech recognition and sensory integration. *American Scientist* 86:236–244.

McNeill, D. 1985. So you think gestures are nonverbal? *Psychological Review* 92:350–371.

Mohay, H. 1983. The effects of cued speech on the language development of three deaf children. *Sign Language Studies* 38:25–49.

Newton, N. 1996. *Foundations of understanding.* Philadelphia, Penn.: John Benjamins Publishing.

Oden, G. C., and D. W. Massaro. 1978. Integration of featural information in speech perception. *Psychological Review* 85:172–191.

Ohala, J. J. 1994. The frequency code underlies the sound symbolic use of voice pitch. In L. Hinton, J. Nichols, and J. Ohala, eds., *Sound symbolism*, 325–347. New York: Cambridge University Press.

Olive, J. 1990. A new algorithm for a concatenative speech synthesis system using an augmented acoustic inventory of speech sounds. In *First ESCA-Workshop on Speech Synthesis* (Autrans, France), 25–30.

Parke, F. I. 1974. A parametric model for human faces (Tech. Rep. UTEC-CSc-75-047). Salt Lake City: University of Utah.

Pelachaud, C., N. I. Badler, and M. Steedman. 1996. Generating facial expressions for speech. *Cognitive Science* 20:1–46.

Reed, C. M., N. I. Durlach, L. A. Delhorne, W. M. Rabinowitz, and K. W. Grant. 1989. Research on tactual communication of speech: Ideas, issues, and findings. *Volta Review* 91:65–78.

Robert-Ribes, J., J. Schwartz, and P. Escudier. 1995. Auditory, visual, and audiovisual vowel representations: Experiments and modelling. *Proceedings of the XIIIth International Congress of Phonetic Sciences* 3:114–121.

Searle, J. R. 1992. *The rediscovery of the mind.* Cambridge, Mass.: The MIT Press.

Summerfield, Q. 1987. Some preliminaries to a comprehensive account of audio-visual speech perception. In B. Dodd and R. Campbell, eds., *Hearing by eye: The psychology of lipreading*, 3–51. Hillsdale, N.J.: Lawrence Erlbaum Associates.

Thompson, L. A., and D. W. Massaro. 1986. Evaluation and integration of speech and pointing gestures during referential understanding. *Journal of Experimental Child Psychology* 42:334–362.

———. 1994. Children's integration of speech and pointing gestures in comprehension. *Journal of Experimental Child Psychology* 57:327–354.

Designing and Evaluating Conversational Interfaces with Animated Characters

Sharon Oviatt and Bridget Adams

II.I Introduction: Ingredients of a Conversational Interface

During the past decade, due largely to progress inspired by the DARPA Speech Grand Challenge project and similar international efforts (Cole et al. 1997; Martin et al. 1997), significant progress has occurred in the development of spoken language technology (SLT). Spoken language systems now are implemented extensively for telephony applications (Spiegel and Kamm 1997), as well as on workstations and even small palm computers. They also are supporting new training systems for learning foreign languages and basic reading skills, as well as the commercialization of numerous automated dictation systems for applications such as medical charting, legal records, and word processing. The rapid maturation of spoken language technology, along with advances in natural language processing, has also stimulated interest in the development of increasingly *conversational interfaces*.

The emerging interest in conversational interfaces presents a particularly intriguing but challenging research agenda. In contrast to alternative styles of spoken language interface, including command language and dictation, conversational interfaces aim to support large-vocabulary spontaneous spoken language to be exchanged as part of a fluid dialogue between user and computer. They also permit the user to take extensive initiative in shaping this dialogue. To accomplish these goals, conversational interfaces support parallel natural language processing for both input and output between human and computer.

However, several other elements of human "conversation" exist that make conversational interface design a challenging direction. First, human conversation is not only an information exchange but also an informal social activity that is inherently reinforcing. In fact, a "conversationalist" is a person who enjoys and contributes to good conversation. As a result, conversational interfaces are considered "social interfaces," and when we participate in them we respond to the computer at some level as a social "persona" or partner (Nass, Steuer, and Tauber 1994). This recognition, in part, has led to the design of new animated software characters, which basically serve as an interface vehicle to facilitate human-computer conversational exchange. The new field of research on animated characters has become an unusually diverse and generative area, as is evident from the range of content in this book.

Another challenging element of human "conversation" that is currently driving conversational interface design is the interest in supporting more transparent, high-bandwidth, and relatively natural multimodal communication (Oviatt et al. n.d.). This movement aims to process human input from two or more modes like speech, pen, touch, gesture, and gaze, while simultaneously generating coordinated multimedia output from text, graphics, animation, speech and nonspeech audio—or their combination in the form of lifelike animated characters (André et al., chap. 8; Badler et al., chap. 9; Ball and Breese, chap. 7; Cassell et al., chap. 2). Such multimodal communication is viewed as a more powerful and expressive means of human-computer interaction, in addition to being well suited to the design of richer and more credible conversational interfaces.

The design of effective conversational interfaces clearly is a wide open research topic. It also is one that relies heavily on multidisciplinary expertise and teamwork, which constitutes a challenge in itself. To design conversational interfaces that function effectively, we need to start at the beginning—by asking a series of deceptively simple questions. Why do we want conversational interfaces in the future? How can we design them to produce the landmarks of a stimulating conversation—engagement, responsivity, reciprocity, synchronization, focus, intelligibility? And how will we evaluate that we have achieved these remarkable but elusive goals?

In this chapter, we introduce a new *Mobile Simulation Environment*, which was developed to support advance data collection and the design of conversational interfaces involving (1) new media (e.g., speech) and multimodal input, (2) portable technology for use in field settings and in situations where users are mobile, (3) diverse user groups (e.g., children), and (4) different animated character concepts. We also describe the results of an initial study based on data collection with this simulation tool and the I SEE! (Immersive Science Education for Elementary kids) educational application. In this study, the spoken language of ten six- to ten-year-old children was compared while interacting with an animated character, and again while interacting with a human adult partner.

The specific goal of this research was to investigate hard-to-process articulatory, lexical, and grammatical features of children's speech, such as spoken disfluencies, which may require specialized language modeling and interface design to build successful interactive systems. Fragmented and disfluent language are known to be particularly challenging features for any spoken language system to process, even in adult language, so the evaluation of children's disfluent speech was a major aim of this research. Since educational technology is typically used in field settings (e.g., school, home) and may best be applied when children are immersed in natural learning opportunities (e.g., marine biology center), the Mobile Simulation Environment was developed as a tool for collecting speech samples in realistic usage contexts. Due to noise levels, collaborative interaction and other factors, the rate of fragmented and disfluent speech would be expected to be higher in such field contexts than in an artificial laboratory one. The general long-term goal of this research is the development of robust conversational interfaces for children, especially ones that can be used in natural environments, and that make effective use of animated characters for purposes like education.

11.2 Tools for Designing and Evaluating Conversational Interfaces
11.2.1 Simulation Techniques

Simulation studies, also known as Wizard of Oz studies, have become an important and flexible tool for investigating human-computer interaction and for designing systems that are still in the planning stages. These studies involve *proactive* and *situated* data collection for the purpose of system design, which is done in advance of actually building a fully functional system. In a semiautomatic simulation, a test subject uses what she believes is a fully functional system, while a programmer assistant at a remote location provides simulated system responses. As the subject works, the assistant tracks the subject's input and simply clicks on predefined fields on his or her workstation to send system confirmations back to the subject. Recently, high-fidelity simulation environments have offered an ideal means of conducting advance empirical work on spoken language and multimodal systems.

A high-quality simulation typically includes extensive automation in order to support accurate and rapid responding by the programmer assistant. For example, simulated recognition errors can be delivered automatically by a random error generator, which is preprogrammed to deliver different base rates and types of recognition error distributed randomly across task content (Oviatt 1996). Simulations also aim to support *speedy interaction,* especially for interfaces that include spoken language. In this type of simulated interface, an emphasis typically is placed on supporting subject-paced interactions that average less than a one-second delay between the subject's input and system response (Oviatt et al. 1992).

One reason that high-fidelity simulations are the preferred method of designing and evaluating planned systems is because they are relatively easy and inexpensive to adapt, compared with actually building and iterating a complete system. They permit researchers and system designers to alter a planned system's characteristics in major ways (e.g., the input and output modes available in a multimedia system) and to study the impact of important interface characteristics in a systematic and scientific manner (e.g., the type and base rate of system errors). In comparison, any particular system with its fixed characteristics is a less flexible and suitable research tool. In a practical sense, simulation research can assist in the evaluation of critical performance tradeoffs and in making decisions about alternative system designs, which designers must do as they strive to create more usable spoken language systems. Using simulation techniques, rapid adaptation and investigation of planned system features permit researchers and system designers to gain a broader and more principled perspective on the potential of whole newly emerging classes of technology, including next-generation conversational interfaces, multimodal/media systems, and animated character design.

Using simulation techniques, researchers are able to collect empirical data that can

- reveal undiscovered phenomena of interest, such as landmark features of interactive speech, that will need to be processed by future spoken language and multimodal systems
- quantify the prevalence of linguistic and other behavioral phenomena observed in users
- establish their causal basis through isolation and manipulation of the factors that drive them
- interpret these linguistic and behavioral phenomena in relation to contextual factors that predict and explain them
- create a solid foundation for next-generation interface design

11.2.2 Mobile Simulation Environment

One limitation of previous simulation environments is that they have focused on supporting laboratory-based research rather than real-world usage contexts. In addition, they have not been tailored to explore interface designs appropriate for a diverse range of more "challenging" users, such as children. Finally, they have yet to be applied to the investigation and design of next-generation conversational interfaces that incorporate animated characters.

In recent years, interest has grown in developing small handheld systems with more natural and powerful interfaces that can be used in varied real-world usage contexts by diverse users. Partly as a result of this trend, the goal of the new Mobile Simulation Environment, which was developed for this research, is to create a high-fidelity tool to support advance data collection and interface design appropriate for (1) new media (e.g., speech, pen, touch) and their multimodal combination, (2) portable technology for use in natural field environments and in situations where users are mobile, (3) diverse user groups (e.g., children or elderly users, accented nonnative speakers), who represent significant market potential, and (4) conversational interfaces that incorporate animated characters and other multimedia output. To further promote these types of future system design, an additional goal of the Mobile Simulation Environment is to develop (5) a toolkit that enables the rapid creation and adaptation of different simulated applications.

One example of an application currently being developed in conjunction with the Mobile Simulation Environment is Immersive Science Education for Elementary kids or I SEE! This application teaches early elementary children about marine biology and simple data tabulation and graphing concepts. Its features include (1) rich National Geographic video segments that kids can query for information, (2) natural conversational interaction with animated video content as well as designed animated characters, (3) control over the video display, and (4) data tabulation and creation of graphic displays. This functionality also is designed to be (5) controlled by children's natural multimodal spoken and pen-based input and (6) used on small handheld systems while children are immersed in natural learning opportunities—whether at school, at home, or passing by exhibits at a marine science center.

Figure 11.1 illustrates the Mobile Simulation Environment's testing setup. During data collection with I SEE!, a child interacts multimodally with the application using a handheld device—for example, while learning about the sea otters that he or she is observing outdoors at the marine science center (fig. 11.1, top

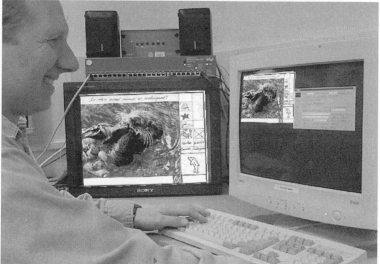

Figure 11.1
Child interacting multimodally with I SEE! on handheld device at Marine Science Center (top), while programmer assistant simulates system and collects user data remotely over a wireless network (bottom).

panel). During this simulation testing, the child believes that he or she is interacting with a fully functional system, although a programmer assistant actually
provides system responses from a remote location as this user data is collected
over a wireless network (fig. 11.1, bottom panel). To ensure high-fidelity data
capture from mobile users, "local calibration" of user's input (e.g., inking and
speech characteristics) also is monitored directly from their portable device
using a small wearable video camera.

This simulation data collection method is based on a distributed agent-
building environment that uses a modified version of the Open Agent
Architecture (OAA) (Cohen et al. 1994), COM, and DCOM. The component agents
include (1) Microsoft "agent" characters, (2) video control, and (3) an inking
agent. The basic architecture for the Mobile Simulation Environment is illustrated in figure 11.2, with the user's display screen on the left and the linked
wizard's screen and control palette on the right. The subject's user interface
accommodates speech and pen-based input, which can be combined multi-
modally. The system's multimedia output includes speech and nonspeech
audio, text, graphics, video, and animated movements. The programmer assistant or wizard's interface is organized with database-driven scenario control
and uses the main OAA agent architecture, COM, and DCOM components.

The Mobile Simulation Environment runs on a PC using WIN 95 or NT.
Using wireless networks, it can receive data from portable computing devices
such as the Fujitsu Stylistic 1200 and DRS machines. Data collection with smaller CE devices also is planned for the near future.

11.3 Talking to Thimble Jellies: How Kids and Animated Characters Converse

11.3.1 Related Literature on Animated Characters

At present, very little is known about how real users will interact with animated characters, especially child users. Most studies performed to date have
focused on adult users' subjective evaluation of animated characters, especially ratings of their social and personality characteristics, general attractiveness,
trustworthiness, persuasive appeal, and so forth (Lester et al. 1997; Nass,
Isbister and Lee, chap. 13; van Mulken, André, and Müller 1998). In a few studies, behavioral measures also have been evaluated to compare adult performance in an interface with and without an animated character. For example, in
an interesting study, van Mulken, André, and Müller (1998) evaluated the
impact of presenting an animated agent with text-to-speech output compared
to presenting the application content via text and object animation. Although

System Architecture

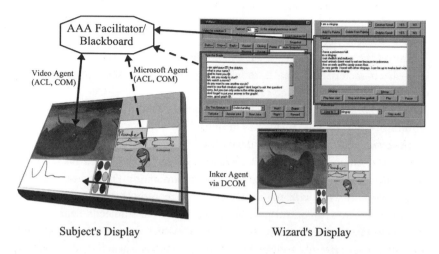

Subject's Display

Wizard's Display

Figure II.2

Mobile Simulation Environment's system architecture, with user's display on the left, and linked programmer assistant's display and control palette on the right.

their subjects preferred the animated character and believed that it helped them concentrate better, it had no actual effect on people's comprehension and recall of technical or nontechnical material. In other studies on educational impact, anecdotal and preference measures again have demonstrated that animated characters are appealing and apparently motivating to students (Lester et al. 1997), although no firm behavioral evidence exists yet that they promote significant learning.

Among the few behaviorally oriented evaluations of animated characters, some have begun examining users' communication patterns during human-computer interaction. For example, during development of the Baldi talking head, Massaro et al. (chap. 10) compared users' perception of different speech sounds while listening to text-to-speech augmented with a view of Baldi's lip movements to their perception of a natural voice. This work has entailed controlled evaluation of the impact of different versions of Baldi's animation on the relative intelligibility of speech sounds, including a thorough comparison of the speech confusion matrices while listening to Baldi versus listening to a human speaker. The results of these numerous iterative evaluations have been used to refine Baldi. More generally, they also have advanced the state of the art on intelligible lip synchronization and animated conversational interface design.

In another recent study, Cassell and Thórisson (1999) investigated users' general communicative responses while interacting with three different types of animated characters, including ones that (1) only supplied propositional feedback, (2) responded with propositional feedback and information on emotional state, and (3) responded with propositional and "envelope" feedback (i.e., nonverbal gaze and gestures). In this research, they examined users' overlapped speech and total dialogue contributions. Their results indicated that the character with envelope feedback promoted the most fluid and efficient interaction. The character based on this design also was rated by users as higher on language ability.

Other recent studies have begun exploring users' speech production while interacting with an animated character. For example, the Swedish August project has collected thousands of samples of human speech from public kiosk users during interaction with an animated character (Bell and Gustafson 1999a). Recent analyses have confirmed hyperarticulate speech adaptations in Swedish users' spoken language to an animated character during error handling (Bell and Gustafson 1999b). This particularly extensive and diverse corpus currently is being analyzed in linguistic detail, so in the future we may learn considerably more about how people actually talk to animated characters.

Although a few recent studies have begun exploring users' communication patterns while conversing with an animated character, a great deal remains unknown about human communication with such interfaces. Furthermore, the specific focus of previous work has yet to address children's spoken language to animated characters. Previous language development literature indicates that children's speech production is considerably more challenging than that of adults, because it is less mature, more variable, and dynamically changing from year to year (Lee, Potamianos, and Narayanan 1997; Shatz and Gelman 1973; Yeni-Komshian, Kavanaugh, and Ferguson 1980). Very recent research also has estimated that children's speech is subject to recognition error rates that are two to five times higher than those for adult speech (Aist et al. 1998; Das, Nix, and Picheny 1998; Potamianos, Narayanan, and Lee 1997; Wilpon and Jacobsen 1996). It therefore is clear that considerable corpus collection, language modeling, and tailored interface design will be needed before successful interactive technologies can be developed for children.

11.3.2 Goals of the Present Data Collection

This study compared the spoken language production of ten six- to ten-year-old children interacting with an animated character in the I SEE! Interface with that of the same children interacting with a human adult partner. The investigation addressed the following general questions:

1. Will children engage in extended "conversations" with an animated character? If so, what kind of content do children initiate during these exchanges? And what are the characteristics of children's speech and language with the animated character?

2. Even though we know adults speak differently to a "computer" than to another person, do children likewise speak differently to an animated computer agent? Or is their speech indistinguishable from the way they speak with a human partner? If their speech differs, then in what respect? Is it simplified or hyperarticulated, as an adult's speech would be?

3. Is children's speech to an animated character harder to process than adult speech to a computer? If so, what is more difficult, and how much more difficult is it?

4. Do children like interacting with animated characters? How lengthy are their interactions, and how absorbed do they become? Can animated characters be used as an effective interface tool for engaging children in conversational interfaces? What potential do they have for use in educational applications, and how should they be designed for such purposes?

Because so little past research has addressed children's spoken language to computers, in this study we were particularly interested in analyzing the different and potentially hard-to-process articulatory, grammatical, and lexical features of children's speech to an animated character. For example, disfluencies have been analyzed quite extensively in adult speech to computers, although to our knowledge they have yet to be evaluated in either adult speech to animated characters or in children's speech at all. *Disfluencies* in spontaneous speech are self-repairs that interrupt the smooth flow of an otherwise coherent linguistic construction. They are widely recognized as presenting a major challenge and source of failure for current spoken language systems. Recently, researchers have become interested in modeling disfluencies as a landmark feature of spoken language, rather than an aberration or linguistic deficiency (Oviatt 1995; Shriberg 1994). Factors that predict disfluent speech have also been identified. Finally, corresponding interface designs have been formulated that are capable of substantially minimizing disfluencies (i.e., by up to 80%), although in a manner that remains completely transparent to users (Oviatt 1995).

For general reference, table 11.1 summarizes estimates of the rate of adult disfluencies per 100 words in a variety of different types of spoken interaction. Among other things, it reveals that disfluencies occur at consistently higher rates in adult interpersonal speech than in human-computer speech. During adult human-computer communication, disfluencies also are known to bear a positive linear relation to utterance length, which accounts for approximately 80 percent of all the variance in spoken disfluencies (Oviatt 1995, 1997). This relation has been attributed in part to the increasing *cognitive load* associated with planning the content and order of information to be articulated, which rises progressively in longer utterances.

In this study, we were interested in comparing the rate of disfluencies in children's speech with that previously estimated for different types of adult speech. For comparable types of spoken interaction, we hypothesized that child disfluency levels might be elevated. We were also interested in directly comparing the rate of disfluencies in children's speech to an animated computer partner with that addressed to a human adult. If young children are mesmerized by animated characters and believe them to be "real," then their disfluency levels should be indistinguishable. On the other hand, if children are engaged but still quite aware of speaking to a computer, then their data should resemble the adult pattern of higher interpersonal than human-computer disfluencies. A third goal was to evaluate whether utterance length bears the same strong linear relation to children's spoken disfluency rates, as it does in adults. Alternatively, if children experience greater cognitive load associated with planning utterances of increasing length, then the slope of their linear function may be steeper than that for adults. In addition to these specific articulatory issues, a further aim of the present study was to explore other potentially hard-to-process features of children's speech, including invented or misapplied lexical content, immature grammatical constructions, and so forth.

11.3.3 Methods

11.3.3.1 Participants, Tasks, and Procedure   Ten children between six years, eight months old and ten years, nine months old participated in this research, including seven females and three males. All were volunteers from the local Portland, Oregon, community.

Table 11.1   Spoken disfluency rates per 100 words for different types of human-human and simulated human-computer interaction

Type of spoken interaction	Disfluency rate
Human-human speech	
Two-person telephone call	8·83
Three-person interpreted telephone call	6·25
Two-person face-to-face dialogue	5·50
One-person noninteractive monologue	3·60
Human-computer speech	
Unconstrained computer interaction	1·74/ 1·87/ 2·14
Structured computer interaction	0·78/ 0·87/ 1·70

Note: Human-computer disfluency rates from left to right represent verbal-temporal content, computational-numeric content, and visual-spatial content.

The study consisted of two data collection phases. During the first part, children interacted with the simulated I SEE! system (see sec. 11.3.3.2) in a room set up as an informal children's bedroom and playroom. The room was designed to be inviting and relaxing, with a sofa, stuffed animals, children's artwork, a toy chest, and so forth. During the session, children sat on the sofa with a Fujitsu 1200 handheld PC angled in front of them, so that they could use pen input and view the screen comfortably. They were introduced to the I SEE! system by the experimenter, who spoke to them using a dolphin puppet. Each child received a ten- to fifteen-minute hands-on orientation to the system and its coverage, including how to (1) use speech and pen input, (2) make corrections, (3) control the movies, (4) use the system to learn about different animals, and (5) make a graph summarizing their findings. During the orientation, children also interacted with three practice animals and graphed information about them.

After this orientation, the experimenter left the children alone to play with the I SEE! system while they interacted with eight unique undersea animals (e.g., manatee, squid, stonefish). In each case, the children were told that they could ask the animals anything they wished but to be sure to ask Spin the dolphin's question each time they met a new animal (e.g., "Are you poisonous or not?"). Spin was available as an animated guide to help the child with any questions about the application's functionality, general interface controls, or graph construction. The children also were asked to enter the answer to Spin's question on their individual graphs, which they could print and keep when done. A video record was made of the interface during the entire interaction, along with a closeup view of the children's faces and a recording of their spoken language as they played. Following this interaction, the experimenter returned and engaged the child in an informal discussion about what they thought of the I SEE! system and its animated characters. During some sessions when several children visited the lab together, an informal brainstorming and "design meeting" also took place between the children, experimenters, and programmers. The general purpose of such meetings was to collect and consolidate children's design ideas during a playful group exchange in which they participated as the "experts" and "advisors" (Druin 1999).

During the second phase of the study, the same children participated in a game of Twenty Questions with the adult experimenter as they attempted to discover the identity of different animals. Children's speech was audiotaped throughout this interpersonal interaction. In both of these phases of the study, children basically were involved in a gamelike interaction in which the goal was to extract information about the features or identity of different animals. For both tasks, children needed to take initiative in asking questions as they retrieved information and solved a simple problem. However, in phase one their resource was an animated software agent, and in phase two it was a human adult.

11.3.3.2 *I SEE! Application and Interface* Figure 11.3 illustrates I SEE!'s interface. The left side of the screen displays movies of marine animals. The child user could control the start, stop, replay, and automatic location of different marine animals on the movie by entering pen input in the white field beneath the movie, or by tapping the pen in this field and speaking. When the movie stopped, the marine animal was embellished with animated eyes that blinked naturally. At this point, the animal became available as a "conversational partner" for answering questions about itself. For example, an animated manatee could identify itself, its diet, habitat, unique behavior, endangered species status, and so forth. Essentially, animated eyes that gazed at the child provided *attentional cues,* and these cues were used to mark the transition from a *passive movie-viewing experience* to *active availability* of the animal as the child's conversational partner.

The upper-right side of figure 11.3 illustrates a graph created by an eight-year-old child after querying six different animals about their endangered species status. After conversing with each animated creature and collecting information needed to classify it, the child entered each animal in her bar graph. In this case, she did so by entering pen input directly into the next available white field on the graph. The I SEE! interface permitted children to construct

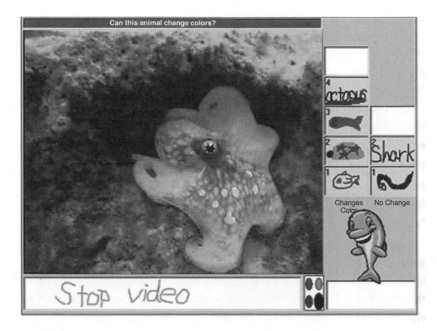

Figure 11.3
I SEE! user interface.

their graph in a direct hands-on manner by using pen input to place symbolic artwork, animal names, or marks on the correct side of the graph or by pointing to a field and speaking their input. The system acknowledged the child's entry by painting the field blue and making a splashing sound as the graph became taller on that side.

The lower-right corner of figure 11.3 also illustrates the animated dolphin character named Spin. The dolphin provided motivation and guidance by answering questions, making suggestions, issuing praise and reminders, and telling jokes. The dolphin was animated with natural eye movements, lip synching, facial expressions, and gestures. Spin also made exuberant large body movements, such as jumping, somersaulting, diving and splashing, and clapping. During conversation, Spin was capable of acknowledging her understanding, or expressing puzzlement and lack of comprehension, through her facial expressions and gestures.

During interaction, both the dolphin and marine animals responded using text-to-speech (TTS). The voices used for this application were female and male ones from Microsoft's Whisper TTS version 4.0, with some hand-tailoring of pitch, duration, volume, intonation, and pronunciation. The voices were crafted to optimize intelligibility and character individuation, which are known to be influential in shaping a user's reactions to an interface (Nass, Steuer, and Tauber 1994). The TTS also was pilot-tested for intelligibility with children and modified as needed.

11.3.3.3 *Transcription and Data Coding*   Each participant's speech was transcribed from the videotapes collected during their human-computer session and from the audiotapes during their interpersonal session. Transcription was done by a native speaker of English and was second scored for reliability. Attention was paid to transcribing verbatim spoken input, without "cleaning it up" in any way. This included recording spoken language phenomena such as nonword sounds, repetitions, disfluencies and self-repairs, confirmations, and so forth. Children's speech in the transcripts was divided into two categories: (1) simple responses to queries elicited by the system (e.g., *System*: "Would you like to hear another joke?" *Child*: "Yes, okay."), versus (2) child-initiated spoken dialogue (*Child*: "Do you change colors rapidly?" *System*: "No, I stay the same color.")

- *Total words.* The total number of child-initiated spoken words was tabulated for each child during both human-computer and interpersonal communication. Since these tasks were driven primarily by the child, less than 5 percent of all spoken language involved simple elicited responses to the system, and these data were excised for analytical purposes. Data on the total number of spoken words primarily provided a baseline for converting disfluencies to a rate per 100 words.

- *Mean length of utterance (MLU).* The average number of spoken words per utterance was tabulated for each subject during human-computer and interpersonal communication. These averages also were based on child-initiated spoken dialogue. MLU primarily was used for examining the relation between utterance length and disfluency rate in children's speech.

- *Utterances per dialogue turn.* The average number of utterances per dialogue turn, or before the system made a dialogue contribution, was tabulated for each child during human-computer and interpersonal communication. This measure in part reflects the degree of interactivity during the conversational exchange.

- *Requests for repetition.* The number of times that each child asked his or her human or animated conversational partner to repeat an utterance was totaled, and a percentage of requested repetitions out of the total utterances for that child's interaction then was calculated. This measure was used as an index of the relative intelligibility of the text-to-speech (TTS) output used in I SEE!

- *Disfluencies.* Spontaneously occurring spoken disfluencies were totaled for each subject during both the human-computer and interpersonal communication sessions, and then were converted to a rate per 100 words. Disfluencies were scored only during child-initiated spoken language, not during utterances involving system-elicited responses. In addition, only spontaneously occurring disfluencies were scored, not cases in which a repetition was elicited by a system interruption or an unusually slow system response. The following types of disfluency were coded: (1) content self-corrections, meaning errors in task content that were spontaneously corrected as the child spoke (e.g., "What kind of fish is that spotted, or no, striped one?"), (2) false starts, or alterations to the grammatical structure of a spoken utterance (e.g., "How many– do you have live babies or lay eggs?"), (3) repetitions—namely, repetitions of a phoneme, syllable, word, or phrase that occurred spontaneously as the subject spoke (e.g., "Are you en– endangered?"), and (4) filled pauses, those spontaneous nonlexical sounds that fill pauses in running speech (e.g.,"Uh, how long does a sea turtle live?"), often signaling the start of a new phrase or self-correction. Scoring included cases in which multiple instances of different kinds of disfluencies occurred within a single utterance, as in "How– do you– do you know how many, uh– different species you have of your kind?" (For further classification and coding details, see Oviatt 1995.) For the purpose of this study, no attempt was made to code minor spoken mispronunciations like elongated or slurred sounds, interjection or omission of individual vowel and consonant sounds, and so forth, which are more difficult to identify reliably during scoring.

- *Idiosyncratic linguistic constructions.* Several types of linguistic irregularity were coded and totaled for each child during the human-computer and interpersonal communication sessions, and then were converted to a rate per 100 words. These linguistic idiosyncrasies were scored only during child-initiated spoken language, and they included the following phenomena: (1) invented words (e.g., "You're the *amazingest* animal I've ever seen. Are you a *tape-eater?*"), (2) incorrect lexical selections (e.g., "Are you endangered or *instinct?*"), (3) concatenated words (e.g., "What are *krill-shellfish?*"), (4) ill-formed grammatical constructions (e.g., "Have you ever *ate* spaghetti?"; "You're the *most smartest* fish."), and (5) distinctly mispronounced or exaggerated articulations, sometimes exclamatory or highly emotive in nature (e.g., "What are *mullooskies?*"; "Are you a stuffed *aminal?*"; "Eeeeeh!"; "Whoooaaaa!").

- *Reliability.* A second scorer independently checked 100 percent of the transcriptions and disfluency codings from both studies, and any discrepancies were resolved before analyses were performed.

11.3.4 Results
The data yielded a child speech corpus totaling over 9600 words, including over 500 spontaneous disfluencies for analysis.

Figure 11.4 illustrates that the same children had significantly higher levels of spontaneous speech disfluencies during interpersonal communication than while conversing with animated characters, paired t-test, $t = 4.55$ ($df = 9$), $p < .0005$, one-tailed. The children's disfluency rate averaged 6.71 percent during interpersonal communication, compared with 2.32 percent during human-computer communication, which represented almost a threefold higher rate during interpersonal communication. Figure 11.4 also clarifies that all ten children had a higher rate of interpersonal disfluencies than human-computer disfluencies. Furthermore, the ranges were very distinct, with the rate of human-computer disfluencies ranging from 1 to 4 percent, and interpersonal disfluencies ranging from 4 to 12 percent. A median-split comparison of children's disfluencies as a function of age (i.e., 6–8 versus 8–10 years) did not reveal any significant change in either human-computer or interpersonal rates within this age range.

Analyses revealed that the ratio of children's speech comprised of verbatim utterance repetitions averaged 20 percent during human-computer communication, but only 7 percent during interpersonal interaction. That is, children's speech directed to animated characters was significantly more repetitive than was their interpersonal speech, paired $t = 3.62$ ($df = 9$), $p < .003$, one-tailed. Since repeated utterances may not require as much cognitive load during utterance planning, children's disfluency rates were recalculated after removing all verbatim repetitions. However, this analysis reconfirmed that children's

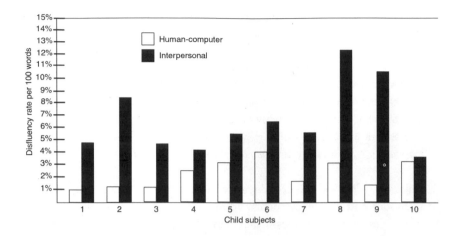

Figure II.4

Rate of spoken disfluencies during children's human-computer and interpersonal communication for each of the ten study participants.

disfluency rates were still significantly higher during interpersonal communication than while talking to an animated character, paired $t = 3.99$ ($df = 9$), $p < .0015$, one-tailed.

Analyses of these data revealed that children's utterance length averaged 4.8 during human-computer interaction and 4.3 during human-human interaction, which was not a significant difference by paired t-test, $t = 1.47$ ($df = 9$), N.S. Although utterance length is known to correspond to disfluency rates, it clearly did not account for the differences between human-computer and interpersonal disfluency rates observed in these data. A comparison of the number of utterances that children spoke per dialogue turn also revealed no difference when speaking to an adult versus an animated character, paired $t < 1$. In these structural respects, then, children's spoken dialogue with an animated character was similar to that with a human adult partner.

Further analyses revealed that children's disfluency rate was higher than that previously reported for adults during unconstrained[1] human-computer interaction involving a visual-spatial task, paired t-test, $t = 2.35$ ($df = 10$), $p < .025$, one-tailed. These comparisons involved child and adult utterances matched on MLU, since children's MLU is shorter than that of adults and MLU is highly correlated with disfluency rates. After matching on utterance length, in this study the overall disfluency rate averaged 64 percent higher for children than the rate previously reported for adults.

A regression analysis indicated that the strength of predictive association between utterance length and spoken disfluency rate for six- to ten-year-old children was $\rho^2_{XY} = .88$ ($N = 11$). That is, 88 percent of the variance in the rate of spoken disfluencies for children was predictable simply by knowing an utterance's specific length. This is similar to, but slightly higher than, the 79 percent strength of predictive association documented previously for adults in a map-based visual-spatial domain. The linear function illustrated in the scatter plot in figure 11.5 summarizes this relation for both children and adults. For children, the y-axis constant coefficient is –0.41, and the x-axis beta coefficient of +0.39 represents utterance length. Children's regression line is the steeper slope shown on the left in figure 11.5. Their disfluency rate rises above 3 percent after an MLU of 7 has been reached, in comparison with an MLU of 12 for adults.

The level of idiosyncratic linguistic constructions in children's speech averaged 1.83 percent overall for this age group, with no significant difference between human-computer (2.42%) and interpersonal speech (1.24%) in terms of rate of occurrence. A median-split comparison of the rate of idiosyncratic language as a function of age (i.e., 6–8 versus 8–10 years) revealed a significantly higher level in six- to eight-year-olds than eight- to ten-year-olds during human-computer interaction, paired $t = 3.12$ ($df = 8$), $p < .01$, one-tailed. Figure 11.6 illustrates the cumulative percentage of children's spoken language that contained hard-to-process disfluencies or idiosyncratic language, which averaged about 5 percent of all human-computer communication and 8 percent of interpersonal communication during the age range studied.

Although children never requested that a human dialogue partner repeat an utterance, half of the children did request at least one repeat when interacting with an animated character that used TTS output. However, only 1.5 percent of all utterances delivered by an animated character resulted in the child requesting a repetition. This indicates that the TTS was adequately intelligible, and children were infrequently distracted by it during their conversation.

11.3.5 Discussion

The following conversation between eight-year-old Edward and the thimble jellyfish demonstrates that children can indeed become very engaged while interacting with animated agents:

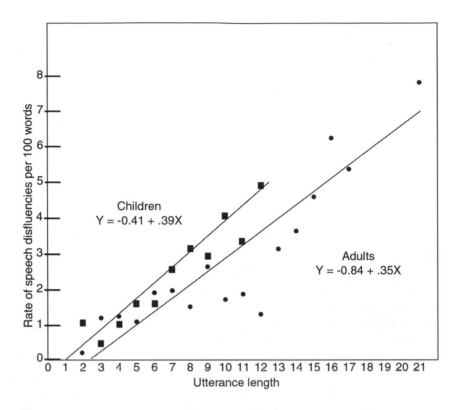

Figure 11.5

Linear regression model summarizing increasing rate of spoken disfluencies per 100 words as a function of utterance length during a visual-spatial task, comparing 6- to 10-year-old children with adults.

Edward: Stop! Hello. What are you? [videotape stops; jellyfish looks at Edward and blinks]

Thimble jelly: I am a thimble jellyfish.

Edward: Cool. Are you poisonous?

Thimble jelly: Yes, I am poisonous. [Edward draws a fish on the poisonous side of his bar graph]

Edward: You kinda look like a jellybean. What is your name?

Thimble jelly: I am Tiny the thimble jelly. I swim with hundreds of other thimble jellies.

Oviatt and Adams

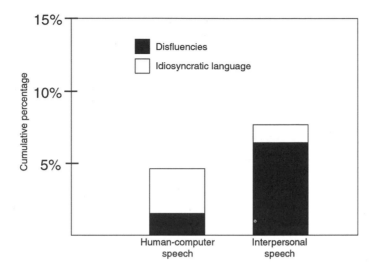

Figure 11.6

Cumulative percentage of children's human-computer versus interpersonal speech that contains hard-to-process disfluencies and idiosyncratic linguistic constructions.

Edward: Are you common or exti- instinct?

Thimble jelly: I am very common.

Edward: Do-um-what- what do you eat?

Thimble jelly: I eat plankton. Sometimes sea turtles eat me.

Edward: Whoa, that's not very much. All I eat is spaghetti, hamburgers. I won't touch fish.

Thimble jelly: Yummy.

Edward: Have you ever ate spaghetti?

Thimble jelly: No way, José!

Edward: Are you a girl or a boy?

During these conversations, children spoke directly to the animals using personal pronouns, and approximately one-third of all the content exchanged involved social questions initiated by the child about the animated character's name, birthday, personal characteristics, friends, and family life. Children typically reported that they enjoyed interacting with I SEE! They often specifically mentioned that they liked "talking to the animals," whom they viewed as "friends" rather than parents or teachers. As expected, however, most of the remaining two-thirds of the conversational content focused on elementary marine biology information.

Edward's conversation with the thimble jelly also illustrates the relatively disfluent, repetitious, and sometimes idiosyncratic linguistic constructions that were typical of six- to ten-year-old children's speech to the computer, which clearly would be difficult for current speech technology to process. In fact, figure 11.6 clarifies that 5 percent of children's spoken language during these interactions involved disfluencies or extreme mispronunciations, invented or misapplied words, and ill-formed syntactic constructions. Given that children's average MLU was five words long, this means that one in four utterances during this application contained hard-to-process language. These data underscore the need for collection of child speech corpora and the development of language models that represent these unique features of children's spontaneous interactive speech. The aim of this approach is to leverage more robust spoken language systems by using models of children's preexisting language patterns, rather than engaging in futile attempts to retrain children's entrenched and immature speech patterns.

This study confirms that children's disfluency rates are substantially and consistently higher during interpersonal than human-computer communication, even though the latter interaction is with an animated and embodied "persona." In fact, the disfluency rate during children's interpersonal communication averaged three times higher, and all ten children had higher disfluency rates when speaking with a real person, as illustrated in figure 11.4. This difference is consistent with the 2.5 to 3 times higher disfluency rate that is typical of adult speech during human-human communication (Oviatt 1995, 1997).

One implication of these findings is that six- to ten-year-old children do distinguish animated from real human partners, even though at times they may seem completely absorbed with their "new friends." Children's speech is not only distinctly different to a computer partner, like adult speech, but also clearer or more hyperarticulated (Oviatt, MacEachern, and Levow 1998). This may indicate that children view their computer partner as a kind of "at-risk" listener, with whom they anticipate needing to work harder to make themselves understood. Children's higher rate of repetitive speech to the computer also provides evidence of linguistic simplification, compared with language directed to a human adult listener.

In some noteworthy respects, children's speech to an animated computer partner was significantly more difficult to process than typical adult speech to a computer. After controlling for utterance length, their disfluency rates averaged 64 percent higher than comparable adult speech during a spatially oriented task. As far as we know, analyses have not yet been computed for adult disfluency rates while conversing specifically with animated characters. Such data will be needed to interpret clearly whether children's disfluency rates are elevated above those of adults in general, or whether disfluency rates may be higher for both children and adults when talking to animated characters than to other types of spatial display.

Children's spontaneous spoken disfluencies also were confirmed to be strikingly sensitive to utterance length. Of all the variance in spoken disfluencies in the present data, 88 percent was predictable simply by knowing an utterance's specific length. This rate is even higher than the 79 percent strength of association found previously for adult speech. These child speech data replicate and extend previous adult findings during verbal, numeric, and spatial tasks (Oviatt 1995, 1997). However, figure 11.5 clarifies that the slope of this function is steeper in children's speech than in adults'. Basically, higher disfluency rates are precipitated at lower utterance lengths in children's speech. In children's speech, the disfluency rate begins exceeding 3 percent after an utterance length of seven words is reached, whereas a 3 percent disfluency rate is not exceeded in adult speech until twelve words or longer. This indicates that the planning load associated with increased utterance length has a greater impact on children, even within the range of relatively brief to moderate sentence lengths.

11.4 Future Research Directions

Developing effective conversational interfaces, especially ones that incorporate animated characters with whom users can interact, will require research on many key issues that still are poorly understood. Among other things, research is needed on the basic functionality and best uses of animated characters, and what their central design elements should be. There is great interest in the apparent power of new conversational interfaces to engage and motivate users, perhaps especially child users. As a result, further research needs to explore much more thoroughly the educational role that such technology could play, as well as how it could best be designed for such purposes.

More careful consideration also is needed of the entire interactive input-output cycle between human and computer. For example, what is the impact of character animation, TTS, and other audio output on subsequent user input? In particular, how is users' speech influenced by animated displays, in terms of the synchronization, complexity, and processability of spoken language that is elicited? And how might the future design of animated characters be used to assist in simplifying or managing the most difficult features of users' spoken language?

The design of interactive technologies for children, especially ones that have recognition rates matching those of adult users, will require a substantial program of research analyzing children's spoken language to conversational interfaces. This research will need to include a comprehensive assessment of the acoustic-prosodic, syntactic, semantic, and discourse-level properties of children's speech. In particular, future analyses should continue investigating features of children's speech other than disfluencies that are especially difficult for current technology to process. This research ideally should be conducted in natural field contexts in which noise levels, collaborative interaction, and other factors are expected to elevate the rate of hard-to-process speech, such as disfluencies, and to reduce system recognition rates. To accomplish the above goals, large corpus collection efforts will be needed on children of different ages while engaged in different types of interaction. In addition, new language models will be needed that represent the central and sometimes idiosyncratic features of children's spoken language. The new Mobile Simulation Environment, in conjunction with the I SEE! application and others to be developed in the future, currently is being used to address these and related research questions.

Acknowledgments

Special thanks to Intel and NSF grant IRI-9530666 for providing funding and equipment donations in support of this research. Thanks to William Fiesterman for designing our dolphin character and eyeball animations, and to the National Geographic Society and its photographers for permission to use videotape footage from *Jewels of the Caribbean Sea*. Thanks also to Jeff Schilling of OGI's television productions for video editing assistance; to CHCC's Josh Clow, Thomas Marsh, Craig Minor, and Joel Pothering for assistance with implementing and testing the new simulation environment; to Jennifer Bruns for assistance with data collection and analysis; and to Phil Cohen for helpful discussions. Finally, special thanks to the children who played with the system, served as design advisors, and inspired this work in the first place.

Note

1. An "unconstrained" interface refers here to one involving a user-initiated interaction, rather than being system prompted or directed. With respect to dialogue initiative, then, these data are parallel to the present child data, in which queries were initiated by the user. This is important because the degree of user versus system initiative is known to influence spoken disfluency rates (Oviatt 1995).

References

Aist, G., P. Chan, X. Huang, L. Jiang, R. Kennedy, D. Latimer, J. Mostow, and C. Yeung. 1998. How effective is unsupervised data collection for children's speech recognition? *Proceedings of the International Conference on Spoken Language Processing* 7:3171–3174.

Bell, L., and J. Gustafson. 1999a. Interacting with an animated agent: User strategies in a spoken dialogue system. *Proceedings of Eurospeech '99* 3:1143–1146.

———. 1999b. Repetition and its phonetic realizations: Investigating a Swedish database of spontaneous computer-directed speech. *Proceedings of the International Conference on Phonetic Sciences (ICPhS '99)* 2:1221–1224.

Cassell, J., and K. R. Thórisson. 1999. The power of a nod and a glance: Envelope vs. emotional feedback in animated conversational agents. *Applied Artificial Intelligence Journal* 13(4–5):519–538. (Special issue on Animated Interface Agents.)

Cohen, P. R., A. Cheyer, M. Q. Wang and S. C. Baeg. 1994. An open agent architecture. *Working notes of AAAI Spring Symposium Series on Software Agents*. Menlo Park, Calif.: AAAI Press. (Reprinted in M. Huhns and M. Singh, eds., *Readings in agents*, 197–204. San Mateo, Calif.: Morgan Kaufmann, 1998.)

Cole, R., J. Mariani, H. Uszkoreit, A. Zaenen, and V. Zue, eds. 1997. *Survey of the state of the art in human language technology*. Cambridge: Cambridge University Press. (Also published as a status report to the European Commission and the National Science Foundation, May 1994).

Das, S., D. Nix, and M. Picheny. 1998. Improvements in children's speech recognition performance. *Proceedings of the International Conference on Acoustics, Speech and Signal Processing (ICASSP '98)* 1:433–436.

Druin, A. 1999. Cooperative inquiry: Developing new technologies for children with children. In *Proceedings of the Conference on Human Factors in Computing Systems (CHI '99)*, 592–599. New York: ACM Press.

Lee, S., A. Potamianos, and S. Narayanan. 1997. Analysis of children's speech: Duration, pitch and formants. *European Conference on Speech Communication and Technology (Eurospeech '97)* 1:473–476.

Lester, J., S. Converse, S. Kahler, S. Barlow, B. Stone, and R. Bhogal. 1997. The persona effect: Affective impact of animated pedagogical agents. In *Proceedings of the Conference on Human Factors in Computing Systems (CHI '97)*, 359–366. New York: ACM Press.

Martin, A., J. Fiscus, B. Fisher, D. Pallett, and M. Przybocki. 1997. System descriptions and performance summary. *Proceedings of the Conversational Speech Recognition Workshop/DARPA Hub-5E Evaluation*. San Mateo, Calif.: Morgan Kaufman.

Nass, C., J. Steuer, and E. Tauber. 1994. Computers Are Social Actors. *Proceedings of the Conference on Human Factors in Computing Systems (CHI '94)*, 72–78. Boston: ACM Press.

Oviatt, S. L. 1995. Predicting Spoken Disfluencies during Human-Computer Interaction. *Computer Speech and Language* 9(1):19–35.

———. 1996. User-Centered Design of Spoken Language and Multimodal Interfaces. *IEEE Multimedia* 3(4):26–35. (Reprinted in M. Maybury and W. Wahlster, eds., *Readings on intelligent user interfaces*, 620–629. San Mateo, Calif.: Morgan Kaufmann, 1998.)

———. 1997. Multimodal Interactive Maps: Designing for Human Performance. *Human-Computer Interaction* 12:93–129. (Special issue on Multimodal Interfaces.)

Oviatt, S. L., P. R. Cohen, M. W. Fong, and M. P. Frank. 1992. A rapid semi-automatic simulation technique for investigating interactive speech and handwriting. *Proceedings of the International Conference on Spoken Language Processing* 2:1351-1354.

Oviatt, S. L., P. R. Cohen, L. Wu, J. Vergo, L. Duncan, B. Suhm, J. Bers, T. Holzman, T. Winograd, J. Landay, J. Larson, and D. Ferro. N.d. Designing the user interface for multimodal speech and gesture applications: State-of-the-art systems and research directions for 2000 and beyond. In John Carroll, ed., *Human-computer interaction in the new millennium*. Reading, Mass.: Addison-Wesley. Forthcoming.

Oviatt, S. L., M. MacEachern, and G. Levow. 1998. Predicting hyperarticulate speech during human-computer error resolution. *Speech Communication* 24:87–110.

Potamianos, A., S. Narayanan, and S. Lee. 1997. Automatic Speech Recognition for Children. *European Conference on Speech Communication and Technology (Eurospeech '97)* 5:2371–2374.

Shatz, M., and R. Gelman. 1973. The development of communication skill modifications in the speech of young children as a function of listener. *Monograph of the Society for Research in Child Development* 38:1–37.

Shriberg, E. 1994. Preliminaries to a theory of speech disfluencies. Ph. D.diss., Psychology Dept., University of California at Berkeley, Berkeley, California.

Spiegel, M., and C. Kamm, eds. 1997. *Speech Communication* 23(1–2). (Special issue on Interactive Voice Technology for Telecommunications, IVTTA '96.)

van Mulken, S., E. André, and J. Müller. 1998. The persona effect: How substantial is it? In *Proceedings of Human Computer Interaction (HCI '98)*, 53–66. Sheffield: Sheffield Hallam University.

Wilpon, J. G., and C. N. Jacobsen. 1996. A study of speech recognition for children and the elderly. *Proceedings of the International Conference on Acoustics, Speech and Signal Processing (ICASSP '96)*, 349–352. Atlanta: IEEE Press.

Yeni-Komshian, G. H., J. F. Kavanaugh, and C. A. Ferguson, eds. 1980. *Child phonology, volume 1: Production.* New York: Academic Press.

Measurement and Evaluation of Embodied Conversational Agents

Gregory A. Sanders and Jean Scholtz

12.1 Evaluation of Interactive Systems

In this chapter, we cover four main topics. First, we consider the overall questions of evaluating interactive systems. Second, we discuss ways in which speech-based systems and embodied conversational agents are both types of conversational systems, and we explain that embodied conversation is nevertheless different from speech-only interaction. Third, we present a detailed formative evaluation that we proposed for a speech-based agent interface: the DARPA Communicator program. Fourth, we correspondingly discuss the ways in which measurement and evaluation of embodied conversational agents is very much a related process, and we present the metrics and evaluation that seem likely to be useful for five important aspects of embodied conversational agents.

When one thinks about the overall questions of measuring and evaluating interactive systems, there are two immediate questions to answer. First, why should we evaluate interactive systems at all? Second, if we do evaluate, how do we accomplish the task?

Measurement and evaluation is a critical piece of both research and development. In order to judge progress in anything, we need a systematic method of evaluation. If we are looking for the best system, then it is necessary that the systems have comparable evaluations. One of the best methods to achieve that is to use the same data and run the various systems on that data. In addition, we need the notion of "ground truth." That is, what answer should the algorithm produce? Then various metrics can be examined such as correctness of answer and the time needed to produce that answer.

Benchmarks, often used for evaluation, are a method of assessing performance. Benchmarks for grade-school children consist of a checklist of what every child should know at a certain level of instruction. In the computer realm, computer hardware is often evaluated by running application benchmarks. A set of applications is run, and the performance for the particular hardware configuration is measured. Software systems can also be benchmarked.

Benchmark or summative evaluations (Nielsen 1993) typically are done after the hardware or software system is completed. Summative evaluations for software involve user testing. Enough users for statistical significance are given a series of tasks to do. Measures of performance and user satisfaction are collected and compared to those from a different system. One source of differences is the expertise of the user. Users can differ drastically, so it is difficult to compare the performance of user A on system A with that of user B on system B. It is best if users use all the systems to be compared in a counterbalanced fashion. Some user differences can be controlled by standard training and by a standard demographics questionnaire for user selection. In comparing systems, we control user differences so that we can be assured that the systems, and not the users, are the source of differences in performance. In conclusion, summative evaluations assess performance and user satisfaction. Summative evaluations tell which systems are better, but not why.

Another type of evaluation, known as formative (Nielsen 1993), is done at various stages of software or hardware development. Formative evaluation focuses on gathering information about specific components for the purpose of improvement. For example, in designing a graphical user interface, one might evaluate the icons proposed for a toolbar. Users could be asked to match names of tools with the proposed icons. Or they could be shown an icon and asked to describe what it would do if selected. Often, software prototypes are completed for specific tasks. Users are brought in and asked to attempt the tasks using the prototypes. Information can be gathered on the steps the users go through, how well they understand the directions, menu choices, icons, and so forth. This information can be used to redesign the interface if necessary.

Usability experts conduct heuristic evaluations. They critique the product using design guidelines for user interfaces and their personal knowledge of factors in user interfaces that cause problems for users (Nielsen 1992). A cognitive walk-through is usually done by experts (or at least people trained in the process). The process is to assess, for each step of a task, what users need to know to accomplish that task and how much of that information is readily available in the user interface (Polson et al. 1992). A more formal analysis technique is the GOMS (Goals, Operators, Methods, and Selection rules) model (Card, Moran, and Newell 1983). A task can be broken down to determine how it is done using a particular user interface. Other formative evaluations are based on user studies. Users may be asked to attempt to do tasks with either computer or paper prototypes of the system and asked to think aloud (Ericsson and Simon 1984) as they do so. The evaluators analyze these think-aloud protocols to determine confusions that the users have about different aspects of the interface. In addition, Wizard of Oz studies, with real users, feature a human expert "behind the curtain" who simulates the intended behavior of the planned system.

Relatively straightforward methods and metrics exist for measuring the performance of algorithms and of computer hardware in a summative evaluation. But when we move to the domain of interactive systems, metrics become less well-defined.

First, people interact with software, and the notion of performance depends on the goals of the users of the software. While the same metrics can be used for different types of software, the priorities of these metrics may change significantly. For example, users of medical imaging software who can devote time to learning the software might place the most importance on how effective it is. But telephone agents using software to place orders or log service information can be judged on how many customers they service; hence, they would be interested in how efficient and error free the software is.

Second, people differ. Novice users are concerned with the quality of the electronic help systems and need more explanations. Expert users want systems that are fast and provide them with the flexibility to skip over many steps that novices find reassuring (Shneiderman 1992).

Third, applications consist of numerous parts, but from the user's perspective the whole system is what counts. The whole system does not equal the sum of its parts in an evaluation from the user's perspective. Good components can be assembled into a bad system, whereas a good interface to mediocre components may make a good system from the user's perspective.

Finally, user interfaces are becoming increasingly complex. Early text-based command interfaces had few components: prompts, commands, and error messages. These were evaluated by how well users could learn and use the commands, and understand the error messages and prompts. Graphical user interfaces added menus, icons, toolbars, multiple windows for displaying information and messages, and direct manipulation features. Adding speech and dialogue further increases the complexity and adds to the number of pieces that produce the end result for the user. Suppose that we had a search engine that one conversed with and a graphical user interface used to display results to the user. We are now concerned with the dialogue, the display of the results, the system response time, and the quality of the search engine. Adding embodied agents to the system adds the look of the agent, the gestures and expressions of the agent, and perhaps the personality of the agent as well. The challenge then is to do evaluations that allow us to identify the effect of individual components on the user's interaction with the system. Embodying the system may well simplify the interaction, but it does not simplify the evaluation.

Our current research focuses on generic evaluation techniques for conversational interfaces: that is, evaluations that are valid, not just for one particular system used for specialized tasks, but valid and useful for evaluation of any conversational interface used for any task. Therefore, the priorities for the different components of user satisfaction will change as the task changes. Other evaluation proposals for speech-based systems—for example, PARADISE (Walker et al. 1997)—treat user satisfaction as the overall goal. We think evaluations often need to optimize for multiple goals, not just user satisfaction, and we would like to break down the user satisfaction metric into several identified components in order to assess which aspects of speech-based dialogue correlate most closely with the various satisfaction components. For example, users of a speech-based banking system might not be pleased if the system gave no confirmations before the user had entered all the information about the transaction desired. But a user trying to browse an online catalog might be happier if the system waited until all information was entered to give a confirmation. If we can correlate various components of user satisfaction to various aspects of dialogue systems, then we can produce heuristics to be used in design and in formative evaluations. These heuristic evaluations could then be used by designers of dialogue systems to determine how well the various components of their system would fare in a summative evaluation. Depending on the use of the system, the heuristics would be prioritized to maximize different components of user satisfaction. The PARADISE framework (Walker et al. 1997) provides one approach to calculate such priorities.

12.2 Two Types of Conversational Agents

By *conversational* agents, sometimes called conversational characters, we really mean agents that carry on a spoken or written conversation with the user (prototypically, spoken rather than written). Creating and evaluating even these linguistic abilities are problems that are by no means solved. By *linguistic*, we mean spoken language (as over a telephone) and/or written language, but without embodied communication. By *embodied,* we mean that a character or agent has at least a face and that the character is endowed with attributes such as facial expression and direction of eye gaze. Typically, these agents also have a body and are endowed with gestures, the ability to point, and the ability to move around the screen or other display space(s).

In discussing evaluation, we will refer to two types of conversational agents: speech-only agents and embodied agents.

12.2.1 Speech and Embodiment Present Related Questions

Embodied conversational agents and speech-only systems are really two classes of conversational systems. Metrics and evaluation are needed for both classes. In the same way that embodied conversational agents can be seen as an extension of speech-only conversational systems, the evaluation of embodied conversational agents can be seen as an extension of evaluation of existing speech-only systems. But exploration of the differences is also important.

We have been involved in metrics and evaluation of speech recognition systems and of human-computer interaction. More to the point of our discussion here, we have been involved in metrics and evaluation of speech-based conversational systems, such as the DARPA Communicator project, as we will discuss a bit later.

There are several obvious questions about the effects of embodiment that evaluation can help answer. For example, are embodied systems more effective than speech-only systems at helping users perform tasks? A common claim for both speech and embodiment is that they both provide more effective ways of interacting with computer systems. If we put both into the same system, is there a synergy between speech and embodiment? In what ways? For example, embodiment might be very helpful in correcting (or simply compensating for) speech misrecognitions and ambiguity. There is some evidence that having an alternative medium available makes for easier and faster correction of speech misrecognitions (Halverson et al. 1999; Karat et al. 1999). Embodiment might help with the mechanics of dialogue, such as turn taking: speech and embodiment certainly cooperate in human-to-human dialogue. Or are speech and embodiment hard to combine in an agent? We are looking for ways to answer such questions and exploring how embodiment changes speech metrics. Note that embodied conversational agents, having a personality as such, can play roles as allies and experts in ways that speech-only systems do not.

12.2.2 Embodied Conversational Agent Interfaces

Embodied conversations imply face-to-face interaction, in contrast to the purely linguistic interaction of a telephone conversation. In addition to the abilities mentioned above, to generate (or output) embodied behaviors, we also have in mind that embodied conversational agent systems will have the corresponding input abilities: getting and understanding the user's eye gaze, facial expressions, gestures, and perhaps even the user's movement around a room. These kinds of *embodied inputs* are currently not as highly developed as the output side. Yet these kinds of embodied inputs are part of the role of an embodied conversational agent because they play a central role in human participation in conversation.

12.2.2.1 Embodied Conversation Is Different   Conversation works better, and the mechanics of conversation are different, when gesture and facial expression are available. Bodily behaviors are the most important means through which human participants in a face-to-face conversation accomplish turn-taking behaviors and assess each other's continued attention and understanding. If embodied conversational agents do not watch and understand these behaviors of human users, then the agents effectively ignore the user to some degree.

To the best of our knowledge, the effects of having agents *understand* these behaviors, when produced by the user, have been researched less deeply than the effects of having the embodied conversational agent *produce* the behaviors. Giving agents these abilities may be expected to help users understand when it is and is not their turn to speak and may lead to the system successfully tracking when the user does and does not understand the system. Human participation in dialogues is characterized by calling gesture into play as a redundant means of communication whenever difficulties arise—for example, due to noise (Rogers 1978). Since all these are areas of known difficulty in systems that incorporate spoken language understanding, it is at least intuitively plausible that these abilities will increase the success of spoken language interaction between human users and computer systems (Oviatt 1995, 1997). To demonstrate this will require evaluation.

The main types of facial expression, or *facial displays*, that play a role in the mechanisms of conversation are movements of the eyes (gaze), eyebrow raises, and nods (Cassell, chap. 1). In contrast, facial expressions such as puzzled looks are not really involved in the mechanisms of conversation but instead play roles that could be filled simply by saying something. Conversational participants use facial displays to perform four main aspects of conversation. First, the turn-taking behaviors (giving up the turn, requesting a turn, holding onto the turn) are primarily a matter of the gaze. Note that it would be a circular problem if one always had to speak in order to get the floor to take a turn speaking, whereas turn-taking regulation, involving the gaze, occurs in parallel with the speaking and listening aspects of conversation. Second, the speaker can indicate that he or she is planning or organizing what to say next, by shifting the gaze away from the other participant. Third, the speaker can indicate emphasis of particular words or phrases (typically marked by vocal stress and pitch), by nodding the head, looking at the listener, and raising the eyebrows. Fourth, the speaker can request, and the hearer can give, feedback by combinations of gaze and head nods. To repeat, what is noteworthy about these aspects of conversation is that they are usually accomplished by facial displays (Cassell and Thórisson 1999).

The presence or absence of gesture is also a strong clue to turn-taking behavior. A participant who wishes to speak will bring the hands into position to gesture. During the turn, the hands stay in use. A participant who is done with a turn drops the hands out of position to gesture (Duncan 1974).

Modifications of linguistic interaction as a result of embodiment (in contrast to, say, telephone conversations) include the ability to physically point. In a phone conversation, one might say, "Notice that a button in the middle of the top row is colored orange," and then go on to say, "That is the valve controller. Press it." But if the row of buttons is shown on the screen, the agent can walk over to the buttons, then point to the correct button while saying, "Press the valve controller." After picking out some physical object in the environment, an embodied conversational participant can say, for example, "Turn it like this," showing how by means of gesture. Similarly, in communicating both manner and path of some motion, one of these aspects can be communicated in words and the other by gesture. This sort of thing is a pervasive difference between how you talk with someone using only language (say, over the telephone) versus having a conversation with an embodied conversational partner, present in the virtual flesh. We will give some attention to what these differences imply for measurement and evaluation of the interaction.

12.2.2.2 Type of Embodied Conversational Agent   Goals really start from the role or purpose of the agent—that is, from the use of the software or agent. We will ignore the types of characters that serve as recreational companions engaging in social chitchat and characters that serve as desktop visual pets (cats, dogs, etc.). Instead, we focus on the types of agents that perform a task: playing roles as teachers/tutors, as experts who can be queried, as agents who act on behalf of the user, and as allies. A teacher/tutor agent might interact with and explain how to operate some machine that is pictured on the screen. A tutor agent is typically intended to act much like a human tutor who is providing one-on-one tutoring. Expert or consultant agents may be intended to provide help to a user who is stuck or may provide expert consultation along the lines of knowledge-based systems or expert systems. An agent who acts on behalf of the user to perform some task might interact with the user to get the user's constraints and goals that define an acceptable plan/solution, then go away and negotiate a solution on behalf of the user. Finally, some agents are allies: a combination of expert consultant and agent acting on the user's behalf. Such an ally can constitute the main human interface to some system that is complex (both to understand and to use). The user interacts with the ally agent and the ally agent knows how to make the system dance on behalf of the user.

In important respects, these embodied ally interfaces present the most ambitious goal: eliminating the need to learn complex interfaces to complex systems (and often a related requirement for the user to have a high level of written literacy). Part of the difficulty of building ally interfaces stems from the complexities of the systems to which they are the interfaces. In place of learning the complex system and interacting with it directly, ally interfaces are intended to substitute interaction with the ally via using one's ordinary human repertoire of human-to-human interactions via spoken language, gesture, eye gaze, and movement (skills almost *everyone* already possesses). This can be evaluated.

12.3 Speech-Based Agent Interfaces—The Defense Advanced Research Projects Agency (DARPA) Communicator Program

We are doing ongoing research on evaluation of task-oriented conversational interactions via language alone (disembodied linguistic interaction) in the DARPA Communicator Project. At the very beginning of the Communicator program, we were asked to formulate metrics and an evaluation approach for the program. We proposed a detailed formative evaluation, which was provided to all research groups that were building Communicator systems, for their use in developing their systems (it seems to have been helpful). A committee is currently formulating a rather different, easier to perform, comparative (more summative) common evaluation, to be carried out over the next several months with a large number of research subjects. The committee is exploring the research issues involved in such evaluations.

The DARPA Communicator as presently conceived is a communication device that can be accessed via spoken natural language (as if over the telephone) to make travel plans, including airplane reservations, car rentals, and hotel reservations. Other task domains will follow. Communicator exemplifies a composite system comprising three areas: content (flight information), search/browse abilities, and interaction with the user.

The Communicator research program addresses the construction of software *agents* that operate in an environment where services are freely distributed in the network, and to which the user can *delegate* tasks. The agent/system will take an active role in performing these tasks: building and exploiting models of context, taking the dialogue and task initiative when appropriate, and handling spoken dialogues that perform these tasks, including information access and creation. The domain complexity and resulting dialogue complexity imply that a successful implementation will have substantial abilities to handle referring expressions, clarifications, and subdialogues to repair misunderstandings. The complexity of the domains that Communicator must deal with can be contrasted with what Hayes and Reddy (1983) described as Simple Service Domains: the abilities that Communicator must have are a superset of those required for a simple service domain.

As an example of an evaluation plan for a purely linguistic interaction, we now present a summary of the formative evaluation for the DARPA Communicator that we proposed. Evaluation of spoken language systems is a problem that is studied intensively (Hirschman 1998; Polifroni et al. 1998). We will discuss metrics as well as how to put the pieces together into a whole evaluation. Evaluation for Communicator makes an interesting illustration of evaluation for purely linguistic task-oriented interaction. We set out to design an evaluation that would allow participants in the DARPA Communicator research program to assess the strengths and weaknesses of their complete systems, with special emphasis on dialogue abilities.

The success of Communicator systems can be seen as having three factors: correct task completion, the cost of completing the task, and the quality of the interaction between the system and the end user. These factors are an extension of the model proposed by Walker et al. (1997) in the PARADISE framework. In addition to our metrics, we proposed to give users a questionnaire to collect ratings for ease of use, efficiency, naturalness of interaction, and so forth, with the goal of finding any correlation of users' questionnaire responses with our metrics for linguistic and task performance.

12.3.1 Heuristic Evaluation for Communicator

We proposed including an interactive heuristic evaluation based on several testing scenarios that an expert evaluator would carry out with the system to explore aspects of its behavior. Such testing can be done early on, when a system is not yet complete and robust enough for user testing. A key weakness of user-based testing is that such testing only covers behaviors elicited by the users (arguably, those are the important behaviors). If one wishes to evaluate specific abilities, however, to determine whether they are present and to see how well they work, it is more efficient to have an expert (say, a developer) simply test those abilities. A corresponding strength of heuristic evaluation is that it can provide systematic thorough coverage of all the desired abilities. We proposed a heuristic evaluation that looks at abilities that experience and Wizard of Oz studies suggest are important for a "successful" dialogue. The heuristic evaluation is interactive in that the evaluator will need to nudge the system into certain states in order to check some of its linguistic capabilities. For example, to determine how the system handles ambiguities in proper names, the evaluator might try to fly to Portland, without specifying the name of the state. On the other hand, heuristic expert reviews will not turn up unanticipated user interactions that cause the system to react in unexpected ways. We believe heuristic evaluation complements user testing and that, generally, both should be done to the same version of the system once the system is sufficiently complete and robust that user testing is feasible.

At this point, we have eight general heuristics for desirable characteristics of the Communicator system (Sanders and Scholtz 1998). For each general heuristic, one lists specific abilities that can be checked for in a system. In general, picking the list of what to check in a heuristic evaluation is part art, part inference from earlier experiments (for example, the human-to-human and Wizard of Oz experiments we mentioned for Communicator), and part long experience with building systems (knowing where problems are likely to be found). A key point about expert heuristic reviews is that they are a purely formative technique.

A written list of heuristics amounts to a compiled version of accumulated experience. The heuristics are to be validated through correlations with user satisfaction ratings and with quantitative metrics. Since the heuristics do not generate a numeric measurement, the correlations must be found informally, in essence by using the heuristics as a source of qualitative explanations for the values of the metrics and for the user satisfaction ratings. Nevertheless, the purpose of the heuristic evaluation is formative, whereas the metrics are typically generated on later versions of the system. Validation accumulates through repeated use. Our proposed heuristics are based on general usability guidelines and include a set proposed by Bernsen, Dybkjær, and Dybkjær (1997). We turn now to our eight general heuristics (Sanders and Scholtz 1998).

1. *The system's functionality and use are clear to users.* The system communicates what it can and cannot do, and users are provided with sufficiently clear instructions that they understand how to interact (e.g., how to have the system listening when they speak) and what the system is supposed to do.

2. *The system takes active responsibility for repair when possible.* When user input is inconsistent or ambiguous, the system should clarify it. When the system's speech recognition or understanding fails, it should seize the initiative and begin a subdialogue to repair the failure or misunderstanding.

3. *The system uses clear, concise, and consistent language.* The same question, or the same name, should be formulated the same way everywhere in the dialogue, to make clear that it is the same piece (or same kind) of information being sought or the same entity being referred to. Superfluous or redundant interactions should be omitted. The system's turns should be reasonably concise.

4. *The system follows the dialogue conventions of natural human dialogues.* The system's use of fully specific noun-phrases versus less specific references, and its use of pronouns, should correspond to the introduction and maintenance of focus. After a task dialogue is interrupted by a repair subdialogue, the system should be able to locate the referent of referring expressions employed by the user to resume the previous topic, and the system should use referring expressions correctly when resuming the previous task, context, and focus. The system should note the user's choices of referring expressions and adopt them if the reference is understandable. The system ought to be able to handle all four main possibilities for what the user may do at the end of a task: the user can

   - end the dialogue
   - do or seek deferred repairs/clarifications, reactivating previous contexts
   - ask a question elaborating the current task (e.g., asking for additional information or checking the truth of something suspected to be true), or
   - initiate a new task by asking a question or stating a desire

Note that each of these four is a common move in human dialogues.

5. *The system gives prompt coherent feedback.* By removing the user's uncertainty about what the system has understood or done, the system gives the user a chance to note and correct misunderstandings immediately, while the relevant context is still active (this is far easier than handling deferred repairs). If the task lends itself to a readback (an organized restatement of the whole final task plan), one should be given. The readback should be semantically and pragmatically coherent.

6. *The system correctly handles answers that give more information than it requested.* The system should remember, and use, the extra information that the user has so helpfully provided.

7. *The system detects conflicting input from the user, notifies the user, and actively clarifies or repairs the problem.* New information that conflicts with something the user has previously confirmed should trigger a subdialogue to clarify the conflict. In general, the system should clarify or repair anything that conflicts with the dialogue history (always seize your opportunities).

8. *The system supports users with different levels of expertise.* For example, the system need not provide experienced users with information about its abilities. The system should allow users to exploit the system's domain knowledge when needed and the system should take into account the users' legitimate expectations about its background knowledge. It should also take into account possible (and possibly erroneous) user expectations and inferences from related domains.

12.3.1.1 The Issue of Deferred Repair We need to elaborate on some issues related to the heuristic about prompt coherent feedback. Situations where the user must notice that the system has misunderstood are difficult. If the user's correction of a misunderstanding occurs when the misunderstood item is still focused, the focus mechanism and dialogue expectations allow an immediate correction that is relatively simple. Prompt coherent feedback will allow the user to see the need for a correction immediately. But if the user's correction occurs later, perhaps at the end of the task, the repair is more difficult: the system must then notice that what the user is saying is not compatible with what it expected the user to say at that point (the system's *current* expectations). So the system must therefore hypothesize a correction of something said earlier, back up an apparently relevant focus, and reinterpret the repair in the context of the utterance being repaired (Danieli, Gerbino, and Moisa 1997). It will be difficult for the system to make such connections successfully, and thus the system will likely fail to follow this sort of context switch. The user could even forget to repair the error. Repairs at the end of a task typically feature some sort of referring expression that will identify (at least for a human participant) the material being repaired, and this implies that the system must have significant facility at handling referring expressions (and perhaps a model of the user's task) if such repairs are to succeed. Note that referring expressions turn out to be important to several dialogue abilities.

When multiple repairs occur back to back, spoiling the tracking of focus and context, the system must be able to recognize or generate referring expressions that recreate (or sometimes just reactivate) focus and context as well as signal resumption of the task dialogue.

Confirmation or feedback from the system about the system's understanding of information the user has provided is also an important factor in maintaining shared context. Clark and Schaefer (1989) discussed the way(s) in which a piece of information provided by one participant in a dialogue gets confirmed as successfully understood, and thus enters the common ground of the dialogue participants. Confirmation takes on added importance because of the less than human accuracy of automatic speech recognition.

12.3.2 Phenomena Examined by the Proposed Metrics

In this section, we describe the metrics that we suggested reporting for Communicator systems. The basic flavor of this evaluation is to do a large number of low-level counts from transcript analysis and then "roll up" the counts into six *composite metrics*. We also give each user a user satisfaction questionnaire. Then (having values for the metrics and user satisfaction) we can do a multivariate linear regression to find correlations between the metrics and user satisfaction, as in the PARADISE framework. In order to provide some context for these results, we also proposed a few descriptive metrics that characterize the tasks/scenarios performed by the users and the style of interaction adopted by the user and system in each session.

12.3.2.1 *The Initiative*   At each point in a dialogue, one participant has the lead or has control, and the other participant is responding. If you ask a question you seize the initiative. When you just answer a question you do not take the initiative. If one analyzes a conversation, looking at the initiative in this sense, one is really talking about having the initiative in the dialogue. This is usually called the *dialogue initiative*. If the dialogue is also performing some task (say, making travel reservations), one can correspondingly talk about the *task initiative*. To see the difference between the dialogue initiative and the task initiative, consider repairs or clarifications of what has been said. Suppose participant A asks, "Where do you want to fly to?" At that point A seizes both the dialogue initiative and the task initiative. Suppose participant B responds, "I'm sorry, are you asking for my destination?" At this point, participant B takes the dialogue initiative but not the task initiative. If participant B had, instead, responded by saying, "I want to take the train, not fly," then B would have taken the task initiative as well. Note that taking the task initiative always also means taking the dialogue initiative (Chu-Carroll and Brown 1997).

12.3.2.2 Pieces of Information to Be Exchanged   The most obvious characteristic of performing specified tasks in Communicator's initial travel domain is that the system and the user must request and provide pieces of information to each other. The most obvious measures of task success turn on whether the information exchanged is complete and correct. But to do actual measurements requires the evaluator to define what counts as a piece of information. For any given task, this concept requires a *detailed* definition, and that definition will be domain-specific. The idea is to count the pieces of information that must be exchanged in a way that corresponds to the intuitions of the human user: for example, the information that a user would refer to with a pronoun. In a travel domain, "Next Monday, October the 18th" is one piece of information (two redundant ways of stating the date). "United Flight 123" is probably two pieces (United and 123) because both attributes are necessary to specify the flight. Further, the user is likely to separately consider the airline (United, in this case) as acceptable or not. These counting principles must be specified in detail. To increase interrater agreement on the raw counts used in formulas, we used a "What constitutes a piece of information" document, including examples, to analyze transcripts for the travel reservation domain. Some such detailed specification is needed for any task domain in which one chooses to count pieces of information as part of some metric(s)—a specification sufficiently specific as to produce good interrater agreement. One should have multiple analysts independently count the pieces of information, then assess interanalyst agreement or at least have the analysts negotiate agreement on the count.

What the dialogue treats as one piece of information is, however, not static. Consider the example, above, of "Next Monday, October the 18th." This is really one piece of information (spoken in a redundant way). Initially, the dialogue would treat this as one piece of information. If we imagine a speech recognition error, "Next Sunday, October the 18th," the error correction process (correcting Sunday to Monday) will cause the dialogue to treat this as multiple pieces of information. If *we* actually count this instance as two pieces, though, that would mean that this particular user's solution of this particular scenario would have more pieces of information than other users' solutions of the same scenario and would make it impossible to calculate our task accuracy metric in a way that would allow the value for this particular user to be strictly comparable to the values for other users. Thus, we recommend counting the pieces of information from the scenario/task to be solved, not from the dialogue.

12.3.2.3 *Turns*   In counting turns, we classify them as various types. Each turn is either a user turn or a system turn. In each case, the turn may be "on task" or not, where on-task turns are those that occur between the dialogue opening exchange (Hello. Hello.) and the dialogue closing exchange (Thanks for using the system; please fill out the user questionnaire; goodbye. Bye bye.). Our evaluation focused on the on-task turns. We classified as *Repair turns* those turns involved in requesting or performing clarifications and repairs. *Good turns* are the on-task turns that are not repair turns, do not consist of *only* echoing misrecognized stuff, and do not consist of only irrelevance/incoherence that will need repair or cause the turn to be ignored. This classification of turns must be done by human analysis of the log files of the interaction, but the categories are relevant to the system's processing of the turns and the analysis/categorization could (conceptually, if not in practice) be done by the system. To recap, we classified each on-task turn as one of three types: good turn, repair turn, or bad turn. We didn't make direct use of any count of bad turns. Note that we can have good user turns with bad speech recognition and good system turns that are off in the weeds due to bad speech recognition that has not yet been repaired by the user.

Another sort of turn class, not really related to the above, is *perseverant system turns* where the system perseveres in a failing tactic that is drawing a response from the user that it cannot deal with. Humans don't really do this. Here is an example:

Syst: What day
User: The Wednesday after next

Syst: What day
User: The Wednesday after next
Syst: What day
User: The Wednesday after next

If you think about this example, a human might ask "What day" for a second time, on the assumption that the first time was not heard, but instead of a third repetition a human user would change tactics. So, on the third repetition this becomes an error. It is probable that every builder of a spoken language dialogue system has seen examples of this sort of problem. The system needs to be able to recognize the need to try a different tactic. We count system turns as perseverant whether or not the wording changes, as long as the content of the system turn is equivalent (inviting the user to repeat the response that the system cannot deal with).

12.3.3 Desirable Properties for a Set of Metrics
You want to pick a relatively small number (usually the minimum number) of relatively cheap metrics that tell you what you want to know. Lean toward metrics that are easy to measure, preferably metrics whose values can be generated automatically rather than metrics that require a great deal of slow, painstaking transcript analysis by hand. By making the evaluation cheap to perform, you increase the effectiveness of evaluation because you will evaluate more frequently, be more willing to evaluate on large numbers of users, and be more willing to compare different versions of a system and different versions of key modules. It turned out that some of the Communicator submetrics about to be described are undesirably expensive to calculate, requiring a great deal of hand analysis of transcripts. But note that the six metrics that we have chosen cover a wide range of phenomena. These metrics are equally applicable to embodied conversational agents.

12.3.4 The Proposed Metrics for Communicator
Six composite metrics constitute our evaluation proper. Each of our six composite metrics is a "rolled-up" combination of submetrics, and the combination is generally done by converting the value for each submetric into its z statistic (units of plus or minus the sample standard deviation for that submetric, e.g., plus 2.12 std. dev.), so that the submetrics are generally equally weighted and the sum of the submetrics is basically zero based. The sign of each submetric is changed if necessary so that positive z statistic values are good and negative values are bad (remember, we want to add them).

Here are the six composite metrics. Note that in assessing the performance of our system, we definitely want to know about each of these items.

1. Quality of speech-recognition and understanding (at the level of simply getting the words accurately)
2. Understanding the user's turns (at the dialogue level, in context)
3. Understandability of the system's own turns
4. Ability to use the system to do the task (usefulness)
5. Efficiency of performing task with the system
6. Task success

We will discuss each of these separately.

For the first rolled-up metric, *quality of speech recognition/understanding at the level of getting the words right*, we calculate the fraction of user turns in which what the user actually said has semantically important task-related content, but *none* of that content made it into the one-best hypothesis generated by the speech recognition process. This is relatively easy to calculate from log files of the interaction plus hand transcriptions (or audio recordings) of what the user actually said. For an embodied agent, one could measure the accurate *acquisition* of the user's facial displays, gestures, eye gaze, and overall movements (even if their meaning is not interpreted correctly).

The second metric, *quality of the system's understanding of the user's turns at the dialogue level in context*, seems to us to reflect the above. The rolled-up metric is basically a sum of submetrics for the following:

- resolving referring expressions, such as pronouns, in the user's turns
- reconstructing ellipses in the user's turns
- the fraction of "good" user turns that are a suitable and relevant response to some question asked by the system and where the speech recognition succeeds, but the system nevertheless does not understand the response
- the occurrence rate of the system failing to follow some context-switch (e.g., change of topic) made by the user

  (NumLostContextSwitches / NumOnTaskSysTurns),

  which is particularly important as a reflection of success at deferred repair (discussed in sec. 12.3.1.1)
- the fraction of the pieces of task information that the user provided in

an overinformative response during apparently successful speech recognition, but that the system failed to remember and exploit in performing the task—if the system asks, "Where do you want to go?" and the user responds, "Denver on Tuesday," then Tuesday is the sort of information we're talking about here. For an embodied agent, one would look at whether the agent correctly understands the meaning of the user's facial displays, eye gaze, gestures, and movement.

In our third rolled-up metric, *understandability of the system's turns*, we sum several submetrics: a penalty for too many pieces of task information mentioned in a single turn (say, more than 5); a penalty for too many (say, more than 3) pieces of *new* task information introduced in a single turn; the fraction of system on-task turns that the user misunderstands or that have some actual deficiency that the user clarifies/repairs; the number of perseverant (third time or more) system turns divided by the number of system good turns; and a somewhat heuristic measure for the total number of things done divided by the number of turns available to do them (sort of an "overloading of system turns" ratio). Specifically, in the overloading of the turns submetric, we sum the number of system turns that provide task information to the user, the number of system turns that request the user to confirm that speech recognition is correct (Did you say "Rome"?), the number of system turns that contain a response to a user initiative (e.g., the user asked a question), and the number of pieces of task information provided by the user that the system either confirmed or specifically solicited. That sum is divided by the number of "good" system turns. This is obviously not a very rigorously justified submetric, but it's fairly useful in practice because high values for this submetric (say, over 2.0) reflect excessively complex system turns. Low values of this submetric are not necessarily interesting, because they may be an appropriate reflection of bad speech recognition or of a noisy acoustic signal, requiring lots of fine-grained repairs. But in the absence of such problems, the system should not prefer an excessively fine-grained dialogue (Hagen and Grote 1997). For an embodied agent, one would look at whether the agent generates appropriate facial displays, eye gaze, gestures, and whether it moves about the display space appropriately. Are these behaviors of the agent easily understood?

The fourth rolled-up metric, *usefulness of the system (ability to use the system to do a task)*, combines the following submetrics: the fraction of the user task information that is confirmed by the system (i.e., the user ends up *knowing* that the system understood the information correctly), the occurrence rate of actively helpful system initiatives (number of such initiatives divided by number of good system turns), the previously mentioned submetric for failures to follow a context switch, the previously mentioned submetric for failures to understand a perfectly good answer given by the user, the fraction of user initiatives (e.g., the user asks a question) that fail, and the ratio of the number of pieces of bogus user task information (explained shortly) to the number of pieces of actual task information provided by the user.

By actual task information, we mean pieces that the user *intended* to provide and that the user *successfully communicated* to the system. By bogus task information we mean pieces of what the system takes to be user task information but which are not really user task information. There are three ways a piece can be bogus: it may be confabulated by the system (the user was not actually trying to provide a piece of user task information), deleted by the system (the user provided it but the system did not get it), or substituted by the system (the user said "Austin" and the system understood "Boston").

The fifth rolled-up metric, *efficiency of performing the task with the system*, combines the actual dialogue length (in turns) and a submetric for the actual response time (tenths of a second from the time the user stops speaking until the system begins responding). It also includes the previously mentioned submetric for the fraction of user task information that was provided in overinformative responses (Where do you want to go? Denver on Tuesday) during apparently successful speech recognition, but that the system failed to remember and exploit in solving the task, thus requiring the user to provide the information again. For an embodied agent, one can try to measure whether its ability to generate and understand embodied behaviors increases the efficiency of the interaction.

The sixth and last rolled-up metric, *task success*, includes submetrics for the following: the number of pieces of user task information that get left ambiguous, wrong, or incomplete (in the judgment of a human analyst); the previously mentioned submetric for bogus user task information; and a submetric for concept accuracy (when a correct solution to the task can be specified). As in the PARADISE framework (Walker et al. 1997), the concept accuracy submetric is a kappa coefficient, from a confusion matrix for the pieces of task information exchanged by the user and system. Kappa is the agreement between the correct solution and the actual solution, with adjustment for chance agreement. Specifically,

$$\kappa = (P(A) - P(E)) / (1 - P(E)),$$

where P(A) is the fraction of the correct solution information (calculated from the scenario) that is present and correct in the solution actually reached by the user, and P(E) is the fraction of agreements that would occur by chance. See Walker et al. (1997) for a detailed explanation of the calculation of a κ coefficient for a task solution from a confusion matrix. Note that using κ here takes into account the task complexity, thus providing some comparability across *different* tasks. We regard this as a key contribution of the PARADISE framework.

12.4 Embodied Conversational Agents

We turn now to measurement and evaluation of embodied conversational agents. We mentioned earlier that embodied conversational agents and speech-based systems are two classes of conversational systems. In what ways is measurement and evaluation of an embodied agent the same as for a purely speech-based system? How is it an extension of speech-based metrics and evaluation? How is it different? In particular, we will consider what aspects of embodied conversational agents seem interesting to measure or evaluate.

12.4.1 Evaluation and Control of Embodied Conversational Agent Dialogues

Embodiment allows physical pointing (which tends to increase the frequency of linguistic deixis), carries the burden of regulating turn taking in face-to-face conversations, and allows embodied back-channel feedback such as nods to indicate a continuing subjective experience that the conversation is being understood and that shared context is being maintained. Thus, it may seem like embodiment has simply grafted additional communication channels onto the conversation without changing the underlying flow of the conversation. That is not so. Clark and Wilkes-Gibbs (1990) gave examples of conversational phenomena that typically turn on watching the facial expression and body language of the other conversational participant. Consider the following example (Clark and Wilkes-Gibbs 1990, 466):

> S: Take the spout—the little one that looks like the end of an oil can—
> J: Okay.
> S: —and put that on the opening in the other large tube. With the round top.

In this example, we presume that, after "Take the spout," S *observed* that J looked lost and therefore produced an expanded noun-phrase identifying the spout. Consider the following example.

S: Okay now, the small blue cap we talked about before?
J: Yeah.
S: Put that over the hole on the side of the tube—
J: Yeah.
S: —that is nearest to the top, or nearest to the red handle.

In this second example, Clark and Wilkes-Gibbs (1990, 466–467) mention that the first utterance by S had a rising inflection, marking it as a trial noun-phrase, and S then waited for J to indicate understanding (the first "Yeah"). We note that this indication of understanding can be a nod or gesture accompanied by appropriate facial expression. The conversation continues with what Clark and Wilkes-Gibbs characterize as an *installment noun phrase*, where the speaker pauses to invite confirmation from the hearer after each installment. Again, we observe that in face-to-face conversation, the confirmation can be nonverbal. In both parts of this example, the speaker's solicitation of confirmation would almost certainly include an inquiring facial expression and/or gestures. A few moments thought about all these examples will persuade you that a disembodied version of the same conversations (say, over the telephone) would be markedly different. Embodied conversation is not just linguistic dialogue plus gestures.

12.4.2 Five Aspects of Embodied Conversational Agents and Possible Metrics for Them

We think the following five aspects of embodied conversational agents seem particularly interesting to measure:

- unconscious embodied mechanics of conversation
- creating accurate user expectations
- individuation (the perceived character or personality of the agent)
- use of gesture to communicate content, and
- functioning as an ally of the user

Much like in our proposed metrics for Communicator, one might think about whether this sort of analysis could be converted into a set of rolled-up metrics.

12.4.2.1 *Unconscious Embodied Mechanics of Conversation*   At the level of mechanics of conversation, does the agent generate and understand emphasis of words or phrases via head nods, beat gestures, and the gaze being directed at the other participant? Does the agent generate and understand turn-taking behaviors relating to the gaze and relating to the hands moving into and out of position to gesture? Does the user understand the agent's embodied behaviors for these purposes? If not, is it that the correct behaviors are missing with incorrect behaviors substituted, or are *noise* behaviors masking the useful behaviors? On a subjective level, does the user think the agent is listening when spoken to, think the agent understands, and think the conversation is fluid and natural— reflecting that the embodied mechanics of turn taking and emphasis are succeeding sufficiently well that (as in human-to-human, face-to-face conversation) they do not rise to conscious attention?

One breaks down these higher-level questions into the obvious lower-level metrics. For example, one could count the changes of turn and the number that are accomplished by embodied mechanisms that occur in parallel with the linguistic conversation, then calculate the ratio of those two counts. With respect to back-channel feedback, one could look at where and how often the agent provides embodied back-channel feedback, and one could look at where and how often the user feels compelled to verify that the character is listening and understanding. Do the points of occurrence (or nonoccurrence) of back-channel feedback correlate with the points where the user believes that the agent is listening or understanding?

12.4.2.2 Creating Accurate Expectations One of the more difficult problems with embodied agent interfaces (as with natural language interfaces in general) is how to create accurate expectations about what the user can say and what topics can be talked about, as well as about what embodied behaviors the agent will exhibit and what embodied behaviors of the user will be perceived and understood by the agent. This relates to the domain of discourse or task and involves both what the users expect the system to be able to do and what the user expects the system to be able to refer to.

In human-to-human interaction, human participants always understand anything they say. Thus, saying something is an implicit announcement that the words, syntax, and metaphors being spoken can be understood. This assumption may be invalid for agents. When an agent violates this expectation, that is definitely an error, so evaluation should probe the agent's ability to understand the metaphors, syntax, and words that it generates.

The appearance (and personality) of the character is also relevant. In the design stage, to evaluate the expectations created by the appearance and personality of the character, one could show the character to potential users and then go through a list of areas in which you want the user and agent to interact. For each area, one can ask the potential user whether the agent would be able to talk about that area. Once a character is implemented, one can note which areas the users unexpectedly never try to talk about with the agent (functionality not expected by the users is present) as well as which topics users bring up that are beyond the actual or intended competence of the agent (functionality expected by the users is missing). To measure part of this more closely, you can look at which referring expressions the users do and do not try with the agent (e.g., will the users say, "Press that" or "Give it to me"? Will the user expect the agent to know about the parts of something shown on the screen?) In embodied interaction, does the agent generate appropriate gestures and pointing? Does the user gesture or point? Does the agent understand when the user gestures or points?

12.4.2.3 *Individuation: Personality, Character, and Appearance* Although some aspects of individuation can be measured (Taylor et al. 1998), more research is needed. The visual appearance of an agent will alter the user's expectations and style of language. Seeing Daffy Duck and Donald Duck pop up is a bit different than seeing a professorial Albert Einstein. Nass, Isbister, and Lee (chap. 13) have shown that characters with a consistent personality have more influence on the user and that when a character appears to be of the same ethnic group as the user, the user will relate more easily, consider the character more trustworthy, and consider its arguments to be better and more persuasive.

It is an empirical fact that people *will* interact with any device endowed with speech as if it were human. Joseph Becker (1975) suggested that casual speech is a process of pasting together lots of canned phrases in somewhat stereotypical ways. This process lies at the heart of parodying someone. It also suggests that phrasal lexical choice and syntax could be used to individuate a character by personalizing its choices, making the choices repetitive so that they typify the character. This sort of phrasing can be measured. Further, in the control or generation of interaction a character could be endowed with habitual phrases to be used whenever vaguely relevant. One could evaluate the effects of this tactic via user questionnaires or interviews.

Does the user adopt language appropriate to the agent? We don't know how to objectively measure that, because "appropriate" is ill-defined. One can measure whether users do or do not adopt the agent's phrases during interaction (known as lexical entrainment). Lexical entrainment is part of the linguistic mechanism of collaborative reference (Clark and Wilkes-Gibbs 1990), but its occurrence or nonoccurrence also reflects (and can serve as one measure of) positive emotional involvement with an agent.

12.4.2.4 *Use of Gesture to Communicate Content*   There are several types of content-oriented gestures (McNeill 1992). Can the user and the agent talk about objects in the domain of discourse with gesture to indicate mode of interaction ("Turn it like this" [demonstrating by gesture])? Can the agent generate and understand gestures that indicate direction or path? Can the agent generate and understand gestures that indicate manner or mode of motion? These questions can be answered by generating a description of the relevant behaviors (a classification of them) and then counting the occurrences of the behaviors.

When pointing, does the agent move to (or reach to) the appropriate place in the display space? Some current help characters are handicapped by being inside a box frame with a fixed location on the screen, so that the character cannot interact with other elements displayed on the screen. Does the agent anticipate its necessary position on the screen? Does anticipatory movement to elsewhere on the screen occur at the wrong times, thus suggesting a seizing of the turn and distracting the user away from the current activity? Is this sort of gesture and movement overlapped with the agent's own speech, or does the agent stop speaking, then turn, then point, then look at the user, then resume speaking? If not overlapped, is the behavior distractingly odd or distressingly inefficient? If it is overlapped, is the import of the gaze and gesture obscured?

12.4.2.5 *Embodied Conversational Agent Interfaces as Allies*   The interface paradigms that are currently dominant, such as command-line interfaces and WIMP/GUI interfaces (WIMP is Windows, Icons, Mouse, Pointing) differ in key ways from ally interfaces (where the user interacts with the embodied ally agent and the ally agent interacts with the application on the user's behalf in order to make the application do what is needed). These differences become obvious when one tries to apply the cognitive walk-through (Polson et al. 1992) or GOMS (Card, Moran, and Newell 1983) approaches to analyzing the required interaction. Evaluating ally interfaces is more difficult than evaluating traditional interfaces for exactly the same reasons that these analyses of the required interaction are difficult. In many cases, talk-aloud protocols and user satisfaction questionnaires must carry heavy weight. Heuristic expert reviews are also helpful. But quantitative metrics appear difficult.

The usual WIMP/GUI interface involves a set of fixed visual metaphors, such as desktops, file folders, trash cans, push buttons, and two-dimensional arrays of objects that can be pointed to. The WIMP/GUI approach breaks down in several respects. First, if the only way you can do an operation is to point and click on each object or if you must drag and drop each object, then there is no way to apply the operation to an entire set of objects specified by description. The user is forced to do the direct manipulation once per object, which is drudgery. In this respect, WIMP/GUI interfaces are a big step backward from command-line interfaces. But even command-line interfaces do not allow you to specify objects by *arbitrary* attributes (for example, delete all files older than 1 year and larger than 2 megabytes).

In contrast, conversational agent interfaces afford the user an apparent ability to construct descriptions with the full power of natural language, and in fact to issue commands that require intersentential context to interpret (e.g., the user could say "I think there are some pictures of Malaysia. See if you can find them."). How is the agent to deal with this? How is the evaluation to deal with it? Evaluation needs to look at what expectations are created by the agent and look at what the agent does to communicate its abilities and limitations as well as the abilities and limitations of the underlying application to which it is the interface. The agent needs a rich representation of the attributes of objects that can be referred to. The earlier discussion about creating accurate expectations about what the user can say and do applies here.

In an ally interface, as opposed to embodied conversational agents in general, one should test the agent's ability to guide the user's expectations. When you consult reference librarians or subject-matter experts, you explain what sort of information you seek and you ask for help. What these human allies will then say or do is basically unpredictable, but you expect a commitment on their part to help and guide you through the interaction. Evidence of this commitment to help and guide can be evaluated. In user testing, users may ask to do things that are not known capabilities of the system or that require referring to items that are not named and thus must be identified by description. If they do, the agent's response can be classified as (1) a total breakdown, (2) an attempt to clarify or otherwise guide the user toward a solution or toward successful shared identification of the item being described, or (3) an attempt to delineate the limits of available functionality. These counts can serve as metrics. In heuristic expert reviews, one can make similar requests of the agent and systematically test the limits of its coverage of the task domain and the limits of its abilities to reach mutual identification of objects being referred to. Because natural language provides powerful abilities to describe sets of objects, one may in particular test whether the agent can deal with such descriptions and can do operations on sets of objects in the domain. Agents must have a rich expressive internal representation of the entities in the domain, and evaluation can look at failures that occur due to the user referring to entities using attributes that the agent does not know about (but could).

Finally, ally agents need an internal model of the tasks that a user might want to perform. In many cases, these internal models need to include models of what the user knows and what the user knows how to do. It appears that the most helpful agent will build a model of what the user is actually doing and will apply its task knowledge to assist. Metrics can look at the occurrence rate of actively helpful initiatives by the agent. They can also look at instances where the agent could have been actively helpful but was not. It is a key attribute of most ally interfaces that the ally agent is supposed to be actively helpful.

12.5 Summary

Embodied dialogues are very different from purely linguistic interaction. Nevertheless, the goals of interaction are roughly the same. Some areas of the interaction between users and embodied conversational agents (for example, the effective integration of both understanding and generating embodied back-channel feedback that occurs in parallel with, and regulates the flow of, the linguistic interaction) are difficult to measure and, in fact, not well understood.

We have shown that metrics are possible for all important areas of embodied interaction. And, as was the case for the evaluation we presented for the DARPA Communicator project, these metrics for embodied interaction can be pulled together into an evaluation yielding useful information that can guide ongoing efforts at developing agents. Building agents and evaluating agents are synergistic activities. Several other chapters in this book discuss important related evaluation issues. Much additional research is needed.

References

Becker, J. 1975. The phrasal lexicon. In R. Schank and B. Nash-Webber, eds., *Theoretical issues in natural language processing (TINLAP-1)*, 60–63. Morristown, N.J.: ACL.

Bernsen, N. O., H. Dybkjær, and L. Dybkjær. 1997. What should your speech system say? *IEEE Computer* 30(12):25–31.

Card, S. K, T. P. Moran, and A. Newell. 1983. *The psychology of human-computer interaction.* Hillsdale, N.J.: Lawrence Erlbaum Associates.

Cassell, J., and K. R. Thórisson. 1999. The power of a nod and a glance: Envelope vs. emotional feedback in animated conversational agents. *Applied Artificial Intelligence* 13:519–538.

Chu-Carroll, J., and M. K. Brown. 1997. Tracking initiative in collaborative dialogue interactions. In *Proceedings of the 35th ACL and 8th EACL* (Madrid, Spain), 271–280. San Francisco: Association for Computational Linguistics and Morgan Kaufmann.

Clark, H. H., and E. F. Schaefer. 1989. Contributing to discourse. *Cognitive Science* 13:259–294.

Clark, H. H., and D. Wilkes-Gibbs. 1990. Referring as a collaborative process. In P. R. Cohen, J. Morgan, and M. Pollack, eds., *Intentions in Communication,* 463–493. Cambridge, Mass.: The MIT Press.

Danieli, M., E. Gerbino, and L. M. Moisa. 1997. Dialogue strategies for improving the usability of telephone human-machine communication. In J. Hirschberg, C. Kamm, and M. Walker, *Interactive spoken dialogue systems: Bringing speech and NLP together in real applications,* 114–120. Somerset, N.J.: Association for Computational Linguistics.

Duncan, S. 1974. Some signals and rules for taking speaking turns in conversations. In S. Weitz, ed., *Nonverbal communication.* New York: Oxford University Press.

Ericsson, K. A., and H. A. Simon. 1984. *Protocol analysis: Verbal report as data.* Cambridge, Mass.: The MIT Press.

Hagen, E., and B. Grote. 1997. Planning efficient mixed initiative dialogue. In J. Hirschberg, C. Kamm, and M. Walker, *Interactive spoken dialogue systems: Bringing speech and NLP together in real applications,* 53–56. Somerset, N.J.: Association for Computational Linguistics.

Halverson, C. A., D. B. Horn, C. Karat, and J. Karat. 1999. The beauty of errors: Pattern of error correction in desktop speech systems. In *Proceedings of Interact '99: International Conference on Human-Computer Interaction* (Edinburgh, Scotland), 133–140.

Hayes, P. J., and D. R. Reddy. 1983. Steps toward graceful interaction in spoken and written man-machine communication. *International Journal of Man-Machine Studies* 19:231–284.

Hirschman, L. 1998. Language learning evaluations: Lessons learned from MUC and ATIS. In *The First International Conference on Language Resources and Evaluation* (Granada, Spain), 117–122. Paris, France: European Language Resources Association (ELRA).

Hirschman, L., and C. Pao. 1993. The cost of errors in a spoken language system. In *Proceedings of the 3rd European Conference on Speech Communication and Technology* (EuroSpeech93, Berlin, Germany), 1419–1422. Grenoble, France: European Speech Communication Association (ESCA).

Karat, C., C. Halverson, D. Horn, and J. Karat. 1999. Patterns of entry and correction in large vocabulary continuous speech recognition systems. In *Proceedings of CHI-99: Human Factors in Computing Systems,* 568–575. New York: ACM Press.

McNeill, D. 1992. *Hand and mind: What gestures reveal about thought.* Chicago: University of Chicago Press.

Nielsen, J. 1992. Finding usability problems through heuristic evaluation. In *Proceedings of CHI 1992* (Monterey, Calif., May 3–7), 373–380. New York: ACM Press.

———. 1993. *Usability engineering.* New York: Academic Press.

Oviatt, S. L. 1995. Predicting spoken disfluencies during human-computer interaction. *Computer Speech and Language* 9:19–35.

———. 1997. Multimodal interactive maps: Designing for human performance. *Human-Computer Interaction* 12:93–129.

Polifroni, J., S. Seneff, J. Glass, and T. J. Hazen. 1998. Evaluation methodology for a telephone-based system. In *Proceedings of the First International Conference on Language Resources and Evaluation* (Granada, Spain), 43–49. Paris: European Language Resources Association (ELRA).

Polson, P., C. Lewis, J. Rieman, and C. Wharton. 1992. Cognitive walkthroughs: A method for theory-based evaluation of user interfaces. *International Journal of Man-Machine Studies* 36:741–773.

Rogers, W. T. 1978. The contribution of kinesic illustrators toward the comprehension of verbal behavior within utterances. *Human Communication Research* 5:54–62.

Sanders, G. A., and J. Scholtz. 1998. Measurement and evaluation in embodied conversational characters. In *Proceedings of the Workshop on Embodied Conversational Characters (WECC 98)* (Tahoe City, Calif.), 114–118, 85–86. (Pagination due to proceedings printing error.)

Shneiderman, B. 1992. *Designing the user interface: Strategies for effective human-computer interaction,* 2d ed. Reading, Mass.: Addison-Wesley.

Taylor, I. C., F. R. McInnes, S. Love, J. C. Foster, and M. A. Jack. 1998. Providing animated characters with designated personality profiles. In *Proceedings of Workshop on Embodied Conversational Characters (WECC 98)* (Tahoe City, Calif.), 87–92.

Walker, M. A., D. J. Litman, C. A. Kamm, and A. Abella. 1997. PARADISE: A framework for evaluating spoken dialogue agents. In *Proceedings of the 35th ACL and 8th EACL* (Madrid, Spain), 271–280. San Francisco, Calif.: Association for Computational Linguistics and Morgan Kaufmann.

Winograd, T., and F. Flores. 1987. *Understanding computers and cognition.* Reading, Mass.: Addison-Wesley.

13

Truth Is Beauty:

Researching Embodied Conversational Agents

Clifford Nass, Katherine Isbister, and Eun-Ju Lee

G. H. Hardy (1941) argues that the sole criterion for excellent research is that the researcher produces "beauty." While this criterion is seemingly ineffable and frustratingly imprecise, Hardy instead suggests that creating beauty is straightforward. First, the work must be accurate: erroneous results are useless. Second, one's peers must recognize the work to be interesting, exciting, elegant, and "cool." While this second criterion might seem arbitrary, there is generally good agreement between scholars in a given community about "interesting" work (see Cole and Cole 1973 for a discussion), so one need not survey numerous researchers to ensure research is beautiful; asking a couple is equivalent to asking them all.

With certain caveats, the work in embodied conversational agents (ECA) can make claims to beauty. ECAs are phenomenologically "accurate" to the extent that the agent's outward appearance objectively matches the appearance, language, attitudes, and behavior of humans. Thus, questions that address manifestation accuracy include "Does the agent walk like a person walks?" and "Does the agent use language and make grammatical errors the same way a person does?"

An alternative approach to accuracy, generally associated more with the artificial intelligence literature than with the ECA literature, assesses the extent to which the *processes* that produce aspects of the ECA are the same as the processes in humans. For example, "Does the muscle model of the character match how human muscles work?" or "Does the character generate language using the same production models that humans have?" With current technology, success in one approach can lead to less success in the other. For example, the most phenomenologically human ECAs often are animated, scripted, and informed by visual "tricks" (Thomas and Johnston 1981), while models that incorporate the best understanding of physical and psychological processes often create representations that are ironically not "lifelike." Under either definition, ECAs are becoming increasingly accurate (and hence beautiful), even though they have not met the standard of absolute accuracy on any dimension of humanness.

Despite the incredible diversity of disciplines, problems, and techniques that are brought to bear in creating ECAs, the research community generally agrees on which work is "interesting" or "cool." Somehow, researchers manage to agree on what "should" be done and when it is done well, even though one might argue that ECA is a preparadigmatic discipline (Cole and Cole 1973; Levitt and Nass 1989). Hence, if a few colleagues endorse a particular ECA, the researcher can be confident that he or she has passed the second beauty hurdle.

13.1 ECA Research Requires a Special Criterion for Beauty

Unlike the simple two-pronged beauty test appropriate to most other areas of research in engineering, physical science, and social science, researchers in ECA have a third beauty test: Does the ECA satisfy *users* of the technology? While this question seems deceptively similar to the question about researchers' reactions, users differ from researchers in two fundamental ways: (1) variance in the community, and (2) to what the ECA should be compared. In contrast to the homogeneity of perspectives in the research community, users responding to ECAs exhibit enormous variety in their assessment dimensions (Nass and Mason 1990) and the particular values they assign to these dimensions. Similarly, while all researchers have exposure to the same relevant range of interfaces, both with and without ECAs, users' experiences vary enormously, which is one of the reasons for the aforementioned heterogeneity in perspective. Thus, a conversation with two or three researchers covers that community; a chat with ten or one hundred times that many users might not provide reliable judgments.

Does this mean that one must abandon practically obtainable definitions of beauty? Happily not. Experimental research (which has its own claims to beauty) provides objective and reliable measures of whether a particular ECA has satisfied users. A detailed discussion of experimental research is obviously beyond the scope of this chapter, but a few general guidelines seem useful.

13.2 Experimental Research and ECAs

The definition and guiding principle of experimental research is as follows: *random assignment to varied conditions*. "Varied conditions" means that one cannot simply show users an ECA and ask questions; instead, responses to a particular

ECA must be *compared* to one or more other instantiations of an ECA, an interface without an ECA, or an actual person. This is often emotionally difficult for a designer. After working so hard to build an ECA, the demands of experimentation mean that the work is only (at most) half done. "Random assignment" means that neither the user nor the experimenter consciously choose the interfaces that they are exposed to, nor do they choose the order in which the interfaces are presented (when a given user experiences multiple instantiations).

Why are varied conditions and random assignment important? Unlike many theories in the physical sciences, for which theories provide absolute values and external metrics, virtually all theories concerning ECAs are *relative* and *comparative*. ECA theories include such statements as "Users will like this ECA more than none at all," "Users will better remember statements by ECAs with synthesized speech than ECAs with word balloons," "My ECA will lead to greater efficiency than your ECA," and so forth. The theories do not make claims such as "users' hearts will beat an average of 72 beats per minute when shown this ECA" or "This ECA will lead to an average of 3.6 errors on the task." Unlike absolute statements that only require the assessment of one interface, relative statements require (empirical) comparison.

The comparison ECAs (or an ECA and a non-ECA or human) can be virtually identical, differing on one or two characteristics (as in the experiments described below), or radically different. When an experiment on ECAs presents limited and well-defined differences (e.g., ethnicity, personality of language, synthesized speech vs. recorded speech), it becomes easy to draw highly specific conclusions, at the expense of failing to capture all of the exciting aspects of a particular ECA. On the other hand, gross differences in interfaces—for example, a particular instantiation of an ECA versus no ECA at all—can generate the very broad conclusions that may be appropriate at the early stages of a technology's development but provide less specific help for designers or theorists.

Random assignment, the second aspect of experiments, is necessary for two reasons. First, if the participants in an experiment are assigned to see a particular ECA based on some systematic criteria (e.g., gender, computer experience), one will not know whether the observed differences between conditions are the result of the manipulation or the prior characteristic. Second, the act of choice has a number of psychological consequences, including the conflicting tendencies of postdecision justification (people like the alternative they choose) and buyer's remorse (people like the alternative they *didn't* choose), so that without random experimental assignment, these effects could obfuscate the results of interest.

Having correctly designed an experiment, an ECA researcher must choose the criteria that define "user satisfaction." In the homogenous research community, satisfaction criteria do not have to be stated because they are shared. In the diverse user community, however, the questions "Are you satisfied?" or "Is it cool?" are much too ambiguous to be answered in a valid and reliable way. In each experiment, the experimenter must choose from an enormous list of user attitudes and behaviors: emotional judgments of liking and arousal, general judgments of similarity (which can be used to impute relevant dimensions), assessments of attractiveness, personality, competence, and similarity to humans, behavioral measures of performance, attention, memory, and so forth. Having chosen the criteria, a researcher has created a "beautiful" ECA when the participants in the experiment provide more positive responses to the ECA than to the comparative agent/interface/human on the dimensions that are of interest to the researcher.

13.3 Examples of Experimental Determination of Beauty in ECAs

To illustrate how to perform the third beauty test, the assessment of user satisfaction, we present two experiments. The two studies address, somewhat tongue-in-cheek, an ECA's *appearance*, the conventional approach to beauty.

The two studies focus on opposite extremes of ECA technology. The first study employs a presently unobtainable ECA: a full-motion video representation of a character with perfect language production and understanding, unequivocal human appearance, and so forth; indeed, they are video recordings of a human face. The second study employs what many would argue is a bare minimum ECA: a stick figure character without a face, communicating through text input and word balloon output. The studies explore very different phenomena with very different metrics, but both incorporate the critical criteria for experiments: clearly specified variation in the representation of the ECAs, random assignment as to which people see which character, and clearly defined metrics that indicate whether one ECA is "better" or "worse" than another.

Both studies are based on the Computers Are Social Actors (CASA) paradigm (Nass and Moon n.d.; Reeves and Nass 1996). This paradigm argues that one can take both theories and methods from social psychology and directly apply them to human-technology interaction. These are, in fact, the first studies to explore the CASA paradigm with respect to human-ECA interaction; previous studies addressed social responses to simple text-based interfaces only (see Reeves and Nass 1996 for a review).

In the CASA paradigm, one does not directly ask users whether they are applying social rules to computers or ECAs; they consistently deny that they do. Instead, the paradigm directs one to place users in a situation in which social rules dictate particular responses, while common sense would suggest different responses. To the extent that individuals apply social rules, even though it is foolish to do so (and they deny doing so), one has evidence for social responses to computers and ECAs (see Nass and Moon n.d.).

13.4 Does the Ethnicity of ECAs Matter?

The first study asked questions about the ethnicity of ECAs (see Lee and Nass 1998 for a more complete discussion of this study). When we meet someone, one of the first things we do is to classify that person as "in-group" or "out-group." This categorization is not always based on a thorough examination of others' beliefs, thoughts, and value systems. Rather, readily observable physical cues such as ethnicity often work as the most salient and strong basis for social categorization (Biernet and Vescio 1993). If one can extend the literature on human-human interaction to human-ECA interaction, as specified by the CASA paradigm, one might expect that users will quickly assess the ethnic identity of an ECA. Having determined the ethnicity of the ECA, the critical question is whether that determination will affect users' attitudes and behaviors. Logically, there should be no effect. Computers do not have ethnicities, and ECAs are not socialized or acculturated into any particular ethnicity. For ECAs, unlike people, ethnicity is essentially arbitrary. Hence, common sense would dictate that ethnicity would be irrelevant to users' responses to ECAs. Conversely, the CASA model would predict the same responses to ethnically identified ECAs as people direct toward ethnically identified humans.

The literature on ethnicity suggests that it does not work monotonically; instead, it operates in conjunction with the ethnicity of the interaction partner. Specifically, individuals assess another's ethnicity primarily to determine whether they are part of the same group or a different group (Tajfel 1978; Turner 1985). Members of the in-group are more "beautiful" on a number of dimensions (Gerard and Hoyt 1974; Whitehead, Smith, and Eichhorn 1982). Individuals agree with in-group members more than out-group members (Clark and Maass 1988) and in-group members are perceived as having the same values as the individual (Allen and Wilder 1979). Furthermore, when someone is identified as part of the in-group as opposed to the out-group, he or she is perceived as more socially attractive and better liked (Lee 1993; Stephan and Beane 1978), more trustworthy (Clark and Maass 1988), and more competent (Stephan and Beane 1978).

If CASA is correct, these effects should be obtained for both participants who believe that they are interacting with an ECA as well as those who believe that they are interacting with a person.

Despite the empirical evidence that demonstrates the critical role ethnicity plays in social interaction, the effects of ethnically diverse computer agents have never been explored. Thus, the first question we address in this study is as follows: *Are agents that ethnically match users more "beautiful" than ethnically different ECAs?* Or, put another way, *Does the ethnicity of a computer agent have an effect on users' attitudes and behaviors?* The experiment also addresses a foundational question for the CASA paradigm: *Does the belief that one is interacting with a person (via video conferencing) as opposed to an ECA affect users' reactions?*

13.4.1 Design of the Ethnicity Experiment

To examine these questions, we created an experiment in which participants interacted with a full-motion video of a person; the only difference in the ECA was whether it was of a similar or different ethnicity than the user. The other varied dimension was whether participants were told they were interacting with a computer agent (HCI condition) or via video conference software with a person in another room (CMC condition). The interactions (described later) were identical for all participants.

To maximize the salience of ethnicity as an identity-defining factor, and because members of the minority tend to identify more strongly with their ingroup than do those of the majority (Wilder and Shapiro 1984), individuals from an ethnic minority (40 Korean students born in Korea and with strong ethnic identity) participated in this experiment. To control for the possible effects of gender, only male participants participated in this study (we were unable to obtain enough female students to permit a balanced design). Participants were randomly assigned to one of four conditions in a 2 x 2 design: HCI-in-group, HCI-out-group, CMC-in-group, or CMC-out-group.

Upon arrival, the participant was told either that he would interact with a computer agent that had speech recognition capacity (HCI condition) or with another participant in another room via a video conferencing system (CMC condition). To emphasize that these were not pre-recorded responses (although they were), the participant was asked to choose one of ten different packets, each composed of eight choice-dilemma situations. In fact, all packets were identical, so that every participant went through the same scenarios. Choice-dilemma situations are hypothetical situations in which an individual has to decide what to do between two courses of actions (Kogan and Wallach 1967), one of which has the potential for both greater benefit and greater harm. For example, one of the situations depicted the dilemma of a college football player who could go for either a risky play that would win or a cautious play that would tie.

After choosing the packet, the participant was instructed to read the situation on the questionnaire silently and then, using the microphone, ask the agent/partner, "Do you think Mr. A (the person in the scenario) should do B (one of the possible choices)?" At this point, one of two Korean (in-group condition) or Caucasian (out-group condition) male confederates popped up on the screen and presented his decision and the arguments in favor of that decision. (We used two different faces to control at least minimally for the fact that every face has unique characteristics that might be more relevant than ethnicity.) After listening to the agent's/partner's decision and arguments (which was prevideo-taped, unbeknownst to the participants), the participant answered a paper-and-pencil questionnaire concerning his perception of the interactant's decision, the quality of the arguments, and his own decision. The questionnaire items were based on a ten-point Likert scale. When he was done answering the questions, he went on to the next scenario. This procedure was repeated for the eight different situations.

In order to make it more like a real-time interaction, a couple of tricks were used. The agent/partner asked the participant on one occasion to repeat his question during the interaction; at another point, the agent/partner asked for more time to prepare his arguments. The choice of packets and the request for repetition of the question and for more time for the interaction were very effective in making people believe that the interaction was not preprogrammed. When the interaction was over, participants filled out a final paper-and-pencil questionnaire regarding value congruence (how much the participant perceived agreement between themselves and the other interactant) and source perception (the participant's assessment of the other interactant).

13.4.2 Measuring the Possible Consequences of ECA Ethnicity

We attempted to measure many of the characteristics of in-group/out-group differences noted above. When indices were created, they were very reliable.

Value congruence was computed by summing two self-reported similarity scores asked after all of the choice dilemmas were completed: "How similar were the computer agent's/your partner's decisions to yours?" (decision similarity), and "How similar were the computer agent's/your partner's reasons for its/his decisions to yours?" (reasoning similarity). Both items were responded to on ten-point scales ranging from "not at all similar"(1) to "very similar" (10) ($r = .77$).

The indices for *social attractiveness* and *trustworthiness* were based on the question "How well does each of these adjectives describe the computer agent/partner you worked with?," which appeared on the final paper-and-pencil questionnaire. Responses were provided on a ten-point Likert scale ranging from "describes very poorly" (1) to "describes very well"(10). The index of social attractiveness was comprised of four items: "likable," "sociable," "pleasant," and "friendly" (Cronbach's α = .88). Trustworthiness was an index comprised of two items: "trustworthy" and "reliable" (r = .65).

The *quality of arguments* (competence) was measured by creating an index based on four adjectives from the final paper-and-pencil questionnaire that described the arguments participants had heard during the interaction: "persuasive," "clever," "analytical," and "creative" (Cronbach's α = .68). To assess *conformity*, we examined the correlation between the agent's/partner's decision and their own decision across the eight situations for each person.

Our analytical strategy was to compare the two HCI conditions directly, followed by the two CMC conditions. We then determined whether individuals reacted to ethnicity differently in the HCI case than in the CMC case; a significant number of interaction terms in the 2 x 2 ANOVA would suggest that they do.

13.4.3 Responses to the Ethnicity of ECAs

Consistent with the equivalence of human-ECA interaction and the social psychological literature, participants who worked with the in-group agent believed that it matched their opinions more than did those who interacted with the out-group agent, $t(18)$ = 2.35, $p < .05$ (see fig. 13.1). Greater perceived in-group value congruence was also evident in the CMC case, $t(18)$ = 2.47, $p < .05$. There was no significant interaction between perceived ontology of the interaction partner and group identity of the source, although CMC participants attributed more attitudinal similarity to their partners than HCI participants did to the computer agents, $F(1,37)$ = 6.54, $p < .05$.

Consistent with the idea that in-group agents/participants are more beautiful, the in-group agents, $t(18)$ = 6.03, $p < .001$, and the in-group partners, $t(18)$ = 2.65, $p < .05$, were perceived to be more socially attractive than their out-group counterparts. There was no interaction and no main effect for HCI versus CMC with respect to social attractiveness.

In-group agents, $t(18)$ = 5.77, $p < .001$, and partners, $t(18)$ = 2.94, $p < .01$, were perceived as more trustworthy than their out-group counterparts. There was no interaction, but CMC participants considered their partner to be more trustworthy than did HCI participants, $F(1, 37)$ = 5.01, $p < .05$. Again consistent with

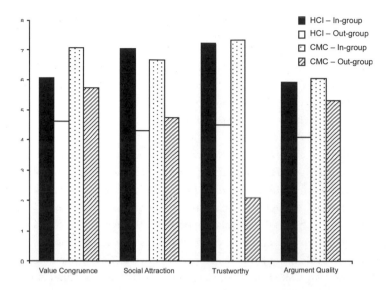

Figure 13.1

Effects of group identity and perceived interactant on perceptions of the interactant.

CASA, in-group computer agents were perceived as providing higher quality arguments than out-group agents, $t(18) = 2.48$, p < .05. There was no effect of group identity in the CMC conditions, $t(18) = 1.31$, $p >.10$, although the results were in the expected direction. There was no interaction and no main effect for HCI versus CMC with respect to argument quality.

Consistent with the expectation that in-group members would obtain greater conformity than out-group members, a higher average correlation existed between the computer agent's decision and participant's own decision for in-group participants, $t(14) = 1.85$, $p < .05$ (see fig. 13.2). Similarly, in-group partners in CMC condition elicited more conformity from the participants than did their out-group counterparts, $t(14) = 2.20$, $p < .05$. Though there was no interaction, there was a main effect for perceived ontology. People agreed more with the computer agents than with the CMC interaction partners, $F(1, 29) = 2.35$, p < .05.

The foregoing results provide convincing evidence that ethnicity of computer agents has significant and consistent effects on user's attitudes and behaviors. In-group participants perceived the computer agents to be more similar to themselves and more socially attractive and trustworthy. Participants

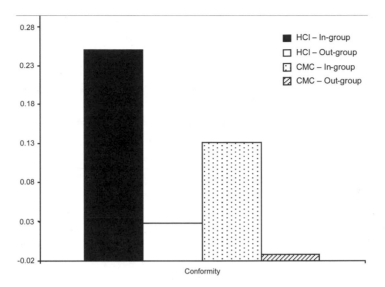

Figure 13.2

Effects of group identity and perceived interactant on conformity.

also conformed more to the decision of their in-group partner and perceived the agent's arguments to be better. Given that in-group favoritism is more likely to occur when the group identity becomes salient due to intergroup conflict/competition (Taylor and Moriarty 1987; Wagner and Ward 1993), our findings obtained in the absence of intergroup contrast lend strong support to the existence of in-group favoritism in HCI.

Before we address the broader theoretical and design implications of this study, we present a second study that uses a very different kind of ECA but also focuses on whether beauty can only be "skin-deep."

13.5 Personality in ECAs

Whether it is a screenwriting guide or a book about how to make successful animated features, artists seem to agree that developing an appealing "personality" is an important part of creating successful characters. What exactly is personality? Media practitioners have working definitions of personality that they use to try to explain what they do. For instance, Thomas and Johnston (1981) discuss how an animated character's personality consists of characteristic attitudes and actions that people learn to associate with that character, as revealed during the story, through the character's motions and conversations and interaction with other characters. Hoffner and Cantor (1981) say that people use a character's physical appearance, speech characteristics, and behaviors to determine what the characters' traits are. Field (1994) contends that one develops a character's personality by establishing attitudes and behaviors people come to expect from the character. Laurel (1993) explains that the traditional Aristotelian understanding of dramatic characters is as "bundles of traits, predispositions, and choices that, when taken together, form coherent entities" (60). Judging from these descriptions, character personality seems to be related to predictability in the character's actions and attitudes that people use to understand how the character works within the media they are watching or reading.

This working definition of personality from the arts is corroborated by the understanding of personality within the field of psychology. The opening definition from a standard psychology textbook reads "Personality represents those characteristics of the person that account for consistent patterns of feeling, thinking, and behaving" (Pervin and John 1997, 4). Consistent with artists' working knowledge of why a character's personality matters, psychologists have found that personality is a predictor of many important things about a person. For example, one's personality is related to the kinds of social situations one is comfortable in, how others will choose to interact with one, and a host of other important life activities (Campbell and Hawley 1982; Eysenck and Long 1986). Personality is something that everyday people recognize and discuss about others and that they feel is a valuable piece of information about a person (Pervin and John 1997).

Because of its importance in both traditional media and in psychology, and informed by the CASA paradigm, we wanted to see whether personality was important in interactive character design as well. To understand how computer users would respond to personality-rich characters in interfaces, we performed an experiment in which the character's appearance and language both presented a particular personality type, although in some cases, the appearance and language suggested conflicting personalities (for complete details of this study, see Isbister and Nass n.d.). Drawing on the CASA paradigm outlined above, we turned to the psychology literature to derive a set of predictions of how people would interact with ECAs that manifested personality in their language and in their appearance.

Which personality trait did we choose to manipulate? Of the many dimensions of personality that trait psychologists have identified, two are particularly important during interaction: extroversion and agreeableness (McCrae and Costa 1989). People quickly assess how extroverted and how friendly a person is, and this affects how they feel about the interaction. Because it is quickly and easily assessed, important to interpersonal interaction, and readily discerned from nonverbal behavior (Gallaher 1992), we selected extroversion as the personality trait that we would examine in our experiment.

13.5.1 Manifesting Personality in ECAs

To manipulate the characters' expression of personality, we were guided by the ways people normally read personality in others. What cues do people use to make assessments about another's extroversion? Confirming artists' intuitions, psychologists have discovered that people use a variety of cues depending upon the situation (Ekman et al. 1980). However, people consistently rely on verbal style and nonverbal cues to guide the determination of personality.

Verbal style includes choice of words and types of sentences and fluidity of speech, as well as how the person refers to another while speaking. For example, an extroverted person might use strong, confident words and phrasing and speak very fluidly, whereas an introverted person might be more hesitant in speech and use less direct and confident phrasing (Jung 1971; Nass et al. 1995).

Nonverbal cues include posture as well as the way the person moves his or her body when interacting with others. For example, an extroverted person is more likely to use gestures that are expansive and may approach more readily, whereas an introvert may keep limbs close to the body and avoid approaching (Gallaher 1992).

In this study, we independently manipulated both verbal and nonverbal cues to convey the interactive characters' extroversion or introversion. No one has yet demonstrated experimentally that people will read personality cues in an interactive character in the same way that they will read them in people, although there is evidence from television research that people apply the same personality traits to TV characters as they do to other people (Hoffner and Cantor 1981; Reeves and Greenberg 1977). We predicted that people would successfully label introverted and extroverted verbal and nonverbal cues from interactive characters, just as they identified the verbal cues of dominance-submissiveness in previous research in human-computer interaction (Moon and Nass 1996; Nass et al. 1995).

13.5.2 Inconsistent Personalities in ECAs

Because people judge a person's personality from a host of different cues, the possibility of conflicting cues arises: What happens if a person is suggesting one personality with the way that he or she speaks, and an entirely different personality with the way that he or she moves? It is clear that people prefer to engage with others whom they can label consistently. Consistency in others allows people to predict what will happen when they engage with them (Fiske and Taylor 1991), makes it easier to remember a person accurately (Cantor and Mischel 1979), and generally lightens cognitive load (Fiske and Taylor 1991). In addition, studies that looked at how people detect deception have found that people turn to nonverbal cues to see if they are inconsistent with the verbal ones. This suggests that discrepancies among cues is a big problem in others (Ekman and Friesen 1974). Cassell, McNeill, and McCullough (1998) note that even though people may not be aware of mismatches between verbal and gestural cues, they will still make combined use of these cues to form an integrated understanding of what was said. Literature also suggests that adults use mismatched verbal and gestural cues in children to help determine the child's knowledge state (Goldin-Meadow, Alibali, and Church 1993).

Character consistency is of great concern to traditional character crafters. Guidelines for creating characters often include a caveat that everything a character does should convey the same general impression about the character to the viewer (Field 1994; Thomas and Johnston 1981). These caveats are needed because it is easy for inconsistencies to creep in during the development process. This is especially the case for complex character creation involving a large team of people, as is often found in the development of interactive characters.

What happens when a person is confronted with inconsistent cues from an on-screen character? From the psychological literature and CASA, one can predict that the person will dislike inconsistent cues and thus will like the character less. This would indeed be a problem that character designers should avoid. However, inconsistency might not work in the same way for characters as for actual people. Perhaps people average the two sets of conflicting cues to arrive at an overall impression of the character. If so, it might be better to design a character with mixed cues, to ensure that all users, regardless of personality, would be at least partially satisfied with the character, on the assumption that all individuals have a preference for one personality type over another. We sought to determine which of these hypotheses would hold true for interactive characters. In sum, the study had two goals: (1) to determine whether users can recognize personality in both verbal and nonverbal cues of interactive characters; and (2) to determine whether inconsistent characters are universally disliked (consistency theory) or perceived as neutral (averaging theory)—that is, whether consistent characters are more beautiful than inconsistent characters.

One complication in addressing these questions is that studies in interpersonal psychology have shown that people tend to prefer others based on the match or mismatch to their own personality. Two conflicting hypotheses exist in this literature: the similarity-attraction hypothesis and the complementarity principle. Similarity-attraction holds that people prefer those with personalities similar to their own (Blankenship et al. 1984; Byrne 1969). Complementarity, conversely, holds that people will tend to behave in complementary ways in their interpersonal interactions and will seek out others who elicit complementary behavior from them (Leary 1957; Sullivan 1953). Both similarity-attraction and complementarity have significant experimental confirmation in the psychological literature (see Isbister 1998). Rather than attempt to resolve these ambiguous results, we simply ensured that an equal number of introverts and extroverts assessed both of the consistent (introverted and extroverted) ECAs as well as the two mixed ECAs (introverted verbal with extroverted nonverbal, or vice versa). This balancing ensured that the effects of user/ECA match or mismatch would be washed out.

13.5.3 Design of the Personality Experiment

To address our two core questions adequately, we created a balanced, between-participants design in which introverted or extroverted individuals were randomly assigned to one of four conditions: (1) wholly matching character (verbal and nonverbal cues were consistent and matched the user); (2) wholly mismatched character (verbal and nonverbal cues were consistent but were opposite the user); (3) matching verbal and mismatching nonverbal; and (4) mismatching verbal, matching nonverbal. Examining the two main effects (verbal personality and nonverbal personality) allowed us to address our first goal of recognizing personality. A comparison of conditions (1) and (2) versus conditions (3) and (4) answered whether consistency was "beautiful" or not, which was our second goal.

Our participants were students from two West Coast universities who had been asked to be in various studies as part of their coursework. There were forty students in all, with students from both schools balanced evenly across the conditions.

We assigned students to conditions in our study based on their own introversion/extroversion (this is not a violation of the principle of random assignment, as equal numbers of introverts and extroverts were randomly assigned to experience each type of character). A few weeks before the experiment ran, we had every student in both classes complete a section of the Myers-Briggs personality inventory (see Murray 1990 for a review) as well as a portion of the Wiggins personality adjective set (Wiggins 1979), as part of a packet of questionnaires administered to the entire class. Students who fell above the class median on the Myers-Briggs (higher than 4 out of a possible score of 9) and on the Wiggins introversion scale (higher than 27 out of a possible score of 54) were classified as introverted; students who fell below the class median on the Myers-Briggs (lower than 4) and above it on the Wiggins extroversion scale (higher than 38 out of a possible score of 54) were classified as extroverted.

Twenty students from the extroverted group and twenty students from the introverted group were asked to participate. They were simply told that they would be participating in a study examining how people work with computer characters to accomplish a task. Everyone signed informed consent forms, was debriefed at the end of the experimental session, and was awarded class credit for participating in the study.

When they arrived, each participant was first asked to complete the Desert Survival Problem (DSP) (Lafferty and Eady 1974) using pencil and paper. The DSP is a problem-solving task that has been used in a variety of studies involving interpersonal interaction and human-computer interaction (see Reeves and Nass 1996). It asks participants to rank a series of twelve items (compress kit, book, raincoat, flashlight, vodka, parachute, water, mirror, jackknife, magnetic compass, salt tablets, and air map), according to their assessment of the items' importance in a desert survival situation.

After finishing this initial ranking, the participant was introduced to an on-screen computer character. The experimenter explained that the participant would get to exchange information about each of the twelve desert survival items with the computer character. In addition, after completing the interaction with the character, the participant would have the opportunity to change his or her initial ranking of all the items.

The on-screen character was in a format similar to comic books: the figure was a still image in each turn, with a word balloon with text in it that represented its own "voice." The character stayed in one place on each screen, creating the impression that one was working through an interaction with a comic-book-like character. The character had no face and was a simple stick

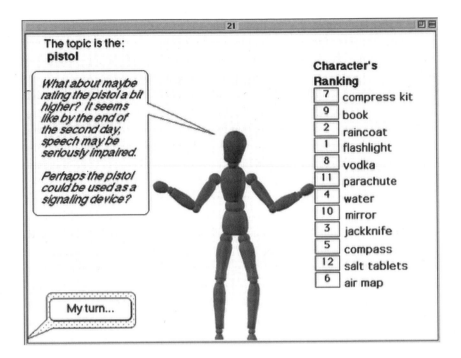

Figure 13.3
Screen shot of the interface (the pistol was the practice item).

figure, in contrast to the rich video images in the previous experiment. Participants typed their own words into their own text word balloon, which also stayed on screen in the same place throughout the interaction (see fig. 13.3).

After a single practice round (discussing the pistol, an item not on the actual list), the experimenter left the room. The participant was left alone to exchange information with the computer character about each of the twelve desert survival items. After the interaction was complete, the student made a final ranking of the desert survival items, on paper. Then, the student was given a questionnaire to fill out. This questionnaire asked for his or her assessment of both the computer character and the interaction itself. After completing the questionnaire, the student was debriefed, thanked, and asked not to discuss the experiment with other classmates until the study was completed.

13.5.3.1 Creating Introversion and Extroversion   Verbal extroversion or introversion was operationalized (implemented) by manipulating the phrasing of the text displayed in the character's word balloons during the interaction. The extroverted computer character used strong and friendly language expressed in the form of confident assertions. This manipulation is consistent with the theoretical definition of extroversion as being the tendency to be assertive, outgoing, and friendly. The introverted computer character used weaker language expressed in the form of questions and suggestions. This manipulation is consistent with the theoretical definition of introversion as behavior that indicates less ease in socializing and less assertiveness.

For example, the introverted computer character would display the following text: "What about maybe rating the pistol a bit higher? It seems like by the end of the second day, speech may be seriously impaired. Perhaps the pistol could be used as a signaling device?" In contrast, the extroverted character would display the following text: "Friend, I'd say the pistol should definitely be rated higher. By the end of the second day, speech will be impaired and the pistol will be an important signaling device." All text for this manipulation was pretested by individuals who did not participate in this experiment, using a web form. Pretest participants were randomly assigned to read one of two sets of statements and to rate the person who made the statements on the same extroversion/introversion scales that we used in the study itself. We tried to control for undesirable personality trait manipulations. To do this, we also asked those who filled out the form to rank the speech giver on adjectives representing undesirable traits ("sly," "conceited," "big-headed").

Nonverbal extroversion or introversion was operationalized by manipulating the postures of the computer characters. The extroverted character body had poses with its limbs spread wide from its body, and some postures made the character seem to have moved closer to the participant (see fig. 13.4). This is consistent with the literature on nonverbal cues of extroversion that indicate that extroverts tend to make wider movements and to approach others more freely in space. The introverted character body had poses with its limbs closer in to its body and did not ever appear to approach the participant. This is consistent with the literature on nonverbal cues of introversion that indicate that introverts tend to keep their limbs closer to their bodies, gesture less freely, and avoid approaching others in space. The character itself was a simple stick figure, which allowed us to avoid possible effects of other cues of personality and personal qualities that arise from things like age, clothing, or gender. As with the verbal cues, the nonverbal cues were pretested to confirm that they were being read properly.

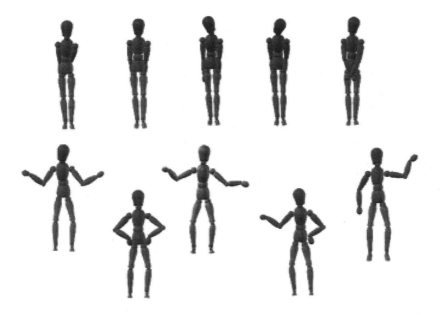

Figure 13.4
Example postures (introverted postures in first row; extroverted postures in second row).

The fundamental information conveyed by the computer character was *not* manipulated; that is, in all four conditions, the computer character conveyed the same type and amount of information about the items being discussed in the task. Only the *style* of communication was manipulated. Moreover, all responses were preprogrammed. No natural language processing or artificial intelligence was employed. To create a smooth interaction, the character always went first in discussing an item, then the participant responded with his or her own information about an item.

13.5.3.2 *Measuring the Possible Consequences of ECA Personality* As in the previous study, the dependent variables were measured using a paper-and-pencil questionnaire.

The first set of questions asked, "For each word below, please indicate how well it describes your interaction with the character on the computer. Note that you are evaluating the actual interaction, not the character itself." This was followed by a list of adjectives (e.g., "fun," "interesting," "useful"), each of which had a nine-point Likert scale that ranged from "describes very poorly" to "describes very well."

The second set of questions, which also used a nine-point Likert scale, was aimed at allowing participants to rank their satisfaction with the character and its perceived value.

The third set of questions asked, "For each word below, please indicate how well it describes the character that you just worked with. Note that you are evaluating the character now, NOT the interaction." This was followed by a list of adjectives (e.g., "assertive," "friendly," "bashful"), each of which had a nine-point Likert scale that ranged from "describes very poorly" to "describes very well." This list of adjectives included all those used in the Wiggins introversion and extroversion scales. Participants then rated the character's *body language* on the Wiggins scales, then its *verbal style* on these same measures.

Based on factor analysis, four indices were created from the questionnaire items. All indices were reliable. *Fun* was an index of four adjectives used to characterize the interaction: enjoyable, exciting, fun, and satisfying (A = 0.90). *Liking* was an index of two items: "Would you enjoy working with this character in another experiment?" and "How much did you like this character?" (A = 0.82). *Usefulness of the Interaction* was an index of two items used to characterize the interaction: helpful and useful (A = 0.91). *Usefulness of the Character* was an index comprised of three questions: "How much did the character improve your ranking of the items?," "How much did you learn from interacting with this character?" and "How helpful did you find this character?" (A = .89).

To assess the perception of the character's personality, we created an index of the Wiggins introversion and extroversion scales for the verbal and nonverbal cues, respectively, to reflect a general extroverted versus introverted assessment (hereafter referred to as "extroverted").

13.5.4 Responses to the Personality of ECAs

Our first goal was to find out if people would be able to identify both verbal and nonverbal personality cues. The results were consistent with previous research, in that participants accurately identified the extroverted language as significantly more extroverted than the introverted language, $F(1,38) = 5.26$, $p < .05$ (see fig. 13.5). (All figures have standardized the indices to reflect nine-point Likert scales.) In results that were consistent with the demonstrated power of nonverbal cues, the extroverted postures were perceived as significantly more extroverted than the introverted postures, $F(1,38) = 8.90$, $p < .01$, even though the characters were faceless stick figures.

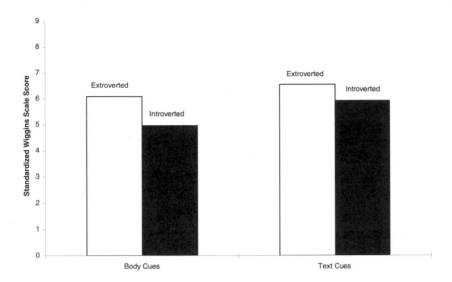

Figure 13.5
Identification of personality in body postures and text.

Our second goal was to better understand the impact of inconsistent verbal and nonverbal cues. If individuals adopt a holistic approach toward the character and are disturbed by inconsistency, we should see significant interactions between the verbal and nonverbal cues. If, however, individuals assess verbal and nonverbal cues independently, no interactions should occur, and main effects should occur only to the extent that similarity-attraction and complementarity have differential effects. Supporting the idea that consistency is important (the CASA prediction), the findings revealed that text and body cues showed consistent interactions for all four indices, giving support to the whole-impression model of how we read mixed cues.

People liked the ECA more when it was consistent than when it was inconsistent, as reflected in a significant interaction, $F(1,39) = 4.21, p < .05$. There were no significant main effects (see fig. 13.6). The interaction was also perceived to be more useful when the ECA was consistent, $F(1,39) = 6.87, p < .02$. There were no main effects. The ECAs with the consistent personality were also more fun to interact with, $F(1,39) = 3.50, p < .07$. The results, consistent with similarity-

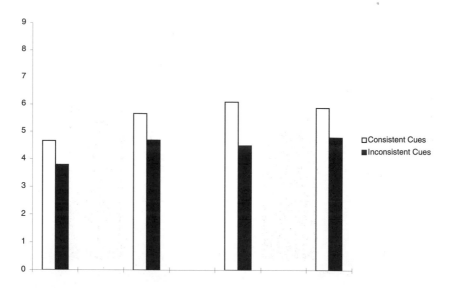

Figure 13.6

Effects of personality cue consistency on assessments of the interaction.

attraction, showed that individuals had more fun with the character whose nonverbal cues matched their own personality, $F(1,39) = 5.47$, $p < .03$. Finally, the consistent character was perceived as significantly more useful than the inconsistent character, even though the content was identical, $F(1,39) = 3.29$, $p < .08$. There were no main effects for text or body.

Another type of confirmation for the superiority of consistent characters comes from an examination of change in the participants' rankings of the items in the desert survival item list. In a comparison of initial rankings to final rankings, a significantly larger change in rankings found in the consistent character conditions, $F(1, 39) = 7.9$, $p < .01$, suggests that the information from the matched character had a greater effect on participants (see fig. 13.7). We then performed an analysis looking at what the direction of the change in rankings was in relation to the character partner and found that participants with a consistent character partner changed their answers much more toward their character partner's answers than those with an inconsistent partner, $M = 14.42$ average change closer to partner after interaction versus $M = 9.75$, $F(1,39) = 11.44$, $p < .05$.

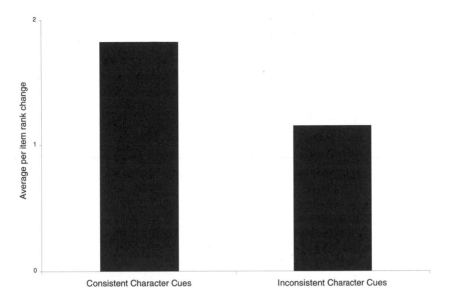

Figure 13.7
Effect of personality cue consistency on user conformity.

This study gives additional support to the growing body of evidence that people apply the same interpretive strategies to interaction with ECAs as they do to interaction with other people (Reeves and Nass 1996). In this study, people labeled postures and verbal styles in interactive characters the same way they would label postures and verbal styles in other people. And, just as is the case in interaction with other people, participants preferred consistency in the characters they interacted with, and they used all the cues from the characters to form an overall impression by which the character was judged.

13.6 Summary and Discussion

This chapter has urged that appropriately designed assessments of user satisfaction, based on experimental methodology, are a critical component of creating beautiful research. Fortunately, a good experiment does more than give one a pat on the back for doing a research job well; it can inform general principles of both theory and design. As an example of the power of the methodology, we briefly highlight a few of the conclusions that can be derived from our studies.

13.6.1 Research Contributions

The two studies presented here show that people apply social rules and expectations to ECAs, even when doing so is not logical. In the first study, participants responded to ECAs as if their ethnicity had meaning beyond an arbitrary representation; the same words meant different things when coming from an ECA that was similar as opposed to different. In the second study, the posture of a stick figure had a significant influence on individuals' assessments of the content and the interaction, even though the character was in no way the "source" of the information. Individuals mindlessly (Nass and Moon n.d.) applied social rules to ECAs, even though they were experienced computer users (though they did not have significant experience with ECAs) who knew that these rules were not logical. Thus, ECAs are clearly social actors.

Each study provides its own unique extension to the CASA paradigm. The ethnicity study is one of the first to directly compare human-computer interaction with computer-mediated communication. Having determined that people treat computers in a social manner, the next step must be to examine *how socially* people respond to computers. For example, people feel good when they are flattered by a computer (Fogg and Nass 1997) but possibly not as much as when they are flattered by a person. Similarly, the gender stereotypes people unconsciously apply to computers (Nass, Moon, and Green 1997) might not be as strong as those they have about people. In other words, CASA had previously replicated the *pattern* of social rules that govern human-human interaction in the context of HCI but had not tested the *degree* of socialness in people's response to computers (Morkes, Kernal, and Nass n.d. and Lee 1999 are exceptions). By juxtaposing HCI and (perceived) CMC, we can now address the "degree" question.

The results provide strong evidence for surprising similarities in the way people respond to ethnicity in ECAs and in humans. Critically, there were no significant interactions between the (seeming) ontology of the source and the source's ethnic identity, suggesting that the processing of ethnicity is similar in the two cases. Thus, this study demonstrates that when one taps into a basic social category (e.g., ethnicity), that category overrides any skepticism the user may have of the relevance of social categories to ECAs as compared to actual people.

The personality study demonstrates that even the most ersatz representation of a person is enough to encourage the user to bring to bear a subtle and complex apparatus that can assign personality to nonverbal cues. In previous CASA studies, the interface was plain text. For users who were experienced with e-mail (virtually all of the participants), this interaction felt no different than an interaction with an actual person. However, the stick figures employed in the present experiment were obviously not human and only moved between screens; indeed, they seemed more like a piece of wood than a person. Yet individuals used their expectation about personality consistency to interpret the meaning of the ECA's words. This provides additional evidence that there is no "on-off" switch in the brain that allows one to process media differently than real people (Reeves and Nass 1996); if there were, the clearly nonhuman representations would surely have tripped it.

13.6.2 Design Contributions

Almost everyone involved in research on ECAs is motivated by the desire to improve interface design. The studies presented here both have numerous implications for design; we will touch on only a few of these implications (for a complete discussion, see Lee and Nass 1998 and Isbister and Nass n.d.).

Perhaps the most general and important take-away from these studies is that "beauty" matters; appearance is a critical component of how people access ECAs. It is perhaps not surprising that individuals prefer to look at or even interact with ECAs that are more "attractive." What is more compelling is that appearance influenced more cognitive assessments, even when the content was identical. ECAs that shared the ethnicity of the user were perceived as more competent; ECAs that presented consistent personality cues were perceived as more useful. Thus, perceptions of seemingly objective criteria, such as intelligence, can be influenced by attractiveness.

These direct assessments of intelligence had indirect effects as well. In both studies, the beautiful characters were more convincing and obtained greater compliance from their users. Thus, designers of interfaces that involve persuasion (Fogg 1998), from an e-commerce web site to medical advice software, should be concerned with whether their ECAs are attractive or not.

Current research also suggests that ECA design must be a highly coordinated activity. Because of the complexity of creating a multimodal ECA, the task is often divided into small groups; integration occurs at a fairly late stage. These results suggest that coordination across functional units is absolutely critical. Each aspect of the ECA should be as similar as possible to the user groups that will be interacting with the agent, requiring interaction with the marketing efforts, and each aspect of the ECA should be consistent with each other aspect, requiring coordinated development efforts in crafting consistent interactive characters.

What should one do when the goals of similarity clash with the goals of consistency, as when there is a varied user base and only one ECA? It is important to note that the desires for consistency were obtained regardless of the characters' similarity to the user. Thus, it may be more important that the character is consistent than that it complement or match the individual using the software. While early industry research and subsequent software (e.g., Microsoft BOB) focused on matching the software user's personality with the character's, given the conflicting picture about similarity versus complementarity, it may in fact be more important that the character sends a clear message about its personality than that it matches the user.

Overall, these studies are an important step toward a more comprehensive picture of how humans use their person perception skills in interpreting and evaluating interactive onscreen characters. As the use of these characters in software increases, it is essential that designers take into account both how person perception works in human-human interaction, and how these skills play out in responses to ECAs.

13.6.3 Final Thoughts on Beautiful ECAs

We began this chapter by establishing three criteria for beautiful research: (1) create ECAs that accurately mirror humans, (2) obtain the admiration of one's peers, and (3) demonstrate that the ECA satisfies users. As the first two criteria have long been goals of the ECA community, this chapter focused on experimental research as the means for objectively and reliably assessing user satisfaction. The principles of varied conditions, random assignment, and clear specification of the satisfaction criteria were shown to be the first steps in ensuring that the creation of ECAs meets the third standard for beauty.

The reader is likely thinking that if that is all there was to experimental research, the ECA research community would have adopted the technique long ago. There is some truth to this concern. There are, of course, numerous other issues in designing experimental research for judging the beauty of ECA research: the number and choice of dimensions that are presented to the participants, and the number and range of values along each dimension; the number of participants in each condition; whether participants will be exposed to all of the conditions (within-participants design) or only a subset of the conditions (between-participants design); the appropriate number and range of effects (dependent variables) to be obtained; the ability to draw conclusions from null results; the ability to generalize from one or more experiments; and so forth. With that said, if researchers simply created more than one stimulus, randomly assigned the presentation of the stimuli, and provided clear metrics for assessments, we would have both beautiful research and beautiful agents, and that, after all, is the justification for the existence of our field.

Note

All authors participated equally in writing this chapter. The ethnicity study was executed by Lee and Nass (1998). The personality study was executed by Isbister and Nass (n.d.).

References

Allen, V. L., and D. A. Wilder. 1979. Group categorization and attribution of belief similarity. *Small Group Behavior* 10:73–80.

Biernet, M., and T. K. Vescio. 1993. Categorization and stereotyping: Effects of group context on memory and social judgment. *Journal of Experimental Social Psychology* 29:166–202.

Blankenship, V., S. M. Hnat, T. G. Hess, and D. R. Brown. 1984. Reciprocal interaction and similarity of personality attributes. *Journal of Social and Personal Relationships* 1:415–432.

Byrne, D. 1969. Attitudes and attraction. In L. Berkowitz, ed., *Advances in experimental social psychology* 4. Orlando, Fla.: Academic Press.

Campbell, J. B., and C. W. Hawley. 1982. Study habits and Eysenck's theory of extroversion-introversion. *Journal of Research in Personality* 16:139–146.

Cantor, N., and W. Mischel. 1979. Prototypes in person perception. *Advances in Experimental Social Psychology*, 12:3–52.

Cassell, J., D. McNeill, and K. E. McCullough. 1998. Speech-gesture mismatches: Evidence for one underlying representation of linguistic and nonlinguistic information. *Pragmatics and Cognition* 6(2):1–34.

Clark, R. D., and A. Maass. 1988. The role of social categorization and perceived source credibility in minority influence. *European Journal of Social Psychology* 18:381–394.

Cole, J. R., and S. Cole. 1973. *Social stratification in science.* Chicago: University of Chicago Press.

Ekman, P., and W. V. Friesen. 1974. Detecting deception from the body or face. *Journal of Personality and Social Psychology* 29:288–298.

Ekman, P., W. V. Friesen, M. O'Sullivan, and K. Scherer. 1980. Relative importance of face, body, and speech in judgments of personality and affect. *Journal of Personality and Social Psychology* 38(2):270–277.

Eysenck, S. B. G., and F. Y. Long. 1986. A cross-cultural comparison of personality in adults and children: Singapore and England. *Journal of Personality and Social Psychology* 50:124–130.

Field, S. 1994. *Screenplay: The foundations of screenwriting.* New York: Bantam Doubleday Dell.

Fiske, S. T., and S. E. Taylor. 1991. *Social cognition.* New York: McGraw-Hill.

Fogg, B. J. 1998. Persuasive computers: Perspectives and research directions. In *Proceedings of the CHI98 Conference of the ACM/SIGCHI,* 225–232. New York: ACM Press.

Fogg, B. J., and C. Nass. 1997. Silicon sycophants: Effects of computers that flatter. *International Journal of Human-Computer Studies* 46:551–561.

Gallaher, P. E. 1992. Individual differences in nonverbal behavior: Dimensions of style. *Journal of Personality and Social Psychology* 63(1):133–145.

Gerard, H. B., and M. F. Hoyt. 1974. Distinctiveness of social categorization and attitude toward in-group members. *Journal of Personality and Social Psychology* 29:836–842.

Goldin-Meadow, S., M. Alibali, and R. B. Church. 1993. Transitions in concept acquisition: Using the hands to read the mind. *Psychological Review* 100(2):279–297.

Hardy, G. H. 1941. *A mathematician's apology.* Cambridge: Cambridge University Press.

Hoffner, C., and J. Cantor. 1981. Perceiving and responding to mass media characters. In J. Bryant and D. Zillmann, eds., *Responding to the screen: Reception and reaction processes.* Hillsdale, N.J.: Erlbaum.

Isbister, K. 1998. Reading personality in onscreen interactive characters: An examination of social psychological principles of consistency, personality match, and situational attribution applied to interaction with characters. Ph.D. diss., Communication Department, Stanford University, Stanford, California.

Isbister, K., and C. Nass. N.d. Consistency of personality in interactive characters: Verbal cues, non-verbal cues, and user characteristics. *International Journal of Human-Computer Studies.* Forthcoming.

Jung, C. G. 1971. *Psychological types.* Princeton: Princeton University Press.

Kogan, N., and M. A. Wallach. 1967. Risky-shift phenomenon in small decision-making groups: A test of the information-exchange hypothesis. *Journal of Experimental Social Psychology* 3:75–84.

Lafferty, J. C., and P. M. Eady. 1974. *The desert survival problem.* Plymouth, Mich.: Experimental Learning Methods.

Laurel, B. 1993. *Computers as theater.* Reading, Mass.: Addison-Wesley.

Leary, T. F. 1957. *Interpersonal diagnosis of personality.* New York: Ronald Press.

Lee, E-J. 1999. *Effects of number, ontology, and representation of influencing agents on public compliance and private conformity.* Ph.D. diss., Stanford University, Stanford, California.

Lee, E.-J., and C. Nass. 1998. Does the ethnicity of a computer agent matter? An experimental comparison of human-computer interaction and computer-mediated communication. In *Proceedings of the Workshop on Embedded Conversational Characters Conference* (Lake Tahoe, Calif.).

Lee, Y. T. 1993. In-group preference and homogeneity among African American and Chinese American students. *Journal of Social Psychology* 133:225–235.

Levitt, B., and C. Nass. 1989. The lid on the garbage can: Institutional constraints on decision making in the textbook publishing industry. *Administrative Science Quarterly* 34(2):190–207.

McCrae, R. R., and P. T. Costa Jr. 1989. The structure of interpersonal traits: Wiggins's circumplex and the five-factor model. *Journal of Personality and Social Psychology* 56:586–595.

Moon, Y., and C. Nass. 1996. How "real" are computer personalities? Psychological responses to personality types in human-computer interaction. *Communication Research* 23(6):651–674.

Morkes, J., H. Kernal, and C. Nass. N.d. Effects of humor in computer-mediated communication and human-computer interaction. *Human Communication Research* 14(4).

Murray, J. B. 1990. Review of research on the Myers-Briggs type indicator. *Perceptual and Motor Skills* 70:1187–1202.

Nass, C., and L. Mason. 1990. On the study of technology and task: A variable-based approach. In J. Fulk and C. Steinfeld, eds., *Organizations and communication technology*, 46–67. Newbury Park, Calif.: Sage.

Nass, C., and Y. Moon. N.d. Machines and mindlessness: Social responses to computers. *Journal of Social Issues*. Forthcoming.

Nass, C., Y. Moon, and N. Green. 1997. Are machines gender-neutral? Gender-stereotypical responses to computers with voices. *Journal of Applied Social Psychology* 27:864–876.

Nass, C., Y. Moon, B. J. Fogg, B. Reeves, and D. C. Dryer. 1995. Can computer personalities be human personalities? *International Journal of Human-Computer Studies* 43:223–239.

Pervin, L. A., and O. P. John, eds. 1997. *Personality theory and research*. New York: John Wiley and Sons.

Reeves, B., and B. Greenberg. 1977. Children's perception of television characters. *Human Communication Research* 3:113–117.

Reeves, B., and C. Nass. 1996. *The media equation: How people treat computers, televisions, and new media like real people and places*. New York: Cambridge University Press.

Stephan, W., and W. E. Beane. 1978. The effects of belief similarity and ethnicity on liking and attributions for performance. *Revista Interamericana de Psicologia* 12:153–159.

Sullivan, H. S. 1953. *The interpersonal theory of psychiatry*. New York: Norton.

Tajfel, H., ed. 1978. *Differentiation between social groups: Studies in the social psychology of intergroup relations*. New York: Academic Press.

Taylor, D. A., and B. F. Moriarty. 1987. Ingroup bias as a function of competition and race. *Journal of Conflict Resolution* 31:192–199.

Thomas, F., and O. Johnston. 1981. *The illusion of life: Disney animation*. New York: Hyperion.

Turner, J. C. 1985. Social categorization and the self-concept. *Advances in Group Processes* 2:77–121.

Wagner, U., and P. L. Ward. 1993. Variation of out-group presence and evaluation of the ingroup. *British Journal of Social Psychology* 32:241–251.

Whitehead, G. I., S. H. Smith, and J. A. Eichhorn. 1982. The effect of participant's race and other's race on judgments of causality for success and failure. *Journal of Personality* 50:193–202.

Wiggins, J. S. 1979. A psychological taxonomy of trait-descriptive terms: The interpersonal domain. *Journal of Personality and Social Psychology* 37(3):395–412.

Wilder, D. A., and P. N. Shapiro. 1984. Role of out-group cues in determining social identity. *Journal of Personality and Social Psychology* 47:342–348.

Contributors

Bridget Adams is a Research Assistant at the Center for Human-Computer Communication (CHCC) at the Oregon Graduate Institute of Science and Technology (OGI). She received her B.A. in Psychology and is a Certified Clinical Research Coordinator. Her current research interests are in human-computer interaction, human factors, and cognitive psychology.

Jan M. Allbeck is a Ph.D. student at the Center for Human Modeling and Simulation in the Department of Computer and Information Science at the University of Philadelphia. She has a master's degree from the University of Pennsylvania and her research focuses on autonomous agents for virtual environments.

Elisabeth André is a principal researcher at the department of Intelligent User Interfaces at DFKI GmbH, Germany, where she has been leading various projects on lifelike characters and multimedia authoring tools. She chairs the ACL Special Interest Group on Multimedia Language Processing (SIGMEDIA). She is on the Editorial Board of Artificial Intelligence Communications (AICOM), and she is the Area Editor for Intelligent User Interfaces of the Electronic Transactions of Artificial Intelligence (ETAI).

Dr. **Norman I. Badler** is a Professor of Computer and Information Science at the University of Pennsylvania and has been on that faculty since 1974. Active in computer graphics since 1968 with more than one hundred technical papers, he focuses his research on human figure modeling, manipulation, and animation control. He is the originator of the "Jack" software system (now marketed as a commercial product by Engineering Animation, Inc.). His expertise includes real-time 3-D graphics, intuitive user interfaces, complex object modeling, and animation systems. Badler received his B.A. in Creative Studies Mathematics from the University of California at Santa Barbara in 1970, and his M.Sc. in Mathematics in 1971 and his Ph.D. in Computer Science in 1975, both from the University of Toronto. He is co-editor of the Journal *Graphical Models and Image Processing* and co-author of the book *Simulating Humans* published by Oxford University Press. He also directs the Center for Human Modeling and Simulation with three full-time staff members and about forty students.

Stephan Baldes is a part-time researcher at the department of Intelligent User Interfaces at DFKI GmbH with a research focus on multimedia presentation planning and automated commentary systems. He is currently involved in the BMBF-funded AiA project and the internally funded Rocco project.

Gene Ball is a Senior Researcher in the Adaptive Systems and Interaction group at Microsoft Research, where he is working toward the creation of conversational computer interfaces. Since 1994, he has organized a series of workshops (Lifelike Computer Characters) that encourage consideration of the psychological, social, and entertainment ramifications of anthropomorphic computer systems. He grew up in Oklahoma, received his Ph.D. in Computer Science from the University of Rochester in 1983, and served on the faculties of Carnegie Mellon University and the University of Delaware before joining Microsoft Research in 1992.

Jonas Beskow is a doctoral student at the Royal Institute of Technology (KTH) in Stockholm. His research interests include computer facial animation and acoustic and visual speech synthesis. He received a M.Sc. in electrical engineering (1995) from KTH. During 1998–1999, he spent eighteen months at the UC Santa Cruz Perceptual Science Lab on a Fulbright scholarship.

Timothy Bickmore is a Ph.D. student in the Gesture and Narrative Language group at the MIT Media Lab, where he is working on the development of conversational computer characters. He previously was a Consulting Scientist at the FX Palo Alto Research Laboratory (FXPAL) in Palo Alto, California, where he led the Office Avatars project, which advanced the development of conversational characters as personal representatives in business applications.

Rama Bindiganavale is a Ph.D. student in the Department of Computer Science at the University of Pennsylvania. She is also the lab and project manager at the Center for Human Modeling and Simulation and is the chief architect for the implementation and integration of the PAR system. She received her B.E. in Electronics from Bangalore University, India, and M.S. in Computer Engineering from Louisiana State University. Her research focuses on motion capture, editing and analysis, action recognition, and intelligent agents.

Jack Breese is Assistant Director of Microsoft Research at Microsoft's primary research facility in Redmond, Washington. Previously at Microsoft, he was a founding member of the Decision Theory and Adaptive Systems research group that develops basic technologies and tools for user modeling, intelligent diagnostics, adaptive systems, and datamining. Recent projects address algorithms for collaborative filtering, pricing of distributed network services, as well as modeling emotions and personality for adaptive user interfaces.

Charles Callaway is a doctoral candidate in Computer Science at North Carolina State University. He holds a B.S. (1993) in Mathematics, a B.S. (1993) in Computer Sciences, a B.A. (1993) in Latin, and an M.A. (1996) in Computer Sciences, all from the University of Texas at Austin. His research in computational linguistics focuses on natural language generation. In addition to the animated pedagogical agents' work described in this volume, in his work with the IntelliMedia Initiative he addresses narrative prose generation, intelligent document generation, multimodal explanation generation, multilingual natural language generation, and embodied agent dialogue.

Lee Campbell is a Ph.D. student at the MIT Media Lab, working in both the Vision and Modeling and the Gesture and Narrative Language Groups. His thesis work involves automated visual classification of discourse gestures for improved understanding of face-to-face conversation. He received his B.A. in

Physics from Middlebury College, and his M.S. in Media Arts and Sciences from MIT. In his other life, he is the proud new father of Benjamin Dunn Campbell, born Oct 14, 1999.

Justine Cassell is faculty at the MIT Media Lab, where she directs the Gesture and Narrative Language research group. She holds a master's degree in Literature from the Université de Besançon (France), a master's degree in Linguistics from the University of Edinburgh (Scotland), and a double Ph.D. from the University of Chicago, in Psychology and in Linguistics. After having spent ten years studying verbal and nonverbal aspects of human communication through microanalysis of videotaped data, she began to bring her knowledge of human conversation to the design of computational systems. She built the very first embodied conversational agent as NSF visiting faculty at the University of Pennsylvania, in the Center for Human Modeling and Simulation, working with their faculty and graduate students. Currently, she and her students are working on the third generation of Embodied Conversational Agent (Rea) and have also integrated the foundations of this work into the design of a 3-D graphical online world (BodyChat). Cassell has also researched how embodied conversational agents, and other kinds of virtual listeners, can encourage and enhance storytelling among children and adults and, with her students, has implemented a suite of *story-listening systems*.

Dr. **Elizabeth Churchill** is a Senior Research Scientist at FX Palo Alto Research Laboratory (FXPAL) in Palo Alto, California. She received her Ph.D. in Cognitive Science from the University of Cambridge, UK. Her current research interests center on computer mediated communication, focusing on the design of virtual environments and virtual embodiments to support collaborative work. With Scott Prevost, she was co-chair for the Workshop on Embodied Conversational Characters (WECC '98). She was also co-organizer of CVE'96 and CVE'98, conferences dedicated to presenting research and development work in the area of collaborative virtual environments. She is currently in the process of co-organizing CVE2000 and is co-editing a book on Collaborative Virtual Environments to be published by Springer-Verlag.

Michael M. Cohen is a research associate in Cognitive Psychology at the University of California, Santa Cruz. His research interests include speech perception and production, speechreading, information integration, learning, and computer facial animation. He received a B.S. in Computer Science and Psychology and an M.S. in Psychology from the University of Wisconsin, Madison, and a Ph.D. in Experimental Psychology from the University of California, Santa Cruz.

Professor **Ron Cole** has studied speech recognition by human and machine for the past twenty-five years, and has published over one hundred articles in scientific journals and archived conference proceedings. Since 1988, Ron has worked to build a multidisciplinary center of excellence at the Oregon Graduate Institute, and in 1990 he founded the Center for Spoken Language Understanding (CSLU). In 1998, he co-founded CSLU Boulder at the University of Colorado.

Linda Cook earned a Ph.D. in Cognitive Psychology from the University of California and a master's degree in Computer Science with an emphasis in Artificial Intelligence from California State University. She is currently a consulting scientist at FX Palo Alto Laboratory, where her work focuses on the role that personality plays in the individuation and believability of synthetic computer characters and the design of evaluation methodologies for character-based interfaces. Dr. Cook was previously associated with the Artificial Intelligence Laboratory at Lockheed, where she was involved in the research, design, and development of intelligent user interfaces.

Patrick FitzGerald is an Assistant Professor of Art and Design at North Carolina State University. He serves as Director of the multidisciplinary IntelliMedia Initiative for NC State's School of Design. Mr. FitzGerald earned his B.A. in Advertising from Southern Methodist University (1985) and his M.F.A. from the Cranbrook Academy of Art (1987). Prior to joining NC State, he served as an instructor, artist, and manager at the Center for Creative Imaging in Camden, Maine. As a multimedia producer for the Providence-based company, AVX, he was a member of the design team responsible for the Lollapalooza Electric Carnival Interactive Experience. He has completed several interactive museum exhibitions. His art has been exhibited across the United States and Japan, including the Tokyo Metropolitan Museum of Art, and his digital work has been published in the Macintosh Handbook for Design.

Peter Hodgson is a Senior Interface Design Researcher at FX Palo Alto Research Laboratory (FXPAL) in Palo Alto, California. He received his Masters in Computer Related Design from the Royal College of Art (RCA) in London focusing on the design of novel and engaging user interfaces. His current task is to extend the visual, interface and interaction design capabilities at FXPAL and to communicate the benefits of a design-led approach to the other research staff. He has previously created interface designs for Apple Computer and the Interval Research Lab at The Royal College of Art. In a previous incarnation, he was a designer in London, conceiving and developing brand identity programs and marketing and communications literature for such corporate clients as *The Economist* and Visa International. He is a member of the Design and Art Directors Association.

Katherine Isbister (Ph.D., Stanford University) is a researcher at the NTT (Nippon Telegraph and Telephone Corporation) Communication Science Laboratories in Kyoto, Japan. Her areas of specialization include the design of social agents and interfaces, social augmentation for online community spaces, and comparative studies of U.S. versus Japanese responses to interfaces.

Lewis Johnson directs the Center for Advanced Research in Technology for Education (CARTE) at the University of Southern California's Information Sciences Institute. He completed an A.B. in linguistics at Princeton University in 1978 and a Ph.D. in computer science at Yale University in 1985. His research interests center on applications of artificial intelligence and cognitive modeling to education and training. Dr. Johnson is past chair of the ACM Special Interest Group for Artificial Intelligence and is current president of the Artificial Intelligence in Education Society.

Martin Klesen is a researcher at the department of Intelligent User Interfaces at DFKI GmbH, Germany, with a research focus on behavior control for lifelike characters and computational models for personality and emotions. He is working full-time on PUPPET, an EU-funded project of the i3 initiative (Intelligent Information Interfaces) on Experimental School Environments.

Eun-Ju Lee is a Ph.D. candidate in the Department of Communication at Stanford University. Her areas of specialization include comparisons of human-computer interaction and computer-mediated communication, social influence processes in HCI, and social identification.

James Lester is Associate Professor of Computer Science at North Carolina State University. He serves as Director of the IntelliMedia Initiative for the College of Engineering. The IntelliMedia team includes computer scientists, animators, educators, and cognitive scientists whose work focuses on intelligent multimedia technologies for educational software. Dr. Lester earned his B.A. (1986), M.S.C.S. (1988), and

Ph.D. (1994) from the University of Texas at Austin. He also holds a B.A. in History from Baylor University (1983). His work has been recognized with the Best Paper Award at the 1997 International Conference on Artificial Intelligence in Education in Kobe, Japan, and the Best Paper Award at the 1999 International Conference on Intelligent User Interfaces. A member of Phi Beta Kappa, he is a recent recipient of a CAREER Award by the National Science Foundation.

Dominic W. Massaro is a Professor of Psychology in Cognitive Psychology at the University of California, Santa Cruz. He received a B.A. in Psychology from UCLA and an M.A. and a Ph.D. in Psychology from the University of Massachusetts, Amherst. After a two-year postdoctoral fellowship at the University of California, San Diego, he was a professor at the University of Wisconsin, Madison, before moving to Santa Cruz. He has been a Guggenheim Fellow, a University of Wisconsin Romnes Fellow, a James McKeen Cattell Fellow, and an NIMH Fellow. He is a past president of the Society for Computers in Psychology and is currently the book review editor of the *American Journal of Psychology* and co-editor of the journal *Interpreting*. His research uses a formal experimental and theoretical approach to the study of speech perception, reading, psycholinguistics, memory, cognition, learning, and decision making. One focus of his current research is on the development and theoretical and applied use of a completely synthetic and animated head for speech synthesis, language tutoring, and edutainment.

Clifford Nass (Ph.D., Princeton University) is an associate professor of communication at Stanford University, with appointments by courtesy in Science, Technology, and Society, Sociology, and Symbolic Systems. He is also Director of the Interface Lab at the Center for the Study of Language and Information at Stanford University. He is co-author (with Byron Reeves) of *The Media Equation: How People Treat Computers, Television, and New Media Like Real People and Places* (Cambridge University Press) and numerous articles in human-technology interaction. His areas of specialization are social-psychological responses to computers and other interactive media, voice input-output systems, and non-parametric statistics. He has consulted on the design of over fifty software and hardware products.

Sharon Oviatt is a Professor and Co-Director of the Center for Human-Computer Communication (CHCC) in the Department of Computer Science at the Oregon Graduate Institute of Science & Technology (OGI). She previously has taught and conducted research at the Artificial Intelligence Center at SRI International and the Universities of Illinois, California, and Oregon State. Her current research focuses on human-computer interaction, interface design for multimodal/multimedia systems and speech systems, portable telecommunication devices, and highly interactive systems. This work is funded primarily by grants and contracts from the National Science Foundation, DARPA, Intel, Microsoft, Boeing, and other corporate sources. She is an active member of the international HCI and speech communities, has published over sixty scientific articles, and has served on numerous government advisory panels and editorial boards. Her work is featured in recent special issues on "Multimodal Interfaces" appearing *in IEEE Multimedia, Human-Computer Interaction,* and *Communications of the ACM.* Further information about Dr. Oviatt and CHCC is available at http://www.cse.ogi.edu/CHCC.

Dr. **Martha S. Palmer** is an Associate Professor in the Department of Computer Science at the University of Pennsylvania. She has been actively involved in research in Natural Language Processing and Knowledge Representation for over twenty years, beginning with her graduate work at the University of Edinbugh. She has investigated the use of lexical semantics in applications at Unisys and from a more theoretical perspective at the National University of Singapore and the University of Pennsylvania. She is currently a member of the executive committee of the Association of Machine Translation for the Americas and was previously on the executive committee of the Association of Computational Linguistics, as well as Co-Program Chair of ACL-96 and Chair of SIGLEX, the Special Interest Group on the Lexicon. Recent grants include a DOD Chinese Treebank grant, Machine Translation of Military messages from the Army Research Lab and two NSF grants on verb representations.

Catherine Pelachaud received her Ph.D. at the Department of Computer Science at the University of Pennsylvania in 1991. For the past ten years, she has been working on the development of systems which simulate conversations between multiple agents with appropriate and synchronized verbal and nonverbal behaviors. Her research interest includes computer animation, conversational agents, human behavior simulation, and multimedia systems.

Isabella Poggi (degree in Philosophy, University of Rome) is an Assistant Professor at the Department of Linguistics of University Roma Tre. She teaches courses in General Psychology and Psychology of Communication. She has worked on First Language Teaching, Pragmatics and Multimodal Communication, particularly interjections, gesture, gaze, face communication and music; she has been carrying on cognitive analyses of communicative phenomena like persuasion, deception, political discourse, and research on the cognitive aspects of emotions like shame, humiliation, guilt, compassion, and enthusiasm.

Dr. **Scott Prevost** is a Senior Research Scientist at FX Palo Alto Research Laboratory (FXPAL) in Palo Alto, California. He received his Ph.D. in Computer and Information Science with an emphasis on Computational Linguistics at the University of Pennsylvania and continued his research in a post-doctoral position at the Massachusetts Institute of Technology Media Laboratory. His current research focuses on building interactive characters with linguistic and behavioral competence to serve as interfaces to complex software and devices. He also served as co-chair for the Workshop on Embodied Conversational Characters (WECC '98).

Jeff Rickel is a Research Computer Scientist at the Information Sciences Institute and a Research Assistant Professor in the Department of Computer Science at the University of Southern California. He has been active in artificial intelligence research since 1985, when he joined Texas Instruments (TI) to study the use of artificial intelligence in industrial automation. During his years at TI, he published on topics ranging from knowledge-based planning and simulation to automated production scheduling and intelligent tutoring. Dr. Rickel received his Ph.D. in Computer Science from the University of Texas in 1995 for his work on automated modeling of physical systems. Since then, his research has focused on animated, intelligent agents for training in virtual reality.

Thomas Rist is a senior researcher at the Department of Intelligent User Interfaces at DFKI GmbH, Germany, with a research focus on adaptive multimedia systems and multimodal interaction. He is currently a member of the European i3 (Intelligent Information Interfaces) co-ordination group and is in charge of various project managing tasks. Within the ERCIM Computer Graphics Network Task II Group, he set up an initiative toward the development of a Standard Reference Model for Intelligent Presentation Systems.

Greg Sanders is a Computer Scientist with the Information Technology Laboratory at the National Institute of Standards and Technology (NIST), where he focuses on measurement and evaluation of spoken natural language systems, particularly on metrics for discourse and dialogue. Dr. Sanders does research on discourse and dialogue in intelligent tutoring systems (ITS) and in information-seeking dialogues, and he is particularly interested in dialogue mechanisms for conversational repair and for the management of cognitive load. He received his Ph.D. in Computer Science from Illinois Institute of Technology, where he worked on control and generation of dialogue in the CircSim-Tutor project.

Dr. **Jean Scholtz** is currently on detail as a program manager in the Information Technology Office at The Defense Advanced Research Projects Agency (DARPA). Dr. Scholtz is a computer scientist with the Information Technology Laboratory at NIST where she focuses on evaluation of interactive systems. Her work at NIST has included tools and techniques for assessing usability of web sites and evaluation of CSCW (Computer Supported Cooperative Work) systems. Dr. Scholtz received a Ph.D. in Computer Science from the University of Nebraska.

William Schuler is a Ph.D. student in the Department of Computer and Information Science at the University of Pennsylvania. He is interested in natural language parsing, translation, and natural language interfaces for instructing simulated humans.

Dr. **Joseph Sullivan** is a Staff Scientist at FX Palo Alto Research Laboratory (FXPAL) in Palo Alto, California. He was recently promoted from being the manager for the Mobile Computing Group to directing the "Invention to Innovation" initiative at FXPAL. The goal of this initiative is to expand FXPAL's research charter to include the development of innovative product concepts arising from research inventions. Joe organized the workshop on "Architectures and Elements of Intelligent Interfaces" held in 1988 in Monterey, California. This workshop is credited as the founding event for the International Conference on Intelligent User Interfaces (IUI). The workshop resulted in the publication of *Intelligent User Interfaces* (Addison-Wesley ACM Frontiers of Science Series, 1991).

Stuart Towns is a character writer and producer at Extempo, Inc. He holds a B.S. in Physics-Engineering from Washington and Lee University (1992) and an M.S. in Computer Science from North Carolina State University (1999). After graduating from Washington and Lee, he taught in the Florida public school system and then joined the graduate program in Computer Science at NC State. The work described in this volume was conducted while he was a graduate student in NC State's IntelliMedia Initiative. After completing his thesis work on multimodal explanation generation, he joined Extempo, where he designs interactive characters.

Susanne van Mulken is a senior researcher at the department of Intelligent User Interfaces at DFKI GmbH, Germany. Her background is in cognitive science and her research focuses on user modeling for adaptive multimedia systems, multimodal interaction, and lifelike interface characters. Currently, she is a member of the European TMR network TACIT, concerned with theory and applications for continuous interaction techniques.

Hannes Vilhjálmsson is working on his Ph.D. in the Gesture and Narrative Language Group at the MIT Media Lab, focusing on embodiment in virtual environments, both for autonomous agents and human controlled avatars. In particular, he is looking at how nonverbal behavior supports face-to-face conversation and how those behaviors can be appropriately animated. He received his M.S. in Media Arts and Sciences from MIT in 1997. His thesis was titled "Autonomous Communicative Behaviors in Avatars." Prior to coming to MIT, Hannes earned his B.S. in Computer Science at the University of Iceland and worked as a programmer and a user interface designer.

Jennifer Voerman is an educational software designer at the SAS Institute. She holds a B.S. in Computer Science from Union College (1994) and an M.S. in Computer Science from North Carolina State University (1997). The work described in this volume on deictic behavior sequencing for animated pedagogical agents was conducted as part of her thesis work with the IntelliMedia Initiative. After completing her M.S., she was a game developer with FarPoint Technologies. She currently designs educational software for secondary schools at SAS inSchool.

Hao Yan is a research assistant in the Gesture & Narrative Language group at the MIT Media Laboratory. His current research interests center on multimodal human-computer interaction and speech applications. With Professor Justine Cassell, he is doing his master's thesis on "Simultaneous Speech and Gesture Generation in Embodied Conversational Agents." Hao Yan was born in Anqing, China. He has a master's and a bachelor's degree in Electrical Engineering.

Liwei Zhao is a Ph.D. student at the Center for Human Modeling and Simulation in the Department of Computer and Information Science at the University of Philadelphia. He received his B.S and M.S. in Computer Science from Beijing University and his M.S. in Computer Science from Ohio State University. His research interests are Virtual Environment Training and Expressive Gestures.

Index